# A HISTORY OF

# FUTURE
# CITIES

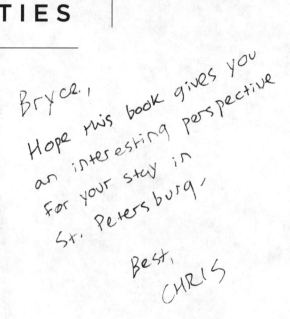

Bryce,
Hope this book gives you
an interesting perspective
for your stay in
St. Petersburg.

Best,
CHRIS

ALSO BY DANIEL BROOK

*The Trap:*
*Selling Out to Stay Afloat in Winner-Take-All America*

# A HISTORY OF

# FUTURE CITIES

## DANIEL BROOK

W. W. NORTON & COMPANY

New York • London

For information about permission to reproduce selections from this book,
write to Permissions, W. W. Norton & Company, Inc.,
500 Fifth Avenue, New York, NY 10110

For information about special discounts for bulk purchases, please contact
W. W. Norton Special Sales at specialsales@wwnorton.com or 800-233-4830

Manufacturing by RR Donnelley, Harrisonburg, VA
Book design by Chris Welch
Production manager: Anna Oler

Library of Congress Cataloging-in-Publication Data

Brook, Daniel.
A history of future cities / Daniel Brook. — First Edition.
pages cm
Includes bibliographical references and index.
ISBN 978-0-393-07812-1 (hardcover)
1. Cities and towns. 2. Cities and towns—Growth. I. Title.
HT111.B76 2013
307.76—dc23

2012045556

W. W. Norton & Company, Inc.
500 Fifth Avenue, New York, N.Y. 10110
www.wwnorton.com

W. W. Norton & Company Ltd.
Castle House, 75/76 Wells Street, London W1T 3QT

1 2 3 4 5 6 7 8 9 0

*For my parents*

# CONTENTS

# AUTHOR'S NOTE

Two of the cities featured in this book—contemporary St. Petersburg and Mumbai—have gone by different names at different points in their histories. The cities will be referred to by the name in use during the period under discussion (e.g., "St. Petersburg in the time of Catherine the Great"; "the Nazi siege of Leningrad").

One of the most captivating aspects of St. Petersburg, Shanghai, and Mumbai is that much of their historic architecture remains extant today. Buildings that have been destroyed will be described in the past tense (on the bells of St. Petersburg's Tercentenary Church, "reliefs were embossed of each member of the royal family"); buildings that still stand will be described in the present tense (Mumbai's "Regal [Cinema] façade boasts bas-relief masks of tragedy and comedy").

All quotations from outside sources are cited in endnotes. All other quotations come from in-person interviews conducted by the author.

**The world, on Mercator's projection, 1840**

### KEY

1. St. Petersburg
2. Shanghai
3. Mumbai
4. Dubai

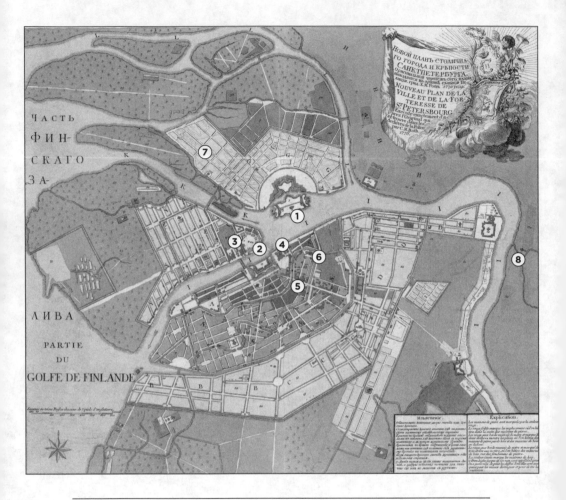

**St. Petersburg, 1776**

KEY

1. Peter and Paul Fortress
2. Kunstkamera
3. St. Peterburg State University
4. Winter Palace
5. Nevsky Prospect
6. Cathedral of Our Savior on Spilt Blood
7. Red Banner Factory
8. Okhta Centre (proposed site)

**Shanghai, 1862**

KEY

1. Shanghai Race Club (now People's Square)
2. Sincere and Wing On department stores on Nanjing Road
3. Great World
4. Cathay Hotel
5. Park Hotel
6. Oriental Pearl Radio and Broadcasting Tower
7. Jin Mao Tower

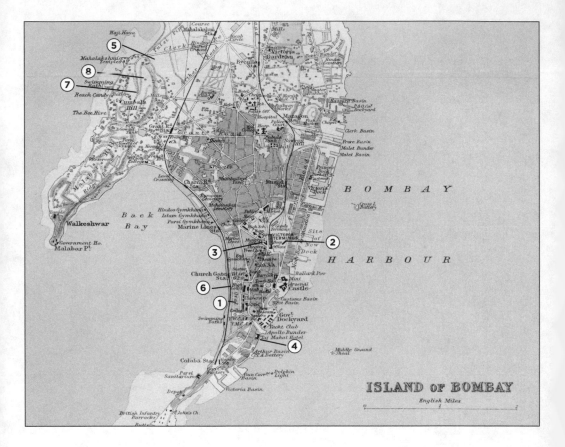

**Bombay, 1909**

KEY

1. University of Bombay (now University of Mumbai)
2. Victoria Teminus (now Chhatrapati Shivaji Terminus)
3. Bombay Municipal Corporation (now Municipal Corporation of Greater Mumbai)
4. Taj Mahal Hotel
5. Willingdon Sports Club
6. Eros Cinema
7. Antilia (Mukesh Ambani residence)
8. Imperial Towers

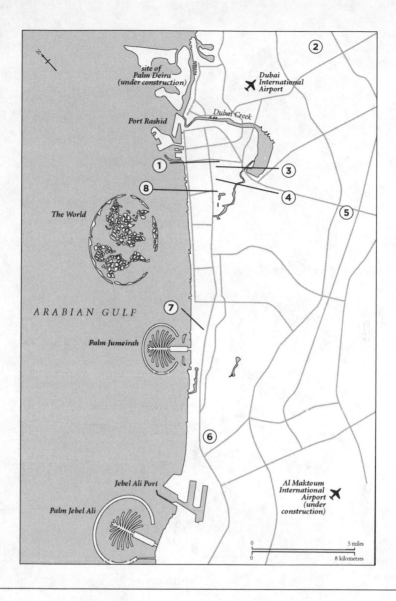

**Dubai, 2010**

KEY

1. Dubai World Trade Centre
2. Sonapur labor camp
3. Emirates Towers
4. Dubai International Financial Centre
5. Dragon Mart
6. Ibn Battuta Mall
7. Twin Chrysler Buildings
8. Burj Khalifa

Introduction

# THE TWENTY-FIRST CENTURY

An Orientation

University of Mumbai Convocation Hall

Where are we?

Walking through the cityscapes of St. Petersburg, Shanghai, Mumbai, and Dubai provokes this same question. Built to look as if they were not where they are—in Russia, China, India, and the Arab world, respectively—each metropolis conjures the same captivating yet discomfiting sense of disorientation. In the heart of St. Petersburg's royal palace sits a lavish room of archways and fresco panels cribbed directly from the Vatican in Rome; only the falling snow outside the window calls its bluff. In Shanghai, 1920s Art Deco hotels look like Jazz Age skyscrapers from Manhattan magically airlifted to a city so far from New York that watches need not be reset—a.m. simply becomes p.m. In Mumbai, the 150-year-old Gothic university campus is an odd Oxford planted with palm trees, while Dubai's twin Chrysler Buildings make visitors wonder: Who thought if one fake Chrysler building was good, two would be even better?

These four unlikely sister cities are unified by the sense of disorientation they impart. They are disorienting cities because each was purposefully dis-orient-ed.

*Orient* is both a noun and a verb—the noun means east; the

verb means to place oneself in space—but its two meanings are intertwined. An individual lost in the wilderness can place herself in space (orient herself) because she knows that the sun rises in the east (the Orient). The disorientation imparted by St. Petersburg, Shanghai, Mumbai, and Dubai results from their being located in the East but purposefully built to look as if they are in the West. Their occidental looks are anything but accidental.

For Western visitors to these cities, love/hate reactions are common. Travelers in India sometimes relish Mumbai, India's most international and developed city, as a respite from the foreignness of the subcontinent. In the Raj-era-built downtown, auto-rickshaws, the cacophonous three-wheeled pods that serve as taxis throughout the rest of the country, are banned. Even roaming street-cows, perhaps the most quintessential feature of Indian urbanism, are rare. Constructed to look like a tropical London, the ruse works as the tidal throngs of commuting stockbrokers and secretaries flow toward their Victorian Gothic office buildings each morning from a train station based on St. Pancras in the British capital. And yet, this ersatz London of stately banks and red double-decker buses often drives Western travelers to the hinterlands to take in the "real" India.

Verdicts on Dubai are typically harsher. Whitewashing away its local traditions by speaking English rather than Arabic, shopping in malls rather than souks, selling pork in its supermarkets, and pouring drinks in its hotels, it is a city where the traditions of the Arab world have been intentionally muted to make way for a placeless, tasteless global future. Without the charm of history, which turns "knockoff buildings" like Mumbai's aped Oxford into "heritage architecture," the "Las Vegas of the Middle East" is mocked as an entirely fake metropolis with no culture at all.

Yet love them or hate them, these dis-orient-ed metropolises matter. They are places to be reckoned with because they are ideas as much as cities, metaphors in stone and steel for the explicit goal of Westernization. Thus the BBC could hold a formal televised debate in 2009 on the resolution, "This house believes Dubai is a bad idea," in a way that they could never devote a similar program to St. Louis. For unlike Dubai, St. Louis is not an idea; St. Louis is just a place.

Whatever visitors—or the BBC's live studio audience—make of the developing world's dis-orient-ed cities, what their own people make of them matters more. The question bedeviling visitors—where are we?—is far less fraught than the question these cities provoke for their own people: Who are we? These global gateway cities raise the question of how to be a modern Arab, Russian, Chinese, and Indian, and whether modernization and globalization can ever be more than just euphemisms for Westernization. In the older cities of St. Petersburg, Shanghai, and Mumbai, different answers to this question have been built into the cityscape over the centuries. Each neighborhood offers a different period's vision of the Russian, Chinese, and Indian future. But even in the most historic of these cities, what is most captivating is not what has been built but what could be built. The reason these cities matter is that their founding promise endures: to build the future.

The world became acquainted with Dubai only a few years ago. The city that launched a thousand magazine features was presented to Westerners as many things: rich, strange, tacky, threatening. But most of all, it was presented as new. The instant global metropolis with a "skyline on crack" captivated the world with record-setting skyscrapers, indoor ski slopes, and a stunningly diverse population. With 96 percent of its population foreign-born, Dubai makes even New York City's diversity—37 percent of New Yorkers are immigrants—seem mundane. As a pair of American observers put it, Dubai is a city where "everyone and everything in it—its luxuries, laborers, architects, accents, even its aspirations—was flown in from someplace else." But for all the breathless coverage of Dubai's supposedly unprecedented emergence, the only truly new thing about Dubai is the "flown in" part. Dubai was touted as a new phenomenon, but it is actually just the most recent iteration of a far older one. For three hundred years, instant cities modeled on the West have been built in the developing world in audacious attempts to wrench a lagging region into the modern world. While the rise of these global crossroads cities was once checked by the speed of ocean liners and locomotives, today their growth is powered by intercontinental jets that can move a passenger from any major city in the world to any other in a single day. So while the *city* of Dubai is new, the *idea* of Dubai is not. It's just that in the age of jet-powered globalization, the idea can achieve liftoff as never before.

This book is about the idea of Dubai—an idea that began in a place as forbiddingly frozen as Dubai is hallucinatorily hot, not far from the Arctic Circle, where the Neva River flows into the Baltic Sea. There, in 1703, on the frigid, fetid marsh, Russian Tsar Peter the Great built a city designed to look as if it were in Western Europe—a model city of columns and cupolas with nary an onion dome in sight. Aping his beloved Amsterdam, the tsar gave his new capital a Dutch name—Sankt Pieter Burkh—rather than a Russian one and had his serfs dig canals so it would more closely resemble the great Dutch port city. He imported top architects from the courts of Europe and had them build the most modern, fantastical structures they could sketch on the virgin land that would become Russia's new capital. In time, St. Petersburg filled with foreign professionals and its Russian elites took to speaking the global language of the age, French, just as Dubai's Emirati power brokers speak English today.

At St. Petersburg's founding, the salon goers of London and Paris chuckled at the twenty-something tsar and his preposterous frozen Venice, with its tangle of unnavigable, iced-over canals.

They soon stopped laughing; within decades, St. Petersburg had become the most cosmopolitan city in Europe. Less than a century after the Russian capital's founding, the bien-pensants of Western Europe had to travel there just to see the finest works of art their own countrymen had produced, for so many of them had been bought up by Catherine the Great and shipped to her Petersburg palace. And yet Russia's autocrats soon had to reckon with the modern people their city had made. The new Russian capital had been built as a stage set of modernity, an experimental metropolis where, liberated from the constraints of budget and existing cityscape, if an architect could draw it, he could build it. But the modern city with its newly erected universities and science museums, all built and initially staffed by imported Western experts, changed the city's people. And as they became broad minded and literate, they grew less willing to accept a social contract that offered them futuristic wonders in exchange for medieval obedience.

Stunned by the rise of St. Petersburg and heedless of its tensions and contradictions, Westerners were soon emulating Peter the Great instead of smirking at him. As they amassed empires around the world in the nineteenth century, the great powers began dotting the globe with Western-style neighborhoods to make their far-flung businessmen feel at home and impress the locals with their technologically sophisticated civilization. The greatest among these became the full-blown Western-style metropolises of Shanghai and Bombay (now Mumbai), the gateways to China and India. In Shanghai, the British, French, and Americans carved up open land to build their colonies, each based on the cities of their home country. The British built a bustling port with a pagoda-free skyline and set aside grassy areas for sports fields. The French built gracious tree-lined boulevards sporting elegant cafés while the Americans slapped together a hodgepodge settlement like something out of their Wild West, all laid out along a central spine they dubbed Broadway. For their gateway to India, the British first built Bombay Island itself, using audacious landfill projects to turn a meager archipelago into a single giant island off the coast of the subcontinent. Then, atop the canvas they had prepared, they painted their tropical London in stone, a Victorian Gothic metropolis of gargoyle-clad train stations and university halls.

While Shanghai and Bombay were intended to be familiar and comforting to the Westerners who designed them, to their Chinese and Indian inhabitants these strange new buildings and the cosmopolitan cities themselves were, by turns, confusing, threatening, and inspiring. It was in Bombay that Indians were first exposed to the technology of the railroad. It was in Shanghai that the Chinese beheld their first skyscraper. Largely excluded from the white societies built on their soil, soon the Chinese and Indian populations were building their own versions of the institutions Westerners had imported but held beyond their grasp. The Shanghainese founded their own business corporations and created China's first elected city council while Bombay's Indians built an indigenous film industry and an anticolonial assembly. These English-speaking cities became the crucibles of Chinese and Indian modernity, where the locals debated and decided what it might mean to be Chinese and Indian in the modern world. These colonial cities forged the men and women who smarted at colonial domination and eventually overthrew it.

Peter the Great and subsequent modernizers, be they foreign imperialists like Old Shanghai's all-white municipal council or indigenous autocrats like Reform-era Shanghai mayor Zhu Rongji, always try to pick and choose exactly which aspects of Western society to import. This requires making decisions about the essential ingredients of modernity—technological sophistication; mass literacy; industrialization; social equality?—and which to add to the society they are cooking up. Naturally, the powerful are keen to import those features they feel will maintain and augment their authority and reject those that could destabilize their rule. Yet for all the meticulous stage directions issued by the self-appointed curators of modernity, their people have a remarkable tendency to go off script. In bursts of creativity not only in architecture, like Shanghai's Jazz Age skyscrapers and Bombay's Art Deco movie palaces, but also in St. Petersburg's literature, Shanghai's fashion, and Mumbai's films, these copycat cities have birthed creations of tremendous originality, the products of a self-determination their rulers had hoped to stave off. What began as copies of Western cities—the replica of a Vatican palace room Catherine the Great commissioned for her St. Petersburg home, the wall from the Doge's Palace in Venice a British architect transposed onto the University of Bombay library, Shanghai's "Big Ching" clock tower, an explicit answer to London's Big Ben—became something entirely new. Built as masquerades of modernity, the trio of historic cities became truly modern when the diverse, literate, cosmopolitan populations they created challenged the parameters by which the cities were run.

Yet each city also experienced periods of loss of faith in modernity. When local people have given up on the possibility of equal exchange between the peoples of the globe, each city has cut itself off from the wider world. It is no coincidence that St. Petersburg birthed the Bolsheviks, Shanghai the Chinese Communist Party, and Mumbai the Indian National Congress, all forces that pared back their nations' ties to the outside world. If its elder-sister cities offer any guidance, the rulers of Dubai are playing a dangerous game with their urban Frankenstein.

The idea of Dubai—which is also the idea of St. Petersburg, Shanghai, and Mumbai—is the idea of our time: the Asian Century, which is also the Urban Century. The journey from countryside to city that has been the archetypal journey to St.

Petersburg for three hundred years and to Shanghai and Mumbai for one hundred and fifty is the defining journey of the twenty-first century. Each month, five million people move from the countryside to cities in the developing world and encounter the Western consumer goods, cultural mores, and architectural fragments that were once limited to these cities. In the early eighteenth century it was only the quixotic Russian tsar who was bringing in scores of Western experts to advise his government; now leaders all over the world solicit the advice of McKinsey consultants and World Bank bureaucrats. In the mid-nineteenth century, only Bombay had the kind of diversity—and its concomitant tensions—that could spur an all-out Muslim/infidel riot over a newspaper's cartoon of the prophet Mohamed; in recent years, such riots have broken out in cities all over the globe. A century ago, only Shanghai hosted an overseas branch of Harvard Univerisity; today, top American universities are opening campuses everywhere from Doha (Cornell) to Singapore (Yale).

The dis-orient-ed looks of these historic East-meets-West cities that were once so unique have now become common. New Jersey–style shopping malls now dot Bangalore and Chennai and Southern California–style subdivisions have sprouted off highway ramps in Beijing and Chengdu. Newly founded cities like Shenzhen, composed entirely of migrants and contemporary buildings, spring up, while historic cities, like Abu Dhabi, all but leveled and rebuilt from scratch, look nearly as new. While a century ago, displaced Western-style cities like Shanghai and Bombay were notable because they were so different from the other cities of the developing world, they are now important because they are so similar. The historic gateway cities are no longer anomalies; they are the original examples of an idea that has gone viral. In today's hindsight, the histories of these precociously modern places can be read as dress rehearsals for the twenty-first century.

In this still-early moment of post–Cold War reglobalization, to be a modern Chinese person means to live in "Orange County," a California-themed gated community in Beijing, and to be a modern Arab means to live in "Beverly Hills," outside Cairo. Today, these stage sets of the West constitute a kind of shorthand for the modern world, though in time more sophisticated amalgams may arise. While acknowledging contemporary historians' often salient attacks on simplistic conflations of "the West" with modernity and on the East-West dichotomy itself as a European creation designed to transmute technological superiority into a justification for colonizing the world, this book will take people's historical self-perceptions—including self-perceptions of backwardness—seriously. When non-Western peoples have de-linked modernization from all-out Westernization to forge non-Western modernities in places like Jazz Age Shanghai and Bombay, they will be recorded, even celebrated. But so too will places like eighteenth-century francophone St. Petersburg or today's Orange County, China, where attempts at outright impersonation predominate.

The reasons that Western Europe developed so rapidly after trailing the Arab world, India, and China for many centuries remain mysterious—that's why there is still such a contentious debate among historians about why it happened. That the ultimate answer remains unclear even today spurs the drive to impersonate. Impersonation is a way to catch up without sorting out precisely why, how, or to what degree one is behind—or even precisely determining what "behind" means. Cognizant of history, it is clear that impersonation is often just a first step, not a final destination, in a place's development. Twenty years into its reintegration with the world, today's Shanghai is more analogous to the imitative 1860s Shanghai, with its British, French, and American settlements, than to the cutting-edge Chinese modernity of 1920s Shanghai. For all of today's skyscrapers and magnetic-levitation trains, Shanghai was in many respects a more futuristic city a century ago. But late twenty-first-century Shanghai may top all of the city's historic highs.

What is truly unprecedented about this century is that the copies have become more important than the originals. While the Doge's Palace in Venice may be a nicer place to visit on vacation, it is in the fake Doge's Palace at the University of Mumbai where the future prime ministers and CEOs of an ascendant India are training. And the goings-on in New York's elegant Chrysler Building, named for the once-mighty American automaker and now 90 percent owned by an Emirati sovereign wealth fund, are of far less import than the dealings in Dubai's chintzy, knock-off twin Chrysler Buildings, where media companies are testing the limits of press freedom in the Arab world every day. While Venice and New York are easier places to live, safely ensconced in wealthy, developed democracies, the fate of the world in the twenty-first century will be determined in places like Mumbai and Dubai.

To truly orient ourselves in our new century—to answer the question, where are we? in time, not just space—we must know the histories of the St. Petersburgs and Shanghais of the world as well as we know the histories of the Londons and New Yorks. Every Shanghai schoolchild knows that the United States once had a colony there; that most Americans are ignorant of this foundational fact of Sino-American relations leaves us flying blind into the future. If the seminal event of the twenty-first century took place three hundred years ago, when Peter the Great, awed by Amsterdam, decided to build what Dostoevsky later called "the most abstract and intentional city on the globe," then that is the place to start.

# NEW AMSTERDAM

## St. Petersburg, 1703–1825

Engraving of the Kunstkamera science museum,
façade and cross section, seen from the east (1741)

In 1697, Peter the Great, traveling incognito, arrived in Amsterdam, the richest city in the world. The cosmopolitan, canal-laced metropolis, with its narrow redbrick townhouses built atop piles in the swampy ground, was the hub of the global trading system. The city was beautiful—some seventy islands linked by five hundred bridges—but its structure was not just a matter of aesthetics. Form followed function, for the wealth and independence of Holland flowed from its maritime prowess. The three main canals the Dutch had dug with such foresight in the early 1600s allowed ships to pull right up to merchants' warehouses, speeding loading and unloading. By the time Peter arrived, the tiny Netherlands boasted the world's second-largest navy and more merchant ships than all other countries on earth combined. The Amsterdam harbor, with its innumerable wooden ships, their masts piercing the horizon, appeared as a vast forest rising up from the sea, heralding the enormous wealth that seemed to spring from Amsterdam's marshy soil.

As Peter walked Amsterdam's streets, he coveted the prosperous Dutch city. He wanted one for himself. And blessed with nearly unlimited power and wealth, what Peter wanted, Peter got.

When he returned to Russia, he would build his own Amsterdam and make it Russia's new capital.

As one contemporary architectural historian put it, "St. Petersburg was built to order [on] the order of one man." Another
quipped that Peter ordered up a city "as you or I would order
lunch." Russian legend insists that the entire city was dropped
from the heavens wholly built onto the banks of the Neva River.
In truth, the young tsar himself vowed, "If God will prolong my
life . . . Petersburg will be another Amsterdam."

Peter did not visit Amsterdam until he was in his midtwenties,
but his obsession with all things European began in his youth.
His first window on the West was Moscow's German Quarter,
the gilded ghetto where all foreigners in the capital were forced
to live in the xenophobic, theocratic Russia into which Peter was
born. To the Russians, "German" was a kind of shorthand for
all foreigners; in the Russian language, the word for a German,
Nemets, is derived from the word for "mute"—one who is silent
because he cannot speak our language. The German Quarter was
an island of Western Europe just three miles from the Kremlin where Peter was raised. The three thousand British, French,
German, and Dutch residents of the neighborhood brought with
them their fashions and architecture. In contrast to the twisting, haphazard alleyways of Moscow, where shoddily constructed
homes with stables and kitchens fronting the street gave the capital the appearance of an overgrown village, the German Quarter
was laid out in broad, orderly tree-lined avenues with columned
two- and three-story brick buildings arranged around courtyard
fountains. To maintain their ties to home, the residents imported
a steady stream of newspapers and books that kept them abreast
of the latest happenings and technological developments. By
contrast, fewer than ten secular Russian books and not a single
newspaper were published in Moscow in the entire seventeenth

century. As a youth, Peter frequented the neighborhood's taverns and talked with the foreigners late into the night, learning to see Russia—and all it was lacking—through their eyes. Soon he was importing foreign experts to gain the latest Western technology. In 1691, he invited twenty shipwrights from the famed Zaandam yards in Holland to work at a shipbuilding facility he'd set up outside Moscow.

Eventually Peter's curiosity about the West could no longer be satisfied by trips to the German Quarter. He wanted to see Europe for himself. Traditionally, there was only one legitimate reason for a tsar to venture into other lands: to kill foreigners in war. In the entire history of Russia, only one prince had ever traveled peaceably to the West and that had been back in 1075. When, on December 6, 1696, Peter announced his intention to journey westward, the assembled nobles were aghast. But Peter argued cleverly that he needed to travel to Europe to master their technology, the better to conquer them in the end. As Peter would later sum it up, "We need Europe for a few decades, and then we must show it our ass." To steal the West's technology, he would travel not as Peter I, Tsar of All the Russias, but as Peter Mikhailov, a simple Russian carpenter hoping to augment his skills. To complete the ruse, on the eighteen-month-long "Great Embassy," as it came to be known, Peter took with him a letter of introduction signed by the tsar himself, supposedly back in Moscow, and made clear to his entourage of 250 advisers that if anyone blew his cover he would have them executed on the spot. The tsar even created his own fraudulent nonroyal seal, a ship's carpenter flanked by his tools with the inscription, "My rank is that of a student and I need teachers."

Peter was most eager to see Holland, the tiny nation with a population of just two million that was Europe's wealthiest and most technologically advanced society. All the treasures of the world—French wines, Norwegian timber, Indian spices—passed through the ports and trading houses of Holland, and the Dutch grew rich taking their cut. It was the Dutch who first figured out that in a global economy, the big money accrues not to those who produce but to those who broker and trade. While their neighbors made goods, the Dutch made money.

Arriving in the Netherlands, Peter had a Dutch friend who did business with the Dutch East India Company land him a four-month internship in the company's famed shipyards. Far more than a simple trading company, through the government-chartered, shareholder-owned Dutch East India Company Holland was conquering the world. The Company, which was granted a monopoly on Dutch trade with Asia, had the power to do far more than just import and export goods. It could establish colonies, negotiate treaties, mint money, collect taxes, even wage wars.

The ultimate source of the company's power was its technology—the massive ships, veritable floating cities, it crafted in Holland and dispatched to the far corners of the earth. It was in those shipyards that Peter the Great trained, mastering the latest maritime technologies like a true shipwright's apprentice. The personal owner of one-sixth of the world's land lived in a tiny wooden house, made his own bed each morning, cooked his own simple meals, and happily reported for work at sunup with his ax and plane. He dressed the part, donning the getup of a Dutch carpenter: a conical felt hat, wide knee breeches, and collarless red jacket. At the internship's end, Peter's supervisor provided him with a certificate that read, "Piter has shown himself a good and skillful carpenter in the construction of the hundred-foot frigate *Peter and Paul*, which he worked on from start to finish. In addition, having under my guidance made a thorough study of naval architecture and the drawing of plans, he has, I think, fitted himself to practice those arts."

Though busy at the shipyard, Peter was captivated by the surrounding city and traipsed from neighborhood to neighborhood.

In the tall, elegant townhouses along the city's tree-lined streets and canals lived Amsterdam's professional class, who managed the banks and insurance companies that serviced the Dutch East India Company. Famously tolerant, Amsterdam took in talented Spanish Jews and French Protestants who had been persecuted in their home countries. The literate and worldly residents of the city ran their own society themselves, as a republic rather than a monarchy.

But it was technology, not democracy, that captivated Peter. One day, the secret tsar studied printing, observing a moveable-type printing press and commanding his entourage to bring one back to Russia. Another day he was off to a lecture on anatomy, to watch a Dutch physician dissect a human body and detail the system of arteries and veins that moves blood throughout the body. In Delft, he visited Anton van Leeuwenhoek to see his breakthrough invention, the microscope. Through his high-tech crafted lens contraption, Leeuwenhoek had examined, among other things, his own sperm, applying scientific rationality to the seemingly divine mystery of human reproduction.

Peter had always had the mind of an engineer, a tinkerer, a gearhead. But in Holland he began to view people themselves as machines. Like machines, people were composed of a series of complex but ultimately rational systems, like circulation and reproduction. And as in any machine, changing the inputs would change the outcomes. He had done this to himself. By exchanging his royal scepter for a hatchet and his golden caftan for knee breeches, he had been transformed from Russian tsar to Dutch craftsman. While it had all started as a ruse, a masquerade, at some point during those months in the shipyards, the felt hat and red jacket had stopped being a costume and just became part of who he was. By the end, he really was a carpenter. He even had the certificate to prove it.

In his travels around Amsterdam, Peter also realized that just like the fashions in which we clothe our bodies, the fashions in which we clothe our structures—architecture—shaped people. They too were an input that could be changed. Thus, Amsterdam was a kind of factory for creating modern people. By living in Amsterdam, walking its crowded streets, sailing its canals, meeting its mix of peoples from every faith and corner of the world, one could not help but become more cosmopolitan, more technologically savvy, more modern. Just as a well-designed sawmill could transform rough timber into uniform, usable planks, so too a city, if properly designed, could shape even the roughest-hewn barbarians into civilized men and women. If human society was a rational system, then social change was just an engineering problem.

Merely importing the West's technology and its experts as he had done at his Moscow-area shipyard would not be enough. Instead, Peter would build a forge of modernity: a new capital for Russia modeled on Amsterdam, where he would force his subjects to dress and act like Westerners. Beyond simply importing Western technologies, he would import the West outright.

And Peter himself would pick and choose precisely which aspects to import. The republican traditions of the Dutch, he felt, had no place in Russia. When Peter attempted to execute two of his staffers for disloyalty, his Dutch hosts informed the no-longer-anonymous tsar that in the Dutch Republic, with its rule of law, only a court could order an execution. Being a good guest, the tsar relented, but he was aghast at the limits on his divine right authority. A few weeks later, on his visit to London, the English king William III, aware of Peter's true identity, invited him to observe the proceedings in Parliament. Sitting in the gallery as the king took impertinent questions from the members of Parliament—William had acceded to the throne in the Glorious Revolution of 1688 by signing a bill of rights limiting his power—Peter remarked to his entourage that it was good to see such forthright advice being given to the monarch, but the idea that he was bound by any of it was an outrage. This sort of thing, he assured them, would never fly in Russia.

In Russia, the autocrat could do anything he pleased—even alter his nation's geography. Peter concluded from his experience in the Netherlands that Holland was modern because it was open to the sea and thus to foreign trade and international exchange. Russia, by contrast, was backward because, by an equal and opposite accident of geography, it was landlocked. If geography was the key, the autocrat would simply decree a change in Russia's geography. To link his empire to the sea, Peter plotted to whip his army into a modern fighting force and send it to capture a west-facing port on the Neva River delta. The Swedes, who were already there, would just have to move.

Peter returned to Moscow in 1698 with a plan for a new capital but without the land on which to build it. Lacking such a port didn't stop him from laying the groundwork. He could make his subjects look like Westerners right away. On his first day back in Moscow, Peter assembled his court in his country palace and, one by one, Peter personally shaved the beards and mustaches off of his noblemen, in keeping with European fashion. Peter then posted barbers at the gates of Moscow. From then on, all male visitors to the capital would undergo a compulsory shave before being admitted to the city.

The beards were just the beginning. At the first state banquet Peter held upon his return, the tsar appeared with scissors and went from noble to noble, cutting the long flowing sleeves from their caftans. "These things are in your way," he exhorted. "At one moment you upset a glass; then you forgetfully dip them in the sauce." But Peter's objection was deeper than long sleeves rendering Russian nobles ill-mannered at formal meals; the impractical sleeves symbolized everything that was wrong with Russia's coddled elite. Russia needed leaders who learned by doing, as Peter had in the Dutch shipyards.

By Peter's time, the Russian royal family, the Romanovs, had amassed so much power that the nobles could hardly be blamed for believing that their only duty in the capital was to enjoy the sumptuous, alcohol-lubricated life of the court. The tsar (or "emperor," as Peter preferred to be called, for its Roman resonance) was the personal owner of all Russian lands. Noblemen, in turn, were the custodians of allotted portions of his property—including the serfs who lived there, who could be transferred from master to master and from estate to estate at will. Without allowing the nobles to check his power, Peter still felt he could tap their atrophying talents. He created a new Table of Ranks for the military and civil service where nobles—and even talented free commoners and foreigners—could gain increasing authority by proving themselves competent on exams and amassing years of experience. Through the Table of Ranks, Peter hoped to import some of the meritocratic ethos he saw in the business world of Amsterdam but safely limit it within the existing system of hereditary power that reserved ultimate authority for him.

Peter similarly pared back the power of the Church. Everything about the Church looked backward. Church architecture drew on the styles of Byzantium, the one-time headquarters of the Eastern Orthodox Church that had been wiped off the map by the Turks in 1453. (Russia's famed golden onion-shaped church domes were an attempt to tweak the sensuous architectural styles of Asia Minor into a shape that could more easily shed Russian snow.) Similarly, Russian church painters aimed to match the styles long-dead Byzantine icon artists had used to depict the otherworldly lives of the saints during the Middle Ages. Meanwhile, a thousand miles away—and seemingly a thousand years into the future—Western painters were learning to represent the world in perfectly accurate dimensions, celebrating the new world of global trade in the dramatic seascapes that had captivated Peter in Amsterdam. Upon his return, Peter successfully decreed that the Church would henceforth be subordinate to the tsar but, fearful of a backlash, he never imported Amsterdam's far-reaching freedom of worship. In his new capital, he would promise only pan-Christian tolerance. Jews, Muslims, and members of other faiths would only be admitted by special dispensation.

Perhaps the ultimate example of Peter's managed modernity was his introduction of newspapers to Russia. When the first Russian newspaper was published in Moscow in 1702, on the imported printing presses Peter had brought home with him to catch up with the West's Gutenberg-fueled information revolution, Peter personally edited and censored the first issue. A press was essential for Russia's modernization, but true freedom of information was unthinkable.

As Peter went about reinventing Muscovite society, his armies set to work reinventing the shape of Russia. In 1703, the Russians conquered the small Swedish fort where the Neva River empties into the Gulf of Finland. There, Peter would build his new capital. He seemed unconcerned that the area seemed so inauspicious for a metropolis. The delta was a near-arctic swamp (Neva means "swamp" in Finnish). It was flood prone, had no reliable source of fresh water, little local timber, and was disease ridden in summer and frozen in the winter, which ran more or less from September to May. But the location had one key advantage: it faced west, away from the Russian hinterlands out toward the modern world. A ship sailing out from the Neva could navigate from the Gulf of Finland into the wider Baltic Sea, crossing into the North Sea through the straights off the Danish coast and, from there, dock at any of the great Western European metropolises: London, Paris, and, most crucially, Amsterdam.

The cornerstone for the new capital was laid on the evening of June 29, 1703, a White Night, as decreed by nature, and the holy day of St. Peter, as decreed by the Church, the anniversary of the day the tsar himself had been baptized and named after the holder of the keys to paradise. The city was christened that day as Sankt Pieter Burkh, Dutch for "St. Peter's City." Giving the new Russian capital a Russian name would have defeated the purpose.

Peter oversaw the construction of his new city from a one-story log cabin he helped build himself on the banks of the Neva. As he had done as a Dutch East India Company shipyard intern, one of the richest and most powerful men in the world chose to get his hands dirty, living in a rustic hut whose ceiling barely cleared his curls. Peter ordered that his three-room wooden cabin be built to look like a redbrick Amsterdam townhouse. With no bricks available, the wood was planed flat and painted red with a grid pattern to resemble brick. To symbolize the new orientation of the city, the first complex completed in the capital, the Peter and Paul Fortress, would be dominated by a golden church spire atop its cathedral. Looking more like a Northern European Protestant church steeple than an onion-domed Eastern Orthodox one was just the half of it; the real purpose of the steeple was entirely secular: to be a beacon to ships sailing into the new capital from the West.

For all its impersonation of Amsterdam, there would be crucial differences between Peter's copy and the Dutch original. While Amsterdam lured migrants with the prospect of tolerance, work, and wealth, St. Petersburg would build its population by royal decree. Peter ordered his nobles as well as merchants, traders, and skilled artisans to relocate to St. Petersburg with their families. While many doubted the tsar's sanity in founding a new capital from scratch at the edge of the arctic, disobedience was not an option. When one nobleman, Prince Golitsyn, resisted, he was brought from Moscow to St. Petersburg in chains.

While serfdom had died out centuries before in Western Europe, its modern cities built by paid laborers and craftsmen,

Peter would build his metropolis with unpaid, unfree serfs. In 1704, he ordered his nobles to send him forty thousand serfs a year, lent out for six-month tours of construction duty. In St. Petersburg, this massive labor force drove the foundation piles into the ground, dug the canals, and built the palaces. During summer's White Nights, they worked near round-the-clock shifts from 5:00 a.m. to 10:00 p.m. Despite his obsession with technology, Peter chose not to import even the most rudimentary tools for his manual laborers. Russia had no wheelbarrows. In fact, when Peter and his entourage had come across the exotic contraptions on their Western European tour, they had raced each other down hills in them, trashing their host's manicured grounds. But rather than import wheelbarrows, Peter had his serfs carry away in their shirts the swampy mud they cleared in building the foundations of his city. Many serfs lacked even shovels, and resorted to digging with sticks and nails. Under such conditions, it is no wonder St. Petersburg became known as "a city built on bones." Peter himself boasted that one hundred thousand people had perished building him his city.

Though Russian commoners would continue to smart under the despotic, feudal system of serfdom for another century and a half, the nobles would be forced to modernize posthaste. Just as Peter dressed his nobles in modern clothing, he forced them to live modern lives. They would no longer walk or ride on horses or in carriages. Instead, they would sail.

To turn pastoral provincials into seafaring cosmopolitans, Peter decided St. Petersburg, even more than Amsterdam, would substitute canals for streets. He prohibited the construction of bridges. For the common people, Peter instituted a system of public ferries. Nobles were given free sailboats, with boat size based on rank. Oars were banned as a form of cheating: after all, with oars one could navigate the water without mastering the modern sciences of physics and meteorology that made a sailboat go.

(Foreign dignitaries used their diplomatic immunity to exempt themselves from the onerous no-oars ordinance.) As the canals froze in winter and silted up over time, Peter's plan faltered. The tsar eventually relented in 1711 and allowed bridges to be built, perhaps taking solace that as scores of bridges sprang up, the Russian capital began to look even more like Amsterdam.

But if Peter's transportation vision was frustrated, his architectural vision was an indisputable success. As usual, Peter first mastered the latest Western techniques and then implemented them on a scale the West could only dream about. In his letters from the period just after the founding of St. Petersburg, Peter feverishly exhorted his diplomats in Amsterdam and Rome to send him "architectural books from which this art can be learned from the beginning." Peter demanded "the new and best architectural books (best if in Latin, but if you can't find that, then in whatever)." In the end, about one-fifth of his enormous collection of foreign books would concern architecture and construction.

In addition to books, Peter imported people. Hundreds of foreign architects and master builders were brought in from Western Europe to construct the new capital and, in turn, hundreds of Western experts were imported to staff the modern institutions they built. Peter's first chief architect was Domenico Trezzini, a Swiss designer who had cut his teeth in Copenhagen, Denmark. Trezzini arrived in St. Petersburg in 1703 and lived there for the rest of his life, becoming a close friend of the tsar's.

More than with any single building Trezzini designed, he put his stamp on the city when Peter had him draw a series of model homes to give the capital a uniform look. For ordinary subjects, called "taxpayers," Trezzini designed a one-story home with a line of evenly spaced windows and an entrance at one side; for "well-to-do persons," he ordered up a grander two-story affair with a central entryway under a pediment and ornamented trim around the line of windows; "grandees" got three stories with a substantial arched entryway and several decorative porthole windows on the top floor. What is striking about the three houses is their commonality. They differ in grandeur but they share the same basic design. All three are anchored by a series of ground-floor windows. And in accordance with the planning regulations Peter and Trezzini issued, all line up together at the street, meeting the sidewalk or canal embankment on the same line. To this day, it is this ordered line of façades and windows stretching off to the horizon or curving around a canal that gives the city its all-encompassing sense of order. For pedestrians—or boaters on the canals—it evokes the feeling of living inside an Italian Renaissance perspective drawing from a book of architectural theory.

And in a sense, in St. Petersburg one really is living inside a drawing. With their vanishing points and perfectly proportioned buildings, the sketches in European architecture books had developed out of an idealization of Italian cities, with their mix of Roman ruins and Renaissance additions. Leading architectural theorists, like Andrea Palladio, gleaned from the historic buildings around them a series of rules for architects to follow. But architectural theory did not arise out of St. Petersburg as it did out of Rome; rather, it was imposed on it. St. Petersburg took Palladio's rules, filtered through Peter's ordinances and Trezzini's design guidelines, and built a city in accordance with them. While the philosophy of architecture moves from the particular to the universal, St. Petersburg moved from the universal to the particular. In this sense, St. Petersburg really was, as the popular legend has it, built in the heavens and dropped whole to earth. Because the city and its modern institutions arose out of imported theory rather than locally rooted processes of development, they tended toward extremes: they could be inauthentic, paint-by-numbers imitations of Western equivalents or cutting-edge institutions that, easily realized on St. Petersburg's tabula rasa, leapfrogged the West.

Trezzini's Twelve Colleges just downriver from the Peter and Paul Fortress is a modern wonder. A protoskyscraper on its side, the salmon-painted structure marches toward the horizon for a third of a mile and resembles twelve Trezzini "grandee" model homes in a row. Inside, the building contains one of the longest hallways in the world, so long it looks as if it truly has a vanishing point. Just as a building of this size would be nearly inconceivable in a European capital like Rome, with layers upon layers of city built atop each other over the centuries, but could be laid down easily on St. Petersburg's virgin land, so the institution it housed could be established without European universities' historical baggage. St. Petersburg State University was founded in 1724 as a secular, coeducational institution. Roughly a third of the students in the university's first class were women. Meanwhile leading Western universities, founded as religious schools to train men for the clergy, took centuries to develop into secular, coeducational institutions. St. Petersburg offered new possibilities. With his new university, Peter, the master architect for a new society, built a hypermodern institution on a blank slate just as much as Trezzini did.

A block away from the Twelve Colleges, Peter built the world's first public museum, tapping a German architect, Georg Johann Mattarnovy, to design a perfectly symmetrical three-story turquoise building with an observatory in its central cupola. Known as the Kunstkamera (Cabinet of Curios) and opened in 1728, the galleries displayed Peter's collection of scientific specimens. Through the Kunstkamera, Peter hoped to educate the ordinary people beyond the reach of his university. The museum was open free of charge and all visitors were given a guided tour. When an aide suggested to Peter that the museum was eating up too large a portion of the state budget, Peter rebuffed him. Henceforth, Peter decreed, not only would the museum remain free but, from then on, he would commit four hundred rubles a year to providing every visitor with complimentary vodka and snacks. Also housed in the Kunstkamera building was a new Academy of Sciences. Though staffed entirely by foreign experts, Peter hoped that eventually Russia would produce great scientists who could replace them.

Just as he had Trezzini model acceptable modes of Western-style housing, Peter modeled Western-style social life for his court. He began hosting concerts of instrumental music—a practice that was still illegal in theocratic Moscow. (The Russian Church maintained that God should be praised by the human voice alone, accounting for the rich Orthodox a cappella tradition.) When Peter returned from his second voyage to the West— a 1717–1718 journey to meet with European heads of state eager to align themselves with the rising power to the east—he instituted a new form of social gathering modeled on coed salons, or "assemblies," he had observed in Paris. To impose this new social ritual on his court, he drew up a manual and issued a decree. "Assembly is a French word which cannot be rendered in a single Russian word," the manual read. "To state it in more detail: it is a voluntary gathering or meeting in someone's home. . . . The manner in which we will conduct these assemblies, until it becomes a habit, is explained in the paragraphs below." The guide goes on to give rule after rule for the who, what, when, where, and how of socializing in the manner of civilized Europeans.

But written manuals on how to act Western were increasingly unnecessary as Russians began to mix with European expatriates on the streets of the capital. To build the new Russian navy, foreign officers had been imported to oversee Russian cadets. And St. Petersburg's shipyards, which by 1715 employed ten thousand men, were supervised largely by Dutch, British, and Italian masters. The foreign maritime experts lived just east of the Admiralty building, whose golden spire matched that of the Peter and Paul Cathedral across the river, in a St. Petersburg neighborhood called the German Quarter. Though it took the same name as the German Quarter in Moscow, this was an entirely different phenomenon. In Moscow, the German Quarter was located several miles from the city center. Foreigners were quarantined there lest they mix with the locals and corrupt them with their un-Orthodox ways. In St. Petersburg, foreigners lived in the heart of the city. In keeping with Peter's policy of tolerance for all variants of the Christian faith, non-Orthodox churches, including some offering foreign language services, sprang up right in the center of town. From the German Quarter sprang the Grand Perspective, later called Nevsky Prospect, a straight street radiating out from the Admiralty and lined with foreign shops. In St. Petersburg, Peter had taken his beloved but marginalized Moscow ghetto and rebuilt it on a magnificent scale as the new capital of Russia. With its cosmopolitan mix of cultures and emphatically Western architecture, St. Petersburg was, in a sense, just one big German Quarter.

By the 1720s, with the city's population at forty thousand, Peter could revel in his accomplishment, blissfully unaware of the city's tensions and contradictions. At a ship launching at the Admiralty not long before his death, Peter summed up his reign:

> Who among you, my brothers, would have dreamed 30 years ago that we would be here together, on the Baltic Sea, practicing carpentry in the dress of foreigners, in a land won from them by our labors and courage, erecting this city in which we live; that we would live to see such brave and victorious soldiers and sailors of Russian blood, and such sons who have visited foreign countries and returned home so bright; that we would see right here so many foreign artists and craftsmen, or that we would live to see the day when you and I are respected by foreign rulers? Historians believe that the cradle of all knowledge was Greece,

from which (with the vicissitudes of time) it spread to Italy and then to all European lands, but this did not go beyond Poland and our ancestors were left in ignorance. . . . Now it is our turn, if only you will support me in my important enterprises, if you will obey me without any reservations . . . perhaps even in our own century you will put other educated countries to shame and raise to a new height the glory of the Russian name.

When Peter died in 1725, he was buried beneath the golden spire of Trezzini's Peter and Paul Cathedral. For all his religious skepticism, Peter was confident that he would spend eternity in heaven. As the tsar had put it in a letter to an underling from the still rough-hewn city in 1706, "I cannot help writing you from this paradise; truly we live here in heaven."

Yet in the city's indisputable successes lay vulnerabilities. How long would the modern people the city forged in its university and science museum—whose whole purpose was to teach Petersburgers to think for themselves—continue to accept autocracy and serfdom? Peter the Great had self-servingly decided that autocracy was the hallmark of modernity in an age when it was unclear whether the popular rule of the Dutch Republic, the modified monarchy of Britain's King William III, or the absolutism of France's Louis XIV was the wave of the future. But as the decades passed, tsarist autocracy would increasingly look like a form of government fit only for barbarian backwaters if not destined for the dustbin of history altogether. By opening Russia to the world and exposing the ship of state to the fast-moving currents of modernity, St. Petersburg would destabilize Russia.

More immediate threats came from those who felt that Russia need not learn anything from the West, that Russia's traditional institutions were all the country needed. Prince Golitsyn, the

Moscow nobleman who had been dragged to the new capital in chains, argued that "Petersburg is like a part of one's body that has been seized with gangrene and which must be amputated so that the rest of the body does not become infected by it." Even Peter's own son, Alexis, agreed. While Peter was on his second trip to the West in 1717, an attempted coup erupted, backed by Alexis, who had vowed to his conspirators, "I shall bring back the old people [and] when I become sovereign I shall live in Moscow, and leave St. Petersburg simply as any other town; I won't launch any ships." Alexis was sentenced to death and died of torture even before his execution could be carried out. Peter had chosen to sacrifice his son to save his city.

After Peter's death, new threats arose from those who loved St. Petersburg only too well, getting drunk on its luxuries. That was always one of the potential pitfalls of building St. Petersburg: in a society ruled by an autocrat with virtually limitless resources, there was always the danger that the city could descend from Peter's high-minded pursuit of modernity to a royal vanity project. Peter had imported the modern world in a bid to rouse Russian society from its stupor, but other royals and nobles saw the wonders of the modern world as their own luxurious playthings. In a cosmopolitan metropolis where the world's peoples are brought together, there is the potential for cultural breakthroughs should people choose to learn from each other, but there is also the concomitant danger that, with so little shared experience, a culture of lowest-common-denominator kitsch can arise instead.

In the winter of 1739–1740, Empress Anna Ivanovna, who had ascended to the throne in 1730, succeeding a short-lived emperor and empress who briefly reigned after Peter's death, decided that while Peter's science museum, university, and shipyard were nice, what St. Petersburg really needed was the world's largest ice palace. The empress hired a German physicist to design the structure. Standard-sized ice bricks were duly cast and fastened together with a layer of water that froze immediately in the near-arctic winter. The building was then adorned with ice sculptures in the form of classical statues. The German scientist also devised several ice cannons that fired ice cannonballs using real gunpowder, and an ice elephant, whose trunk could shoot water or, at night, flaming oil twenty-four feet in the air.

The system of construction was detailed in a monograph, complete with architectural drawings of the palace, published in German and French by the St. Petersburg Academy of Sciences based in the Kunstkamera. In the self-seriousness of the work, the Petrine principles of St. Petersburg are subverted from within. The best Western minds had indeed been brought to the new Russian capital, but they were being tasked with the most decadent and inane assignments, which they dutifully took up with complete scientific rigor.

Yet even when Westerners were tasked with frivolity—building ice palaces, styling Russian noblewomen's hair in the latest styles from Paris, or putting on formulaic comedies in the city's French-language theaters—the simple fact of their presence was changing the unofficial culture of the city even as the official culture of fire-and-ice spectacle verged on self-parody. As the foreign-staffed Russian capital became the most diverse city in Europe, a vast population for whom Russian ways were not the norm now called the city home. A pair of visiting Irish sisters complained that St. Petersburg was "overrun with French as with locusts. . . . Dancing masters are of course French, so are the multitudes of Physicians . . . Tailors, Mantua-makers, Milliners, Waiting Maids, Cooks, [and] Book-sellers."

The Russian elite may have learned French to enjoy a night at the opera or simply to brand themselves as modern, global Russians (demoting their native tongue to a patois for ordering around the servants), but they ended up able to read all the serious works published in Paris. The idea that a government could link its capital to the outside world, import thousands of expatriate professionals, teach its educated population the global lingua franca, and yet still control what they read and thought seemed remarkably hubristic. And so the ultimate threat to Peter the Great's delicate balancing act came not from an open enemy like his son Alexis or an intellectual lightweight like Anna, who reigned until her death in 1740, but from one of the city's greatest champions: Catherine the Great, the German-born empress who had married Peter the Great's grandson, Peter III, and then, in 1762, swiped his throne.

Inside the massive Winter Palace, the main royal residence in the heart of the capital that Anna had commissioned of baroque architect Bartelomeo Rastrelli, the son of an Italian sculptor Peter the Great had imported to St. Petersburg, Catherine overhauled room after room. Out went the gold-leaf-encrusted curlicues favored by Anna and in went Catherine's sober granite Doric columns, which sought to link her reign and her capital back to the font of Western civilization, ancient Greece.

More than just classing up and toning down her own palace, Catherine began an ambitious program of urban improvements in St. Petersburg that she admitted became a compulsion. "The more you build, the more you want to build," she confessed. "It's a sickness somewhat akin to being addicted to alcohol." Catherine raised St. Petersburg's building height limit to accommodate its growing population, which hit the one hundred thousand mark early in her reign. In the city center, she paved the streets and made streetlamps standard. And she turned the Crooked Rivulet, a naturally occurring semicircular stream that encircles the central city about one mile out from the Winter Palace, into the Catherine Canal. To make it worthy of bearing the empress's name, stately granite embankments with elegant steps extending from the curb down to the water were built and iron ship-mooring rings were added at equal intervals from one end to the other. Soon Catherine's signature embankments flanked every river and canal in the city, a symbol of human ingenuity imposed over untamed nature. To add a classical order to her capital, Catherine imported the architect Giacomo Quarenghi, a disciple of Palladio's meticulously symmetrical forms, to design dozens of landmark projects including the new Smolny Institute for the Education of Young Women of Noble Birth, a pioneering institution for female education.

As an addition to the Winter Palace itself, Catherine had Quarenghi design a theater whose interior was modeled on Palladio's Teatro Olimpico in Vicenza, Italy, and whose exterior was held aloft by a series of columns chiseled in the shape of loincloth-clad Herculean figures, perhaps a nod to the empress's legendary collection of younger lovers. Attendance at the theater, which performed works written by Catherine herself as well as leading European playwrights, was by royal invitation only.

The renovated Winter Palace became, under Catherine's exacting eye, a repository of the world's finest in arts and letters, filled with the world's greatest paintings and frequented by its greatest minds. Fancying herself an enlightened despot, Catherine felt she should solicit the advice of the wisest foreign experts—again, by invitation only—and then implement their most advantageous ideas for her empire by fiat. Open debate would reign within the Winter Palace even as autocracy prevailed outside its walls. If Peter's hubris had led him to build the modern world in one city, Catherine did him one better: the modern world in one building. As the Great Curator, Catherine would bring the best the world had to offer to her palace where she could weigh its merits and accept or reject it.

Catherine's curatorial impulse began with art. As a precocious teen, Catherine had subscribed to French philosophe Denis Diderot's handwritten periodical, *Literary and Artistic Correspondence*, which offered gossipy dispatches from Europe's cultural capital, Paris. Early in her reign, she enlisted Diderot himself, a man who knew the Paris art world like few others, as her personal scout. From Paris, he would alert her of major collections for sale. Catherine bought and bought and bought. She collected the modern masters: Rembrandt, Rubens, Poussin. The geniuses of the Renaissance—Raphael and Michelangelo—found a place in her collection, too. In just thirty years of amassing art, buying collections whole at the auction houses of Paris and London and shipping them to St. Petersburg by the boatload, Catherine's collection of four thousand paintings rivaled what generations of French kings had collected in the Louvre over four centuries. Catherine had to build additions onto the Winter Palace, called Hermitage wings, just to hold all the acquisitions.

Intent on importing the West, just two Russian paintings were declared worthy of Catherine's collection. Russia's greatest art collection contained virtually no Russian art, just as Russia's greatest city all around it had virtually no Russian buildings. Immensely proud of her haul, Catherine never paused to consider whether her people should be proud that Russia contained the world's greatest art collection or ashamed that it was nearly 100 percent foreign.

What Catherine could not buy, she had no qualms about copying. Catherine coveted the Pope's loggia, a long hallway in his Vatican palace lined with panel after panel painted by Renaissance master Raphael, that was, tragically, not for sale. Naturally, to copy a Roman building, Catherine tapped her Italian architect, Giacomo Quarenghi. He in turn hired an Austrian artist to copy each of Raphael's paintings in Rome onto canvas and ship the paintings to St. Petersburg, where they could then be duly copied onto Catherine's walls. Each of Raphael's sumptuous Bible scenes was copied faithfully. The only difference between the Pope's loggia and Catherine's was the insertion of her royal seal—the double-headed Russian eagle and inscription "EII" for

Ekaterina the Second—in the central panel. With its series of concentric arches extending toward a vanishing point and filled with copies of the best from the West, the loggia was like the entire city of St. Petersburg crystallized in a single room—stunning in its grandeur but also in its unhinged ambition.

Tempting fate most brazenly, Catherine imported Western philosophers who dreamed of a world without serfs or monarchs to her palace to advise her. While Peter had imported foreign scientific experts who could help him modernize Russian technology, Catherine imported social and political thinkers, confident they could advise her safely and privately on modernizing society. Catherine's first target was Europe's greatest intellectual celebrity, Voltaire. Initially the empress had ingratiated herself to the French philosophe by granting a license for the radical *Encyclopédie* to be published in St. Petersburg after the conservative French authorities had revoked its Parisian publishing license. The French royal censors had objected to articles by Voltaire and other contributors on politically charged subjects like "rights," "liberty," and "equality." Impressed by Catherine's gesture, the greatest wit of the Enlightenment ingratiated himself to the empress by presenting her with a hot-off-the-presses copy of the latest volume from his hagiographic work, *The History of the Russian Empire under Peter the Great.* Voltaire was captivated by the story of Peter's reforms and his elegant new capital—how Peter had "civilized so many people . . . and made them fit for society," as Voltaire put it in his biography. To Voltaire, Peter the Great's reign in Russia had been a perfect test case of Enlightenment social theory. Voltaire and fellow Enlightenment partisans were arguing that if only people freed themselves from the superstitious teachings of religion and trusted in science, they could build wonders here on earth. (In Immanuel Kant's 1784 essay, "What Is Enlightenment?," the German philosopher defined the term *enlightenment* as "man's emergence from his self-imposed . . . inability to use [his] understanding without guidance from another" and offered the Latin dictum, *Sapere Aude!*—Dare to know!—as "the motto of enlightenment.")

To Voltaire, Peter's inquisitive, youthful journey to the West embodied the scientific spirit of the Enlightenment. Rather than trust in bearded priests' biased descriptions of the infidels to the west, Peter had gone to see for himself. Upon his return, Peter had pared back the power of the Orthodox Church and modernized a country many Europeans thought hopelessly barbaric. To answer those who dismissed Voltaire and his fellow philosophes as impractical dreamers, he could point to St. Petersburg, as if to say, "Go there, and then get back to me."

Catherine was ultimately unable to bring Voltaire to St. Petersburg—his advanced age made him too frail to make the journey—but she did manage to purchase his personal library at auction. Upon his death, she moved it to the Hermitage, where it was posthumously looked after by a marble likeness of the philosopher that Catherine had commissioned from French sculptor, Jean-Antoine Houdon. In the sculpture—one of the Hermitage's prized holdings—a seated octogenarian Voltaire, a classical robe draped over his fragile frame, looks out at the world with bemusement, his grand hopes for it dimmed by experience but not extinguished.

Though Catherine failed to lure Voltaire, she successfully imported his collaborator, her Paris-based art scout, *Encyclopédie* editor Denis Diderot, for a stint as her personal philosophy tutor in 1773. Diderot scandalized the Russian court with his radical egalitarianism and head-to-toe black attire. Though sixty years old, the philosopher was still a dynamo. When he would get particularly exercised about a point, he would tear off his wig and throw it across the room. But Diderot's insistence on radical political reforms soon got him into trouble. To Diderot, just as St. Petersburg had been a space on the map that could be built whole as a modern city, so Russia was a "blank sheet" that could be more easily reformed than Western countries.

When Diderot suggested that Catherine dismantle what he termed Russia's system of "masters and slaves," it was the last straw. Catherine, whose belief in the institution of serfdom was so unquestioning that she had been known to give serfs to her lovers as tokens of affection, replied that there were no "slaves" in Russia, only peasants tied to a land they loved and free in spirit if not body. As they spoke, a peasant rebellion was sweeping Russia. Catherine banished the philosophe back to Europe. "Monsieur Diderot," she told him, "I have listened with the greatest pleasure to all the inspirations of your brilliant mind; but all your grand principles, which I understand very well, would do splendidly in books and very badly in practice. In all your plans for reform, you are forgetting the difference between our two positions: you work only on paper, which accepts anything, is smooth and flexible and offers no obstacles either to your imagination or to your pen, while I, poor Empress, work on human skin, which is far more sensitive and touchy." To increasing numbers of Russians beyond the palace walls, it seemed the most demeaning of all possible situations. Not only was the empress seeking advice from foreign experts decades after Peter the Great had vowed that Russia would show Europe its ass, but when they offered advice for empowering the Russian people, the empress refused to take it.

Only the most favored Russians were permitted to speak freely in front of the empress—and even then, only for a night. Catherine's handpicked guests were invited to gatherings in the tradition of Peter's "assemblies." For her own take on the Parisian salon, held in an addition to the Winter Palace that Catherine had commissioned from one of her favorite French architects, Catherine composed ten rules and had them posted on the door. In keeping with the theories of the Enlightenment, she insisted on complete equality between the guests (rule 1: "On entering, titles

and rank as well as hat &, especially, sword will be left behind";
rule 2: "Pretentions based on prerogatives of birth, pride & other
similar sentiments will also have to remain outside"). Catherine
listed penalties for the violation of each of the rules. The most
severe was for violating rule 10 ("Leave all quarrels behind on
entering. What goes in one ear must go out of the other before
you cross the threshold"). Those who broke this rule were banished from her parties for life. Catherine had complete confidence
that Russians could treat each other as equals in one room for one
night and then leave to resume their roles in Russia's hyperhierarchical society. She thought a space for social equality could be
created for an evening in the Winter Palace without ever reaching the city streets beyond.

The French Revolution of 1789 changed all that. When news
of the storming of the Bastille reached St. Petersburg, the French
ambassador to Russia recorded the scene on the cosmopolitan
streets of the Russian capital. "I cannot describe the enthusiasm
which was excited among the merchants, the tradesmen, the
citizens, and some young men of a more elevated rank, by the
destruction of that state-prison, and the first triumph of a stormy
liberty," he wrote. "Frenchmen, Russians, Danes, Germans, Englishmen, Dutchmen, all congratulated and embraced one another
in the streets, as if they had been relieved from the weight of
heavy chains." Radical chic soon swept the capital. Revolutionary French songs were all the rage; a society lady was seen in
the English Club wearing a red Jacobin cap, the symbol of the
most radical faction in France. While the *St. Petersburg Gazette*,
an official government mouthpiece published by the Academy
of Sciences editorialized, "The hand trembles with horror in
describing events in which people could show such lack of duty
to the ruler, and to humanity," Catherine herself was not overly
concerned at first. She attributed the unrest to "the frivolous and
flighty spirit and the inborn recklessness of the French nation." It

was just the French being French. She knew these people. They get all wrapped up in their philosophical posturing, call you a despot, throw their wig across the room, and the next day you're friends again.

What alerted Catherine to the full implications for Russia of the events in France was the publication of a book, written anonymously by Alexander Nicolayevich Radishchev. Radishchev was in many ways a model of the new global Russians the new capital had made. Catherine had dispatched him, the bright son of a provincial noble family, to the West for training in 1766, sending him to study law and philosophy in Leipzig, Germany. When he returned, he worked his way up the St. Petersburg civil service ranks, ultimately becoming the head of the St. Petersburg Customs House, an institution that, in the most tangible way, linked Russia to the West. In his spare time, Radishchev translated works of the French philosophes into Russian and penned an homage to the American Revolution entitled, "Ode to Freedom."

As a student in the West, Radishchev had imbibed Enlightenment values and turned against autocracy. The institution of serfdom that had built Russia's modern capital, Radishchev came to feel, was an anachronism. In Germany, where he had studied, serfdom had died out along with catapults and jousting knights in the late Middle Ages. Radishchev codified his dissent in his *Journey from St. Petersburg to Moscow*, published in 1790, which used the conceit of a journey through the rural expanse of Russia between the old and new capitals to attack the serfdom that reigned there. Using the literary device of a found document, he even included a plan for freeing the serfs. While Westerners like Diderot had been urging Russia to abolish serfdom for decades, Radishchev was the first Russian to do so.

When Catherine got ahold of his book, she flew into a rage. Her copy, with its increasingly infuriated margin notes, exists to this day. "The questions brought up here," she jotted down in her copy, "are the ones over which France is now being ruined." Catherine ordered the anonymous author found out, arrested, and all copies of his book seized. Radishchev was, in short order, tracked down, detained, interrogated, and charged with publishing a book "filled with the most mischievous doctrines destructive of public order . . . tending to arouse among the people indignation against their rulers and government . . . and containing insulting outbursts against the imperial dignity and power." On July 24, 1790, Radishchev was tried by the Central Criminal Court in St. Petersburg and condemned to death. Still clinging to her identity as an enlightened monarch, Catherine commuted his sentence to ten years' exile in Siberia.

As Radishchev was duly roused from his cell in the Peter and Paul Fortress and sent to the Russian Far East, he became the first in a long line of political dissidents who had come to the capital filled with hope for a modern Russia only to end up imprisoned for their dreams. The Peter and Paul Fortress, the first structure Peter the Great built for his new capital, came to loom over the city as its torture chambers grew more famous than its shining cathedral spire. What had been built as a beacon of Russian progress became a symbol of Russian repression, as the autocrats' loyal henchmen struggled to put the genie of modernity back in its bottle.

As the revolution in France grew increasingly radical—stripping more and more powers from the aristocracy and then executing them outright—Catherine grew increasingly reactionary, closing many of the intellectual windows to the West that she had cultivated earlier in her reign. In 1791, Catherine ordered that all bookstores in St. Petersburg register their catalogue with the state-run Academy of Sciences. In 1793, when Catherine heard of the execution of the French king Louis XVI, she banned the importation and distribution of French publications, including the works of Voltaire, whose library she had purchased, and the

*Encyclopédie* that she had had published. Catherine smashed a bust of Voltaire in the gallery at her summer palace and had Houdon's masterpiece portrait banished to the Hermitage attic. In her old age, she would repudiate the philosophes she once embraced, even as they were elevated to secular sainthood by the French revolutionaries. She wrote to an old friend with regret that she hadn't trusted the warnings of her fellow monarchs. Remember, she wrote, "that the late King of Prussia [Frederick II] used to say that . . . the aim of the *'philosophes'* was to overthrow all the European thrones, and that the *Encyclopédie* had been created with the single aim of destroying all the kings and all the religions."

In 1796, Catherine set up the first formal system of censorship in her reign, ordering every foreign book to be inspected at the border. Later that year, Catherine, who had once so optimistically kindled the flame of reason, confident she would never be singed by it, died, embittered and adrift in a world that had spun beyond her control.

With the revolution in France, the internal contradictions of Peter's project were becoming clear. At the time of the French Revolution, St. Petersburg's population was roughly two hundred thousand, including thirty-two thousand foreigners. The cosmopolitanism of the capital was exposing Russia to destabilizing ideas from the West. And another, still undiagnosed, fault line had developed: the up-to-date capital, an island of modernity in a medieval Russian sea, had also opened up a wide and potentially destabilizing gulf between it and the rest of the country. In Western Europe, the gap in development between the capitals and the hinterlands was not nearly as great as in Russia. In the 1790s, over 95 percent of Russia's population was still rural while Western Europe was rapidly urbanizing. Male literacy in Russia stood at between 2 and 7 percent, compared with 47 percent in France, 68 percent in Britain, and 80 percent in Prussia (northern Germany). Even in bibliophilic St. Petersburg itself most commoners were illiterate, creating a massive social division within the supposedly modern capital. Peter and Catherine had proved the naysayers wrong: a model modern capital could indeed be built. But could it endure?

Peter had hoped Russia would join the modern world on the tsar's terms through a window on the West that would let in the light of science and technology but keep out the winds of political change. But the French revolutionary army crashed through that window in 1812 when Napoleon Bonaparte, the military dictator who had arisen out of the revolution's turmoil, invaded Russia. Napoleon made the tactical mistake of first taking out Russia's spiritual heart, Moscow, before attacking its administrative brain, St. Petersburg. Regrouping as Moscow burned, the Russian army and their allies ultimately pushed the French all the way back home and St. Petersburg escaped unscathed. In 1814, the Russians took Paris, and Catherine's grandson Tsar Alexander I rode down the Champs-Elysees on a white steed. Just over a hundred years earlier, Peter the Great had promised the Russians that by copying the West's technology, they could become a great power. Here was conclusive proof that Peter was right: they had defeated the West's mightiest army and were occupiers of Europe's finest capital.

In the aftermath of the French Revolution, Peter's implicit goal of Russia being modern without being democratic became explicit. As such, Alexander embraced a new model: the Roman Empire. As Rome was the hub of the greatest empire of the ancient world, so St. Petersburg would be the capital of the modern world's colossus, stretching from Eastern Europe to Northern California. And like imperial Rome, Russia would be technologically sophisticated but ruled by a single autocrat. Returning triumphant to St. Petersburg, Alexander embarked on a building spree, reimagining and rebuilding his capital in Roman imperial style.

To build the new Eternal City, Alexander tapped architect Carlo Rossi, who had trained in Rome and brashly declared that the Russians shouldn't "fear to be compared with [the Romans] in magnificence." Alexander appointed him head of the Commission for the Development of the Square Opposite the Winter Palace, charged with turning that space into the city's premier parade ground. It would get plenty of use. As one tsarist-era source records,

> During the period [following the fall of Paris], parades and reviews in Russia . . . singularly occupied the mind of Tsar Alexander I. . . . In St. Petersburg parades were held on the flowing days: on the day of Bogoiavlenia-Kreshchenski [Epiphany]; on March 13 in memory of the battle of Fer-Champ; on March 19, the day of the conquest of Paris; on May Day; the summer parade on August 17 in memory of the battle of Kulm, and the autumn and winter parades. Apart from the preceding ones, further parades were held for special occasions, such as the parade in honor of the arrival of Prussian potentates in St. Petersburg. Finally many parades were held in honor of each return of Alexander I to the capital from his many tours of Russia and abroad.

To create the central parade ground of the capital, Rossi framed the end of the square opposite the Winter Palace with a new military headquarters, the General Staff Building. The edifice, which still stands today, is the length of six football fields. In keeping with the panoramic feel of the city, Rossi used a perfectly flat façade. To shape the square, the pale yellow building wraps around it. Its only flamboyant feature—the central archway—is built in service to the parades, as a grand entrance to the square through which marchers entered from Nevsky Prospect. The arch itself is studded with niches filled with sculptures of Roman armor and topped by a statue of the angel of victory riding a chariot and holding a wreath with which to crown the victor. When the building was nearing completion, locals began to doubt that such a massive archway could support itself. For the opening of the building, Carlo Rossi, with his rosy cheeks and bushy side-whiskers, boldly stood atop the arch as the supports were removed.

With the name Carlo Rossi—the Italian equivalent of John Smith—he seemed the perfect man to rebuild St. Petersburg as a new Rome. He relished the role of the hot-blooded, operatic Italian. And yet Rossi himself was not all that Italian. He had been born in St. Petersburg, the son of an Italian ballerina who had been brought to St. Petersburg to dance and decided to retire there. Rossi's father was unknown but rumored to have been Tsar Paul I, Alexander's short-reigning predecessor. Raised in the St. Petersburg household of Paul's favorite architect, Vincenzo Brenna, who trained him, it was not until Rossi was twenty-six that he went to study in Rome. When he returned to Russia, he began his career in Moscow during the Napoleonic Wars and arrived in St. Petersburg at just the right time to transform his real hometown into a fantastical version of his presumed hometown. Neither entirely Italian nor entirely Russian, Rossi was a true Petersburger—a natural product of the attempt to create a modern city by importing talented Westerners like his mother.

Contemporaneous with Rossi's vision of St. Petersburg as the new Rome was a rival, stillborn vision for St. Petersburg as a global city whose architecture could import not just the best of the West but the best of the entire world. That vision came from French architect Auguste Ricard de Montferrand, a veteran of Napoleon's Grande Armée who, seeing greater opportunities serving the victorious Russians than his defeated countrymen, duly relocated to St. Petersburg after the war. In addition to building a victory column in front of the Winter Palace pointedly taller than the Petit Caporal's on Place Vendôme in Paris, Montferrand was tapped to redesign St. Isaac's Cathedral at the western end of Alexander's gigantic parade ground. To win the commission from the tsar, Montferrand had created a series of stunning miniature paintings to illustrate various styles in which he could build the church: Greek, Roman, Renaissance Italian, Byzantine, Indian, and Chinese. The emperor was impressed by his renderings, but there was no question in the royal mind about the style. The emperor demanded a neoclassical church with a giant gilded dome. After all, every other European capital already had one—London had St. Paul's, Paris had St. Genevieve's (which became the Panthéon with the revolution), and, most crucially, Rome had St. Peter's. St. Petersburg had to be like the other European capitals, only better. No question about it, its skyline needed a dome.

The disconnect between the emperor and his architect is intriguing. The Russian capital struck Montferrand, upon his arrival in St. Petersburg from France, as a global city with huge foreign populations, polyglot masses, and a French-speaking elite. The Russianness of it, just one cultural strand among many, added a frisson of Eastern exoticism. For the architecture of such a city, Montferrand wondered, why not have a sampling of the best the world had to offer? Why not a magnificent Chinese-style edifice or Indian temple? But to the Russians, St. Petersburg had to look like Europe. And Montferrand duly got with the program. In the book of plans he published in 1845—an enormous, sumptuously illustrated book worthy of the tsar's coffee table—Montferrand ran through the history of Western sacred architecture from the temples of the ancient Greeks and Hebrews through the masterpiece cathedrals of Europe, implicitly presenting his St. Petersburg church as the culmination of the Western tradition. In its dedication to the tsar, Montferrand cites all the great domes of Europe. He does not mention that he ever even considered building in a non-Western style.

But while the Romanovs benefited greatly from a fresh influx of Western experts from defeated France, occupying Paris also destabilized the regime in unforeseen ways. The Russian army could conquer France, but the values of the Parisians would conquer St. Petersburg.

The educated officer elite who had trained in St. Petersburg, Europe's most diverse city, and had been raised to believe it the equal of anything Western Europe had to offer were stunned by their experience abroad. For all Russia's military might, the defeated Western societies they occupied seemed centuries ahead of Russia socially, educationally, economically, and politically. Their months spent as an occupying force in Western Europe were a kind of study-abroad semester for the Russian officers. They read widely and attended lectures. Even for the common soldier, the experience of seeing the West was striking. "During the campaigns through Germany and France our young men became acquainted with European civilizations, which produced upon them the strongest impressions," one officer wrote. "They were able to compare all that they had seen abroad with what confronted them at every step at home: slavery of the majority of Russians, cruel treatment of subordinates by superiors, all sorts of government abuses and general tyranny." As another Russian wrote at the time, "There was only one subject of conversation in the army from generals down to the humblest private—how wonderful life was abroad." Their homeland's showcase modern capital seemed nothing but an oversized Potemkin village.

In 1816, six young officers from the elite Imperial Guards formed a secret society to bring constitutional government to Russia. St. Petersburg, they believed, deserved a government as modern as its buildings and its people. And St. Petersburg deserved to be run by Petersburgers: the officers called for the expulsion of foreign experts from the Russian government. When Peter the Great had first imported Western ringers, he assured his people that eventually Russians would acquire the expertise needed to run their own country. But over a hundred years later, the tsar's government was still filled with foreigners, some of whom could barely speak Russian. While the officers hoped to import many of the social and political ideas they had discovered abroad, restoring Russian honor would have to be done by Russians themselves.

The officers plotted that when the tsar died, their secret society would announce itself and refuse to swear allegiance to the new tsar unless he abolished autocracy and created an elected national legislature. Waiting for a succession was a remarkably timid strategy for reform. At the time the conspiracy was formed, the current tsar, Alexander I, was only thirty-nine years old and in excellent health. But in 1825, Alexander suddenly took ill during a trip to the southern edge of his empire. His doctors' prescription of laxatives and leeches only seemed to make him worse. On November 19, the tsar died. Modern experts suspect he had contracted a tropical disease, likely typhoid or malaria.

As Alexander had no children, his untimely death set off a crisis. The army pledged allegiance to Alexander's eldest brother, Constantine, unaware that when Constantine had married a commoner in 1820, he had, secretly and willingly, renounced his right to the throne. Younger brother Nicholas was only too happy to take charge, but he asked Constantine to come to the capital to clear up the confusion and publicly renounce the throne.

On November 24, when news of the tsar's death finally reached the capital, the secret society's hand was forced. They'd been waiting for nearly a decade, but they had no real plan. The cosmopolitan St. Petersburg conspirators decided on subterfuge, assuming that lecturing their illiterate rural enlisted men on Enlightenment political philosophy would be a lost cause. (Only one lone conspirator, Sergei Muraviev-Apostol, who had been raised in France, tried to educate his men, telling them to rebel for "divine liberty and sacred justice.") Rather than openly explain their aims and call for a republic or constitutional monarchy, the officers would instead paint Nicholas as a usurper and support Constantine. Since the officers knew Constantine didn't want to rule anyway, they figured he would be easier to sideline in favor of a provisional government.

On December 13, the conspirators, who would become known as the Decembrists for the month of their revolt, learned that the army would be asked to swear allegiance to Nicholas in St. Petersburg the following day. Early the next morning, the officers summoned their troops in full battle regalia and stood them in serried lines on a parade ground in front of St. Isaac's Cathedral dominated by an equestrian statute of Peter the Great, commissioned by Catherine. Then nothing happened. The Marine Guards, who were supposed to seize the Winter Palace, simply massed with the others on the square. Soldiers began shouting for Constantine. Others, confused about what they supported and why, supposedly cried out, "Long live Constantine and his wife, Constitution!" Another befuddled soldier reportedly exclaimed, "I'm all for a republic, but who will be our tsar?"

Nicholas watched the farcical revolt with glee. He had been tipped off about the conspiracy two days before and had positioned loyal troops around the square. While he hoped to avoid bloodshed, the early winter sunset left no time to defuse the situation. Nicholas gave the order to fire. Grapeshot tore through the crowd. As soldiers ran for their lives out from the square and across the iced-over Neva, Nicholas ordered cannons to shell the river in order to crack the ice and drown the men. The official death toll was 1,271.

Overnight, the authorities worked feverishly to erase all evidence of the revolt. Blood was scrubbed off the paving stones of the square. The city police chief, in haste, ordered the dead bodies thrown into the river through holes in the ice. They would reappear gruesomely on the riverbanks during the spring thaw. At the center of the square, a silent sculpted Peter watched as his grand project went awry, his pedestal now stained with the blood of the officers who had fulfilled his greatest hope by making Russia a great European power but also his greatest fear: autocracy betrayed.

The sculpture, unveiled in 1782 on the hundredth anniversary of Peter's coronation, depicts him riding a wild stallion rearing up on its hind legs, an allegory of the enlightened tsar taming wild Russia. The monument, called the Bronze Horseman, was a perfect encapsulation of Peter's city. It had been designed by a Westerner, the French artist Etienne-Maurice Falconet, who had written the article on "sculpture" in the *Encyclopédie*. Like the city, its construction combined modern technology with medieval barbarism. An engineering marvel, the sculpture is balanced on just three points—the horse's tail and two legs—but sits on a base carved from a 1,500 ton piece of granite hauled to the site pharaonic-style from five miles inland by hundreds of serfs. Befitting its East-meets-West location, the inscription, "[To] Peter the First [from] Catherine the Second," appears in Russian on the east-facing side of the pedestal and in Latin on the west-facing side. Like Voltaire, Falconet saw Peter's project as universal. To make the point, he purposefully made Peter's clothes nondescript, "that of all nations, of every man in any time," as he put it. The philosophes believed St. Petersburg would propel Russia toward reason and human progress. Yet viewers debate whether the horse is going forward or backward.

The new tsar resolved to break the unruly Russian horse once and for all. The trial and execution of the Decembrists marked the beginning of all-out repression in Russia. Dangerous as his ideas had been, Radishchev, Catherine's antagonist, was a lone scribbler; the Decembrists were an organized conspiracy. In 1826,

Nicholas formed the Third Section of His Majesty's Own Chancery, an ostentatious title for a simple concept: the tsar's secret police. The Third Section, from its stately offices above the red granite embankments of St. Petersburg's Fontanka Canal, built a massive spy ring that reached throughout the capital and into the depths of the empire. It censored books and intercepted mail. At St. Petersburg State University, Nicholas's regime pared back the teaching of philosophy and the liberal arts, mandating that instruction focus on technical subjects instead. Nicholas banned access to Voltaire's library in the Hermitage. And he strictly limited study-abroad opportunities, noting that Russian students "return from [Europe] with a spirit of criticism." To Nicholas's mind, building a window on the West had been a grave mistake. He resolved to slam it shut.

# SHANGHAI RACE CLUB

## Shanghai, 1842–1911

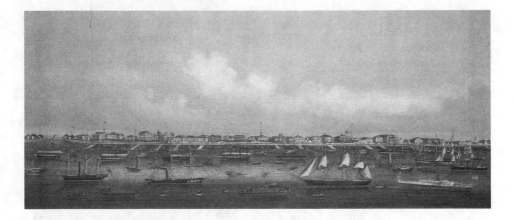

The Bund, mid-1860s

A thirteenth-century Mongol emperor is credited with naming the city of Shanghai, which means "above the sea" in Chinese. The emperor was describing the city physically—it sits on bluffs above the Huangpu River, a tributary of the Yangtze, just a few miles from where it empties into the ocean—but the name also embodies a deeper, albeit less literal, truth. Presiding over the innumerable trade routes of the world's largest ocean, the city of Shanghai reigns over the Pacific. If geography is destiny, the city where the Yangtze meets the Pacific—the gateway to the world for one-tenth of humanity—is, by rights, the leading city on the planet.

When Hugh Lindsay of the British East India Company first laid eyes on Shanghai, he understood its importance immediately. On his 1832 journey, Lindsay was floored by the hundreds of junks, some from as far away as Siam, plying the Huangpu by Shanghai. Then a regional market town of around two hundred thousand people hailing from all over China packed within a small circular city wall, Shanghai was already grander than the small fishing village that would be written into the self-serving lore of its Western imperialists. But Lindsay saw rightly that it could be much more than it already was. The scale of Asia's landmass, population, and natural resources, he realized, could make even the greatest European ports, like Amsterdam and Liverpool, into also-rans. "The advantages which foreigners, especially the English, would derive from the liberty of trade with this place are incalculable," Lindsay wrote.

The British East India Company functionary appreciated the tragic irony of this geographic fact: the world's greatest potential trading city sat squarely in its most insular, xenophobic empire. Imperial China was the least eager to trade of all the world's major countries. While China had once explored the world—the Chinese navigator Zheng He voyaged to India and the Middle East in the early fifteenth century with a fleet that made Columbus's three-boat flotilla look primitive by comparison—by the eighteenth century, the country had turned inward. What had been the world's leading shipbuilding facility, in Nanjing, had been shuttered by closed-minded emperors. Young Chinese who aced the national exams were made to master a self-referential canon of ancient Confucian texts rather than explore new technologies and parts of the world. In the Chinese system, the smart brothers who passed the exams made the rules for the dumb brothers who had failed them and had to make their living through trade. Domestic commerce was tightly regulated by the imperial bureaucracy, and international trade was strictly circumscribed.

While Britain ached to find new markets for its manufactured goods, the Chinese weren't buying. "We possess all things," Emperor Qianlong had informed a British envoy to his court in 1793. "I set no value on objects strange or ingenious and have no use for your country's manufactures. Our ways bear no resemblance to yours." The only product the British could find a market for in China was opium, a narcotic produced in their Indian empire that physically addicts its users, eroding their powers of free will.

In the early nineteenth century, the limited trade the Chinese emperor permitted with the West was done through Canton (now Guangzhou), on the Pearl River Delta nearly one thousand miles south of Shanghai. Canton had historically been China's international gateway. In the Middle Ages, Arab traders plowed its waters. With the rise of the West, first the Portuguese and later the Dutch, British, French, and Americans began trading with China through Canton. Opium in, tea out.

Western traders in Canton lived under the emperor's tight restrictions. Since the Chinese considered themselves the only civilized people on earth, the imperial authorities mandated that all barbarians be closely watched to prevent their contaminating the indigenous population with their inferior ways. A dozen Chinese men, appointed by the emperor, were given a monopoly on trade with the foreigners. In exchange for their monopoly, the Canton traders—known as the *cohong*—agreed to police the foreigners' behavior and collect their customs duties. Only the *cohong* could so much as communicate with the barbarians; the fate of human civilization itself depended on maintaining the quarantine.

Each *cohong* set up a trading house along the Pearl River, about two hundred yards outside the city. During the summer trading season, the river filled with ships and the warehouses with goods. Built up by the profitable commerce, the trading houses soon grew into substantial edifices, each flying a different foreign flag and equipped with vast verandas where sweaty Europeans could seek relief from South China's subtropical climate. When the monsoons came, the trading season was over and the foreigners had to leave—at the very least for the nearby Portuguese colony at Macau, if not for their home countries.

The Europeans grumbled over the emperor's restrictions, but the money was good so they kept their complaints to themselves. That all changed when, in 1839, the emperor outlawed opium, which he rightly saw as a public health menace and an economic drain on China. The emperor dispatched a hard-line governor to Canton to crack down on the trade. Spurred on by the British opium trading firms and their allies in Parliament, who feared a hideous trade deficit with the Chinese should they stop buying the only British product that interested them, the British struck back violently. For three years, the royal navy alongside British merchant ships fought the badly outmatched Chinese. In 1842, the emperor sued for peace, signing the Treaty of Nanjing. It was the first of what became known as "the unequal treaties," in which the emperor remained on the throne but made ever-greater concessions to the Western powers. The document was negotiated in a Nanjing temple dedicated to explorer Zheng He and signed aboard a sophisticated British warship, both painful reminders of the self-destructive inward turn that had set the stage for China's humiliation. As part of the peace deal, five Chinese coastal cities were opened up to trade, including Shanghai.

The emperor's negotiator had assured his boss that though "the demands of the foreigners are indeed rapacious . . . they are little more than a desire for ports and the privilege of trade. There are no dark schemes in them." He could not have been more wrong. For the new Shanghai, the Westerners had a mad dream: to undo the irony that had placed the world's greatest trading post in its worst trading empire, they would wrest Shanghai from China and build a Western city that just happened to be in the Far East. The city would initially be built to look like London and Paris and later Chicago and New York—but that was just the half of it. The Western traders who would live in Shanghai would reside in China physically, but legally, they would still be in Europe or America.

From the start, the Westerners saw Shanghai as far more than just another trading post. Though China's negotiators hoped for a system with a fixed trading season, with Westerners living on ships and leaving their families back home or in Macau, the British rejected this outright. Instead, they won the right to live in Shanghai year-round with their families and "whatever personnel the merchants might consider necessary to have on hand . . . for the purpose of carrying on their mercantile pursuits without molestation or restraint." This clause—with its enormous loophole— meant that the foreign population of Shanghai would be unlimited. An addendum to the Treaty of Nanjing, signed in 1843, made this explicit. The provision allowed Britons to buy or rent land and houses and put no restriction on the number of properties they could obtain. "The number cannot be limited," the treaty read, "seeing that it will be greater or less according to the resort of the merchants." Incidentally, the Treaty of Nanjing never mentioned opium, the ostensible cause of the war. In Shanghai, opium trafficking became an officially illegal open secret, regulated by informal agreements with the Chinese authorities that required ships holding the drug to dock downriver from Shanghai rather than in the city itself.

The 1843 addendum also established the diplomatic anomaly that birthed global Shanghai, a novel legal principle known as "extraterritoriality." Foreign merchants had always resented being bound by imperial China's strict criminal code, with its famously fetid jails and torture-induced confessions. Having won the Opium War, they decided they would no longer accept the fate of foreign travelers and businessmen in every country on earth: the requirement to abide by local laws. Under a stipulation in the Treaty of Nanjing, British subjects involved in criminal cases in China were subject only to British law. America's unequal treaty, signed in 1844, expanded this protection to civil cases as well. "Citizens of the United States," the treaty read, "who may commit any crime in China shall be subject to be tried and punished only by the[ir] consul . . . according to the laws of the United States. All questions in regards to rights, whether of property or person, arising between citizens of the United States in China shall be subject to the jurisdiction of and regulated by the authorities of their own Government."

Extraterritoriality soon took on spatial dimensions as sections of Shanghai were carved out as foreign-run zones called foreign settlements or concessions. In 1845, the 140-acre British Settlement was created at the confluence of the Huangpu River and the Suzhou Creek, half a mile north of the Chinese walled city. The British chose their site with trade in mind much as the Chinese had chosen theirs centuries ago for security. In 1849, the French Concession was established on the remaining land between the walled Chinese city and the canal that marked the southern border of the British Settlement. And in 1854, the American Settlement was created on the land across the Suzhou Creek to the north of the British Settlement.

While the Chinese initially saw the foreign zones as just more ethnic enclaves in an already diverse city—by the time the Opium War broke out, there were already twenty-six different Chinese regional guilds in Shanghai where migrants spoke their native dialects and preserved their folkways and foodways—the foreigners saw them differently. Their ultimate goal was to build Shanghai as a kind of Canton turned inside out. While Canton had been a large Chinese city with a tiny foreign ghetto, Shanghai would be an enormous white city built around a tiny Chinese ghetto. In the foreigners' early maps of Shanghai, the walled Chinese city was often left blank, a spot of uncharted territory; when it was included at all, it was often labeled "Chinatown," as if it were an immigrant enclave on a far-flung continent rather than a mainland Chinese city.

While the walled Chinese city was an organic tangle of streets, as the British Settlement grew, the foreigners laid out their thoroughfares in an orderly grid. The Land Regulations of 1845 agreed to by the British and Chinese authorities stipulated that the

British Settlement's riverfront—the towpath along the Huangpu River—must remain a public right of way. The British upgraded the towpath into a proper waterfront avenue. Soon construction sites dotted the Bund, as it was called, derived from a Hindi word meaning "embankment" that British East India Company hands had picked up in their prized South Asian colony. Chinese manual laborers were hired for a pittance to drive piles deep into the muddy, swampy towpath to lay foundations for the new trading houses along what would become the Wall Street of Asia. As one Westerner observed, a "dirge-like chorus depressing to the spirits" sounding like "Ah ho! Ah ho!" echoed through the Bund as the workers, called "coolies," from the Chinese *kwei-li* meaning "bitter strength," drove the spikes into the ground. Bitter strength would ultimately sum up the city itself. Built on the backs of the Chinese, it would become China's mightiest metropolis, rendering it at once China's greatest pride and greatest shame.

By 1843, eleven foreign merchant companies had already set up shop on the Bund. Designed by local builders, their offices looked like Chinese buildings, with the upturned eaves and courtyards typical of the Middle Kingdom. By 1846, Western-style buildings had begun to appear. Largely designed by a Cantonese contractor who went by the name Chop Dollar, they resembled the *cohong* trading houses of Canton, built with prominent verandas set in yards blooming with English roses, magnolias, and tulip trees. Most Chinese found the Westerners' buildings odd. Why, they wondered, would anyone want a courtyard-less building where you had to sit out front to enjoy fresh air? Where's the privacy? After a few bitter Shanghai winters, the Westerners found them odd as well. Breezy verandas made sense in near-tropical Canton; in temperate Shanghai, they realized, they'd do better to build as they did back home. While St. Petersburg's Western architecture was part of a grandiose plan conceived in the mind of its autocrat, Shanghai's occidental looks came from a trial-and-error attempt to create practical, comfortable surroundings for its far-flung traders. In contrast to "the most abstract and intentional city on the globe," Shanghai began as a pragmatic, ad hoc settlement essentially designed by committee with nary a thought as to what it would mean for China.

By 1847, the Bund was looking like an urban downtown in the West. A hotel, a clubhouse, and several stores had joined the trading firm headquarters. Commerce was booming: in 1844, 12.5 percent of all goods bound for Britain were shipped out of Shanghai; by 1849, it had already reached 40 percent. A British traveler who visited Shanghai in 1847 wrote, "Shanghae [sic] is by far the most important station for foreign trade on the coast of China. No other town with which I am acquainted possesses such advantages: it is the great gate—the principal entrance, in fact, to the Chinese empire . . . there can be no doubt that in a few years it will not only rival Canton, but become a place of far greater importance."

The foreign settlements were soon growing physically as well as economically: in 1848, the British used a diplomatic spat involving missionaries who were attacked while proselytizing in the countryside to expand their settlement to 470 acres from the original 140. By 1850, the Anglophone *North China Herald*, Shanghai's first newspaper in any language, could editorialize prophetically, "Canton has been the cradle of our commerce with this wonderful country [but] it is the destiny of Shanghae [sic] to become the permanent emporium of trade between [China] and all nations of the world."

Soon Western residents of Shanghai were referring to the city as their "eastern home" and their colony as the "Model Settlement." Indeed, by the 1850s, foreign Shanghai, with its revolving cast of expatriates, was nearly indistinguishable from a Western city. The only Chinese-style building remaining on the Bund was the temple-like Imperial Customs House, a symbol of the

Chinese governmental authority. The hub of foreign power was the British Consulate. Located on the best site in the city—the northernmost end of the Bund where the Suzhou Creek meets the Huangpu—the site was so good that the British consul put up $4,000 of his own money to secure it when his superiors in London balked. Opening in 1849, the consulate was built in the neoclassical style then in vogue in London in a collaboration between an American contractor and a British architect. Two blocks back from the Bund, the British erected their Anglican church, Holy Trinity Cathedral. In part designed by Sir Gilbert Scott, Britain's leading proponent and practitioner of the Gothic Revival style, the church, with its gargoyles and pointed arches, looked as if it had been airlifted in from the English countryside.

Ironically, as Shanghai's foreign concessions became more and more Western looking in this period, their populations became more and more Chinese. Seeking shelter from the fighting and civil instability sweeping the interior, Chinese refugees poured into the foreign settlements of Shanghai. The unequal treaties had made the weakness of the imperial authorities plain for all to see. So when a strange, charismatic leader named Hong Xiuquan, a serial flunker of the national exams who claimed to be Jesus Christ's little brother, rose up to topple the ineffectual Qing dynasty emperors, an army of hundreds of thousands backed him. From 1851 to 1864, Hong's Taiping Rebellion forces held large swaths of China, leaving millions dead and sending hundreds of thousands of refugees fleeing to Shanghai. The influx turned the foreigners' peculiar trading post into the fastest-growing city on earth.

At first, both Shanghai's foreign and Chinese authorities tried to restore the city's system of segregation by razing squatter camps in the foreign concessions. Soon they gave up as the foreign landlords realized there was more money to be made in housing the Chinese refugees than in evicting them. "My problem is how to amass a fortune as quickly as possible," one foreign landlord explained. "Renting plots of land to the Chinese and . . . constructing dwellings for them [can earn] 30% to 40% profits. . . . Within two or three years at the most, I hope to leave. What do I care if Shanghai is subsequently engulfed in fire or floods?" With this attitude prevailing among the foreigners, by 1854 there were twenty thousand Chinese living in the foreign concessions. Chinese nationals would remain the largest single ethnic group in the foreign settlements for the rest of their history.

To accommodate the influx, a new type of mass housing was created, called *lilong*. Derived from the Chinese words *li* (neighborhoods) and *long* (lanes), each development was a block, walled off from the main city streets, composed of lines of identical row houses extending along pedestrian alleyways. *Lilongs* were made of stone, like Western buildings, rather than wood, in the Chinese manner, and used an English row-house structure rather than a Chinese courtyard plan. But their urban planning, with the housing colony built behind walls and closed to through-traffic, was characteristically Chinese, reminiscent of the *hutong* neighborhoods of Beijing and other historic Chinese cities. By 1860, the British and American Settlements contained 8,740 *lilongs* compared with just 269 Western-style houses. As the homes and the gardens that once dominated the foreign settlements were razed to build dense *lilong* compounds, the concessions lost the feel of a gracious colonial town. Instead, their teeming streets took on the aura of a great metropolis.

With the influx of Chinese refugees, the Westerners' mad dream of building an all-white city around a Chinese ghetto foundered—but their dream of creating a city on Chinese soil that wasn't really part of China came true as never before. Not only did Shanghai look like part of the West but, as Chinese imperial power faltered throughout the 1850s, it began to function that way. Foreign Shanghai took on the powers of an autonomous state within a state, with its own armed forces, taxation authorities, and city councils. In 1853, Chinese Shanghai's anti-Imperial Small Swords rebels, a local faction supporting the larger Taiping Rebellion, seized the walled city of Shanghai from the emperor's officials. But when the emperor's forces tried to retake the city, the foreigners claimed neutrality in the civil dispute and forbade the Imperial troops from crossing through their settlement en route to the Chinese city. When the demand went unheeded, the self-styled Shanghai Volunteer Corps, a force of 250 Britons and 130 Americans, marched out to defend the boundaries of their concession and expel the Imperial troops. After a small skirmish that left thirty Chinese soldiers and four foreigners dead, the Chinese forces withdrew to the concession boundary. While the Imperial general likely backed down because of a diplomatic deal rather than out of any fear of the meager Western units, the "Battle of Muddy Flat" would enter the lore of the foreign settlement. If the most basic definition of a state is the entity that holds a monopoly on the use of force, by 1853, the foreign settlements were no longer parts of China.

The foreigners soon usurped the power to tax, another defining feature of a sovereign state. In 1854, when the Small Swords ransacked the Chinese customs office on the Bund, the foreigners debated how to respond. Many Western merchants decided it was the perfect excuse to stop paying the import and export duties levied by the imperial government. The French consul brazenly declared, "Until such time as I see established and recognized in Shanghai a regular authority able to guarantee the observation of the treaty articles . . . I consider myself free to allow my nationals' vessels to enter and leave without paying any dues." Other, craftier Westerners saw an even greater opportunity. Under the pretext that suspending customs payments would be tantamount to "consent[ing] to the abrogation of all treaties and to the utter destruction of our trade with China," British diplomats created a system whereby the Westerners would manage the customs office themselves, collecting the taxes on behalf of the Chinese government. As Shanghai cemented its status as China's global trading hub, these collections soon amounted to half the customs revenue for all of China, allowing the British to hold the emperor by the purse strings. The Westerners initially cloaked their new power by continuing to operate out of the restored Chinese-style customs house; in 1893, they ended the ruse and replaced the Bund's only Chinese-style building with a collegiate Tudor office complete with a clock tower whose chimes matched Big Ben's in London. Henceforth, British Shanghai not only looked like home, it sounded like it, too.

Even as the foreigners collected import duties on goods passing through the port on behalf of the Chinese government, their own Shanghai-based companies operated income tax–free. Though no provision of the treaties gave foreign companies immunity from Chinese corporate taxes, the foreigners' extraterritorial privileges meant that they couldn't be prosecuted for breaking Chinese tax laws. So they simply broke them with impunity.

The capstone in the creation of foreign Shanghai was the all-white Shanghai Municipal Council (SMC), founded by the British in 1854. A full-scale sovereign government to rule and tax their settlement in lieu of the Chinese authorities, the SMC was a merchant oligarchy cloaked in democratic clothing. The right to vote in SMC elections was restricted to the foreign landowners who paid the highest rents and taxes to the concession government; the property qualification was so high it excluded over 80 percent of the foreigners. Chinese were barred from voting outright, simply for being Chinese. And yet all residents of the foreign settlements—and already by this time most were Chinese—were required to pay taxes to support the SMC. In 1862, the French Concession established its own all-white municipal council. In the same year, the American Settlement merged with the British Settlement to form the International Settlement under the assurance of American seats on the SMC. With the creation of full-scale governments in the concessions, the foreign settlements of Shanghai completed their transformation, as one contemporary historian put it, "from mere residential zones into veritable enclaves that eluded Chinese sovereignty." These foreign zones carved out of China would endure for nearly one hundred years, a period the Chinese refer to as their "Century of Humiliation."

The foreigners who sought their fortune in Shanghai had every intention of creating a global business hub, but they created a global society almost in spite of themselves. As one British trader confessed, "Commerce was the beginning, the middle, and the end of our life in China—that is to say, that if there was no trade, not a single man, except missionaries, would have come there at all." Another put it even more crassly: "You must not expect men in my situation to condemn themselves to years of prolonged exile. . . . We are money-making practical men. Our business is to make money, as much and as fast as we can." That lure of instant wealth drew men from all over the world to Shanghai, the "El Dorado of the East." The fortune seekers came to call themselves, cheekily, "the Shanghailanders," to distinguish themselves from the Shanghainese locals.

Shanghai's extraterritorial status made it the most open city in the history of the world, with neither passport nor visa required for entry. All were welcome, albeit at different levels in the Shanghai pecking order. By 1870, the International Settlement's census showed myriad nationalities present. In addition to British, French, and Americans, there were Austrians, Prussians, Swedes, Danes, Norwegians, Portuguese, Spaniards, Greeks, Italians, Mexicans, Japanese, Indians, and Malays. Though all groups lived side by side, a clannishness pervaded the city's economy. Trading houses were typically organized along ethnic and national lines with Scottish firms and American firms, German firms and Jewish firms.

Shanghailander society was more meritocratic than back home in London or Paris or Boston. It was a city of self-made men whose pasts, however shady, were considered irrelevant. "Shanghai is tolerant," wrote one resident. "The mixed population is so good-natured that any one but a murderer may rehabilitate himself or herself after a long period of industry, repentance, and quiet."

At the top of Shanghai's slapped-together society sat the taipans, the great traders and captains of industry. The taipans' ideal was the Scotsman William Jardine. A doctor by training, Jardine initially went to Asia as a ship's surgeon on board a British East India Company vessel. Perhaps it was his medical expertise that made him realize opium's potential as a money maker; soon he'd retired his stethoscope and become a full-time drug trafficker. While proper British society looked askance at drug running, Jardine assured his potential investors that opium was the "most gentleman-like speculation I am aware of." Still, as he grew wealthier and more established, eventually attaining a title of nobility and a seat in the British Parliament, Jardine's firm—Jardine Matheson and Company—diversified into aboveboard businesses including textiles, real estate, and insurance. It was Jardine's meteoric rise from déclassé drug lord to landed aristocrat that other Shanghai newcomers hoped to emulate.

The would-be taipans who flocked to the city were known as "griffins," young newly arrived assistants hoping to impress their bosses and succeed them one day. By tradition, "griffin" status lasted for one year, one month, one day, one hour, one minute, and one second after arrival in Shanghai. Below the griffins were the "goosers," essentially office "gophers." Sometimes called "white boys," these office assistants were usually mixed-race Eurasians from Macau—part Portuguese and part Chinese. Aiding the Western traders were compradors. Literally "buyer" in Portuguese, compradors were the Chinese fixers who helped negotiate the imperial bureaucracy and communicate with local contractors and customers. Compradors were typically Cantonese whose families had migrated to Shanghai as the new treaty port displaced China's historic East-West exchange hub in the Pearl River Delta.

There were clear racial hierarchies in the foreign city, a continuum with whites on top and Chinese on the bottom. Even after residential segregation broke down, with Chinese living in the foreign concessions, public places remained segregated by a system similar to America's Jim Crow laws. When the British built a "public garden" on the Bund riverfront near their consulate, it was, despite its name, closed to the Chinese who constituted most of the public. It would remain segregated until the late 1920s, the only exception being made for Chinese nannies, called *amahs*, caring for foreign children.

Above the Chinese but below the whites were an array of groups, many of whom the British brought in from their other colonies for specific purposes. In the International Settlement, the British shipped in Sikhs from India—whom they prized for their martial traditions, not to mention their regal height, turbans, and mustaches—to serve as policemen. Among other duties, they patrolled the public garden to keep out the Chinese. A small Parsi community, a diaspora group of Persian Zoroastrians who had settled in India in the Middle Ages, also made their way to Shanghai following British trade routes. As "foreigners" in Shanghai, Parsis had full use of the public garden and other spaces from which the Chinese were banned. Still, given the city's racial hierarchies, passing not just for foreign but for white was of great importance. Shanghai's Jewish community, with roots in Baghdad, was careful to identify themselves as Sephardim, a Hebrew term literally meaning "Spaniards," denoting the descendants of Jews expelled from Spain in 1492. Though the Baghdad community's historical ties to Spain were dubious, by linking themselves to the Iberian Peninsula Shanghai Jews could claim the privileges of being "European" rather than "Oriental," whites rather than Arabs.

Each group brought its own world to Shanghai. "Peruvians do not behave like Germans, nor Frenchmen like Yankees," one resident explained. "With twenty nationalities to please nearly everybody ends up by submitting to the inevitable, and, whilst living, letting." In the foreign concessions, the Americans continued to celebrate July 4; the French, July 14; and the British, Queen Victoria's coronation day. If a German immigrated to Milwaukee, he became an American. But if he moved to Shanghai, he remained a German.

Entrepreneurs thrived importing products to recreate their far-flung homelands in Shanghai. One British-owned Shanghai department store guaranteed its customers everything they'd need to have a Christmas dinner "just like home," as its *North China Daily News* advertisement crowed. Americans flocked to the San Francisco–based Getz Bros. & Co., which opened up a Shanghai store in 1871, offering, as a 1903 ad put it, "A complete line of American Products and Manufactures." Beyond just importing Western products, the wealthiest trading firms imported chefs for true home cooking. The American opium-trading firm Russell & Co. shipped in African-American cooks from Mississippi to whip up Southern specialties like barbeque, grits, and fried green tomatoes. Not to be outdone, their Scottish opium-trade rivals, Jardine Matheson, opened up the dining room in its Bund headquarters to the entire foreign community. In the interest of keeping their tables full, they shrewdly imported a French chef rather than a Scottish one.

For most Shanghailanders, each group's organizations and clubs formed the core of local society, more than any official institutions. Germans congregated at the Club Concordia, founded in 1865, which eventually commissioned lavish murals of Berlin and Bremen over its bar. The French gathered in their sports club, the Cercle Sportif Français, while the Scots' Saint Andrew's Society was famous for its annual Caledonian Ball, which hundreds of men attended in kilts.

As usual, the Britons' Shanghai Club, which opened on the Bund in 1864, was first among equals. The famed bar in its renovated digs, built at the turn of the twentieth century, clocked in at 110 feet long and was reputed to be the longest in the world. More important, it was the yardstick by which Shanghai society was measured. The taipans congregated at the far end while the griffins grouped near the entrance. Social-climbing in Shanghailander society was measured by one's movement down the bar.

More than any club, it was the horse racing track that was, as a contemporary historian put it, "the social heart of British Shanghai." The city's first modest racecourse was laid out behind the Bund just after the Opium War in the 1840s, so the Western traders who made a living from gambling on the price of tea could spend their leisure hours gambling on the speed of horses. A larger course was built in 1854 and an even bigger one constructed in 1863, with a proper British cricket pitch in the middle. Eventually, the Shanghai Race Club grew so successful it became the third-wealthiest foreign corporation in China. As its name inadvertently implied, the Race Club was open only to members of the white race. With the Chinese pointedly excluded from the city's main park and social space, the metropolis itself could be seen as a kind of whites-only race club, with the Chinese on the outside looking in.

While Shanghai's Westerners bragged of their luxurious gambling venue, with its stately clubhouse and manicured lawns, they were quieter about their other great vice: prostitution. The get-rich-quick dreams Shanghai kindled had resulted in a foreign population that was over 90 percent male in the mid-nineteenth century as young men went to seek their fortune. An official survey taken by the British Consulate in 1864 showed that Shanghai's foreign settlements contained 688 brothels. But prostitution was more than just a way to spend a lonely night in the foreign settlements; it was, in a very real sense, what Shanghai was all about. The city became known not as the "whore capital of Asia," though that surely would have been a statistically accurate description, but rather as "the Whore of Asia."

The Westerners' only interest in Shanghai was in making money for their own gratification or, as they would sometimes put it in their stilted, nod-and-a-wink Victorian English, "opening up" Shanghai for "intercourse." Few Western residents of Shanghai even bothered to learn Chinese beyond the missionaries eager to save Chinese souls and wipe out practices like female foot binding. The attitude of most Shanghailanders was get in, get satisfaction, and get out. As the Westerners dressed Shanghai up as their fantasy of the perfect city, foreign Shanghai came to resemble a kind of adolescent boy's dreamworld. It was a Pleasure Island where the main green space wouldn't be a city park but a racetrack and whose civic pride wouldn't be the world's greatest art museum but the world's longest bar.

To enable the foreigners to conduct business without learning Chinese, a lingua franca—pidgin English—arose from a mixture of English, Portuguese, and various dialects from China and India. While a few Shanghainese pidgin phrases, like "no can do" and "chop chop," endure in colloquial English, in Old Shanghai, pidgin English was a complete business language. A Shanghai-based American journalist illustrated this in a hypothetical pidgin conversation he wrote up for his readership back home in the 1930s. In it, a taipan asks his comprador, "How fashion that chow-chow cargo he just now stop godown inside?" The comprador replies, "Lat cargo he no can walkee just now. Lat man Kong Tai he no got ploper sclew." In this exchange, the taipan wants to know why his mixed ("chow-chow") cargo is still in the warehouse ("godown"). The comprador answers that the cargo can't be moved ("no can walkee") because its buyer hadn't provided proper security ("ploper sclew").

This bizarre language embodies Shanghai's unique form of multiculturalism. Clearly the English are on top, making only the concessions to the Chinese that are absolutely necessary. And yet, this is not simply an English colony but an admixture of the whole world—hence the Iberian and South Asian influences. The foreigners of Shanghai may have wanted to simply recreate home, but they ended up creating a new kind of global city with its own Esperanto-esque language. It was a leap into the modern world even beyond St. Petersburg, whose elite, aspiring to verisimilitude with the West, spoke perfect French.

With the varied groups in Shanghai all able to do business with each other and an enormous, low-wage labor force of desperate Chinese refugees, the city's economy boomed. Even more than an ordinary business hub, Shanghai's business was all about location. Within the stone boundary markers that demarcated the borders of the foreign concessions, the economy operated under much freer rules than on the bureaucratic mainland. And the foreign powers that ran the concessions offered a level of stability available no place else in the imploding Chinese empire. As trade took off in what was indisputably China's best place to do business, the metabusiness of buying and selling the city itself— real estate speculation—took on a life of its own. "Land mania" ensued, as one early twentieth-century Shanghailander's history put it. *Lilongs* sprouted like mushrooms throughout the foreign settlements as land values spiked. The price of a hectare of land increased 3,000 percent from the 1840s to 1860s, twice that if it bordered the Bund. Major banks in the city moved their capital from opium into real estate and from real estate into shipping and back again in what looked like a virtuous cycle of ever-increasing profit. The Chartered Bank of India, Australia, and China (now Standard Chartered) opened its Shanghai office in 1858; the Hongkong and Shanghai Banking Corporation (now HSBC) opened in the city in 1865.

As with all great booms, in Shanghai, too, eventually the music stopped. When Imperial forces ultimately put down the Taiping Rebellion with the aid of European commanders that the beleaguered emperor had enlisted to lead his forces, peace broke out all over China. The refugees who had pushed up Shanghai real estate prices soon returned to their ancestral provinces. The Chinese population of the International Settlement fell from over five hundred thousand to seventy-seven thousand in less than a year. As the Shanghailanders lost their shirts, they grew enraged at their paying guests' exit. The *North China Herald* sneeringly speculated that

> the paternal government under which they found themselves, the impossibility of doing as they liked, of being as dirty as nature intended them to be, of shouting in the streets, of forming cess pools before each door, of firing crackers and tom-tom-ing in the middle of the night, of periodically taking the gods for an airing accompanied by fifes, gongs, drums and clanking chains—all the absurd limits which the Municipal Council assigned to the legitimate enjoyments of the Chinese must have seriously interfered with their comfort, and led them to look forward anxiously to the happy day when a benign heaven would restore them to their filth, disease and general noisomeness.

Almost overnight, the real estate boom went bust. Many of the Shanghailanders hadn't been producing anything other than paper wealth. As one observer wrote, "The bulk of the population is composed of a number of lively spirits who call themselves brokers, but whose occupation is apparently gone." Postcrash, the *Herald* editorialized on the "land speculators, some of whom made their first investment with borrowed capital, clothed themselves in purple and fine linen, and fared sumptuously every day.

Happy they who seized the auspicious moment, and shifted the responsibility of landed possessions to shoulders other than their own before the crash came [and] a striking change fell immediately on the complexion of land speculation. No longer were eager purchasers to be found, each holder was anxious to 'sell a bargain.' "

The formerly bustling metropolis began to look like a ghost town. The warehouses along the waterfront lay empty and the wharves abandoned. Six of the eleven banks in the International Settlement suspended payments. Destitute Shanghailanders who had lost everything in the crash wandered the empty streets amid half-built buildings still covered in bamboo scaffolding but devoid of workers. "Building operations were suddenly stopped," the *Herald* recounted in its year-end summation of 1864, Shanghai's annus horribilis. "Reeds and long grass commenced to grow in profusion of the lower floors of the dwellings occupied a month before by crowds of industrious natives. . . . Long lines of wooden tenements stand forlornly exposed to every blast, to the decomposing action of the elements."

With the economic panic, the Shanghai Municipal Council found itself facing a sovereign debt crisis. During the boom, with tax money flowing in, the SMC had borrowed even more to build a modern metropolis for the millions of residents the city would surely house one day. Now the city was shedding hundreds of thousands of people every year. "The Council have got into a sad mess in their money matters," the British consul admitted. "Their money, while they had a large frightened Chinese population of refugees willing to pay heavily for their protection, came in readily enough and was as readily spent, and now with a falling revenue they find themselves [deeply] in debt."

Shanghai would not experience a similar boom until the 1920s. But for the Chinese, even postbust Shanghai, even with all its racism, embodied the possibility for a new, modern China. Foreign Shanghai was inadvertently creating a new kind of global Chinese person—a Shanghainese—who spoke a hybrid language and was familiar with the cultures of many faraway nations. Like the *lilongs* in which they lived, which combined Western and Chinese architectural forms to create a building type unique to Shanghai, the new hybrid people that the city forged were different from their country cousins who languished in the Confucian backwaters of the empire. For the city's Chinese population, foreign-dominated Shanghai was uniquely humiliating but also uniquely liberating. In Shanghai, all the features and institutions of modern society were presented to the Chinese—but held just beyond their reach. Though Shanghai was designed by Westerners, for Westerners, its most enduring significance would be for the Chinese themselves.

Contact with the foreigners was changing the Chinese population of the city, estranging them from the traditional Chinese culture of their ancestral villages and initiating them into the modern world of trade, travel, and technology. Though the racecourse at the heart of the Westerners' social life was segregated, that didn't mean that the Chinese were fully cut off from this new pastime. As a writer for the American magazine *Harper's Weekly* reported from the races in 1879, Chinese men and women, banned from the stands at the racecourse, created their own informal races on the streets of the city: "At Shanghai on race-days vast crowds of this dark-haired people, of both sexes and of all ages, stream along the thoroughfares that lead to the race-course," the reporter informed his readers across the Pacific. "The majority are on foot, some are mounted on scragglylooking ponies, and many are conveyed on wheelbarrows, while the better-dressed people occupy carriages of various shapes and colors. Interspersed amongst them are to be seen the splendid equipages of Europeans. . . . On returning from the races this curious concourse seems imbued with the spirit which animated the jockeys, for . . . races with wheelbarrow [and] all the different sorts of vehicles vie with each other to get home first." Though barred from the Race Club's gates, the Chinese created an ersatz Western social space in their own streets, where adults engaged in games that would have been dismissed as child's play in the rest of the country and men and women mixed in public—a scandal in and of itself in imperial China.

Chinese capitalism was born in Shanghai in a similarly imitative manner as upstart Chinese businessmen began hawking bootleg copies of Western products. As early as 1863, the British food company, Lea & Perrins, was taking out ads in the *North China Herald* to warn Shanghai consumers of "spurious imitations of their celebrated Worcestershire sauce [with] labels closely resembling those of the genuine Sauce" and threatening lawsuits against anyone who dared to manufacture or sell the knockoff product. But Chinese business soon blossomed beyond its roots in cut-rate imitations. In time, Chinese businessmen were building legitimate companies and reinventing themselves as taipans, growing as rich as the foreigners and enjoying similar lifestyles.

Taking advantage of the capitalist island the foreigners had built with their imported extraterritorial legal system, compradors initially multiplied their earnings by investing their money in Western companies. Much of the capital for HSBC's Shanghai operations came from Chinese investors. Similarly, when the American firm Russell & Co. launched its Shanghai Steam Navigation Company, hoping to diversify its opium-heavy portfolio by bringing the steamship technology that worked so well on the Mississippi to the Huangpu, one-third of the capital came from the company's own Chinese compradors. Flush with returns, soon Chinese businessmen were buying and founding companies of their own. The steamship startup was bought outright by Chinese investors in 1877. Dubbed the China Merchants Steam

Navigation Company, the Chinese firm took over the Shanghailanders' fleet as well as their Bund headquarters, making it the
first Chinese-owned company to have a presence on the prestigious riverfront thoroughfare.

In Canton, compradors had been little more than glorified
domestic servants guiding Western businessmen through governmental red tape, translating documents, and fixing deals.
No matter how much wealth they amassed, they never gained
any social prestige in a Confucian society that valued scholar-
ship over business acumen. In Shanghai, however, compradors
like Tong King-sing, the mastermind behind the creation of the
China Merchants Steam Navigation Company, could become
taipans themselves. Educated at a missionary school in Hong
Kong, the young Tong, who reputedly "spoke English like a
Briton," moved to Shanghai to work as a salesman for Jardine
Matheson, cutting deals for raw materials with Chinese merchants up the Yangtze on behalf of his Scottish bosses. By 1863,
he had been named chief comprador of the firm. When he left
a decade later to found China Merchants, he was already one
of the richest men in Shanghai, overseeing a business empire in
banking, insurance, and newspaper publishing. Similarly, Hsu
Jun, who had begun his career as a comprador to a British trading firm, went into business for himself, first dealing tea and
silk, then founding his own bank and, by the late nineteenth
century, amassing a Shanghai real estate empire of over two
thousand rental properties in the International Settlement. By
the end of his career, Hsu lived like a Shanghailander magnate in
a sprawling Western-style mansion with polished marble floors
on Bubbling Well Road, the most fashionable residential street
in foreign Shanghai. A staff of eighteen servants kept the place
up to Hsu's exacting standards.

As more and more Chinese struck it rich, Bubbling Well
Road became a see-and-be-seen promenade for the Chinese

elite, including Chinese women whose counterparts in imperial China were generally confined to the home, physically disabled by their bound feet. "Celestial beauties drive along this road, arrayed in splendid silks and satins, got up in the height of Chinese fashion," one Shanghailander gushed.

Surrounded by their success, the wealthy Chinese merchants of Shanghai began to see their society as a microcosm of a modern China. Just as they had adopted certain aspects of Western modernity—new technologies, social mores, and business practices—and in doing so beat the Westerners at their own game, so too could China, as one reformist official put it, "learn the superior techniques of the barbarians to control the barbarians."

Even China's generally conservative and insular imperial officials began to take notice. Modernizing factions within the Qing dynasty began supporting a Shanghai-centered "Self-Strengthening" campaign, championed in the city by Li Hongzhang, an official and businessman who backed the creation of a series of commercial joint ventures between the local government and Shanghai merchants. The first joint venture was a munitions plant and arsenal run by the Chinese but stocked with the latest imported American machinery. While the plant adopted Western methods of production, it kindled the dream of one day turning the modern weapons it forged on the Western occupiers themselves. Li also founded Shanghai's Interpreters' College to teach gifted Chinese students Western languages and science. Beginning in 1868, the college's publishing house began issuing translated editions of Western works on science, law, and history—a repository of information that became a tremendous resource for Shanghai's growing community of worldly, reformist intellectuals.

Still, there were limits to what the increasingly wealthy, Westernized merchants of Shanghai could accomplish. While they saw their pioneering businesses—among them the first

Chinese-owned paper mill, shipyard, and telegraph company—
as part of a larger "Self-Strengthening" program, they were
never scaled countrywide. Conservative factions in Beijing,
jealous of the Shanghai merchants' success and still skeptical of
their vision of a China empowering itself through imitation of
the foreigners, limited their businesses to Shanghai-based quasi-
governmental monopolies, eschewing the chance to develop
China more generally.

And while the Chinese elite could benefit from the modern economy of Shanghai and insulate themselves from its humiliations—
the sting of the foreigners-only one-acre Public Garden on the
Bund didn't sting as much for those with private yards twice its
size—the Chinese masses could not. For them, living in Shanghai was an experience of being surrounded by an alluring modern world built by them, for others. Shanghai was China's most
modern city, but it was not a modern city for most Chinese.

With voting in the Shanghai Municipal Council's elections
limited to a small, white merchant oligarchy, the councilmen's
main goal was to keep taxes low on their wealthy constituents,
not to build a modern city for all. Apart from the Bund and a few
major streets, road construction was left to the local inhabitants.
The streets of the rich were well paved while the streets of the
poor remained muddy ruts. When modern conveniences were
brought to the city—gaslights were introduced in 1862, electricity in 1882, running water in 1883, and a tramline in 1902—they
arrived on schedule with such improvements in leading Western
cities like London and New York. But, as they were brought by
private companies rather than public utilities, the modern world
was only available to those who could pay the going rates. Most
Chinese couldn't afford running water, gas, and electricity so
they simply didn't have any. Surrounded by the bright lights of
one of the world's greatest cities, most Chinese literally lived in
the dark.

Since most British families sent their children back to the United Kingdom for boarding school, the Shanghai Municipal Council, for all its pride in being a sovereign government, viewed building schools as beyond its mandate. The only educational institutions for Chinese students were built by Western missionaries. It was not until 1900 that the Shanghai Municipal Council finally built a public school for Chinese children and a public hospital for Chinese patients.

In perhaps the most extreme expression of the Shanghai Municipal Council's philosophy of government for profit, Shanghai entered the twentieth century without a sewer system. Instead, people placed buckets of their excrement, euphemistically called "night soil," outside their homes for collection by a company that sold it to farmers as fertilizer. The night soil company paid the municipal council for the privilege of collecting the free feces. It seemed the perfect privatized sanitation system—rather than pay to build a sewer system, the International Settlement authorities were getting paid not to build one. Needless to say, the vegetables grown in the night soil routinely infected Shanghai diners with cholera, typhoid, and dysentery. And yet the system endured until the 1920s, a jarring reality that caused the *Far Eastern Review* to observe wryly, in a 1919 article, that Shanghai boasted "every modern convenience, except sewerage."

While modern conveniences were unequally distributed in Shanghai, they were completely unknown in the rest of China. Foreign domination of the city and unusually business-friendly local officials like Li Hongzhang gave Shanghai a power and wherewithal to modernize found nowhere else in the empire. Under the gloss of Chinese cultural chauvinism, the emperor used his authority to quarantine technology in Shanghai, the modern world in a single city. For decades, the emperor refused to allow the foreign taipans of Shanghai to build railroads in China, wary that they would help the foreigners rob his empire blind, as they seemed to be doing in India. A proposal made by foreign merchants in 1863 to build a railroad linking Shanghai and Suzhou, a city sixty miles inland, was rejected, as was a grander proposal for a Chinese national rail system the following year. In 1876, foreigners added an unauthorized tramline to a road that the Chinese authorities had commissioned them to build, linking the burgeoning foreign settlements to the hinterlands. When a pedestrian was killed a few weeks after its opening—a probable suicide—the Chinese authorities bought the track in a forced sale and promptly tore it up.

Similarly the emperor's top representative in Shanghai, the *taotai*, did his best to quarantine both the telegraph and electricity within the concessions. In 1866, the American firm Russell & Co. had built a telegraph connecting Shanghai's French Concession with the former American Settlement that had just merged with the British. As the wire was routed entirely within the foreign settlements, it did not need Chinese approval. But when the company proposed to build a regional system beyond the confines of the foreign settlements, the *taotai* stopped it after a man died under the shadow of a telegraph pole. He blamed the telegraph for interfering with the man's feng shui. The *taotai* similarly tried, unsuccessfully, to ban the few Shanghai Chinese residents who could afford it from using the electricity they saw all around them in the foreign concessions, arguing that the new technology was untested and dangerous.

From this nose-pressed-to-the-glass experience of modernity, the question for the Chinese became whether to build upon or to destroy the modern society in their midst. And foreign-dominated Shanghai allowed them more freedom to debate this question than anywhere else in China. Just as international Shanghai's extraterritorial legal system opened up opportunities for Chinese businessmen unknown elsewhere in China, so too did it open up space for Chinese intellectuals. Though the unequal treaties never mandated it, Chinese residents of the foreign settlements began to enjoy some extraterritorial privileges, including more freedom of speech, thought, and the press than their mainland countrymen. A judicial forum called the Mixed Court, initiated in 1864 to hear cases involving Chinese imperial subjects arising in the International Settlement, was presided over by a Chinese judge and a Western magistrate's assistant from the settlement's consulate. As time went on, the "assistant" became more powerful than the judge. By the early twentieth century, the Chinese authorities had lost the power to arrest Chinese subjects in the foreign settlements or even have them extradited for crimes committed on Chinese soil.

Beyond the arm of the emperor's law, critical Chinese newspapers that would have been censored elsewhere were published in the foreign settlements, bankrolled by Shanghai's wealthy Chinese merchants. When the nostalgic Boxer Rebellion failed at the turn of the century, crippling China with reparation debts to the Western powers and further discrediting the Manchu dynasty, the anti-imperial Shanghai modernizers seemed to offer a viable way forward.

Winning over public opinion with the pro-modernization editorials in their newspapers, Shanghai's leading Chinese citizens endeavored to construct a parallel modern world for the Chinese by mirroring the Western settlements' institutions. First, the traditional Chinese guild and community institutions took it upon themselves to get the Chinese city's infrastructure up to the standards of the foreign concessions. The "Impartial Altruism" society organized a system of street cleaning, while the "Efficient Care" charitable association created a fire brigade of fifty firefighters. A formal, public Office for Commercial Affairs was created in 1895 to spearhead economic development, and an Office for the Construction of Roads was created to extend and pave the Bund along the waterfront by the Chinese city, south of the foreign settlements.

In 1905, Chinese citizens went a step further, rising up to demand representation on the all-white Shanghai Municipal Council. Crowds of Chinese rioted through the International Settlement, sparring with British and Sikh policemen and burning a police station to the ground. To restore order, the Shanghai Municipal Council agreed for the first time in its history to meet with representatives of the Chinese population. No Chinese would be permitted to serve on the council, the white leaders explained, but the feasibility of a "Chinese advisory committee" would be considered. Once order was restored in the city, the white taxpayers voted down the proposed committee.

Though the Chinese were rebuffed in their effort to join the council, they successfully set up their own government to oversee the walled Chinese city. In 1905, the Office for the Construction of Roads became the General Office of Public Works, a municipal council for the Chinese city of Shanghai. Modeled on the International Settlement's Shanghai Municipal Council, the General Office of Public Works consisted of a sixty-member council elected by Chinese taxpayers. It was a totally unprecedented new form of representative government in China. Dominated by merchants and compradors, the civic government created a public sector for the Chinese city, including an eight hundred–man police force and an indigenous volunteer corps explicitly modeled on the foreigners' militia. As a veteran of the corps, present at the creation, later recalled, the founder "proposed that a voluntary militia like this one in the International Settlement should be organized in Chinese Shanghai." The council also initiated urban improvements, dredging canals, building roads and bridges, installing public lighting, and creating a system of garbage collection. Part of the drive to modernize the Chinese city was the humiliation of having its fetid alleyways constantly compared to the modern city that lay just beyond its walls. As one Chinese newspaper editorialized, "When strangers first come to Shanghai, wander about the Settlement, and see how clean and broad the streets are . . . they cannot help asking in delight: 'Who had the power to do this?' We tell them: 'The Westerners.' . . . If the Chinese area is compared to the Settlement, the difference is no less than that between the sky above and the sea below."

While the ultimate goal of creating Chinese versions of the Western institutions was sending the foreigners home, the question of how exactly to retake their city divided Shanghai's Chinese elite. Some wanted to make the emperor powerful enough that he could restore China's independence; others hoped to overthrow the emperor and create a Chinese republic. In the early twentieth century, the anti-imperial faction gained the upper hand.

The call to revolution roared out of Shanghai from a pair of dissident journalists, Zou Rong and Zhang Binglin, who, in an anti-imperial screed published in 1903, called for the assassination of the emperor. The crux of Zou and Zhang's rhetorical attack was to tar the imperial family themselves as foreigners, conflating their rule with the Western domination of China. Indeed, the Qing dynasty had been founded by invaders from the north in the seventeenth century. Coming from Manchuria, the rulers were known as the Manchus to distinguish them from the Han people, China's ethnic majority. As the centuries passed, most Chinese had come to accept the Manchus as the legitimate rulers of the nation, no different from the earlier imperial dynasties. But as humiliation after humiliation befell China from the Opium War onward, a new intellectual space had been opened up in which a Chinese person could be pro-Chinese but anti-emperor. And with the extension of extraterritorial privileges like anti-Qing free speech and assembly to Chinese residents of the foreign concessions, Shanghai became the physical space where this view could be most freely expressed. When Zou and Zhang were sentenced to death in absentia by an imperial court, the concessions' foreigner-dominated Mixed Court refused to extradite them. Instead, it gave them mild prison sentences, arguing that the death penalty could not be applied for holding dissident opinions. Ironically, anger at the emperors was rooted in their allowing China to be humiliated by foreigners, but the freest place to express or publish such opinions was in Shanghai's foreign-administered concessions; the Chinese nationalist backlash against Western domination was born in Westerner-dominated Shanghai.

While the first Chinese-language newspapers in Shanghai had been published by Western missionaries and were generally concerned with proselytizing (though one British paper did spur modernization by exposing Chinese readers to the accomplishments of Russia's Peter the Great and Japan's Westernizing Meiji emperor), by the first decade of the twentieth century, revolutionary Chinese-owned newspapers dominated the Shanghai media market. The Revolutionary Alliance, an anti-imperial political party that had been founded by Chinese expatriates in Japan, inspired by their host country's modernization, and later headquartered in Shanghai's foreign settlements, put out a succession of papers—*People's Sigh*, *People's Cry*, and *People's Stand*—that gave Shanghai's Chinese readers a slant on the news that they could never have found in the rest of China. Local newspapers spurred protests against a series of foreign humiliations, including the 1904 murder of a rickshaw coolie by a Russian navy man who disputed his fare and the 1905 extension of the agreement between the Chinese emperor and the United States that barred Chinese immigration to America. In pamphlets published by student radicals, the nuanced arguments of Shanghai's nationalist intellectuals were boiled down to simple incendiary imperatives: "All press ahead! . . . Kill! Kill!" incited one flyer, calling on China's people to wipe out both the foreign colonialists and the Manchu imperial interlopers. "Revolution, revolution! Achieve it, then you may live . . . fail in it, then you may die," another exhorted.

A spat over the right to build railways in China united the city's business elite, nationalist intellectuals, and student radicals with the masses of the hinterlands in anti-imperial, anti-foreign fury. In 1898, the weakened Chinese emperor had finally granted the foreigners the right to build railroads beyond the foreign concessions. But the increasing wealth and sophistication of the Shanghai business elite meant that by 1905, Chinese Shanghai firms had the wherewithal to build a railway system themselves. The prospect of the modern Chinese of Shanghai being capable of building a modern nation, as symbolized by the railroad, only to be held back by Westerners in league with a Manchu emperor led to nationwide demonstrations. Though the demonstrations were suppressed by 1907, the same urban-hinterland alliance would topple the emperor just four years later.

The Chinese revolution of 1911 that ended the two millennia of rule by emperors broke out inland, but it was very much a Shanghai revolution. Newspapers and political groups in Shanghai had laid the intellectual groundwork for the uprising; its lodestone was a vision of modern China born in Shanghai; it was organized by the Shanghai-based Revolutionary Alliance; and Shanghai's merchants bankrolled the revolt. When news reached Shanghai of the inland uprising against the Manchus, the city's elated, irate populace bid up the cost of a copy of *People's Stand* to ten times its cover price. Only three weeks after the outbreak of the revolution, rebels easily seized the arsenal Li Hongzhang had built decades before, and Shanghai's Chinese city declared its independence from the emperor. The "Shanghai rising," as it came to be called, was a largely bloodless affair. In less than a month, most of the country had slipped beyond imperial control, and on January 1, 1912, the birth of the Chinese republic was declared.

With the fall of the emperors, the Chinese merchants of Shanghai could finally implement the full-scale modernization plans that the Luddites in the Forbidden City had forbidden for so long. The circular wall that had cut off the Chinese city from the foreign settlements was demolished. The tramlines that foreigners had built in their concessions were extended into the Chinese city. Physically, at least, Shanghai, which had for seven decades been two cities—one Chinese-administered, the other foreign—was united as one.

Socially, Chinese and foreign Shanghai were drawn together as well. At the news of the empire's collapse, the Chinese men of Shanghai promptly cut off their queues, the mandatory long braids that signified submission to the Manchu emperors and, in multicultural Shanghai, served to underscore the difference between Chinese and foreign residents. Chinese police patrolled the streets with scissors, shearing laggards. Those who failed to comply typically did so more out of ignorance than imperial sympathies. As a Shanghai missionary wrote at the time, "Many a poor innocent farmer, who had never heard of revolution, found himself rudely nabbed and clipped as he came into market." Meanwhile, Shanghai sophisticates reveled in their newfound freedom, slicking their hair down with oil in the trendy Western style. Imitative though those first styles were, a new space for self-definition had been opened up that would eventually lead to the hybrid fashions of Shanghai's Jazz Age modernity.

But if postrevolutionary Shanghai was more unified than ever, the revolution's aftermath made clear that China's international, modern hub was deeply estranged from the rest of the nation—an estrangement embodied by the bewildered country farmer set upon and sheared of his queue on the streets of the metropolis. The rest of the nation was ill prepared for the idealistic visions of the Shanghai nationalists who, unlike their countrymen, had already had a test run at electoral democracy through the local council. As the revolutionary factions turned on each other, the most authoritarian ended up on top, in league with the Western powers who still held China by the purse strings.

A series of political assassinations rocked Shanghai and paved the way for dictatorship. In January 1912, a young army officer named Chiang Kai-shek, who would ultimately rule postimperial China as a military strongman, executed his revolutionary rival, Tao Chengzhang, while he was recuperating in the city's Sainte-Marie Hospital. When, in March 1913, the Nationalist party leader tapped to be prime minister, Song Jiaoren, was assassinated in the Shanghai train station before he could board the train to his Beijing swearing in, dreams of a republic gave way to the reality of dictatorship under a series of despots.

Shanghai's Chinese merchants, who had been so instrumental in fomenting the revolution, ultimately backed stability over democracy. "As Shanghai is a trading port and not a battlefield . . . whatever party opens hostilities will be considered an enemy of the people," the Chinese General Chamber of Commerce declared. In a nation still struggling to catch up with the West, they concluded, strong central authority was the only choice. They would content themselves to live in a dictatorship as long as they could get rich.

# *URBS PRIMA IN INDIS*

## Bombay, 1857–1896

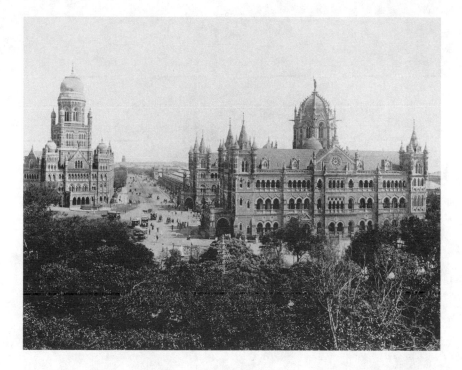

Bombay Municipal Corporation (left) and Victoria Terminus (right)

On the afternoon of October 13, 1857, a crowd of hundreds of Europeans and thousands of Indians gathered on the Esplanade, the wide grassy expanse between the Arabian Sea and the British East India Company's Bombay Fort, as two sepoys, Indian soldiers enlisted under British officers, were led out onto the field. On the order of Captain Bolton of the Royal Artillery, both Sayyad Hussein, a Muslim, and Mangal Gadiya, a Hindu, were publicly stripped of their uniforms and tied to the ends of loaded cannons. "Then was seen a flash," the *Bombay Times* reported, "and the unhappy men were launched into eternity. The bodies of the traitors were blown to pieces and their mangled remains fell in bloody fragments on the ground. It was a ghastly and horrible spectacle and one which must have carried terror to the heart of the miserable wretches who may be hatching treason against us."

The British authorities in Bombay counted themselves lucky that the Sepoy Mutiny, as they termed it, had not been even worse in their city. Earlier that year, the Bengal Army, headquartered at Calcutta and stationed throughout North India, had risen up against its officers when rumors spread through the units that their new ammunition cartridges were greased with hog and cow fat. Since loading their muskets required biting off the end of the cartridge, this would violate religious tenets for both Muslims, who were forbidden from eating pork, and Hindus, who were forbidden from eating beef. When soldiers who had refused to load their weapons were publicly humiliated, some even dishonorably discharged, revolt swept the ranks as Indian enlisted men turned on their British officers.

When news of the revolt reached Bombay, the British East India Company authorities inside the Bombay Fort had grown worried, in particular about the city's large, restive Muslim population. It had only been five years since the city was engulfed in the harrowing Mohammed cartoon riot. In 1852, a Parsi-owned Bombay newspaper published an article on the life of the founder of Islam, Mohammed, accompanied by a hideous illustration of the prophet. An agent provocateur pasted the cartoon to the door of the city's main mosque, the Jama Masjid, during Friday prayers. When the congregants emerged, they grew enraged and attacked Parsis indiscriminately. Moreover, Muslims influenced by the austere Wahhabi movement, the brainchild of a conservative theologian on the Arabian Peninsula named Mohammed Ibn Abd al-Wahhab, had been restive throughout the British Empire in the nineteenth century. The British worried Bombay's Islamic community merited what they termed their "Wahhabi phobia"— imperial fear of radicalized anti-Western Muslims—especially now that rumors ran rampant that the British had forced Indian Muslims to unwittingly consume pork. Yet the Eid al-Adha holiday commemorating Ibrahim's willingness to sacrifice his son passed without incident in the summer of 1857.

Many Indian Bombayites actively backed the British in the revolt. As writer Govind Narayan, who had been brought to the city from Goa at the age of nine by his parents, put it in his 1863 chronicle of his adopted hometown, during the rebellion, "members of all communities offered prayers in their respective temples on three occasions to seek victory for the English, that their rule continue unharmed." When the small plot among the Bombay sepoys for a citywide uprising on Diwali, the Hindu festival of lights, was personally discovered and thwarted by Bombay's British police chief, the leaders met their fate on the Esplanade two days before the holiday, and that was that. Since the Bombay Army remained loyal to the British, its troops were dispatched to more rebellious parts of India to restore order.

Though the British ultimately quelled the Sepoy Rebellion, the uprising had taken the imperialists by surprise. India had been quiescent under the thumb of the British East India Company for a full hundred years, since the Battle of Plassey in 1757. And the Parliament-chartered Company had long prided itself on its light hand. Even after establishing its authority over the subcontinent, the Company left the Mughal emperor on the throne in Delhi as a figurehead. Instead of foisting British laws and social norms on the Indians, the Company had taken pains to codify existing Hindu and Muslim legal traditions, only imposing its own values in the most extreme cases, like outlawing sati, the ritual suicides in which widows threw themselves on their husbands' funeral pyres. But the uprising, during which portions of North India defied British control for an entire year, had discredited British East India Company rule. On August 2, 1858, Parliament passed the Government of India Act, revoking the British East India Company's authority over the subcontinent, ending the Mughal dynasty, and transferring all power over India to Queen Victoria herself. The British Raj, nine decades of direct royal rule over the jewel of the empire, had begun.

On November 1, 1858, the Queen's Proclamation was read on the steps of Bombay's neoclassical, British East India Company–built Town Hall. In the proclamation, Victoria promised her Indian subjects tolerance for their varied faiths and modernization of the country (what she termed "social advancement" and "peaceful industry," which we would today call "development"). Following an honorary salvo from the assembled troops, the crowd watched as the ever-so-slightly-asymmetrical Union Jack was raised over Town Hall—upside down. Though it was immediately righted as the first chords of "God Save the Queen" rang out, the image of the city that would become the greatest metropolis of the Raj fanned out beneath an upside-down British flag was all too apt for Bombay. For try as they might, the British never quite created their tropical London on the Arabian Sea. Rather Bombay, the second city of the empire, would rise as a kind of bizarro London, where the punctiliously planned efforts of the British were refracted in the fun-house mirror of the teeming, multicultural subcontinent.

The archipelago off the coast of India that became Bombay was initially taken by the Portuguese in the sixteenth century. They thought it a good bay (*bom bahia* in Portuguese) and named it as such. When the islands passed into English hands as part of the dowry the Portuguese princess, Catherine of Braganza, brought to marry Charles II of England, the name was anglicized to "Bombay." In 1668, the Crown leased the islands to the British East India Company for the bargain-basement sum of ten pounds a year.

The site the Company had rented was a great port but not yet a great port city. The seven islands that made up the archipelago were fully distinct only at high tide, when they were divided by open sea. At low tide, when the waters receded, a marshy wetland divided the green hills. Watching the tides roll in and out, the shrewd new British rulers of the islands deduced that by blocking off the points through which the sea flowed in, they could triple the area's landmass—all without increasing their rent. By reclaiming land from the sea, they would turn these marshy islands into one of the world's greatest metropolises. As Salman Rushdie, the finest novelist the city has yet produced, would later put it, the

British "turned the Seven Isles [of Bombay] into a long peninsula like an outstretched, grasping hand, reaching westwards."

The reclamation effort began in 1708, as Indian laborers under Company direction built a massive stone causeway that cut off one of the key points through which the waters came rushing in. The largest and most important floodway was sealed in 1782 on the order of Governor William Hornby, the British East India Company's point man in Bombay. To Hornby, the benefits of reclamation were so self-evident that he ordered causeway construction to begin without approval from the Company board in London. The directors refused to sign off on his plan, balking at its steep 100,000-rupee price tag, but by the time they sacked Hornby for insubordination, the reclamation had already been completed. The erstwhile governor would be vindicated from beyond the grave: in the great city that rose atop the swamp he had drained, the main commercial thoroughfare would be named in his honor.

To populate their giant island, the British East India Company authorities in Bombay promised newcomers the physical protection of their fort and the spiritual solace of religious freedom. Religious communities that had sought refuge in India from the fractious Middle East in earlier centuries, including Persian Zoroastrians (Parsis) and Yemeni Jews, flocked to Bombay. Envisioning the West-facing port as the principal trade link between Europe and the subcontinent, the British lured traders from all over India to set up shop on the island. To sell the teakwood of South India, Keralites came to Bombay; to deal the gems of the North, Gujaratis. Trading different goods, speaking different languages, and wearing different clothes, all the peoples of the subcontinent poured in to seek opportunity as the port grew. As an economic hub, Bombay lured a disproportionate number of young men; the first census, taken in 1864, revealed the city to be nearly two-thirds male.

To the young migrants, Bombay was a kind of social escape hatch. In the traditional villages of the Indian mainland, ossi-fied social structures were religiously codified through explicit hereditary castes for priests, merchants, landlords, and manual laborers. Sons were expected to do as their fathers did, usually subsistence farming. With, at best, a few simple tools and a water buffalo, a lifetime of hard work would yield a simple, largely veg-etarian diet of lentils, rice, and wheat. Daughters did like their mothers, churning butter, baking bread, and turning cotton into cloth with the aid of a simple hand-powered spinning wheel. Children were raised to fulfill their destiny, not seek their for-tune. But while the rest of India moved at the pace of a bullock cart, Bombay rushed into the future, opening Asia's first railroad, which linked the island city to the mainland, in 1853. On the offshore metropolis, the son of a farmer could become a merchant or a clerk. A person's social status could rise through education, wealth, and accomplishment. Success in life mattered more than accident of birth. As Govind Narayan recorded in his 1863 book, "Those who used to do odd jobs earlier are now learning Eng-lish. Many have left their traditional trades to learn English and obtain employment." As disconcerting as the modern city could be, its magnetic pull meant a newcomer could rest assured that a community from his home region already lived on the island.

While Europeans occupied the top rung of Bombay society, each group had its own community leaders and patrons, creat-ing a multivalent metropolis. And segregation was not nearly as total as it was in other Indian cities. Too many of the peoples of Bombay, like the Parsis, couldn't be fit neatly into binary racial schemes of "black" and "white," "native" and "foreign." By the 1857 rebellion, Bombay was already a distinct cosmo-politan mixture of peoples and cultures found nowhere else in India—a cosmopolitanism written into the city's urban fabric. Though the Bombay Fort, which had stood since 1769, physically resembled the British forts in other major Indian cities, with its thick, foreboding stone ramparts and guarded gates, it always reflected Bombay's unique social realities. While in most British East India Company settlements, the fort was synonymous with the segregated "white town," and the precincts outside the walls with the "black town," Bombay's fort included both "white" and "black" neighborhoods. A 1772 ordinance decreed the central east–west artery, Churchgate Street, as the line of demarcation: Europeans lived south of Churchgate, non-Europeans lived to the north.

Favored for their relatively fair complexions and trade links with communities of coreligionists throughout Asia, Parsis were the dominant non-European group within the city walls, comprising fully 46 percent of the walled town's population. Parsis mixed more easily with the British because, unlike other Bombay religious groups (Muslims, Hindus, Jains, Buddhists, and Jews), the Parsis had no food taboos. Moreover, for austere Hindus, the Europeans were technically untouchables since they stood outside the caste system; contact with them had to be limited out of fear of spiritual pollution.

The other variegated Indian communities lived and worked in the bustling market neighborhoods north of the fort—the bazaars, where each group had its own residential enclave. As Govind Narayan recorded, all the peoples of the city and all the goods of the world were on display in the market. "In the hours that follow dawn," he wrote, "one can see a procession of hawkers each loudly proclaiming their wares . . . in various languages." Narayan's list of items available for purchase ran the gamut from coriander and turmeric to keys and Chinese bangles, but he was particularly proud of the proper shops selling European and American manufactured goods that had arrived in port. "Clocks and watches are so common-place in Mumbai that it would be difficult to find even a third of their number in the rest of India," Narayan wrote, flaunting his adopted hometown's Westernized sophistication.

Even more than the variety of goods on its streets, it was the variety of peoples that struck Bombay's chroniclers. Calling them "the hatted races," to distinguish them from his turbaned countrymen, Narayan listed, besides the English, the "Portuguese, French, Greek, Dutch, Turkish, German, Armenian and Chinese." Louis Rousselet, a Frenchman who visited Bombay in the 1860s, similarly gushed over the "world of peoples and races, of perfectly distinct types and costumes [that] are crowded together in the streets of this capital. . . . Beside the indigenous races which still present such varieties, we see the Persian, with his high cap of Astrakan; the Arab, in his Biblical costume; the Tomali negro, with fine intelligent features; the Chinese, the Burmese, and the Malay. This diversity gives to the crowd a peculiar stamp, which no other town in the world can present. . . . The Tower of Babel could not have assembled at its foundation a more complete collection of the human race." What struck Rousselet even more was the degree to which the groups mixed. "The refreshment-rooms in the taverns are thronged by Europeans, Malays, Arabs, and Chinese," he observed. "Far into the night will the songs resound."

Bombay's stunning diversity was breeding a new culture unique to the world's most cosmopolitan cities. "Not only is one entertained by the variety of strange costumes worn by these tribes, but the sight of them inspires yet other thoughts in the mind," Narayan wrote. "You do not come across people of so many castes in any other city. One would not be wrong in terming it a melting pot for all cultures." And yet, in this city of Indians checking their shiny new watches as they caught the train to ESL class, it seemed the melting pot was doing far more to Europeanize the Indians than to Indianize the Europeans. Rousselet noted this trend when he wrote, "The rich Hindoos lead here a very different life from that of their ancestors. Without changing anything provided by their religious code, they adopt quite a European style of luxury." While the British East India Company had made an explicit policy decision not to foist Westernization on India, Westernization was sweeping Bombay, largely powered by Indians themselves seeking the social and economic advantages it offered.

Notably, the adoption of luxurious European urban lifestyles predated Bombay's reconstruction as a luxurious European-style city. Visitors were puzzled that this place, for all its wonder, didn't quite look like a proper city. Though it had a uniquely vertical urbanism—with some buildings as many as six stories tall—that was unknown elsewhere in India, Bombay lacked civic monuments worthy of its urban dynamism. "It cannot be considered a city, in the full acceptation of the term," Rousselet wrote. "It is rather a conglomeration of vast districts, situated a short distance from each other, on an island which gives them a generic name."

The Frenchman had visited just a few years too soon. He noted that the old fort walls in the center of town were "in the course of demolition," but he could scarcely fathom the scale and beauty of the buildings that would replace them. Atop the rubble a new governor of Bombay, Sir Henry Bartle Edward Frere, had grand plans to build a physical city worthy of the remarkable society already present on Bombay Island.

Sir Bartle Frere had been dreaming of turning Bombay into Britain's greatest imperial city for years before his 1862 appointment as governor of Bombay gave him the power to finally do it. Frere had first arrived in India just shy of twenty years old, quickly rising through the ranks to serve as the private secretary to the British East India Company governor of Bombay. In 1844, he coined the moniker *urbs prima in Indis* for his new hometown. This Latin phrase, meaning "first city of India," embodied Frere's aspirations for the island: that it would be India's first city both in the sense of being its leading metropolis but also in the sense of its being the country's first true city, a modern municipality that could legitimately be considered the peer of a London or an Amsterdam. It was an audacious vision for such a young man and for a city that, for all its potential, was still a far-flung frontier trading post physically dominated by a defensive fort.

Between his Bombay stints as private secretary and his appointment as governor, Frere served as a member of the viceroy's council in Calcutta, the city from which the British East India Company ruled India. Administering the colony from a series of neoclassical buildings, the Company hoped to establish itself as heir to the great empires of Greece and Rome, which had similarly straddled Europe and Asia. A British visitor to Calcutta in 1781 wrote that the "long colonnades, with open porticoes and flat roofs [create] an appearance similar to . . . a Grecian city in the age of Alexander." In the 1820s, the British Bishop of Calcutta compared the city to St. Petersburg, which Carlo Rossi had just rebuilt as a new Rome. But if Calcutta was a tropical version of the Russian capital, as the bishop insisted, it was only a pale shadow of Russia's "Venice of the North." Before the Raj, India was a trading post run by a multinational corporation rather than a full-fledged colony run by a monarch. As such, the grandeur of the architecture was always hemmed in by the Company's corporate bean counters.

When the Calcutta Government House, completed in 1803, included a state dining room decorated with life-size marble busts of the Twelve Caesars, the London board members reprimanded the Calcutta office for squandering Company profits on their own luxury. While one British lord who had attended the opening of the building countered that India should "be ruled from a palace, not from a counting-house," prevailing opinion held that British East India Company officials should live like civil servants, not Roman emperors or maharajas.

Just as Frere had declared Bombay India's first city decades before it could legitimately make such a claim, during his time in Calcutta he was already living in a Bombay-bred manner that foreshadowed the paternalistic ideology of Raj rule—that even Indians could be properly civilized through exposure to Western culture and education. In Calcutta Sir Bartle Frere and his wife were known for their good relations with the city's Westernized Indian elites, inviting them over for dinner and treating them with the same courtesies they extended to their white friends. Frere and a faction of other Britons had long favored policies that would, in the words of one imperialist, "[create] a class of persons, Indian in blood and colour, but English in taste, in opinions, in morals and in intellect." Still, many looked askance at the white couple's fraternizing with the locals—until the uprising. The lesson the British took from the Sepoy Rebellion was that the Company's strategy of not imposing Western culture in the hope that the Indians wouldn't resent the British presence had failed. As it turned out, the most Westernized Indians were the most loyal.

In the aftermath of the rebellion, as the British pondered what had gone wrong, they came to adopt policies more in line with Frere's Bombay-style attitudes. What George Campbell, a young British official posted to India, had observed in 1853 now looked prophetic: "The classes most advanced in English education, and who talk like newspapers, are not yet those from whom we have anything to fear; but on the contrary they are those who have gained everything by our rule, and whom neither interest nor inclination leads to deeds of daring involving any personal risk." Postrebellion, the British adopted a policy of allowing Anglophone Indians to rise higher in the ranks of the military and civil service, and of giving Indians more input on the administration of India. Frere championed "the admission to the legislative body of non-official [Indian] members," arguing that they could "advise us as to the opinions and wants of our native fellow-subjects." When Frere became governor of Bombay, he enlisted Indian merchants and professionals as advisers, thereby winning their support and considerable resources for his modernization schemes.

Bombay's relative quiescence during the uprising vindicated its cocktail of religious tolerance, nonwhite elite class of well-to-do traders, and technological progress. Now viewed from London as the city that worked, Bombay went from anomaly to model. In many ways, the Raj was an attempt to spread the Bombay model to the other major cities of the Indian empire. The queen would rule India by awing its population with Britain's sophisticated technologies and modern institutions, not by cowing them with British terror, strapping men to cannons and the like. A bid to be loved rather than feared, the Raj was a massive hearts-and-minds campaign. So while the Sepoy Rebellion was a protest against Western power in India, it didn't halt the Westernization of the subcontinent—it sped it up.

In Bombay, Frere would create a kind of factory for producing Westernized Indians—people who, though they still practiced their non-Christian religions and wore their distinctive fashions, would be English on the inside. Frere would win over the locals by building them the greatest city of the greatest colony of the greatest empire in the history of the world, a new London with edifices worthy of Her Majesty. At the end of his term as governor, Frere would brashly declare that before him there was no British architecture in India worthy of the name.

Like Peter the Great, the debonair, mustachioed Sir Bartle Frere combined the most grandiose visions for his city with a spartan lifestyle and a hands-on mode of municipal management. Frere was famous for riding daily through Bombay's Indian neighborhoods to take the pulse of his city. A paternalist, he believed his charge to care for his Indian subjects came from the

Lord himself, by way of Her Majesty. British rule in India was "a trust from God for the good government of many millions of His creatures," Frere declared. "However firmly England may resolve that no force shall wrest from her the Empire of India, the root of that resolve has always been a deep conviction that to surrender that Empire would be to betray a high trust."

To rebuild the trading post of Bombay as the *urbs prima in Indis*, Frere destroyed the fort, chartering a Ramparts Removal Committee to level the walls and plan a new metropolis. To be India's first modern city, Bombay would need the institutions of modernity, so Frere brainstormed a list of fourteen must-have public buildings that would "meet the most pressing wants of the military and civil administration." His list included a telegraph office and a railway station, a hospital and a courthouse, a customs house and a records office. While in Europe these institutions had developed and evolved over centuries, in Bombay, they would all be built simultaneously. Modern Bombay would spring whole from the mind of Sir Bartle Frere.

To design his new city, Frere imported top architects from Britain, like T. Roger Smith, a lecturer at the prestigious Royal Institute of British Architects in London, to staff his Ramparts Removal Committee. He ordered the committee to draw up a set of design guidelines for the city. While Smith thought he was simply bringing European architecture to India in a grander and more up-to-date manner than had been done at Calcutta, he ended up laying the groundwork for a new hybrid style of architecture in spite of himself. In a London lecture, Smith described his style as purely European: "As our administration exhibits European justice, order, law, energy, and honour—and that in no hesitating or feeble way—so our buildings ought to hold up a high standard of European art. They ought to be European both as a rallying point for ourselves, and as raising a distinctive symbol of our presence to be beheld with respect and even with admiration by the natives of the country." And yet from the start, Smith realized that simply airlifting in British Gothic—the spires-and-gargoyles style of the Middle Ages that was then experiencing a revival—didn't make sense for Bombay's climate. Instead, he endorsed importing the styles that had "grown up in sunshiny regions [like] the Renaissance and Gothic of Southern Italy or Spain, or the early Gothic of Southern France." But Bombay, with its intense heat and pounding monsoons, was hardly Venice or Nice. As such, Smith ordered that stone walls be extra thick to keep interiors cool and that every floor include a veranda. These would not be the verandas of gin and tonics on the porch in Canton or the early Shanghai Bund, but rather amped-up versions of the shaded, arched walkways of the Mediterranean monastery. The Ramparts Removal Committee's design guidelines coupled with the influence of Indian architects like Muncherji Cowasji Murzban (a Parsi whom Frere appointed assistant to the secretary of the committee), the craftsmanship of the Indian workers who built the buildings from European plans, and the palette of stones from local Indian quarries gave rise to a new, unique hybrid style in Bombay unlike anything found in Britain or on the Indian mainland. It became known as Bombay Gothic.

Soon the fort walls were coming down and the construction-obsessed Governor Frere was personally choosing the plots for the imposing new buildings he'd planned. To create the sense of an open, peaceful city where all the diverse communities lived in harmony, Frere converted the Esplanade, long kept empty to create a clean line of fire against potential invaders and the site of the grisly public executions in 1857, into a series of parks. Called the maidans, on these much-beloved green spaces Bombay's masses could escape the close quarters of their neighborhoods and enjoy the sea breeze or a nice cricket match.

Frere placed his most crucial institutions in a half-mile-long row, lined up along what was now the Oval Maidan, literally looking westward toward the sea. The serried Gothic row—"one long line of array, as if on parade before the spectator," as one nineteenth-century observer recorded—constituted the first planned architectural ensemble ever built in colonial India. At the center was the University of Bombay.

It had been the British East India Company, in the final years of its reign, that had proposed building universities in the major cities of Bombay, Madras, and Calcutta. But it was only under Frere that the University of Bombay took on the remarkable ambition to be a training ground for the Indian elite modeled on Oxford and Cambridge, the crown jewels of British higher education. To Frere, the university was "a most powerful lever to move the great mass of popular ignorance." In his 1862 convocation address, he explained how the university, like his city, would create a new man, who looked like an Indian but thought like a Briton, and who could, in turn, Westernize all of Indian society:

> Remember, I pray you, that what is here taught is a sacred trust confided to you for the benefit of your countrymen. The learning which can here be imparted to a few hundreds or at the most to a few thousands of scholars, must by you be made available through your own vernacular tongues to the many millions of Hindustan [India]. The great majority of your countrymen can only learn through the language which is taught to them at their mother's knee and must be through such language mainly that you can impart to them all that you would communicate of European learning and science. . . . Remember, too, that not only the character of the University, but the character of your whole people, is to a great extent in your hands.

Before the completion of the university, Govind Narayan had lamented the low level of indigenous participation in the city's intellectual life. Of the local branch of the Asiatic Society, he wrote, "The number of native people is so few that it is almost shameful to mention." But the rising generation of cultivated, Anglophone Indians the university educated would change the social and physical fabric of the city.

To build an institution on par with Oxford and Cambridge, Frere enlisted Sir Gilbert Scott, the British Gothic Revival architect. It was a coup made possible through the connections of the British architects whom Frere had already recruited to Bombay for the Ramparts Removal Committee. As Scott understood the commission, he had been hired to drop a British university onto the subcontinent. He already knew very well how to design a British university—after all, he had previously completed buildings at both Oxford and Cambridge—so site visits in India were unnecessary. Scott simply drew the plans, built the scale models in his London office, and sent them via ship to Bombay. The result is the palm-bedecked Oxford on the Oval Maidan.

The two core campus buildings Scott designed—the library and convocation hall—use the Collegiate Gothic style to hearken back to the medieval buildings at Oxford and Cambridge. Unlike the emphatically secular St. Petersburg State University, which shunned any acknowledgments of the religious roots of Western universities, the University of Bombay embraced but tweaked them. Scott's convocation hall looks like a Gothic cathedral but with secular imagery substituted for religious. The rose window includes Sir Bartle Frere's coat of arms in stained glass in lieu of symbols of the Four Evangelists; the carved stone faces that decorate the church represent European and Indian ethnic groups rather than saints. And the floor plan is rectangular rather than cross shaped, befitting a lecture hall rather than a church.

At the center of the library building, begun in the late 1860s, a bell tower rises 280 feet into the air. Based on Renaissance master Giotto's unbuilt proposal for a tower in Florence, the structure—the tallest in the city when it opened—was intended as Bombay's answer to Big Ben. After all, how could Bombay be a tropical London without a clock tower to dominate its skyline?

The exterior façade of the library is a near-perfect replica of the side of the Doge's Palace in Venice—two stories of shaded walkways framed by Gothic arches. The only difference from the original is the upper deck's arch shape. In Venice, they are sensuously curved arches reflecting Venice's connections with the Muslim peoples of the eastern and southern Mediterranean; in Scott's Bombay University building, they are replaced by more typically British convex Gothic arches. Architectural historians surmise that Scott found the Venetian arches too Islamic. Ironically, for a university that would always have a large population of Muslim students, Scott felt the need to make his building emphatically Western. His design is the physical embodiment of the Raj-era notion that West and East are two utterly distinct cultures, one ascendant, the other in need of guidance and of the university as the conduit for transmitting what Frere termed "European learning and science." Thus any hint that historically the Christian West and Muslim East are, as a contemporary scholar put it, "cultures that overlap, borrow from each other, and live together in far more interesting ways than any abridged or inauthentic mode of understanding can allow" must be expunged.

And yet for all its architectural intentions, the University of Bombay was never a fully British institution. The funding for the university came not only from the British government but also from the private philanthropy of Indian businessmen who endowed the campus buildings. Through philanthropic donations to new civic institutions like the university, local merchants gained higher social status as the British rewarded them with titles of nobility; they also bought access to the city's British imperial rulers, turning the construction of colonial Bombay into less of a top-down imposition and more of a "joint enterprise," as one contemporary historian has termed it, between the British authorities and the native elite.

The Jain commodities trader and stockbroker, Premchand Roychand, was the library's chief donor, and the main funder of the convocation hall was his business partner, Parsi shipping magnate Sir Cowasjee Jehangir. (The noted Parsi philanthropist eventually bowed to popular demand by legally adopting his laudatory nickname, "Sir Readymoney.") Though the blueprints were drawn up in London and many of the materials, including the floor tiles and stained glass, were imported from Britain, Indian craftsmen built the buildings. The Indian artists who made the carvings were given free rein to incorporate local flora and fauna among the heads of Shakespeare and Homer in the library.

The university's craftsmen had trained at the Bombay art and architecture academy known as the Sir Jamsetjee Jeejeebhoy School of Art, itself a joint enterprise institution. The institute was endowed by a Parsi shipping tycoon who, after becoming the first Indian to be knighted, in 1842, was invariably known as "Sir JJ." The source of Sir JJ's fortune was opium, which he shipped out from Bombay to China. He'd gotten into "the China trade," as drug running was euphemistically known, when, as a young man sailing to the Middle Kingdom, he fortuitously befriended his ship's doctor, none other than the Scotsman William Jardine. When the wily physician gave up prescribing pharmaceuticals for dealing narcotics, founding Jardine Matheson and Company, Sir JJ became his South Asian supplier. The opium fortune he amassed became the endowment for his art school, which he charged with modernizing the traditional Indian arts and crafts so that they could survive in an industrial age dominated by European manufactured goods. It was the graduates of this school who ended up imbuing the city's buildings with their distinctive Bombay Gothic decoration.

For all the beauty of the new Bombay Gothic edifices, for Frere's hearts-and-minds campaign to succeed his city had to do more than just *appear* to be the equal of Europe's cities—it had to truly match them. If the British were seen to be giving Indians anything less than they gave themselves, the scheme would fail. During Frere's governorship, Bombay always got the latest technology right on schedule with the West. Gaslights were introduced in 1865. As *The Times of India*, the British-run Bombay-based newspaper, reported with a hefty dose of Raj paternalism, "As the lamp-lighters went from lamp to lamp they were followed by crowds of inquisitive natives who gazed in mute astonishment at the new Western Wonder that had appeared in their midst."

Sanitation was miraculously improved through a coordinated system of night-soil collectors, street sweepers, and the creation of designated public market halls where meat could be sold during the day and the stalls cleaned at night. In the 1850s, Bombay had been considered among the most fetid cities on earth, with "700,000 human beings . . . living in the midst of the putrefying filth they [were] generating day by day [and] fever lurk[ing] in every lane and alley," as one observer recorded. But Frere's leadership led nursing pioneer Florence Nightingale to gush in a fan-mail letter, "Bombay has had a lower death-rate on the last two years than London—the healthiest city in Europe. This is entirely your doing."

Most crucially of all, Frere understood that the key to Bombay's future was to solidify its centrality within the global trading system. Bombay had already established itself as the hub of India's first railroad system, but to improve shipping from the interior, Frere presided over the expansion of rail service to link offshore Bombay deeper into the fertile Indian hinterlands. The

Bombay railroads' 1865 alphabetized guide for shippers testifies
to the riches pouring in and out of the city. The pamphlet runs,
literally, from A ("Aerated waters, in bottles") to Z ("Zinc ore"),
moving through everything from "Cannon balls" and "Cotton" to
"Onions" and "Opium" in between. And Frere ensured that the
city was linked by telegraph to the mother country. The Bombay-
London telegraph was inaugurated on March 1, 1865, before even
the United States and United Kingdom were connected. The
visionary governor ensured that the *urbs prima in Indis* truly lived
up to its swaggering motto.

Frere's grand plans for Bombay fortuitously coincided with an
unprecedented economic boom. The root of this prosperity was
the American Civil War, which made cotton a more lucrative
cash crop for Bombay even than opium. While not a single boll
of cotton ever grew on the island of Bombay, the city was the
export hub for the subcontinent's bounty. When the cotton that
had flowed from New Orleans to Liverpool to supply England's
Lancashire mills was halted by the Union's naval blockade, Britain looked to South Asia for a new source of the raw material.
As *The Times of India* bluntly put it in 1862, "The 'difficulty' of
America has been a golden 'opportunity' for India." Frere's city
was built on cotton profits, as he wisely leveraged fortunes like
Sir Readymoney's and Premchand Roychand's into building his
colonial metropolis. One Bombay Briton observed the causation
clear as day: "Splendid buildings sprang up on all sides during the
four years the [American] war lasted."

Between 1859 and 1864, the price of cotton surged fourfold
and the amount India exported to Europe more than doubled.
Rumor had it that Bombayites took to ripping apart their mat-
tresses to sell the cotton inside for a windfall. The cotton boom
also lured a massive influx of eager workers from the mainland to
work in Bombay's bustling port. The city's population more than

doubled between 1852 and 1864 to over eight hundred thousand people. With the increased demand for housing, Bombay real estate prices skyrocketed. On Malabar Hill, one of the city's most desirable areas, set high atop a breezy spit of land jutting out into the Arabian Sea, plots that went for less than five hundred rupees in the 1830s were selling for thirty thousand by 1864. Even typical plots in less fashionable districts sold for fifteen times what they had cost less than two decades before. A real estate and construction boom soon created its own momentum, luring ever more workers who needed ever more housing. It was only a matter of time before someone came up with a manic new proposal: If land was so valuable in Bombay, why not create more land?

Bombay had already undergone a series of massive land reclamation projects to turn the original archipelago into a single island, but now people were proposing to reclaim more land from the sea purely as a speculative real estate venture. Along with the banks and insurance companies that were springing up with the Bombay boom, several land reclamation corporations formed as well. The most prominent was the Back Bay Reclamation Company, which planned to reclaim land from the Arabian Sea for a new railroad station and housing development. Headed by a British partner in the firm of Sir Readymoney and Premchand Roychand, the company launched with a massive initial public offering in 1864. As one observer recounted later, "The whole community, European and native, went perfectly mad over . . . leveling and filling up Back Bay, and speculation rose to such an unheard of height that shares were actually sold at a profit of £2,500 before a load of gravel had been emptied into the bay."

Roychand was the leading booster for the Back Bay project, in particular, and the Bombay boom, more generally. Shifting easily between the official European world of the Bombay stock exchange and the informal Indian world of the Share Bazaar—a shaded spot under a banyan tree near Town Hall where each day

a group of traders gathered to wheel and deal stock certificates—
Roychand was nicknamed the "Supreme Pontiff of Share Speculation." Always offering market tips on the sixty-two joint stock
companies that had arisen since 1855, he was particularly fond
of touting his own portfolio of a dozen banks and reclamation
companies. As the most prominent businessman of the Bombay
boom, Roychand was the de facto head of the government-
chartered Bank of Bombay, entrusted with a blank book of
promissory notes he could issue at will, often on the collateral of
share certificates in one of his other companies.

As "Share Mania," as it came to be known, swept the city,
"time bargains," what we would today call futures contracts or
derivatives, proliferated. Time bargains offered a way to place
bets on fluctuations in the price of, say, cotton or Back Bay Reclamation Company shares. Speculators with no actual interest in
owning the underlying asset would simply resell the contract as
a commodity in itself. As the boom crested, Bombay corporate
lawyers were in such demand to draw up incorporation charters
and securities contracts that they began demanding a place on the
board and stock options in any company they advised. Frere tried
to reign in the rampant speculation. But even when he succeeded
in passing a bill to ban "time bargains," approval of the measure
was held up by his Raj superiors in London. In the words of
one observer, "Everyone became suddenly a millionaire. . . . The
whole community was debauched."

Fortuitously, Roychand and other paper millionaires made a
habit of banking a portion of their profits throughout the boom
and making massive philanthropic donations. Roychand endowed
the university library in 1864, following Sir Readymoney's donation of 1863. Similarly, in 1863, the Jewish shipping tycoon David
Sassoon endowed a new library specializing in architecture, science, and engineering that was erected on a major avenue of
Frere's new city.

Those who hadn't cashed out in time lost everything in April 1865 when, a world away, General Robert E. Lee surrendered at Appomattox. With the American Civil War over, the global cotton market changed overnight. No longer was India the sole or best source of raw material. The price of Indian cotton immediately collapsed to a quarter of its wartime value. With layoffs looming, it was only a matter of time until Bombay workers began returning to their inland villages, leaving the local real estate market to implode. Parsi business magnate Byramjee Hormusjee Cama was the first to be ruined. As the default of his business empire rippled through the Bombay markets, the entire speculative edifice collapsed. July 1, 1865, the designated day for "time bargain" futures contracts to be delivered, became known as "Black Day," the day Share Mania died. The contracts were unsellable and those left holding the bag were ruined as the near-worthless cotton and joint stock company shares were delivered. As *The Economist* reported in its coverage of "The Crisis at Bombay," " 'Woe to the last holder,' is the motto of the panic." As an eyewitness later recalled, "Men who had been reputed millionaires . . . were left penniless. [T]he lawyers swept up the débris."

In 1866, the Back Bay Reclamation Company was partially bailed out by the Bombay government, which bought out the shareholders at a fraction of its one-time trading price. That same year, the Bank of Bombay, which had been issuing loans backed with Back Bay shares, went belly-up. Premchand Roychand, once a celebrated philanthropist and business mogul, became reviled as "the best abused man in Bombay."

Yet for all the excesses of the boom, Bombay had laid a foundation for future prosperity. Frere had built civic institutions like the university and invested in the new railway and telegraph infrastructure that firmly established Bombay as India's gateway to the world. When the Suez Canal opened in Egypt in 1869, green shoots finally appeared after the long economic bust. The new shortcut between Europe and Asia put Bombay at the center of the global trading system. Recognized by his superiors, Frere was promoted to the India Council, which oversaw the jewel of the empire from London. As Frere sailed from Bombay to Britain, the buildings he had commissioned, which would come to be known as "Frere Town," were rising on the skyline behind him. Back in England, Oxford gave him an honorary degree. His ersatz Oxford on the Arabian Sea had apparently met their standards.

In the 1870s, a veteran Western journalist, long posted to India's financial hub, fretted over the impossibility of explaining to young Bombayites what the city had been before its breakneck transformation. "To the present generation," he wrote, "it would be difficult to convey an idea of the aspect of Bombay in 1822. It can only be done by negatives. There was . . . no educational establishment of any kind for the natives, no boarding houses, no banks . . . no daily newspaper . . . no steam engines of any kind, and of course no railroad. . . . Civilization, as we now understand, was positively stagnant."

Frederick William Stevens arrived in India just as Sir Bartle Frere was leaving. The young architect from Bath, England, with close-cropped black hair and a mustache edging toward handlebar status, arrived in India in 1867 as a lowly assistant engineer in the Public Works Department of Pune, a provincial city one hundred miles inland from Bombay. Within a year and a half, Stevens had been promoted to work in the *urbs prima in Indis*, the city he would stamp as his own in a three-decade career, and the city where he would be buried. For Stevens, design was an obsession. "His profession," a friend recounted, "was not merely the labour, it was also the delight of his life. Even on his holidays he was never happy unless his drawing board accompanied him. The mental recreation which other men find in reading or in conversation was found most of all by him in the intellectual absorption of design-ing." Stevens's joy and obsession are evident in the plans he left behind, which blur the line between blueprints and art in a way reminiscent of the Renaissance masters who saw no distinction between being an artist, an engineer, and an architect.

Arriving in Bombay, the young Stevens worked on several Ramparts Removal Committee projects—a perfect fit for a man who shared its administrators' passion for the Gothic style. Hav-ing made his reputation on committee projects, the publicly chartered, privately owned Great Indian Peninsula Railway cor-poration requested to hire Stevens out from the city government to design their new office-cum-terminal on a massive plot at the northern edge of downtown. Built on the spot where the old fort's Bazaar Gate had stood, it would be the largest and most expensive building yet erected in Bombay, grander than anything constructed under Frere. Tagged simply the Great Indian Penin-sular Railway Terminus on Stevens's drawings, the station was renamed Victoria Terminus on Queen Victoria's Golden Jubilee in 1887, the fiftieth anniversary of her coronation.

Giving pride of place to a train station speaks volumes about British intentions for Raj-era Bombay. Above all, Bombay was a transportation hub, the link between Britain and India. It was the city where the ships from Europe docked and the trains to the Indian mainland departed. At the time Stevens received his com-mission, Bombay was the largest city in the empire after London, and its international trade amounted to a stunning £45 million a year (the equivalent of several billion in today's pounds or dollars).

To handle such an important project, the government granted Stevens a leave of absence and, in 1878, he headed back to Europe to conduct a study-tour of the latest in railroad station design. From Sir Gilbert Scott's Gothic-style rail-terminal-cum-hotel, St. Pancras Station, which had just opened in London, Stevens got some practical ideas about how to orient a major building around a massive rail yard and the aesthetic notion of creating a counterpoint of spires in a vast Gothic structure. Perhaps even more influential was Scott's unbuilt proposal for a house of parliament in Berlin, where the master architect proposed topping a Gothic Revival office building with a central dome. Stevens's return to his native Bath, England, with its ensemble of honey-colored stone buildings, may have given him the color for the terminal he would erect in Bombay.

Other than a few nods to the East, in particular the bicolor arches over the carriageway for first class passengers, reminiscent of the arches in the Great Mosque of Cordoba, in Spain, Stevens's design was Gothic. The materials are a mix of Indian and European: Italian marble is interspersed with the rich yellow sandstone and blue-gray basalt from the local quarries of Western India. As was typical of Bombay construction projects by this point, Stevens, the British-born architect, was assisted by two Indian draftsmen, and the carved details on the building were executed by Indian students from the Sir JJ School of Art. In the carvings that decorate every spare inch of the station, fantastical English gargoyles and griffins frolic with Indian peacocks and cobras. The mix of the grand and the intricate is what makes the building so engrossing. The station's orderly rows of peaked windows and identical arches topped with such a varied array of carved creatures evoke an almost musical counterpoint. As a pair of contemporary architectural historians aptly summarized, "The viewer's eye constantly shifts from the mass to the detail—towering spires, arches, verandas, balustrades and pillars and the plethora of fine ornamental carvings of flowers, animals, [Great Indian Peninsula Railway company] symbols and the innumerable gargoyles."

The largest and most prestigious sculptural commissions were reserved for Thomas Earp, an eminent Victorian artist, who carved them from Indian stone in his London studio and shipped them to Bombay. The carriage gateway to the railroad company offices is guarded by two of Earp's pieces: a lion representing Britain and a tiger representing India. Other Earp sculptures top the gables of the station, including *Science* and *Trade* personified as toga-clad women.

The climax of the building is its octagonal forty-foot-wide dome—the first masonry dome ever adapted to a Gothic building—which is topped by Earp's statue, *Progress*, a fourteen-foot-tall goddess bearing the first two great engineering advances of humanity, the torch and the wheel. Just as Tsar Alexander I had felt that St. Petersburg needed a massive dome on its skyline to match the great cities of Europe, so Bombay needed one, too. But with Queen Victoria's proclamation of Crown rule over India guaranteeing tolerance for India's varied faiths, a church dome would be unacceptable. Thus Bombay is crowned with the dome of a church to Britain's true faith—the religion of progress. While a statue of Jesus towers over Rio de Janeiro, the symbol of an Iberian empire built upon the conversion of the natives, it is the goddess Progress who stands high atop Bombay. The station is built to win converts to the Western faith in progress, not in Christ.

Fittingly, the ticket office of Stevens's station looks like a cathedral, with groined arches forming the ceiling and extending down into thick marble columns anchored to the floor. Along the interior walls, ticket booths take the place of confessionals. The stained-glass lancet windows of the dome—all made in London and shipped to India—give glory not to God but to the Great Indian Peninsula Railway company. Alongside the company's GIPR monogram logo are an elephant and a locomotive, elements of its heraldic crest. The elephant reminds passengers of India's means of transportation before the British came. As magnificent as it is ponderous, the lumbering pachyderm embodies the backward grandeur of preconquest India while the sleek locomotive embodies the British-forged progress that was modernizing the subcontinent. Another of the stained-glass windows includes the company's motto, *Arte non ense* (Latin for "by art, not the sword"). It would be a fitting motto for the British Raj itself. While the British had once conducted public executions on the very site where the station rose, in the ideology of the Raj the right of the British to rule was no longer imposed by force but earned through modernization. The stained-glass windows of Victoria Terminus are essentially imperial propaganda posters with higher production values.

British hopes to convert Bombayites to the religion of progress worked, if only too well. The modern city forged modern people who rode its trains and read the latest English books. But if the city was on par with London, Bombayites began to wonder, why were they still ruled like children? The British claimed that they needed to run India until their Indian apprentices had imbibed enough of their civilization to administer the subcontinent themselves. But as the Indian elite trained at places like the University of Bombay grew more numerous and sophisticated, the question of how much authority should be handed over to them and how soon became points of contention. While conservatives always argued that more time was necessary—as one British official put it, "That there should be one law alike for the European and the Native is an excellent thing in theory, but if it could really be introduced in practice, we shall have no business in the country"—progressives, both in India and England, kept pushing to turn over more authority to the Indians sooner rather than later.

Even among the British administrators of India, there were those who took the British ideology of progress and apprenticeship at face value. While to many, bringing the benefits of progress to the subcontinent was just a cover for white rule and resource extraction, a significant segment within the bureaucracy wanted the Raj to live up to its own rhetoric. One such administrator was Allan Octavian Hume. The son of a left-wing British politician, Hume had spent an entire thirty-two-year career in the Indian Civil Service. In 1883, he secretly wrote to a group of recent Indian university graduates and suggested they hold a national conference of educated, Anglophone Indians. Such a group, he wrote, could "form the germ of a Native Parliament which, if properly conducted, would constitute in a few years an unanswerable reply to the assertion that India is still wholly unfit for any representative institution." He described this organization as crucial for achieving "social and political progress in India," shrewdly redefining the raison d'etre of the Raj—"progress"— not as the technological advancement embodied by Victoria Terminus but as the political advancement embodied in an elected legislature. To Hume, the British ought not just bring the railway to India but representative government as well.

The time was ripe for proposing such a group. Lord Lytton's reactionary 1876-to-1880 reign as viceroy, the top Raj official in India, had angered educated Indians. Most infuriating was his draconian 1878 Vernacular Press Act, which had censored criticism of Britain in non-English newspapers and magazines, of which there were dozens in Bombay alone. In 1885, spurred by Hume's secret letter, the founding conference of the Indian National Congress was held in Bombay with seventy-two delegates in attendance.

The conference's purpose, as stated in the official invitation, was to "discuss questions of national importance." While this proposal sounds like mundane mission-statement boilerplate, it bespeaks how radically the British had transformed the subcontinent. The fact that men from all over India could plan their meeting was testament to the postal system the British had built; that they could so easily assemble in Bombay for a meeting was the result of the British-built rail system; that they could discuss anything with each other was the fruit of British imperialism as well, for the British had imposed upon a polyglot subcontinent a unified common language—English—known by elites of every region and used in over a hundred newspapers. That their discussion would focus on questions of "national importance" bears the imprimatur of Britain as well, for India had long been a subcontinent of warring kingdoms and princely states, not a unified country. It was the British treatment of the subcontinent as a single colony that imparted to the indigenous peoples a national consciousness, the sense that they all inhabited one country.

The majority of the conference delegates were lawyers, many of whom had trained in England. Newspaper editors and educators were well represented, as were industrialists, in particular from the multicultural Bombay business elite. The attendees were hardly radicals; they made no demands for Indian independence and took pains to pledge loyalty to the Crown. They simply asked that the Raj principle of apprenticeship be more than rhetoric. As one delegate explained, Britain had given India "order, . . . the Railways, and above all . . . the inestimable blessings of Western education." What was still needed, though, was for Britain to rule India "according to the ideas of government prevalent in Europe."

To the delegates, British rule in India simply wasn't British enough. The host city of the conference, Bombay, was an incomplete imitation of London. Sure it had a Big Ben. But while London's Big Ben was on the Houses of Parliament, Bombay's version was on its university. Why? Because Bombay didn't have a parliament—a rather suspicious omission, it was beginning to seem, from Frere's list of fundamental modern civic institutions. When Bombay delegate Dadabhai Naoroji later penned an attack on the British, he accused them, in the words of his title, of "Un-British Rule in India."

The assembled group made mild demands for fuller Indian representation on legislative councils. One delegate called for an Indian "nonofficial parliament" to be formed that would study the laws and budgets passed for India by the real Parliament in London and make suggestions for improvement.

But even with all the pledges of loyalty to the queen, elements within the British Raj took the founding conference of the Indian National Congress, the political party that would one day lead India to independence, as a threat. "It is by force that India must be governed," *The Times of India* editorialized of the meeting. "If we are to withdraw, it would be in favour not of the most fluent tongue or the most ready pen, but the strongest arm and the sharpest sword." And the paper scoffed at the preposterous notion of Indians running India. "If India can govern itself, our stay in the country is no longer called for. All we have to do is to preside over the construction of the new system and then to leave it to work. The lawyers and schoolmasters and newspaper editors will step into the vacant place and will conduct affairs with no help from us. Those who know India will be the first to recognize the absurd impracticability of such a change."

The wiser among the British realized that if there was any hope of winning back the Western-educated, Anglophone elite they had created, they were going to have to accommodate them. Indian demands were appeased with an increase in the number of elected representatives on the governing Bombay Municipal Corporation in 1888 and, symbolically, with a hybrid new building that opened in 1893. Designed by Frederick William Stevens and sited across the street from Victoria Terminus, the new city hall mirrors the station's Gothic base but blossoms into a euphoric dance of minarets and voluptuous domes that draw from the Mughal architectural palette of buildings like the Taj Mahal. By the end of the nineteenth century, the monumental core of Bombay was growing less Gothic, increasingly incorporating forms found in Indian architecture before British domination. The style that resulted reflected the city's increasingly assertive indigenous populace. Called "Indo-Saracenic" architecture, it clothed modern buildings in styles lifted from the pre-British architectural traditions of India—both Hindu ("Indo") and Muslim ("Saracenic" from Saracen, the archaic term for Arab).

In the 1890s, when a portion of the vast plot of land reclaimed from the sea by the bailed-out Back Bay Reclamation Company was finally used for its original stated purpose—as the site for a new terminal for the Bombay, Baroda and Central India Railway (BB&CI)—the company had Stevens build an emphatically Indian building. Stevens's design for the BB&CI employed a similar layout to Victoria Terminus—a palatial office with a rail yard and platforms to one side. But unlike Victoria Terminus, with its polite nod to the East, the BB&CI headquarters went all out to acknowledge its Indian location. The sober, Gothic base in blue-gray local stone retreats into the background while the blindingly white domes and domelets on top steal the show. *Progress* again puts in an appearance, this time holding a locomotive atop the central gable, but she is dwarfed by the Mughal-style tower behind her, with its array of minarets flanking a central onion dome.

Though Bombay was never the true replica of Europe that the Ramparts Removal Committee architects intended, in the early Raj, Bombay was built as a city where an Englishman could feel at home. The arriving Briton pulling into the harbor would see Sir Gilbert Scott's tower and be reminded of Big Ben. After docking, he would be ferried past the university, a palm-studded Oxford, and hear its carillon chiming "Rule, Britannia." Arriving at Victoria Terminus, he couldn't help but reminisce about St. Pancras. Only when his train crossed the bridge over the creek between the island of Bombay and the mainland would he feel himself truly in India.

By the turn of the century, this was no longer the case. Architects like Stevens were designing a city that physically mirrored the people the Raj had made and was now struggling to manage—Indian on the outside, European on the inside. As a guidebook published by the Great Indian Peninsula Railroad at the turn of the last century explained, "A man dressed in a coarse homespun coat and *dhoti* (sheet draped about the legs), and wearing a little black cap, walking quietly in the street, may be carrying, stored in his memory, the contents of a large library, and if, perchance, his voice were raised in the Municipal Corporation . . . he would astonish the visitor with his command of English and still more so with his knowledge of Western political institutions and procedure." Without missing a beat, the guidebook goes on to the analogous architecture: "The public buildings are large, spacious and handsome, seeking to combine the arches and domes and turrets of the East with the telephones and filing cabinets of the Western world."

"What would India look like if it were modern?" Stevens and his contemporaries seem to be asking themselves. Yes, it would have modern institutions—train stations, city halls, post offices, banks—but they might not look like their Western counterparts. In the hybrid architecture of turn-of-the-century Bombay is a glimpse of a new idea—that Asian modernity might not look like Western modernity—as well as the first dawning of its logical corollary: that Asians might design their modernity themselves. Only then would it truly be progress.

# 4

# CITY ON SPILT BLOOD

St. Petersburg/Petrograd/Leningrad, 1825–1934

The Cathedral of Our Savior on Spilt Blood,
under construction and today

S t. Petersburg had been intended as a city of controlled modernization, but the modern people the city made—literate, worldly Russians—would not be easily controlled. The Decembrist revolt had proven that. In its wake, Nicholas I endeavored to turn St. Petersburg into a city of enforced stagnation. He hoped to bring the once-dynamic capital down to a sociological absolute zero, the point at which all progress stops. Nicholas endorsed a reactionary state ideology named "Official Nationality" that called for an eternally stable motherland resting on three conservative pillars: Orthodox Christianity, autocratic rule, and Russian nationalism. Under Nicholas I, Russia would wear the backward qualities European bien-pensants sneered at—its superstition, authoritarianism, and xenophobia—as badges of honor.

While his greatest Romanov predecessors, Peter and Catherine, had prided themselves on matching, if not outpacing, the West in infrastructure improvements in the capital, Nicholas held the city back. When Nicholas opened Russia's first railroad with tremendous fanfare in 1837, it laughably connected St. Petersburg with the tsar's suburban summer home at Tsarskoye Selo. One critic mocked it as linking "the capital with the cabaret," as there was a dance hall and restaurant built at the suburban station. Designed by an English architect, the Tsarskoye Selo station complex took the name of the Vauxhall station in London. The transliteration, *vokzal*, entered the Russian language as the generic word for train station, a permanent reminder of Russia's cribbed modernity at its most blatant. Russia's railroad reduced transformative modern technology to a royal vanity project. While the tsar enjoyed taking the train to his suburban estate, time and again he nixed proposals for a nationwide railway network, barring from Russia the transportation breakthrough that was transforming Europe. To the people of St. Petersburg, though, the lone railway line remained tantalizing: a glimpse of a world of progress held just beyond their reach.

The restrictions on railroad technology were part of a larger strategy aimed at keeping the modern industrial world out of Russia. As Nicholas's finance minister made plain, the problem with railways was how they changed people, broadening their horizons beyond their neighborhood or village and threatening the social order. Linking the nation by rail, the minister advised, would encourage "frequent purposeless travel, thus fostering the restless spirit of our age." The shrewd Nicholas understood that social modernization would undermine his rule. In France, economic development had created a new middle class and a new working class, both hostile to the old aristocratic regime. Since industrial revolution and political revolution were linked, Nicholas was determined to prevent both in Russia.

A contradictory feeling of possibility and frustration lay at the heart of the St. Petersburg experience in the mid-nineteenth century. It was a city whose residents were too sophisticated for both their rulers and their nation. And the stage on which the tensions played out was the avenue at the center of the capital, the world's greatest shopping street, Nevsky Prospect. Predating Baron Georges-Eugène Haussmann's grand boulevards in Paris, Nevsky concentrated the whole city, even the whole world, on a single promenade. Orginally called the Grand Perspective, then inappropiately renamed under Empress Anna Ivanovna for Alexander Nevsky, a Russian prince who fought off Western invaders during the Middle Ages, the avenue offered generations of Russians a grand perspective on the world beyond their borders.

To Nicholas and the Petersburg nobles, Nevsky Prospect served a simpler function: its stores allowed them to enjoy the luxurious manufactured goods of Western Europe without importing the threatening industrial economy that produced them. They could live the genteel life of *ancien régime* aristocrats—attending lavish balls at the royal court, summering in elaborate country estates—without giving up the bounty the Industrial Revolution produced. In the Nevsky shops, all the world's goods, from imported clocks to carriages, were available for purchase. A lithographer's complete panorama of the street, published in the 1830s, shows that more than half of the signs on the Prospect were bilingual or foreign-language only; French bookstores *(librairies)* and barbers *(coiffeurs)* lined the avenue. When the weather was harsh, as it so often was, shoppers could take refuge in the Gostiny Dvor. The vast, block long, neoclassical, Rastrelli-designed complex fronting Nevsky was one of the world's first shopping arcades, an antecedent to the contemporary megamall. But while the shopping on Nevsky was exclusive, catering to aristocratic budgets—and a serf might not be welcomed to roam the covered, climate-controlled halls of the Gostiny Dvor—the promenade itself was open to all. On Nevsky, the whole social panorama of nineteenth-century St. Petersburg came together.

Even without industrial workers or industrialists, it was a stunning assembly of people. By the 1840s, St. Petersburg's population was nearly twice that of Moscow. Despite Nicholas's xenophobia, the city remained 10 percent foreign. At the top of its social structure, fifty thousand aristocrats lived lives of luxury funded by their productive estates in the interior. Urban serfs, who made up over 40 percent of the population, worked sixteen-hour days on massive, multidecade construction projects like Montferrand's St. Isaac's Cathedral. Military men drilled daily along the streets of the capital. Shipped in from the Russian heartland, many had never seen a paved road before in their lives. But mid-nineteenth-century St. Petersburg was, above all, a city of bureaucrats. Every day in the capital, thousands of government functionaries processed forms from dawn till dusk. Between 1800 and 1850, the staff of the imperial bureaucracy increased fivefold. In 1849, the Ministry of the Interior alone produced thirty-one million official documents.

The bureaucracy was staffed with educated, ambitious young men from the provinces—and they were all men (seven in ten city residents were male). Many were the sons of the country doctors and teachers employed in the provincial hospitals and schools that Catherine the Great had built to enlighten her benighted empire. So strong was the capital's magnetism for young men on the make that the novelist Mikhail Saltykov-Shchedrin remarked of the city's totemic power, "We provincials somehow turn our steps towards Petersburg instinctively . . . as if Petersburg all by itself, with its name, its streets, its fog, rain, and snow, could resolve something."

While St. Petersburg lured talent from the entire empire, it never fully delivered on its promise. No matter how bright, the son of a country doctor was indelibly stained with a social rank below that of the sons of country aristocrats. And there were modern thoughts that could never be expressed. While the city's literate population read the daily newspaper just like in other European cities, the paper of record, the *Northern Bee*, was so strictly censored that it rarely offered anything substantive at all. As its editor, a careerist who kowtowed to the censors told his staff, "Theater, exhibitions, shopping mall, flea market, inns, pastry shops—that's your field and don't take a single step beyond it."

The eager meritocrats who flocked to the city soon grew frustrated as they bumped up against its aristocratic glass ceilings. Some sought refuge in politics—a dangerous choice—while others turned to the arts. From the city's stunted reality grew a limitless dreamworld.

Among the ambitious provincials drawn to the imperial capital was Nikolai Gogol, from Ukraine. In his 1835 story "Nevsky Prospect," the bachelor narrator initially extols the wonders of St. Petersburg's grand promenade. Strolling along Nevsky, he spies a beautiful woman and surreptitiously pursues her as she drifts off into the less prestigious sections of the city. His love-at-first-sight experience is dashed when he follows his seemingly chaste beloved to the brothel where she works. Heartbroken, the protagonist disavows the street and, by implication, the city as a fraud. "Oh, do not believe this Nevsky Prospect!" he exhorts the reader.

In Gogol's world, St. Petersburg is a mirage—nothing more than its beautiful façades. And the people of the city are like the metropolis itself: so focused on keeping up appearances of prestigious rank that all substantive matters are neglected. Gogol relished mocking Petersburgers' slavish mimicking of French fashion. Just as Peter the Great had forced Petersburgers to shave to look like Westerners, once Westerners began wearing beards, so too did Petersburgers. In "Nevsky Prospect," Gogol tells his readers of the facial hair you will "meet" on the eponymous street: "Here you will meet wondrous mustaches, which no pen or brush is able to portray; mustaches to which the better part of a lifetime is devoted—object of long vigils by day and by night; mustaches on which exquisite perfumes and scents have been poured, and which have been anointed with all the most rare and precious sorts of pomades, mustaches which are wrapped overnight in fine vellum, mustaches which are subject to the most touching affection of their possessors and are the envy of passers-by."

Gogol skewered the absurdity of the bureaucracy's minute divisions of rank, informing his readers that only foreign ministry bureaucrats were permitted to wear black side-whiskers; all others must wear red ones. For Gogol and his ilk, Peter the Great's bureaucracy, with its Table of Ranks for promotions, only made the whole system more insidious by giving it a patina of legitimacy and modernity: St. Petersburg was an aristocracy posing as a meritocracy. Through satire, he savaged a society where many wore their ranks on their sleeves—literally, on the epaulets of their military uniforms—as they walked the streets of the capital and where each man schemed to enhance his own status. In the novel *Dead Souls*, Gogol tells the story of a middling aristocrat who grossly exaggerates the number of "souls" (serfs) he owns to raise his social standing. In his surreal short story "The Nose," the title character becomes detached from the protagonist's face and begins cavorting about the capital on his own. When the noseless protagonist finally confronts his wayward proboscis in a cathedral on Nevsky Prospect, it won't even deign to acknowledge him—for the nose has somehow achieved a higher civil service rank than its erstwhile owner. To Gogol, St. Petersburg's senseless division of the body politic into the finest gradations of rank was worthy of farce. But left to atrophy indefinitely, as the decades passed, the city's divisions began to tear it apart.

With the world's premier shopping street, constant theater openings among the resident Russian, French, and German troupes, and the breathless reviews of the latest diversions in the *Northern Bee*, the Petersburg elite could flatter itself that its city was among the leading European capitals. But Russia's humiliating loss in the Crimean War to an alliance of Britain, France, and Turkey gave the lie to this belief. When the Russian generals signed the peace treaty in Paris in 1856, the contrast with the victory over Napoleon just a few decades earlier was painful.

Nicholas I died in 1855, as Russia was losing the war. Hopes for reform and modernization were pinned on his side-whiskered son Alexander II, who quickly repealed the most repressive policies of his predecessor. The capital was roused from its consumerist slumber as censorship was relaxed, foreign travel became easier, restrictions on the university were lifted, and political prisoners, among them the surviving Decembrists, were granted amnesty. Most important of all, Alexander unleashed the modernizing reforms that would transform St. Petersburg into a great industrial city.

Alexander understood that Russia could not keep up with the West without industrialization, infrastructure improvements, and corporate capitalism. To create the labor force for the Russian industry he hoped to build, he broke with previous monarchs and freed the serfs. Alexander's emancipation proclamation of March 1861 freed twenty-two million people, who had been owned by one hundred thousand nobles.

While to American ears, this sounds almost normal—Russia's emancipation proclamation and America's came just two years apart—in the European context, Russia's backwardness was more shocking. In Western Europe, serfdom had broken down centuries before from economic change and development, not royal decree (even as the European powers remained loathe to extend full liberties to their colonial subjects). In Britain, the labor shortage resulting from the Black Death of the fourteenth century largely wiped out the system of serfdom, which could no longer bind peasants to the land when there was demand for their labor elsewhere. In France, Louis XVI officially proclaimed serfdom abolished in 1779, but this was just a ratification of reality: French serfdom had largely disappeared hundreds of years earlier. In Germany, centuries of movement by peasants to cities winnowed down the number of serfs. Runaway serfs who sought refuge in the cities became free, customarily after a year and a day. The first German free city, Bremen, was chartered in 1186. In Western Europe, free labor was an essential part of the modern city: in the countryside, one was bound by custom and tradition, working the land as one's ancestors had for generations on behalf of the same noble family one's ancestors had served. In the city, life was different. Workers did whatever job needed to be done; when they saw better opportunities, they took them. The liberating ethos of the city became embodied in the German expression, "Stadtluft macht frei" (City air makes you free).

But in Russia, city air most certainly did not make you free. When Peter the Great built his new Amsterdam-themed capital on the Neva, he built it with serfs, shipped in for six-month tours of construction duty and then, provided they were still alive, returned to their feudal lords. The whole secret to Russia's breakneck modernization, the key to its ability to build a cutting-edge capital practically overnight, was that it retained a premodern labor system. But now, in a new experiment in breakneck modernization, Russia scrapped that labor system literally overnight—just as quickly as it had scrapped centuries-old Moscow for St. Petersburg in 1703.

News of Alexander's edict was initially greeted with celebration by both St. Petersburg's serfs and its progressive intellectuals and bureaucrats. But as the details became known, dissatisfaction grew. In the countryside, peasants revolted, displeased with the amount of land the edict gave them, which was less than they had farmed as serfs. A frightened Alexander backpedaled on his earlier reforms. But this only served to radicalize St. Petersburg's frustrated liberals, who soon called for even more dramatic change: an outright revolution.

On September 1, 1861, a mysterious horseman rode down Nevsky Prospect, leaving a flurry of pamphlets behind him before he disappeared. Addressed "To the Younger Generation," the leaflet exhorted bluntly, "We do not need either a Tsar, an

Emperor, the myth of some lord, or the purple which cloaks hereditary incompetence. We want at our head a simple human being, a man of the land who understands the life of the people and who is chosen by the people. We do not need a consecrated Emperor, but an elected leader receiving a salary for his services."

Three weeks later, Nevsky saw its first political demonstration. A group of students from St. Petersburg State University, men and women alike, marched up the avenue and over the bridge to campus. They were protesting new regulations that barred meetings of student groups and the end of scholarships for poor students, whom administrators feared were likely to become radicals. As one participant later remembered it, "A sight like it had never been seen. It was a wonderful September day. . . . When we appeared on the Nevsky Prospect, the French barbers came out of their shops, and their faces lit up, and they waved their arms cheerfully, shouting 'Révolution! Révolution!' "

As usual, the authorities reacted with repression. After a series of confrontations between the students and administrators—student strikes, expulsions, arrests—the university was closed outright for two years. Stifled, the brightest young people that the university had lured to the capital turned to clandestine, radical politics and schemed to overthrow the tsar.

To St. Petersburg's leftist intelligentsia, it was the destiny of Russia's most modern city to bring the conservative Russian empire up to speed. In the 1870s, a group of radical students organized a plan to go to the countryside and foment a peasant revolution. They became known as the Narodniks, from a Russian phrase meaning "going to the people." In the "mad summer" of 1874, over two thousand students fanned out over the countryside. At a meeting in St. Petersburg the winter before, the students had decided to adopt en masse an itinerant trade that would be their cover as they traveled from village to village. They voted to become cobblers and had a politically sympathetic master cobbler give them a few tutorials. In the spring, the urbane students left the capital for a Russia they hardly knew.

To fit in better in rural Russia, the students took on new appearances. In place of their Westernized, Petersburg fashions, the students put on peasant shirts and the women wore heads-carfs. The spectacles of the library dweller were removed and boots of the farm laborer donned. Just as St. Petersburg had been architecturally designed to mimic a Western city, so Petersburg-ers had been dressed up in European styles. But now, as they removed their costumes, they found that there was a problem: the Western garb that Petersburgers wore was no longer a ruse; it was a part of who they were. And when they dressed up as Russians, they weren't very believable.

In the villages, the undercover radicals ran into a problem. There were already plenty of cobblers in rural Russia, so their services weren't needed. As a fallback, they pretended to know other trades, but when asked to perform them, they invariably failed. In an attempt to politicize the peasantry, the students dis-tributed illegal revolutionary pamphlets. These were of little use since the peasants were illiterate. When the students tried instead to incite their countrymen with radical speeches against the tsar, the peasants reported the radicals to the tsar's secret police. By 1877, sixteen hundred students had been arrested. Many ended up imprisoned in the Peter and Paul Fortress.

In the wake of the Narodniks' failure, the radicals adopted a new strategy: if the peasants of the hinterlands didn't have the good sense to rise up, the intelligentsia of St. Petersburg would rise up for them. Calling themselves People's Will, a small, con-spiratorial cell of men and women—many of whom had initially moved to the capital for higher education—plotted to assassinate key regime officials. In a system as hierarchical as Russia's, they imagined, decapitation of the body politic would set the coun-try free. On August 26, 1879, the anniversary of Tsar Alexander

II's coronation, People's Will formally sentenced him to death. Though enemies of autocracy, the radicals were, in a sense, very much the children of Peter the Great and his city. St. Petersburg had been created as an attempt to instantly modernize Russia from above; the terrorists hoped to hurtle Russia into the future through bold actions in the capital. And the inquisitive, worldly Russians who made up People's Will were exactly the type of modern Russians the capital bred.

By November 1880, Tsar Alexander II had already survived half a dozen assassination attempts, seemingly by divine providence. Shocked and terrified by what the radicals brazenly called "the emperor hunt," Alexander considered appeasing them through reform. He had his liberal interior minister draw up a proposed set of new laws that included easing censorship, abolishing the secret police, and allowing elected representatives of the people a voice in national affairs.

On March 13, 1881, the tsar was heading home to the Winter Palace in his royal sleigh to review the reform proposals, after his customary Sunday visit to the palace of his brother, Grand Duke Mikhail Nikolayevich. People's Will operatives staked out the tsar along several possible paths to the Winter Palace. When the tsar's entourage turned the corner down the Catherine Canal heading toward Nevsky Prospect, People's Will member Nikolai Rysakov threw a bomb under the royal carriage. An explosion rung out and a cloud of white smoke billowed up. When the haze lifted, the tsar emerged unharmed, crossing himself, as he had six times before, looking like an icon of a saint floating on a cloud. His bodyguards quickly tackled the assailant. As they held him, the tsar personally confronted him, wagging his finger smugly after yet another failed attempt.

While the tsar's handlers urged him to get into one of the undamaged sleighs and return home, the sovereign pensively paced along the canal. Another young man, Ignati Grinevitsky, stood along the red-granite canal embankment, waiting for the tsar to draw near. When he did, Grinevitsky dropped a second bomb at his feet. This time when the white smoke cleared, all beheld the tsar's shattered legs. Blood poured from his lower body. Alexander's entourage packed him in a sleigh and set off for the Winter Palace. As the bleeding emperor was carried through the halls of Rastrelli's thousand-room palace, his grandson Nicholas, just thirteen, trailed behind. In the room where Alexander had signed the emancipation edict twenty-five years before, he died. The liberal reforms his interior minister had prepared died with him.

With their successful assassination, People's Will expected revolution. Instead, as one radical later wrote, "The people were completely indifferent to the fact of regicide. There was nothing else—no barricades, no revolution. A dreary longing for our failed dream entered my heart." St. Petersburg was swarming with radicals, but beyond the gates of the capital, Russia was in mourning.

To the conservative Alexander III, who succeeded his father at age thirty-six, the path of Westernization had led to this point. Though some advisers clamored to move the capital back to Moscow, Alexander III had a shrewder idea: he'd bring Moscow to St. Petersburg. In the heart of the great European city, Alexander would build a monument to the Russia that existed before Peter the Great that would remind St. Petersburg of its sin forever.

The project that became the Church of the Resurrection of Jesus Christ, more commonly known as the "Cathedral of Our Savior on Spilt Blood" or even "Christ on the Blood," would have been a simple shrine if not for the personal demands of Alexander III for a large-scale church fit for a thousand worshippers. The new tsar had announced an architectural competition for a cathedral to be built over the site of his father's assassination just weeks after the crime, but when the proposals came in,

Alexander III refused to pick a winner from among the varied styles. Instead, he decreed that only one style would be acceptable: seventeenth-century Russian.

The architects duly revised their proposals in keeping with the tsar's stylistic demands. But in the end, Alexander selected a design not by an architect but an archimandrite, an Orthodox Church official one rank below bishop. Archimandrite Ignaty Makarov claimed to have been overcome by the compulsion to design a building while preparing for Holy Thursday services just after the tsar's assassination. In a frenzy, he said, he sketched his church design miraculously in a single sitting, despite having no training as an architect beyond auditing a few architecture courses at the Imperial Academy of Arts as a young priest. The hierarch's story was moving, and the tsar loved Ignaty's nostalgic sketch. The archimandrite's proposal was approved by the tsar's architectural committee on the condition that it be turned into workable plans by Alfred Parland, a professional architect who had been a runner-up in the competition, and then be submitted to David Grimm, professor of architecture at the Imperial Academy, for final review.

The St. Petersburg architectural establishment looked askance at the whole competition, but most Russians were happy to see their priest, Makarov, win over experts with names like "Parland" and "Grimm." (Parland, though identified as a British subject in press coverage at the time, was actually a St. Petersburg native who had retained the surname and Anglican faith of his immigrant forebears.) Yet the public's xenophobia was oddly appropriate, for xenophobia was what the cathedral was all about: turning away from Amsterdam toward Moscow. Parland himself openly admitted the fact apparent to even the most architecturally ignorant observer of the redbrick, onion-domed building: the exterior was cribbed from St. Basil's Cathedral on Moscow's Red Square.

The inside of the church, however, is nothing like St. Basil's. In keeping with the tsar's desire for a thousand-parishioner space, its interior is a single, vast central nave, rather than St. Basil's series of intimate chapels. Fresco and mosaic icons on the theme of the resurrection decorate the walls, drawing a parallel between Christ's sacrifice for humanity and Tsar Alexander II's for the Russian people. St. Basil's prayer, which begs God to forgive his people, is given pride of place beneath the central cupola. As one architectural historian has written, the cathedral begs forgiveness for "the weakness, the tolerance, and the laxity presumably responsible for the murder. The cathedral [is] an act of repentance for Western culture."

Rising up along the Catherine Canal and reflected in its waters, the redbrick cathedral—"a notoriously out-of-place landmark," as one architectural historian aptly described it— stands out against the city's pastel-painted stucco, its onion domes clashing with the city's neoclassical triangular pediments. But beyond the purposeful stylistic mismatch, the building stands out from the city quite literally. While the rational order of St. Petersburg had always mandated that buildings line up to meet the streets and canals in a row (the so-called red line), the Church of the Resurrection steps out into the canal. The bloodstained embankment sidewalk where the tsar was attacked is encompassed within the church, marked by a small, flower-strewn altar, built to look like Ivan the Terrible's throne in Moscow's Kremlin. Outside, the embankment of the Catherine Canal was extended out around the church. With the cathedral pulled out of the frame of the city's rigid order, the vista from Nevsky Prospect was transformed into the one vista in the city where the geometry of the buildings, the embankment, and the canal is not symmetrical. The cathedral tears the fabric of the city and its Renaissance perspectives and offers a rebuke: the egalitarian humanist values of the Western Renaissance and Enlightenment lead here—to regicide. A gash in the urban fabric of the capital, the cathedral is, as one contemporary architectural historian put it, "a deliberate intrusion of the 'real' Russia onto the Petersburg scene."

Notwithstanding Alexander III's nostalgic dream, embodied in his new-old cathedral, St. Petersburg was changing in the late nineteenth century. Alexander II's emancipation edict had brought floods of former serfs to the city. Freed to leave their lords' estates but given inadequate land to farm by the reforms, rural migrants flocked to the capital, eager for jobs. Between 1860 and 1900, the city's population more than doubled to well over a million people. By 1900, more than two out of three Petersburgers had been born elsewhere.

Employment opportunities were plentiful for the new arrivals. To spur economic development, Alexander II had subsidized heavy industry and finally built the national railroad network Nicholas I so disdained. Alexander had also dispatched his finance minister, Mikhail Reutern, to the West to relentlessly promote Russia as an emerging market. Reutern touted his country as a Wild East where returns could dwarf anything offered in the developed world. In St. Petersburg, Western businesses could enjoy all the modern technological conveniences they enjoyed back home, Reutern explained, but without the inconveniences of their more egalitarian homelands. In Russia, workers had no rights. They couldn't speak freely, publish, march, or vote. And they'd work for a pittance.

The pitch worked. By 1870, foreign direct investment in the Russian economy was ten times higher than it had been in 1860; by 1900, it was one hundred times the 1860 figure. In the 1890s, the Russian economy averaged 8 percent growth per year—likely the highest in the world at the time. Multinationals built giant factories in the Russian capital. The Russian-American Treugolnik Rubber Company alone employed eleven thousand workers in its St. Petersburg plant.

Industrialization brought the same Dickensian conditions to St. Petersburg that it had brought to the cities of Western Europe, but in an even more virulent form. In Britain, the birthplace of the Industrial Revolution, scores of cities industrialized simultaneously—Manchester and Liverpool, Birmingham and Leicester. In Russia, with its single modern city, heavy industry concentrated more thoroughly in St. Petersburg, as did urban migrants.

The center of working-class life was the Haymarket, less than half a mile from Nevsky Prospect. Founded by Catherine the Great as a market for peasants from the nearby countryside to sell their produce, the wagon-strewn open-air Haymarket became an agglomeration of peddlers and pickpockets. More like a Middle Eastern bazaar than a European market hall, the Haymarket betrayed the dirty secret of St. Petersburg: despite its modern façades and up-to-date urban improvements—a waterworks in 1862, electric streetlights on Nevsky Prospect by the 1880s—working-class St. Petersburg was a metropolis of peasants. There was always a pastoral element to life in St. Petersburg that had no equivalent in the capitals of Western Europe, as if the city were staffed by actors—country folk who played urbanites on stage.

At first, aside from the burgeoning crowds at the Haymarket, the industrializing Russian capital didn't physically look any different; migrants just crowded in the interstices of the urban fabric. By 1871, thirty thousand people were living in cellars, typically dank and rat infested. Single men slept on cots hidden underneath staircases and slept in shifts in hallways. Since the annual rent on a posh apartment was equivalent to what a workingman made in a decade, migrants overloaded homes built for wealthier tenants. A mid-nineteenth-century government report found fifty men, women, and children living in a single room. Soon the number of people crammed into each apartment in St. Petersburg was twice that in Paris, Berlin, or Vienna. Behind the "red lines" of the aristocratic city, hidden hovels were sprouting up.

As industrialization took off—the city had just 12,000 factory workers in 1840, but 150,000 in 1880—a fetid industrial belt of factories and wooden tenements rose up around the edge of the capital. A city built as an island of privilege for the royal family, the nobility, and the top ranks of the military and civil service was now encircled by a notorious slum. The mortality rate in the poor neighborhoods was three times higher than in the city center. And all—rich and poor—had to breathe the haze of industrial smog that now hung in the air.

St. Petersburg had wanted to be a city of superlatives, boasting the world's grandest university building and greatest art collection, but now it was taking first place in all the wrong categories. The Russian capital attained the dubious distinction of having the highest death rate of any major city in Europe by the 1870s. Sanitation was atrocious. An 1870s study of a working-class district found that just one resident in fourteen had access to running water—and it was usually a spigot in a courtyard rather than indoor plumbing. A public health report from the period estimated the amount of human feces piled up in the courtyards of St. Petersburg buildings at thirty thousand tons.

Bleak life in the factories and the slums drove men to drink. By 1865, the city had 1,840 taverns, and Petersburgers topped the nation in per capita vodka consumption. "Drunkenness is unprecedented, even for Russia," wrote one observer at the time. "There have been cases of fatal alcohol poisoning . . . even among fourteen- and fifteen-year-olds." Without the gracious homes of the rich or even, for some, a bed that was their own for more than an eight-hour sleeping shift, public intoxication was a chronic problem; there were 35,000 arrests for drunkenness in 1869. Crime more generally was rampant. In 1866, 130,000

Petersburgers were arrested and jailed—nearly a quarter of the city's population.

Prostitution was legal and ubiquitous. During the mid-nineteenth century, there were 150 officially licensed brothels. The number of registered sex workers topped 4,400 in 1870. By the early twentieth century, roughly one in every forty Petersburgers was a prostitute.

The city's social problems were typically met with malign indifference from the men who ran it. Ultimately, industrial age St. Petersburg was run by the tsar, but day-to-day management fell to a merchant oligarchy. Under Alexander II's 1870 reforms, men over twenty-five who owned real estate or businesses could vote for a city council, which in turn chose the municipal executive. Since the government represented the very people who were benefiting from the poverty of St. Petersburg's desperate, low-wage industrial workers, little inroads were made in improving conditions. The only truly successful social program pioneered by the city in the late nineteenth century was the introduction of public education through the creation of dozens of new schools. By 1910, literacy in St. Petersburg stood at nearly 80 percent, well ahead of Moscow and off the charts compared to rural Russia. But mass literacy was a social innovation the Petersburg elite would come to regret.

Industrial St. Petersburg was really two cities—one of the wealthy and another of the working poor. And yet the two cities existed cheek by jowl. The world of flea-market hawkers, even the Dostoevskian phantasmagoria of propositioning prostitutes and passed-out drunkards, stood a brief stroll down the Catherine Canal from the onion domes of Christ on the Blood and the lavish shops of Nevsky Prospect. Long the most international street in Russia, in the industrial age, Nevsky Prospect became even more luxurious, catering to the new capitalists with fine French restaurants and, on a side street, the Fabergé gallery, where the

St. Petersburg–born son of a French Huguenot jeweler sold his famed gilded Easter eggs. Befitting a city at once both richer and poorer than any in the West, a single egg cost more than a mansion in Paris or New York.

With industrialization, the city was becoming a site where wealth was made, not just spent. Among the upscale shops of Nevsky Prospect, American-based multinationals like Singer Sewing Machine Company and International Harvester established their Russian headquarters. The Singer Building, which opened at the intersection of Nevsky Prospect and the Catherine Canal in 1904, stands six stories, serviced by three Otis elevators. Its façade is decked out with bronze larger-than-life, nude, helmeted Valkyries—most fighting, one sewing—and a giant American eagle. On top, a glass-and-steel cupola culminates in a globe hoisted on the shoulders of Atlas. Part salute to America (the eagle), part paean to the ravenous ambition of global capital (Atlas with his arms around the globe), the building, designed by Pavel Siuzor, the reigning dean of St. Petersburg architects, tips its hat to its historic St. Petersburg surroundings. For all its modern glass and steel, the façade's swirling art nouveau vines-and-flowers ornamentation is just a modern gloss on the exuberant curlicues that Rastrelli applied to his Russian baroque masterpieces.

To finance such industrial concerns, turn-of-the-century Nevsky Prospect was lined with twenty-eight banks. Alongside multinationals like Crédit Lyonnais stood the elegant fin-de-siècle headquarters of the St. Petersburg–based Banque Russo-Asiatique. The façade boasts a carved head of Mercury, the Greek god of trade, and two ship prows, each with an ornate, oversized anchor below and a caduceus—Mercury's snake-and-wings staff—above. The tribute to shipping was already a tad anachronistic when the building opened in 1898, for it was Russia's railways that were increasingly central to trade. And indeed, the Banque Russo-Asiatique owned a large stake in the crown jewel of Russia's belatedly built rail network, the Trans-Siberian Railway.

The Russian bank with the French name was ultimately acquired as a capstone for the commercial empire of the Putilov family, the top merchant clan in industrial age St. Petersburg. It was fitting that the Putilov family purchase the railroad-financing bank, since they had made their money producing rails and locomotives. When Russia embraced industrialization under Alexander II, Nikolai Putilov, a civil engineer who had established his reputation designing steam-powered gunboats during the Crimean War, won the government contracts to build the system. Soon the Putilov family's wealth rivaled that of Russia's great noble dynasties.

The Putilovs' ironworks in St. Petersburg's burgeoning industrial belt was the largest in the city, employing over twelve thousand workers. And the plant itself was completely up to date, its methods of production on par with factories in the West. Yet in its design, the plant seems embarrassed by its modernity. The enormous works of brick and steel is hidden behind a green-painted wall of repeating stone archways and elegant glass-and-ironwork streetlamps stretching off into the distance as if the factory owners wanted to pretend it wasn't really there—that behind the wall was just another nobleman's palace. The Putilov Works—much like the city itself—was uncomfortable in its own skin, in denial about its development. This discomfort was underscored by the two-story church, modeled on St. Basil's in Moscow and dedicated to Nikolai Putilov, the late founder of the commercial dynasty, that once stood next to the factory. It was one of several churches built by the government (but funded by "contributions" from Putilov employees) in an effort to intensify religiosity among industrial workers. Like the nostalgic wall, the church was built in the hope that the factory workers would remain traditional, mystical, patriotic peasants, even though they had left their ancestral farms for a factory in the city.

The effort backfired spectacularly when the state-approved chaplain at the Putilov Works, Grigori Gapon, began organizing the plant workers. While Gapon's union, the Assembly of Russian Factory and Plant Workers, had been founded by the government as a way of controlling worker unrest, it soon took an unauthorized turn toward independence. When four Putilov workers were fired for being members of the assembly, Gapon tried to intercede with the company. But when management refused to rehire them, 12,500 Putilov workers went on strike on January 3, 1905. By the end of the week, strikes had spread to 382 factories in the capital. One hundred twenty thousand Petersburgers refused to report to work. The increasingly sophisticated and literate men who toiled their lives away just to rent a bed for an eight-hour shift in a hallway had had enough.

With industrial St. Petersburg on strike, Gapon, a charismatic Ukrainian-born priest with an intense gaze and majestic mane of wavy jet-black hair, organized a petition and hatched a plan to deliver it in a mass march on the Winter Palace. The petition demanded civil rights, including freedom of speech, the press, and assembly; social rights, including free public education for all; and workers' rights, including an eight-hour day, a minimum wage, and the legalization of independent labor unions. "Sire," it read, "We, workers and residents of the city of St. Petersburg, of various ranks and stations, our wives, children and helpless old parents, have come to Thee, Sire, to seek justice and protection. We have become beggars; we are oppressed and burdened by labor beyond our strength, we are humiliated; we are regarded, not as human beings, but as slaves who must endure their bitter fate in silence. . . . If Thou dost not . . . respond to our pleas we will die here on this square before Thy palace."

On Sunday, January 9, the workers assembled at various points around the city and resolved to march up Nevsky Prospect and the other radiating avenues to the steps of the Winter Palace, assembling on Rossi's enormous square around Montferrand's gigantic victory column. The tsar they intended to petition was Nicholas II, who as a boy had watched his assassinated grandfather expire and who, on the eve of his own coronation in 1894, had confided to a cousin that he was not ready to rule. By 1905, popular discontent with Nicholas was raging over Russia's ineptly fought border war with Japan, which had exposed the supposedly European Russia as a second-rate Asian power. While Nicholas had welcomed jingoistic demonstrators from the balcony of the Winter Palace at the war's auspicious beginning, he now spent as little time in St. Petersburg as possible, preferring to live with his family in the suburban palace at Tsarskoye Selo. True to form, when Nicholas heard of the preparations for the march, he left for his Tsarskoye Selo compound, putting his police and soldiers in charge of the capital. The new authorities promptly ordered Father Gapon's arrest.

Wearing a white cassock, Gapon led his band of Putilov workers from the slums near their factory on the subfreezing day. The workers, dressed in their Sunday finery, carried religious icons and portraits of the tsar. At the Narva Gate, the triumphal Roman arch that marked the border of the imperial city, the cavalry ordered the procession to stop. When the march continued, a bugle sounded and shots rang out. One of Gapon's bodyguards was hit and slumped into him, knocking the priest down. "There is no tsar!" Gapon uttered before fleeing to safety.

The other columns of marchers converging on the Winter Palace had similar confrontations with the police and military, but survivors of the skirmishes made it to Palace Square on time. The five thousand marchers on Nevsky Prospect were joined by the Sunday-morning crowds of shoppers and curious onlookers. Soon sixty thousand people were assembled in front of the

Winter Palace, but at two o'clock, the time when the petition was to be delivered, Father Gapon failed to show. A hush settled over the bewildered crowd, which was surrounded by troops. A bugle sounded and a volley of fire cut down nearly a thousand men, women, and children, staining the snow red with blood. The crowds scattered, and for the rest of what became known as "Bloody Sunday," the capital was in disarray.

Over the months that followed, chaos gripped St. Petersburg—and the rest of Russia along with it—as its shallow-rooted modern institutions ceased to function one by one. Strikes crippled the factories. The stock exchange closed down. The universities were shuttered. Doctors and lawyers—and even the ballerinas at the Imperial Mariinsky Theater—went on strike.

Faced with the crisis, Nicholas was indecisive as liberals called for constitutional monarchy, radicals argued for a republic, and conservatives sought salvation in a military dictatorship. In August, Nicholas publicly proposed creating a parliament with extremely limited suffrage and a solely consultative role, but the capital's strikes and protests went on. Then the tsar approached his uncle, the Grand Duke Nicholas Nikolayevich, and inquired whether he might serve as dictator. The grand duke refused. Scrambling, on October 17 Nicholas decreed a true constitutional monarchy with civil liberties and a parliament, the Duma, elected by universal male suffrage. With the 1905 Revolution, autocracy was finally abolished. The form of government Peter the Great had observed in London two hundred years before and purposefully chosen not to import had finally come to Russia through the sheer will of the people Peter's city had made.

In April 1906, members of Russia's first legislature arrived in St. Petersburg. For many Petersburgers, it was a case of buyer's remorse. While the principle of having a national legislature, like a normal European country, had its appeal, the composition of the chamber brought home the fact that Russia was hardly a normal European country. Nearly half of the Duma's nearly five hundred representatives were rural peasants, a veritable foreign presence in the Venice of the North. One reform-minded official referred to the new Duma as "a gathering of savages . . . as if the Russian land had sent to St. Petersburg everything that was barbarian in it."

For his part, Nicholas never truly made peace with the end of autocracy. After just seventy-two days, the tsar dissolved the Duma and called for new elections. Over the next decade, Nicholas would dissolve the Duma twice more and unconstitutionally meddle in its composition to limit the growing number of socialists in its ranks.

Even more than usual, Nicholas was hiding from a modern world in which he had never felt at home, barricading himself in his suburban compound at Tsarskoye Selo with his sickly son, four daughters, and his wife, Alexandra. His entire life, Nicholas had been nostalgic for Russia before Peter the Great—"the ancestor I like least," he called him, "for his enthusiasm for Western culture and violation of all purely Russian customs." Upon coronation, Nicholas had adopted the old-fashioned Russian title "tsar" in lieu of the Westernized "emperor" favored by Peter. He named his only son, Alexis, after the last great tsar to reign in Moscow before Peter built his new capital. From early in his reign, at royal balls, Nicholas would dress in the long, gold-embroidered caftans of medieval Moscow with the impractical sleeves Peter had so vehemently clipped. And Nicholas grew a beard reminiscent of the facial hair of seventeenth-century Russia that Peter had personally shaved off his empire.

Besieged by liberals and radicals after the 1905 Revolution, playing dress-up was no longer enough. Nicholas began living in the past quite literally. On his grounds in Tsarskoye Selo, he commissioned his architects to build the Feodorov village, a miniature walled town designed to look as if it had been built in the seventeenth century. As one observer wrote at the time, "As if by magic you were transported to the era of the first Romanov. Your feet sank into thick carpets. You were met by soldiers dressed in [medieval] Russian costumes." Nicholas seemed to want to undo Peter's reforms by living in his own inverted St. Petersburg. While Peter had endeavored to build a modern European city from scratch to modernize the country, Nicholas built a medieval Russian village to pull the nation back to its roots. But the tiny royal compound at the Feodorov village lacked the audacious aims of metropolitan St. Petersburg. Nicholas's village would never be more than a royal hideout. While he hoped it would be a model of autocracy reborn, as the latest imported automobiles sped incongruously past its thick, white, turreted walls, the project came to seem ineffectual and preposterous. Peter had understood that his mad vision would be mocked unless he made it grand enough to be reckoned with. Feckless Nicholas simply didn't possess that kind of ambition.

In the heart of the capital, Nicholas ordered up the nostalgic Tercentenary Church to commemorate the three hundredth anniversary of Romanov rule. As its architect, Stepan Krichinsky, openly said, "The idea was to create an entire corner of the seventeenth century." A corner, rather than a whole city—that was about the scale of Nicholas's vision. Krichinsky's cathedral was an oversized replica of the seventeenth-century churches in the historic city of Rostov, but built out of reinforced concrete to make it large enough to accommodate four thousand worshippers. One wall boasted an enormous family tree of the Romanovs. On the church bells, reliefs were embossed of each member of the royal family with his or her patron saint. The church, which opened in 1913, stood at the base of Nevsky Prospect, on the square in front of the city's main train station, where the Moscow–St. Petersburg line terminates. Now passengers planning to travel from traditional Moscow to modern St.

Petersburg would emerge from the station to find an enormous monument to Muscovite nostalgia.

In July 1914, World War I offered Nicholas the opportunity to turn Russia even further inward. When Nicholas and Alexandra appeared on the balcony of the Winter Palace after declaring war on Germany and Austria-Hungary, a crowd of 250,000, gripped by patriotic fervor, fell to their knees singing the national anthem, "Bozhe tsaria khrani" ("God Save the Tsar"). Later that week, crowds trashed the German embassy, prying the bronze equestrian statues off the roof and throwing them down into the square in front of St. Isaac's Cathedral. The following month, Nicholas seized on the rampant xenophobia to change the city's name to Petrograd, Russian for "Peter's City." That the original name had been Dutch, not German, and that Russia was not at war with Holland was beside the point.

The nationalistic mood did not last long. The war was a disaster. Within the first ten months, there were nearly four million Russian casualties along the thousand-mile front. Army deserters began roaming the streets of the capital. During the harsh winter of 1916–1917, blizzards severed the rail links that provided Petrograd with food and supplies. The Putilov Works, which had been converted to military use, winning massive government contracts to produce artillery shells for the front, ceased production in February for lack of fuel. Bread riots swept the city. On February 24, a large rally unfolded in front of the newly completed Tercentenary Church, with crowds chanting, "Down with the autocracy!" The next day, the city was crippled by a general strike. Students marched down Nevsky Prospect singing the battle hymn of the French Revolution, "La Marseillaise."

Nicholas II and the aristocracy remained in denial. On Saturday night, February 25, the cream of St. Petersburg society went to the Carlo Rossi–designed Alexander Theater to watch a revival of Mikhail Lermontov's *Masquerade*, a Gogolian satire of hyperhierarchical St. Petersburg written in 1835 as Lermontov himself grappled with Nicholas I's censors. Despite the shortages plaguing the city, the Imperial Treasury had shelled out thirty thousand gold rubles for the sets alone. As one historian later wrote of the event, "Autocratic Russia was collapsing . . . the entire solemn ritual of the Court, the magnificent uniforms, the bewitching power of rank, the strict etiquette, the indestructible preeminence of tradition, the arrogance of the nobility, heraldry, orders, epaulettes, review parades."

In the city outside the theater, the authorities were losing control over the industrial districts. Local police stations were set afire. In the morning, crowds marched down Nevsky Prospect despite a curfew. Soldiers fired on them, killing about four dozen on the square between the Tercentenary Church and the main train station. But as the disorder continued into the night, rather than fire on their starving countrymen, unit after unit mutinied. The next morning, a crowd torched an infamous courthouse and prison a few blocks south of the Neva, and that evening a disconnected Nicholas, holed up in Tsarskoye Selo, received a disturbing telegram from the general in charge of Petrograd: "I beg you to inform His Imperial Highness that I am not able to carry out his instructions about the restoration of order in the capital. . . . The majority of army units . . . have refused to fire on the rebels. . . . Other units have joined with the insurgents and have turned their weapons against the troops still remaining loyal to His Highness."

Inside the Winter Palace, Duma leaders announced the formation of a provisional committee to restore order in the capital. On March 2, Nicholas abdicated in favor of his brother, Mikhail. Faced with word from Petrograd of crowds rallying for "no more Romanovs," Mikhail abdicated the following day. Just three years after the completion of the church marking their dynasty's three hundredth anniversary, the Romanovs were finished.

The Provisional Government of Alexander Kerensky, a St. Petersburg State University—educated attorney and former Duma member, was ineffectual from the start, and as the short months of its administration passed, conditions on the ground in the beleaguered capital worsened. Just a few days after the February Revolution, Petrograd workers had won the right to an eight-hour day through an agreement between the Petrograd Society of Industrialists and the radical Petrograd Soviet of Workers' and Soldiers' Deputies. But progress soon stalled. By mid-May, forty thousand Petrograd workers were unemployed, real wages were plummeting, and mass layoffs were accelerating. On top of that, the Provisional Government chose to continue waging the deeply unpopular world war. The Petrograd masses wondered, is this the new Russia we have risen up to create?

Humiliated in the Great War by the European powers of Germany and Austria-Hungary, Russia was again ready to double down on a leader with a transformative vision for the country's breakneck modernization. It would come from one of the ambitious, worldly Russians the capital had lured in with its opportunities but stifled with its restrictions. Vladimir Illyich Lenin (born Vladimir Ulyanov) first came to the capital as a young man to study law at St. Petersburg State University. The youthful Lenin was radicalized by the execution of his brother, Alexander, a People's Will splinter group operative who was arrested on Nevsky Prospect carrying a bomb intended for Tsar Alexander III. Hounded by the tsar's secret police as an enemy of the state, Lenin lived mostly in exile in Western Europe, but the promise of the city where he had come of age remained in his mind: the possibility that foreign ideas imported into Russia could once and for all modernize the lagging country.

In his 1902 manifesto, *What Is to Be Done?*, the goateed, wolf-eyed revolutionary had laid out his central political ideas. While accepting Communist founder Karl Marx's critique of capitalist exploitation and faith in the coming of a communist future, Lenin disagreed with Marx that communism could only arise in the world's most advanced economies. Rather, Lenin argued, a revolutionary vanguard could impose communism on developing countries, like Russia, from above. Though Lenin acknowledged that his homeland was "economically most backward," stunted in its development, and socially and technologically far behind the West, he believed bold leadership by an elite cadre of visionaries could catapult Russia forward to communism. Lenin's call for national transformation from above echoed Peter the Great's conviction that he could autocratically wrench Russia into the modern world without having to wait for more organic development from below. Leninism was forged as Marx's theories were refracted through St. Petersburg, the model modern city built to revolutionize a backward country. The revolutionary hubris of Leninism parallels the revolutionary hubris of the city of St. Petersburg itself.

To make his revolution from above, Lenin split his followers off from Russia's larger democratic socialist movement to form the Bolsheviks. While other factions on the Russian Left had faith that the Russian masses could shape their own better future through trial and error and open debate, the Bolsheviks plotted a top-down revolution.

In 1917, unconcerned with Lenin's larger philosophy of communism but cognizant that the Bolshevik platform called for pulling Russia out of World War I, German authorities gave Lenin safe passage to Petrograd from his exile in Switzerland in an armored train car. Once in the city he knew so well from his student days, Lenin began plotting a coup.

With conditions declining in the city even after the ousting of the tsar, Lenin found a sympathetic audience in Petrograd's workers. On the night of October 24–25, Bolshevik units of radical soldiers and armed industrial workers took over key institutions throughout the city, including train stations, the main post office, and the telephone exchange. In unceremoniously taking over these modern institutions of the capital, in most cases without a fight, the Bolsheviks essentially took over Russia. While subduing the hinterlands would take years of civil war, Russia was so unevenly developed, its nerve center so completely concentrated in a single city, that simply taking over the centers of power in that city alone constituted a revolution.

At 9:00 a.m. the next day, Alexander Kerensky fled the Winter Palace in a car provided by the American Embassy. That night, Bolshevik-supporting troops fired a volley of shells at the lightly defended former royal residence. Only two hit the building. By 2:30 a.m., the palace was secured. At 3:00 a.m., across town at the Bolshevik headquarters in the Smolny Institute, Catherine the Great's school for young noblewomen, Lenin announced the end of the Provisional Government and the dawn of Soviet power.

The Bolsheviks made good on their promise to withdraw from the world war, signing a peace treaty in March 1918. But there was no peace in Russia. Civil war erupted as the Bolsheviks' Red Army clashed with a broad alliance of opponents, called the Whites, made up of everyone from constitutional democrats to tsarist dead-enders and aided by forces from several anticommunist Western powers including Britain, France, and the United States. Faced with enemies to the west, St. Petersburg's geographic orientation became a liability; Lenin moved the capital to Moscow in 1918 for military reasons as the civil war raged.

Even after the Red Army vanquished the Whites, the capital remained in Moscow, for it was more than military necessity that dictated the demotion of Petrograd to second city of the Soviet Union. Lenin had never trusted the cradle of the revolution. Though Peter's city was the gateway through which European ideas, including Karl Marx's, flowed into the country, once Lenin seized power, new ideas became a threat. The city whose cos-

mopolitan streets and flourishing universities had inspired generations of Russians to ponder a new future for their country
had to be silenced lest its revolutionary possibilities unseat the
new regime. The capital was moved back to the Kremlin, where
a bearded theocratic elite had once overseen Russia, guided by
the eternal truths of Church teaching; soon a new class of gray
men would monopolize power inside the redbrick Kremlin walls,
intent on ruling Russia in accordance with a new holy canon of
official Bolshevik doctrine.

Petrograd's Soviet transformation began immediately. The
day after the coup, non-Bolshevik newspapers disappeared off
the streets of the city. Within weeks, the Cheka, the Communist successor to the tsar's infamous secret police, was founded
in an office just off Nevsky Prospect. Its mandate was to stifle
what Lenin called Petrograd's "embittered bourgeois intelligentsia." In addition to liberal intellectuals, soon the very
Petrograd workers who had led the revolution were being suppressed by Party leaders as the chaos of revolution and civil
war, coupled with brutal winters, took its toll. As wages fell
and food became scarce, the peasants-turned-workers who
had flocked to the capital for jobs during the prewar industrial
boom returned to their ancestral villages. The population of
Petrograd dropped from 2.3 million in 1918 to 720,000 in 1920.
Those who remained became openly critical of the Bolshevik leadership. In 1918, the workers in the now-nationalized
Putilov Works introduced a resolution in the Petrograd Soviet
demanding free speech and independent trade unions. And on
the fourth anniversary of the overthrow of the tsar, a flyer
appeared on the streets demanding freedom of speech, press,
and assembly. "Workers and peasants need freedom," it read.
"They do not want to live by the decrees of the Bolsheviks."
But when bread riots similar to those that caused the February
Revolution broke out in Petrograd, Bolshevik troops clashed

with workers on Nevsky Prospect and the Cheka arrested hundreds of striking workers.

Finally, in the winter of 1921, the ten thousand sailors at the nearby naval installation of Kronstadt, whom Lenin's right-hand man, Red Army commander in chief Leon Trotsky, had called "the pride and flower of the Revolution," rose up against Bolshevism. In their unauthorized version of the official Soviet daily, *Izvestia*, they wrote, "In carrying out the October Revolution the working class hoped to achieve its liberation. The outcome has been even greater enslavement of human beings . . . a new serfdom."

The Bolsheviks violently crushed the Kronstadt revolt, but the unrest pushed Lenin to ease up on control over Petrograd's economy and culture, creating some space for those who had hoped that Petrograd, freed of tsarist backwardness, could finally fulfill its destiny as the birthplace of a new global culture. When Lenin died in 1924 and the metropolis was renamed Leningrad in his honor, it still remained unclear how the city would develop. For all the brutality of the Bolsheviks, many observers saw tremendous potential in the new Soviet state. After the revolution, Russia again, as under Catherine the Great, captivated the world's visionary thinkers as an enormous blank slate where the future could be built in one fell swoop. Brilliant architects and philosophers poured in from the West with ambitious plans to forge a hypermodern society. And to a far greater extent than in the eighteenth century, these foreign experts were joined in their projects by talented Russians.

In the early twentieth century, avant-garde architects, many affiliated with the German architecture and design school, the Bauhaus, founded in 1919, were pioneering a style known as modernism. Inspired by industrial technologies, the modernists experimented with new materials, making chairs from steel tubing and designing austere homes and offices that embraced the stripped-down form–follows–function aesthetic of factories. While cognizant that modernity could be discomfiting, as people are unmoored from the solace of tradition, and dehumanizing, as workers are turned into cogs in the wheel of assembly-line production, the architectural avant-garde held onto a hope that modernity could ultimately liberate humanity. If only we could harness our new tools to serve us rather than we serving them and share the bounty we all produce, they believed, everyone could live a decent life. For a time, these hopes were pinned on the new Soviet state. And in the period when progressive internationalists in the Soviet Communist Party still held some power, idealistic architectural modernists flowed into Russia, and the nation's own indigenous modernists won major commissions.

When plans were made to hold the third Communist International, a conference of the world's communist parties, in the city on the Neva in 1921, culturally progressive officials tapped avant-garde architect Vladimir Tatlin to create a monument. In his design, officially called the Monument to the Third International but invariably known as Tatlin's Tower, the architect envisioned a twentieth-century answer to Paris's Eiffel Tower—a structure that could similarly thrust a historic city stalked by nostalgia and dowdiness back to the cutting edge. Tatlin envisioned a skeletal ziggurat well over a thousand feet tall—larger than the Eiffel Tower—jutting out at an angle like a rocket about to lift off. The spiral of steel, Tatlin said, represented "the line of advance of free humanity." Within the twisting exoskeleton he planned three halls—a cube housing a conference hall, a pyramid of executive offices, and a cylindrical media and visitor center. The cube, pyramid, and cylinder—the exoskeleton's proverbial internal organs—would all rotate based on the frequency of meetings in each body. The cube would turn once a year, the pyramid once per month, and the cylinder once per day. No longer would Petrograd be a mere window on the West; the leapfrog city would be the center of a new modern world.

The tower, though indisputably one of the most important designs of the twentieth century, was never built. The Soviet state was too burdened by the costs of fighting the civil war to fund such a project. But even with its most famous creation unbuilt, the cradle of the revolution did birth many works of revolutionary architecture in the early Soviet period. By the Narva Gate, near Putilov's nationalized factory, city authorities built a new model neighborhood for the industrial workers who had been so instrumental in the 1905 and 1917 revolutions. Along the rechristened Strike Avenue (Prospekt Stachek), they built the institutions of a new world in a new style—Constructivism. Russia's distinctive variety of modernism, Constructivism was deeply imbued with the imperial capital's centuries-old architectural obsession with geometry and perspective. In the late 1920s and early 1930s, new buildings were erected throughout the working-class neighborhood, offering a vision of a new and better society. A "Palace of Culture" with an arched glass curtain wall soon stretched along Strike Avenue, offering "collectives," cultural enrichment courses for neighborhood workers. Across the street rose a gray industrial "kitchen factory" where meals were mass-produced in an effort to free women from the drudgery of housewifery. Down the avenue, a school honoring the tenth anniversary of the revolution was built in the shape of a hammer and sickle. Inside, students were broken into creative pods that solved problems together using a new pedagogy emphasizing teamwork.

While in the imperial heart of the old city the vast apartments of the wealthy were divided into shared collective apartments, in the neighborhood by the Narva Gate, the city administration built the Soviet Union's first worker housing on Tractor Street (Traktornaya Ulitsa), named for the machinery the workers made at the plant. Unlike the soulless slabs that later became synonymous with Soviet housing, the Tractor Street homes were an innovative, humane updating of classical Petersburg forms. The three-story apartments, which were painted a typical Petersburg color—pale salmon—break the "red line" of the imperial city but do so in an ordered way, taking one step forward for each set of apartments. This provides each unit with a dignified outdoor balcony, curved at the end to give the whole structure a streamlined industrial appearance. Viewed from the end of the street, the long buildings with their ordered setbacks mimic the vanishing-point-perspective of the imperial city but in a new, Constructivist way. Similarly, the decorative half arches that divide the fronts of the buildings from the green space behind constitute a modernized version of Rossi's Roman arches downtown.

Early Soviet Leningrad also experimented with a new architectural aesthetic in the buildings where its workers labored. While the Putilov factory had hid behind a long stone barrier wall of nostalgia, the new Soviet factories embraced the industrial age with excitement and wonder. To design the Red Banner Factory, a Leningrad textile works, in 1925, the German-Jewish Bauhaus architect Erich Mendelsohn was brought in. Mendelsohn drew up a building like a giant ocean liner plowing forward into the future, with a redbrick prow, topped by a decorative zigzagging, sand-colored stucco cornice to cut through the air. In his mind, a factory need not be a massive, plodding building; Mendelsohn's factory looks ready to set sail.

But soon cultural conservatives gained the upper hand within the Party. The few daring projects that were realized in the early Soviet period came to serve only as eerie reminders of the idealistic ambitions the revolution never fulfilled. Today, the Tractor Street homes and the Red Banner Factory stand as symbols of Leningrad's short-lived experiment with avant-garde architecture and global culture, crushed by leaders, chief among them Joseph Stalin, whose only imagination was for amassing their own power.

In 1933, Mendelsohn's Bauhaus colleague, Walter Gropius, visited Leningrad. As Mendelsohn wrote at the time, "Gropius is back from Leningrad, horrified and shaken by what he has seen and experienced. The great idea has been ground down by bureaucracy." Heartbroken, the architect concluded that Bolshevism "is the destroyer of socialism." As in the Age of Enlightenment, Russia's window on the West birthed dreams of a glorious future only to smother them. While the city did build a smattering of futuristic wonders, the larger vision it inspired, of a wondrous future, would remain unbuilt.

# GREAT WORLD

## Shanghai, 1911–1937

The Bund, mid-1930s, with Cathay Hotel (at right)

Shanghai, the Paris of the East!
Shanghai, the New York of the West!
Shanghai, the most cosmopolitan city in the world.
—*All About Shanghai*, English tourist guidebook, 1934

With the fall of the Chinese emperor in 1911, Shanghai, the city famously divided into Chinese, French, and Anglo-American sectors, came together as never before. The walls around the historic Chinese city were torn down. And the canal that had divided the French Concession from the International Settlement was filled in to become Avenue Édouard VII, using a French name to honor an English king.

In the treaty port where the Chinese had long been reduced to second-class citizenship, in the new century, they began to create a coequal world for themselves. In 1911, a group of well-to-do Shanghainese set up their own International Race Club as an alternative to the Shanghai Race Club that refused them entry. And the growing city was increasingly being taken seriously as a global hub. In 1912, when a group of recent Harvard Medical School graduates opened the school's first-ever overseas branch, they did so in the most logical place: Shanghai. The modern world, knit together by trade and travel, needed a few international crossroads cities—a role that Shanghai, the most open city in the world, where neither passport nor visa was required for entry, seemed destined to play.

But by the 1920s, Shanghai was more than just a place where

Western institutions like Harvard Med were airlifted in, or where the Chinese created their own versions of Western institutions like the International Race Club. It was the crucible for a distinct Chinese modernity—not a simple mimicry of the West but a new culture altogether. And by the 1930s, Shanghai was forging a truly global modernity, reflected in its architectural styles of modernism, Art Deco, and pastiche. While modernism embraced the stripped-down aesthetic of the industrial age, the more flamboyant global style of Art Deco drew on the actual technologies that were tying the world together, applying the streamlined forms of ocean liners and airplanes to buildings through swooping balconies and porthole windows. Though named after the 1925 Parisian art fair, the Exposition Internationale des Arts Decoratifs et Industriels Modernes, the style soon went global, leaving a greater stamp on the rising cities of Asia and the Americas than on Europe. Meanwhile, pastiche embraced the world by sampling various designs from other times and places and weaving them together in a patchwork style. Generally regarded as an architectural innovation of the "postmodern" 1970s and '80s, pastiche was all the rage in Shanghai half a century before it came into vogue in the West. In the aftermath of World War I, Shanghai's rivals in Europe were already in decline, while America's great cities were hamstrung by a perfect storm of the religious fundamentalism of Prohibition in 1919, the isolationism of the xenophobic 1924 immigration act, and the economic collapse of the 1929 crash. Pre-Communist Shanghai wasn't just the most modern city in China; it was the most modern city in the world.

And yet the humiliated status of Shanghai's Chinese population was never quite undone. Extraterritorial privilege, which allowed Westerners to live in Shanghai without being bound by Chinese law, was pared back but never fully eliminated. And a staggering gap between rich and poor haunted the city throughout the exuberant era. Jazz Age Shanghai was a house divided, a city, as the British tourist guidebook *All About Shanghai* put it in 1934, of "modern skyscrapers [and] straw huts shoulder high."

In the dynamic world of early twentieth-century Shanghai, the simple European-over-Asian racial hierarchy of the treaty port began breaking down. The late-model limousines honking their way past hand-pulled rickshaws now often ferried Asian tycoons around town, and the rickshaws were occasionally pulled by impoverished whites. The Asian magnates usually were Japanese, relative newcomers to Shanghai who had transformed its economy. While mercantile Shanghai had been created by the Western powers of Britain, France, and America, industrial Shanghai was a Japanese invention. In the second half of the nineteenth century, the Japanese emperors who had long been as isolationist as their Chinese counterparts embraced industrialization with a vengeance. During the Meiji period (*meiji* meaning "enlightened rule" in Japanese), they accepted a constitutional monarchy and imported thousands of Western experts to help develop the country. By the 1890s, Japan was far more developed than China, a reality made plain by China's defeat in the Sino-Japanese war. The war-ending Treaty of Shimonoseki, signed in 1895, guaranteed Japanese companies the right to "carry on trade, industry and manufactures" in China's treaty ports, forcing industrialization on a reluctant Middle Kingdom. From the principle of "most favored nation" status, anything the Japanese negotiated for themselves, the major Western powers automatically won as well. Almost immediately, Shanghai experienced a massive boom that doubled the city's population in fifteen years and ringed the city with a swath of industrial areas, most dramatically in Pudong, the east bank of the Huangpu River, directly across from the Bund.

As word spread in Japan of a newly opened market brimming with opportunity, just a short trip from the home islands, where you could move without papers, Japanese businessmen flooded

Shanghai. In a nod to their growing influence, the Western powers eventually welcomed the Japanese into their race club, giving them two seats on the Shanghai Municipal Council in 1918. The Chinese remained excluded. Numbering nearly fourteen thousand by 1925, the Japanese became the largest foreign community in Shanghai. Japanese foremen, who, unlike Western managers, generally learned to speak Chinese, developed a reputation for efficient labor management that pidgin-speaking Shanghailanders, assisted by Chinese compradors, could not match. Of course, what looked like managerial efficiency on a balance sheet often felt like slave driving on the factory floor, and Sino-Japanese tensions arose.

Soon after the jarring Chinese encounter with high-status Asians, they were shocked again by the new phenomenon of low-status whites: the Russian refugees who fled to the open city of Shanghai from Lenin's Bolshevism and civil war. Many of the pale newcomers, particularly rural Russians unaccustomed to urban life, had no marketable skills. These penniless refugees often ended up homeless and drunk on the streets. Others took menial jobs, like pulling rickshaws, that Europeans had never before deigned to do. For women, prostitution beckoned—especially as the fair-haired Russians could trade on their exotic appeal to charge higher rates. A 1930s League of Nations report found that one in four Russian women in Shanghai was a sex worker.

Petersburgers tended to fare better than their rural countrymen. For them, China's international gateway was oddly familiar, and they seized its opportunities accordingly. Anatol Kotenev, a former Petrograd constable, landed a job with the Shanghai Municipal Police, since policing Russia's most cosmopolitan city had prepared him well to police China's. And the Russian-owned and -managed Banque Russo-Asiatique, the crowning achievement of the Putilov dynasty of St. Petersburg industrialists, continued doing business in Shanghai for a full decade after its Nevsky Prospect headquarters had been shuttered by Lenin's decree "confiscating all the real and personal property of Mr. Alexei Putilov." The Russian refugee bankers who took jobs in the Banque's three-story Italian Renaissance–style office on the Bund, which housed China's first elevator, already had plenty of experience advising companies seeking to profit in a freewheeling emerging market.

The new communities of high-status Asians and low-status whites emboldened wealthy Chinese to argue that Shanghai's institutions be restricted by class instead of race. After all, "respectable" Chinese certainly trumped white beggars. And the "respectable" Chinese were growing wealthier and more numerous in early twentieth-century Shanghai. After the Treaty of Shimonoseki opened up Shanghai to foreign-owned industrial concerns, the imperial authorities eased restrictions on would-be Chinese industrialists; after all, it was no longer a question of whether Shanghai would industrialize—only who would reap the profits. The revolution of 1911 abolished the remaining restrictions outright. Just as whites were taking jobs heretofore reserved for the Chinese, the Chinese increasingly did work once reserved for whites, branching out far beyond the comprador-cum-financier roles they'd pioneered in the nineteenth century and enjoying the lifestyles to match.

Nanjing Road, Shanghai's Nevsky Prospect, had been home to Western department stores since the nineteenth century, but after World War I, Chinese merchant families began opening their own stores. The first, Sincere, opened in 1917; its archrival, Wing On, opened the following year on the opposite side of the street. Near mirror images of each other, and designed by rival Shanghailander architecture firms, both were massive Renaissance-style edifices topped by elegant spires. Illuminated at night, they appeared like two sentries staring each other down across a disputed border while the rest of the street erupted in a riot of flashing lit-up signs in a style that came to typify the East Asian city. An estimated two hundred thousand pedestrians a day passed by the stores' entrances, which were placed at an intersection where several major tramlines converged. Inside, the rivals sold merchandise from all over the world—China's finest silk and porcelain packed the shelves alongside whiskeys from Scotland, cameras from Germany, and leather wallets from England. More than just stores, both buildings housed elegant restaurants, theaters, and hotels as well. As one visitor exclaimed, "To call Wing On's a department store is like calling Barnum and Bailey's an elephant show."

Sincere and Wing On were establishments created by a newly Westernized Chinese elite for a newly Westernized Chinese elite. Both the Ma family who founded Sincere and the Guo family who founded Wing On were Cantonese migrants who had learned the Western-style retail trade—fixed, displayed prices rather than bargaining; systematic organization of goods; courteous service—while living as diaspora Chinese in Australia. Both families founded their retail empires in colonial Hong Kong and then opened flagship stores in Shanghai as the city prospered after the 1911 revolution, safely stabilized under the foreign powers even as the rest of China remained fractious with various warlords vying for control.

As Wing On prospered, the Guo family moved into a lavish Tudor-style mansion in the foreign concessions and adopted English first names. A formal family portrait from the period shows several generations of Guos gathered on their expansive lawn like English aristocrats. In the front row, an imperious young woman sits cross-legged with her hair in a modish perm while a young man rakishly leans in on the end, sporting a jaunty bow tie and pocket square. Through their establishment, the Guos offered Chinese customers a taste of their elegant lifestyle.

As the *Far Eastern Review* explained to its Anglophone readership, Sincere's Oriental Hotel catered to Chinese "accustomed to foreign manners" while Wing On's Great Eastern Hotel promised unparalleled service to its Chinese clientele "accustomed to Occidental . . . customs." At the Wing On hotel's Great Eastern cabaret, Chinese theatergoers were initiated into the jazz music craze that had swept the Shanghailanders. Chinese women, who had initially shunned ballroom dancing out of Confucianism's strictures against public displays of affection, soon overcame their inhibitions.

For the average Chinese newcomer to Shanghai, who could only afford to window-shop at Sincere or Wing On, the city offered downscale versions. Just a few blocks off Nanjing Road, bordering the Shanghai Race Club, stood Great World. Dubbed "a department store for amusement," Great World opened in 1923 as a profit-seeking pleasure palace built by Chinese entrepreneur Huang Chu-jiu and designed by Zhou Hui Nan, considered to be Shanghai's first Chinese architect. Within the four-story building that grandly curves around its corner site, beckoning passersby to enter beneath its wedding-cake spire, was a labyrinth of theaters, beach boardwalk–style shooting galleries, food stalls, even a roller skating rink and a wrestling ring. Inside, fortune-tellers, magicians, puppeteers, acupuncturists, and acrobats competed for visitors' attention and money. While Sincere and Wing On assumed a familiarity with Western culture on the part of its sophisticated clientele, Great World taught it explicitly: on one floor, a row of commodes were displayed with guides explaining to Chinese patrons, accustomed to Asian squat toilets, how to use the exotic contraptions. In this "hodgepodge of the most déclassé elements of East and West," as one historian put it, was the rawest essence of what came to be known as Haipai, the Shanghai style of commercial, cosmopolitan Chinese modernity.

The central concept of Haipai was a Shanghai neologism: *modeng*, a transliteration of the English word *modern* grafted onto the ancient Chinese language. In Jazz Age Shanghai, *modeng* denoted the new and fashionable, ranging from the tawdriness of Great World to the elegance of the city's upscale cabarets. At the center of this new culture was the Shanghai Girl, the single young woman who was the city's answer to the Western world's cigarette-smoking, nightclub-hopping, independent-thinking flapper. Everything about the Shanghai Girl was *modeng*: her permed hair, her job outside the home, her social life organized around dating rather than the arranged marriages of the traditional Chinese village. And when a Shanghai Girl did get married, to a man of her choosing, she wore a *modeng* white dress and veil rather than a traditional red tunic and diadem. To bring dating to China, another new word was coined: *daling*—a transliteration of the English word *darling*.

White weddings aside, Haipai was more than a simple appropriation of the West. Shanghai men typically mixed Western garments with Chinese ones, often wearing European trousers under their black scholar's robes. For women, the height of fashion was neither the latest designs from Paris nor the old flowing imperial robes of traditional China, but the *qipao*, a form-fitting dress with a high collar and prominent, often distractingly high slit. An updated version of an old Manchu outfit, it was both modern and uniquely Chinese. Its exact origins are debated, but according to urban legend a Chinese actress complained to a band leader in the Majestic Hotel that her long dress wouldn't let her do the Charleston, the latest dance craze to sweep the city. The solution, he suggested, was to cut slits. The range of *qipao* fashion was best recorded in advertisements for branded consumer goods, typically painted by Chinese artists for Western-owned companies and reproduced in freebie calendars. Cigarette ads of the era were famous for showing sophisticated *qipao*-clad Shanghai Girls lighting up, with city icons like the racecourse, the Bund, or Nanjing Road illuminated behind them.

Print advertising also fueled the new Chinese magazine industry, overwhelmingly based in Shanghai, which helped shift the center of gravity in Chinese literary life from Beijing to Shanghai's foreign concessions. By the 1930s, most Chinese publishers and nearly all of China's magazines were based in the international sections of Shanghai. Continuing political instability in Beijing pushed intellectuals to relocate, but more than that, the old order that had long anchored Chinese intellectual life in the capital had broken down. For centuries, the ablest scholars in China aced the national exams on the Confucian classics and moved to Beijing for civil service sinecures that left time for intellectual pursuits like composing poetry, fiction, plays, or philosophical treatises. Now writers supported themselves by selling their work to magazines and publishing houses in Shanghai. And the lifestyle of the cosmopolitan foreign concessions, where tiny apartments were more common than multigenerational family homes and the nightlife never stopped, was conducive to the writer's life of feast-or-famine fortunes and unconventional work schedules.

To appeal to a Shanghai readership, the new writers wrote in the vernacular, engaged the themes of city life, and embraced the new individualist values of the metropolis. "I am the splendor of the moon, / I am the splendor of the sun," proclaimed Shanghai poet Guo Moruo, channeling Whitman and challenging Confucius with his embrace of unbridled individualism over collectivist humility. Lu Xun, the leading light of the Shanghai literary scene, lived in a Western-furnished town house in the International Settlement's Continental Terrace development. From this perch, he wrote of his provincial upbringing and chronicled the city to which he'd moved. Fancying himself the Gogol of Shanghai, he named his first story

"Diary of a Madman," a title borrowed from the St. Petersburg master. In Lu Xun's "Diary," the protagonist is driven mad by China's stagnant, outmoded Confucian traditions in the same way Gogol's diarist is destroyed by Russia's backward system of aristocratic rank. Yet for all the skewering of Confucius, Lu Xun was not anti-Chinese any more than Gogol was anti-Russian. He simply hoped China could grow powerful through modernization and ultimately liberate itself from foreign domination and saw his own literature—contemporary in its language and unsparing in its social criticism—as a spur to that modernizing project.

Lu Xun and other like-minded Shanghai intellectuals were, as one contemporary historian put it, "cosmopolitan nationalists" who experienced an "ambivalent love-hate relationship . . . with the city." They were "critical of imperialism and viewed the unequal treaties and the existence of foreign-run enclaves as a source of national humiliation [yet] they were anything but parochial or xenophobic." When Chinese people moved to Shanghai, they were exposed to American movies and Russian novels, they met in French cafés and English pubs, and attended lectures by the globetrotting intellectuals who visited the city, including American philosopher John Dewey and feminist Margaret Sanger, British novelist Aldous Huxley, and Indian poet Rabindranath Tagore. The Chinese literati who flocked to Shanghai were thrilled to live in the most dynamic city in China but humiliated by the knowledge that it was the creation of foreign imperialists.

Even as they worked to forge a modern culture for China, Shanghai intellectuals were plagued by doubts that it could ever be understood by their country cousins. Haipai, in its uniqueness to Shanghai, seemed irrelevant to the vast Chinese hinterlands. And those hinterlands began just beyond international Shanghai's stone boundary markers: as an observer noted, within "fifteen minutes one can leave behind the second largest bank building in the world and stand beside a mud-hut."

Hinterlands aside, Shanghainese intellectuals wondered aloud if Haipai could be made relevant to the working class of Shanghai itself. While the city boasted modern conveniences on par with any city in the world, the impoverished masses made the bitter joke that they got around town on the "number 11 bus"—their own two legs. Just steps away from the Bund or off Nanjing Road was all the poverty of rural China with none of its rustic charm. And more disturbingly, it seemed the modern trappings of the elite were derived directly from the abject poverty of the masses. While the British American Tobacco company was upgrading its International Settlement office building as one of Shanghai's first modernist edifices—completed in 1925, its double-height windows are abstract but unmistakably cigar shaped—the company's workers toiled as virtual slaves in its factory across the river, in Pudong. Though the Chinese market accounted for more than a third of British American Tobacco's global revenue by the 1920s, its Chinese workers lived in appalling conditions. Children were bought from their parents for twenty dollars to work twelve- to fourteen-hour shifts, often for no money at all—just grim grub and a place to sleep. As one British journalist wrote in the *Manchester Guardian* in 1926, the Shanghailanders "look round on their magnificent buildings and are surprised that China is not grateful to them for these gifts, forgetting that the money to build them came out of China."

For many Chinese workers, even overcrowded *lilong* homes were unattainable. Thousands of Shanghai residents lived in shantytowns of clustered huts, handmade from mud and bamboo, often slapped together without authorization on vacant land abutting industrial areas and railroad tracks. By 1929, an estimated twenty-one thousand such hovels dotted the city. On the Suzhou Creek, across the street from British American Tobacco's fancy new offices, recent migrants unable to rent even a shack lived on the rough-hewn wooden boats that had brought them to the city.

Each major Shanghai industry became notorious for a particular ailment. Battery factory workers got lead poisoning; cotton mill workers got tuberculosis; factory girls who worked in silk-spinning mills developed a white fungus on their fingers. Some did not live long enough to develop such symptoms: a hundred women died in a silk plant fire when their boss locked them in on their shift—a practice that had been banned in the West after New York's notorious 1911 Triangle factory fire but which the Shanghai Municipal Council continued to tolerate. Similarly, in Shanghai match plants, a type of phosphorus long banned in Europe for causing painful skin inflammations was still used instead of a safer, but costlier, alternative.

Other jobs simply worked people to death. In 1934, the life expectancy for a Chinese person in Shanghai was just twenty-seven. The typical career of a Shanghai rickshaw puller lasted only four years. Perversely, the official regulations for rickshaw pullers in the International Settlement mandated "that the ricsha [sic] coolies be strong [and] healthy" and "that no old, dirty, or opium smoking coolies . . . be allowed to pull ricshas [sic]." In a vicious cycle, coolies poured their strength into a brief career as a rickshaw puller only to have their livelihood taken away when they were no longer "strong [and] healthy." And these rickshaw men, who so regularly expired from exhaustion on Shanghai's streets, all for just ten cents a day in earnings, didn't even own the rickshaws they pulled. At the top of an unconscionable racket of contractors and subcontractors sat a wealthy French company called Flying Star.

The brutality and exploitation that might have seemed almost normal for a remote colonial outpost—sugar plantations on a small Caribbean island, rubber-tree farms in the jungles of Southeast Asia—seemed shocking for a major world metropolis.

In 1934, Shanghai, with 3,350,570 people, was the sixth-largest city in the world. Only London, New York, Tokyo, Berlin, and Chicago were larger. And yet, Shanghai was rife with Dickensian conditions that other major world cities had already put behind them—or never even experienced, as in the case of human-pulled rickshaws. The Chinese metropolis, one of the most densely populated cities in the world, averaged 600 people per acre, while Manhattan's densest ward hit 696. But Shanghai achieved its density differently. While nineteenth-century Manhattan's densest neighborhoods were low-rise tenement slums, by the 1930s, they were high-rise neighborhoods of upscale apartments all fitted with the latest modern conveniences. Shanghai's density, by contrast, grew out of shantytowns and a level of degradation even nineteenth-century Manhattan had never experienced.

The yawning rich-poor divide had made Shanghai fertile ground for the communist organizing that first shook the city in the 1920s. But the crucial ingredient in making communism relevant to Shanghai was Lenin's transmutation of Marx's political theory from one pitched to the industrial workers of the wealthy imperial powers into one aimed at the intellectual elite and tiny industrial class of developing economies. Tellingly, Marx's *Communist Manifesto*, originally published in German in 1848, was only translated into Chinese in 1920, after Lenin's Russian Revolution. But despite the manifesto's Euro-centricity, with its paean to the transformative power of capitalism, wonder at the birth of global culture, and outrage at the exploitation of the impoverished masses, Marx in Mandarin translation seemed to describe industrial-age Shanghai from beyond the grave.

In addition to Lenin's claim—and with the Russian Revolution, seeming proof—that an elite cadre of committed revolutionaries could bring communism to an underdeveloped country, the Bolshevik leader had argued in a 1917 pamphlet, *Imperialism: The Highest Stage of Capitalism*, that the path to ending the West-

ern powers' domination of the globe was likewise through communist revolutions in their colonies. It was another remarkable
revision of Marx, who had always maintained that colonization,
for all its exploitation, was the only way to bring underdeveloped
countries into the modern world of capitalism from which they
could, one day, progress to communism. Lenin's new vision of
communism as anti-imperialism was pitched perfectly to Shanghai, a capitalist city where most capitalists were foreign imperialists rather than indigenous industrialists.

The new Bolshevik regime in Russia masterfully ingratiated
itself to the Chinese masses by renouncing Russian extraterritorial privileges in China. For the Bolsheviks, renouncing extraterritoriality was a no-brainer. They had no interest in protecting
their White Russian enemies who had fled to Shanghai, and
the policy gave the Soviets anti-imperialist credibility by exposing the hypocrisy of self-proclaimed democracies like Britain,
France, and the United States, which insisted that while all men
are created equal, they need not be bound by the same laws. To
Shanghai's cosmopolitan nationalists grasping for an intellectual
battle plan to retake the concessions and undo China's humiliation, Marxism-Leninism beckoned.

In 1920, on the third anniversary of the Bolshevik revolution,
a new Chinese magazine called *The Communist* was published in
Shanghai, the first use of the Marxist term in the Chinese language. The following summer, the Chinese Communist Party
(CCP) was founded in a French Concession girls' school.

Marxism-Leninism fit Shanghai like a glove. Like Russia's
Petrograd, Shanghai was China's gateway to the West, the
city where European ideas, including Marx's, flowed in—and
where the bounty that the impoverished working class produced flowed out to the foreign shareholders of companies like
John D. Rockefeller's Standard Oil, which had a massive industrial facility in Pudong and an office building across the river a

block behind the Bund. And like Petrograd, Shanghai was the only city in its peasant-dominated nation that had the types of people to whom communism would appeal—radical industrial workers and left-wing intellectuals.

But beyond Shanghai, communism initially had little appeal. Rural Chinese were largely illiterate, culturally conservative, and wedded to the hierarchical structures of the past that were given sanction by Confucianism. In the hinterlands, through-out the 1920s, Chiang Kai-shek's vision of a strong independent China reunified under his dictatorial rule held more appeal than Marxism-Leninism. He gained followers accordingly.

Meanwhile, in Shanghai, workers and intellectuals flocked to the newly founded Chinese Communist Party. Among the most remarkable Party operatives was Gu Shunzhang. Born working-class, Gu held a series of arduous jobs in Shanghai, including mechanic at a cigarette factory, before becoming a juggler at the Sincere department store on Nanjing Road. On the rooftop garden at Sincere, Gu performed magic tricks, typically appearing in whiteface as a "foreign devil," wearing a Western suit and a big prosthetic nose. The experience of par-ticipating in Nanjing Road's nascent Chinese consumer cul-ture as paid help, dressing up like a white man for the laughs and tips of upscale Chinese for whom dressing like whites was no joke at all, helped radicalize Gu. He was soon putting his skills as an illusionist to work for the Party as an undercover agent and assassin.

The newly formed Shanghai University was also a breeding ground for Communists, much as St. Petersburg State University had been. One of the first Chinese Party leaders was Qu Qiubai, a Shanghai University professor who had met Lenin personally while abroad and is credited with translating "The Internatio-nale," the Communist hymn celebrating the unity of the global working class, into Chinese. Many Shanghai University students, particularly those who had studied abroad in Europe, also joined the Party.

A series of Communist-instigated strikes, including one at British American Tobacco's Pudong factory, shut down Shanghai in the early 1920s. But the local Communists' real coming-out party was a general strike that rippled through the metropolis in 1925. On May 15, a labor-management dispute at a Japanese-owned textile mill escalated until a Japanese foreman shot and killed a Chinese plant worker who was also a Communist Party organizer. Rather than arrest the Japanese foreman, the authorities of the Shanghai Municipal Council, which included Japanese representatives but no Chinese, arrested six Chinese workers as they attended a protest memorial for their slain colleague. In response, on May 30, a busy Saturday, three thousand protestors massed among the shoppers on Nanjing Road. With the Sino-Japanese nature of the original dispute now layered with general antiforeign tensions after the SMC's arrests, the protest was less about an individual Japanese man getting away with murder and more about the colonial nature of the foreign settlements themselves. Marchers demanded an end to extraterritoriality and Chinese seats on the SMC. They carried banners reading, "Take Back the Concessions" and "Down with Imperialists."

While the young police lieutenant in charge of the area was enjoying a long lunch at the British-only Shanghai Club on the Bund, his underlings frantically debated how to respond. Eventually, the two British officers on the scene panicked and ordered their Chinese and Sikh policemen to open fire. Several protestors were killed. Though Anatol Kotenev, the old Petrograd policeman, wrote approvingly that "the shooting had the immediate effect of dispersing the crowd and traffic became normal shortly afterwards," firing on unarmed protestors did as little to stop the forces of change in Shanghai in 1925 as it had in St. Petersburg in 1905.

The Saturday massacre led to a mass boycott of Japanese and British goods and a strike by over one hundred thousand workers against over a hundred foreign-owned factories. The International Settlement administration, staffed at its lower levels by Chinese employees, was paralyzed as its workers walked out; municipal services ground to a halt. On the streets of the Shanghai concessions, Chinese spat on foreigners from balconies as they walked below and seized them at random for beatings. As an American Shanghailander wrote, "I could not believe it. The Shanghai I knew and enjoyed . . . had suddenly vanished. . . . I was living in a strange, unfriendly world thousands of miles from nowhere." It came as something of a revelation to the foreign residents: Shanghai was in China, after all.

Sensing opportunity, as the job action shuttered their foreign competitors' factories, the Chinese merchants' General Chamber of Commerce contributed to a strike fund to support picketing workers. Moreover, the strike had been transformed by nationalism into a cry for political reforms, with the strikers' demands addressed not to the factory owners but to the Shanghai Municipal Council. The workers' calls for an end to extraterritorial privilege and the addition of Chinese seats to the council were demands the Chinese industrialists wholeheartedly supported.

Sensing the uneasy nature of the alliance between Chinese workers and bosses, the members of the SMC schemed to divide them. At the suggestion of a British cotton mill manager, the council decided to shut down the Shanghai Power Company electric plant, the city's main source of electricity. Soon the Chinese-owned factories, blacked out and powerless, were as crippled as their foreign competitors', devoid of workers. Outfoxed, the General Chamber of Commerce promptly stopped contributing to the strike fund and the strike duly collapsed. But in its wake, the Shanghai Municipal Council made one major concession: for the first time, it would allow Chinese to serve as councilmen.

The leaders of the foreign settlements opted to admit the increasingly assertive Chinese into the power structure of the concessions rather than risk the destruction of the near-century-old edifice that was international Shanghai.

Dissatisfied with the Chinese elite's separate peace, Shanghai's Communist leaders like juggler/assassin Gu Shunzhang and Zhou Enlai, the future People's Republic diplomat, continued to organize in the city. The movement flared again in March 1927 with an October Revolution–style uprising. Over half a million Shanghai workers went on strike. Forming "armed pickets," radical strikers seized strategic intersections and key institutions in the Chinese city. In the foreign concessions, forty thousand American, British, French, Japanese, and Italian troops stood guard, having already amassed, prepared to rebuff Nationalist general Chiang Kai-shek, who had vowed to close down the Shanghai concessions and unify postimperial China's patchwork of warlord- and foreign-administered regions under his rule. While Chiang had explicitly called for the end of the foreign concessions—and had made good on his promise in Nanjing and Jiujiang, where he reclaimed the British zones—Shanghai's foreign powers, faced with the prospect of another Communist uprising, were able to make common cause with Chiang against the Communists. In Chiang's Nanjing headquarters, the leaders of the Chinese General Chamber of Commerce, with the backing of the Shanghai Municipal Council, literally bargained with the generalissimo over the price he would be paid to clear the Communists out of the city.

True to its moniker, "city for sale," coined by a Shanghai-based American journalist, Shanghai was simply purchased by its wealthiest factions and the dirty work subcontracted out to an organized crime syndicate. With $10 million from Shanghai employers, Chiang in turn hired Du Yuesheng (a.k.a. "Big-Eared Du"), the Pudong-born boss of the Green Gang mob that held day-to-day authority on the streets of Shanghai. (With Shanghai's three-cities-in-one structure, police couldn't pursue suspects who fled across concession borders, so uniformed police had long paid gangsters to enforce the law.) Once Chiang had hired the Green Gang to crush the Communists, it was a fait accompli.

With the special permission of Sterling Fessenden, the American lawyer who served as president of the Shanghai Municipal Council, Big-Eared Du sent his goons, disguised as workers, through the International Settlement and toward the Communist strongholds. At dawn on April 12, the mobsters' massacre began as the Green Gang attacked the General Labor Union headquarters. The strike collapsed the next day. For the next three weeks, the White Terror, as it came to be known, swept through Pudong and other industrial areas as thousands of workers, trade unionists, Communist sympathizers, and their family members, including women and children, were slaughtered in the streets by Green Gang thugs, ultimately acting on behalf of Chiang Kai-shek, the Chinese General Chamber of Commerce, Sterling Fessenden, and the Shanghai Municipal Council.

With the city in the hands of the Nationalists, the leaders of the Communist Party deserted Shanghai for the hinterlands of China. Regrouping in the countryside would radically reshape the CCP's ideology. Rather than a revolution led by urban workers and intellectuals, it envisioned one led by radicalized peasants. Though the Party had been founded in China's most modern city, in its decades of exile from the metropolis, its ideology would take on a deeply antiurban cast. Mao Zedong's army of peasants that would eventually "liberate" Shanghai in 1949 had little in common with the urbanites who founded the Party in the French Concession in 1921 and little love for China's greatest city.

As most of China fell into line under his authoritarian government, formally established in Nanjing in 1928, Chiang abandoned his call to close down Shanghai's foreign concessions. Dependent upon loans from the city's international financiers to fund his government, Chiang, who had risen to power railing against the foreign domination of China in general and the foreign concessions of Shanghai in particular, allowed them to remain in place.

Though the concessions were preserved, foreign privilege was pared back and the Chinese elite, if not the Chinese masses, attained a certain measure of equality. The very day after the Green Gang's murders at dawn established Nationalist authority in the city, the Shanghai Municipal Council agreed to integrate the Public Garden on the Bund, though it soon added a ten-copper-cent admission charge. Equivalent to half a day's pay for a common laborer, the ticket price kept out poorer Chinese as well as Russians and other impoverished foreigners. More foreign prerogatives were dismantled in 1930: the number of Chinese representatives on the Shanghai Municipal Council was increased from three to five, customs authority was returned to the Chinese, and nine countries lost their extraterritorial privileges, although not the leading powers of Britain, the United States, France, and Japan. The new Chinese government in Shanghai also began taxing the profits of foreign companies for the first time.

In tandem with negotiating these changes, Chiang pursued a softer strategy to roll back foreign power in China. Because the weakness and incompetence of the Chinese authorities had provided the pretext for the Westerners' nineteenth-century power grab in Shanghai, Chiang believed that by demonstrating competence in running the Chinese city, the rationale for the concessions could be upended. To this end, the new Nationalist regime worked to turn Chinese Shanghai into a model city on par with the Shaghailanders' model settlement.

In the Chinese neighborhoods of Shanghai, utility improvements and a 1929 regulation limiting residency to three families per house helped bridge the shameful development gap between the Chinese city and the foreign settlements. But the ultimate physical embodiment of Chiang's vision for a new, fully Chinese Shanghai was his plan for a civic center at Jiangwan on the northern outskirts of the city, four miles from the Bund. There, the government proposed to build a model district of nine grand public buildings, modern on the inside but clad in traditional Chinese architectural forms lifted from historic Beijing. The project mandate ordered that "scientific principles developed from Europe and America" be merged with "excellent aspects of the artistic tradition of our nation." For all its "practical use" of Western technology, the project was to have a Chinese "essence."

To accomplish this feat, there could only be one choice of builder—not a traditional Chinese craftsman but an American architect named Henry Killam Murphy. While most Western architects in China had without a second thought imposed Western architecture on the nation, Murphy, a New Haven native and Yale graduate, became fascinated by traditional Chinese forms on his first trip to the country in 1914. In his designs for the Yale-in-China campus at Changsha, he clad modern classroom and administrative buildings in traditional Chinese forms, even dressing up the Protestant campus chapel as a Chinese temple. The architect with the oversize glasses and mad scientist shock of white hair was put in charge of architectural policy for the new Nationalist government in Nanjing. He in turn placed his Chinese protégé, Dong Dayou, in charge of the Shanghai civic center project. One of the most promising of a rising generation of Western-educated Chinese architects, Dong had studied at the University of Minnesota and Columbia, and worked at architecture firms in New York and Chicago, before returning to his native China to join his mentor's bicontinental firm, Murphy & Dana.

In 1933, Dong's new Shanghai City Hall opened. With its upturned eaves, dragon-headed roof ridge icons, stone stairway approach, and red-and-gold painted wooden panels, it looks like a temple from the Forbidden City—only bigger. In 1935, Dong's Shanghai Library was completed nearby, with its distinct double-tiered roof based on Beijing's thirteenth-century Drum Tower. The coup de grace was Dong's sports complex, which incorporated elements from Chinese fort and city wall architecture into its pool, indoor arena, and outdoor stadium. Had the Ming emperors been keen to build an Olympic-sized swimming pool, it might have looked something like Dong's natatorium. The building's heavy, gray stone arched entrance, which echoes a traditional walled city gate, draws the eye away from the nakedly modern redbrick exterior behind. The venues' interiors look like those of top-of-the-line athletic facilities anywhere in the world. Only the Ping-Pong tables that are so frequently set up beneath the steel-trussed, barrel-vaulted ceiling of the indoor arena give away its Chinese location.

In their construction of the civic center, the Nationalists' message was clear: China could learn from the West without being enslaved to the West—either culturally or politically. Indeed, the overall purpose of the civic center project was to physically relocate Shanghai's downtown from the International Settlement's Bund to the Chinese-controlled city, as well as to move it architecturally from the Western skyscrapers of the concessions to the Chinese-style institutions of Jiangwan.

But the Nationalists' plans to replace the Bund with an alternate downtown were not to be. As Jiangwan took shape, the Bund was essentially rebuilt, bigger and better than before. With the Nationalists firmly in charge and the concessions' autonomy preserved, the International Settlement experienced a boom, the likes of which it had not seen since its early years as a treaty port. The Bund was completely rebuilt over the 1920s and '30s, and in the rebuilding, the skyline of Shanghai was transformed from a copy of a Western city to a new kind of global metropolis. The buildings of the Jazz Age Bund herald the dawning of a new, global, multivalent world order. The International Settlement was finally living up to its name.

As much a triumph of the human will as of engineering, the new Bund's row of skyscrapers defied experts who had long dismissed Shanghai's soil as too marshy to support tall buildings. An engineer who had compared Shanghai's mud to Manhattan's bedrock in the early twentieth century said, "Shanghai can only stand six floors, London sixty floors, New York and Hong Kong any number." But just as engineering breakthroughs had allowed Chicago's muddy lakefront to support some of the tallest buildings on earth, so Shanghai's muddy riverfront was overcome. Thousands of piles cut from Oregon pine trees were shipped in across the Pacific and driven into the ground below while new, stronger, lighter building materials like steel beams and concrete were used to construct the edifices above. The wooden piles' combination of strength and buoyancy held the buildings up in the mud. As with St. Petersburg's serf-built palaces, Shanghai's inexhaustible supply of cheap coolie labor allowed skyscrapers to be built without the modern construction techniques being pioneered by builders in America. Cement was generally mixed by hand. And yet, with armies of ill-paid coolies, the pace of construction wasn't slowed down a bit. In 1934, an elegant fourteen-story steel-framed hotel with a gray-stone façade and New York–style setbacks—the building tapers back in blocky segments as it rises—was erected in Shanghai in just three months.

Hotels were being built as quickly as possible in a feverish attempt to keep up with demand from a new social segment: tourists. While the global market had long connected far-flung regions through trade—eighteenth-century St. Petersburg courtesans drank coffee grown in Latin America with sugar grown in the Caribbean; nineteenth-century British mill workers spun cloth out of cotton picked in Gujarat and Mississippi—in the Jazz

Age intercontinental travel became accessible to the merely well-to-do rather than just aristocrats, diplomats, and businessmen. As round-the-world luxury cruises became fashionable among the global leisure class, China's foreign-run metropolis became a standard port of call and the Bund skyline became China's front door much as Lower Manhattan was America's. Cities like Shanghai were becoming crossroads of modernity, where a new global class met to work and play.

When boats pulled in from the Pacific, headed up the Huangpu, and docked at the customs jetty on the Bund, no one could refrain from remarking how un-Chinese the city looked. As a Shanghailander historian wrote in 1928, "When a traveller arrives in Shanghai to-day he is struck by the fact that to all intents and purposes he might be in a large European city [on account of] the tall buildings, the well paved streets, the large hotels and clubs, the parks and bridges, the stream of automobiles, the trams and busses, the numerous foreign shops, and, at night, the brilliant electric lighting,—all are things he is accustomed to in the homeland." But a look behind the façades to the interiors of the buildings—the stages upon which the social life of the city was acted out—revealed a metropolis that was more vital than anything Europe could offer. With the desegregation of public spaces—even the famously restricted Shanghai Race Club had been integrated during World War I—the balkanized metropolis where each community created its own separate world gave way to a city where all the groups came together.

No building embodied this new Shanghai modernity more than the Bund's tallest building and greatest Jazz Age skyscraper, the Cathay Hotel. Opened in 1929, the Cathay stood at Shanghai's premier location, where Nanjing Road met the Bund, formerly the site of the office of Augustine Heard & Company, an American tea and opium trading firm. Other hotels in Shanghai, like the hostelries inside Sincere and Wing On just down Nan-

jing Road, claimed to be "European class," up to the standards of
the West; the Cathay exceeded them. The height of luxury, each
room was outfitted with its own telephone, a convenience still
unknown in the hotels of Europe. A simple call to the British-
accented Chinese concierge and the Cathay's famed room-service
opium was on its way. Another discrete call and the city would
live up to its reputation as the Whore of Asia—by the 1930s,
Shanghai had an astounding three thousand brothels and more
prostitutes per capita of the female population than any city on
earth. On account of its pyramid-shaped tower and sleek twelve-
story trapezoidal floor plan (the front of the plot, on the Bund,
is slightly smaller than the rear), one architectural historian has
described the building as "an Art Deco rocket ship." The met-
aphor is even more apt than the historian intended. With the
Cathay Hotel, the architecture of Shanghai achieved liftoff, moving from its roots in cut-rate imitations of the West through a
phase of extraordinarily accurate impersonations of the West to
become truly global.

In period advertisements for the hotel, its name, "The Cathay,"
is typically rendered in faux-Asian script alongside a Deco-style
print of the building—a reminder to the potential customer that
though this looks like an edifice that could easily be in mundane
Chicago, it is in exotic Shanghai. But inside the hotel, the entire
world—East and West—was recreated. Top-end guests could
choose from among nine deluxe suites, each decorated in the
style of a different country. There was the wood-paneled British suite where guests could warm themselves by the fireplace as
in a countryside hunting lodge and an Indian suite that offered
patrons the chance to stand on an authentic subcontinental rug
and fix their hair in a Mughal-arched mirror. In the Chinese
suite, guests moved from the sitting room to the dining room
by passing through a traditional moon gate, the oversized circular pedestrian passageways common in Chinese gardens and

homes. Craftsmen who hailed from the respective countries were hired to ensure the authenticity of each room. For dining, guests could ascend to the ninth-floor Chinese restaurant, which was entered through a frosted glass door carved with koi and featured Chinese decor, including antique bronze Buddhas, and a ceiling painted by Chinese temple artists. Alternately, on the tenth floor a European meal could be downed in a medieval English-style banqueting hall. Though tempting to dismiss as proto–Las Vegas kitsch, all of the cultures recreated in the Cathay's suites were actually present on Shanghai's streets. And the creator of the hotel was a man who moved effortlessly between all of the places his hotel channeled, as at home in London as he was in Bombay or Shanghai.

The Cathay Hotel was the brainchild of Sir Victor Sassoon, who kept a private apartment in the building. Victor was the great-grandson of the Baghdad-born, Bombay-based Jewish shipping magnate, David Sassoon, and the grandson of Elias Sassoon, who had moved onward from Bombay to Shanghai in 1844 to expand the family's commercial empire. Going legit from opium into real estate in the 1870s, the Sassoons began amassing the Bund parcels where the Cathay Hotel would eventually be built. By 1880, the family was Nanjing Road's largest landholder. Standing to inherit the real estate empire, Victor was shipped off to Harrow, a prestigious English boarding school where the great-grandson of turbaned Mesopotamians was clad in the school's nostalgic country outfit, a near parody of upper-crust Englishness topped off by a straw boater hat. Victor went on to don the black academic dress of Cambridge before returning to Shanghai with dreams of transforming its skyline, and the wealth and land to do it. Educated in Britain, with family roots in Bombay and Baghdad, Sassoon stood beyond the East/West dichotomy.

Sassoon ensured that the Cathay Hotel wasn't just a theme park of the modern world but a stage on which Shanghai's people could move toward the cosmopolitanism he embodied. Initially following the early treaty port pattern of segregated worlds, Baghdadi Jews like the Sassoons had built their own network of communal institutions. The most prominent was Shanghai's Jewish Country Club, which stood on property owned by the Kadoorie family, another clan of Jewish real estate barons with Baghdad roots and Bombay branches. But when Victor Sassoon was denied a table at one of Shanghai's poshest nightclubs, he didn't storm off to drown his sorrows at the Jewish Country Club. Instead, reflecting the city's increasingly open-minded outlook, he founded his own unrestricted nightclub, Ciro's, which opened in 1936, directly across Bubbling Well Road from the restricted British Country Club. And in the ballroom and Tower Club of the Cathay Hotel, under the exacting eye of a manager he had swiped from Bombay's legendary Taj Mahal Hotel, Sassoon threw his own parties and invited notables from all of Shanghai's communities, including its Chinese majority. At his bawdy costume balls the monocled bon vivant, who walked with a cane on account of an accident as a British pilot in World War I, always cast himself in leading roles that blurred the line between sadomasochism and social revenge. At his "school days" party, the Cathay ballroom was decked out with blackboards and maps while the cap-and-gown-clad Sir Victor made rounds with a birch cane. At the circus party, the host played the ringmaster and wielded a whip. Sassoon found satisfaction as the proper Britons who had excluded him (one had snidely asked him whether, for his frequent trips to London, he went by camel) now all clamored for invitations to his fêtes.

Fittingly, the sound track for this new cosmopolitan city was the world's first global music—jazz—that gave its name to the age. The New World amalgam of African rhythms and European instrumentation with a distinctly modern sense of making it up as you go along had burst forth from America to conquer a world that was becoming more and more like America as people from every continent got jumbled together in places like Shanghai. For anyone who wanted to dance the Shanghai night away in an integrated setting, Sir Victor's Ciro's was just one of many choices.

The largest nightclub in the city, opened in 1933, was called the Paramount in English and Bailemen (Gate of a Hundred Pleasures) in Chinese. It had been financed by Chinese businessmen and designed by a Chinese architect, Yang Xiliu. Taking up nearly an entire city block in the International Settlement, from the outside it looked like an Art Deco cinema topped by a scalloped tower remarkably similar to the one then rising across the Pacific on San Francisco's Telegraph Hill. The trans-Pacific vibe pervaded the inside as well, where an American bandleader, Harlem-bred trombonist Ernest "Slick" Clark, presided over the in-house orchestra. It took Slick's big band sound to fill the vast venue, with its balcony and second-tier dance floor above the main hall. The two-tiered structure allowed the club to feel full even when half-full, architect Yang explained, showing his mastery of the club promoter's art of making a joint feel packed and exclusive even on a slow night. "According to crowd psychology," Yang said, "groups of people enjoy a ruckus and detest loneliness, so if the dance hall is too spacious, only during a special holiday or special event will the guests feel enjoyment."

Yang was prized as much for his stylistic flexibility as for his clever use of space. While the Paramount embraced the global Art Deco aesthetic, in his Metropole Gardens Ballroom, which opened across town in 1935, Yang clad a modern jazz club in the styles of imperial China. A giant red lantern hung at the entrance, and the band played beneath a mural of frolicking dragons.

With the Chinese continuing to gain wealth and status during the Nationalist period, soon a Chinese-owned hotel and nightclub was giving the Cathay Hotel's Tower Club stiff competition. While the Cathay was the tallest building on the Bund, in 1934

a hotel that rose even higher opened across town, where Nanjing Road passed by the Shanghai Race Club. The tower was
commissioned by the leading Chinese-run financial institution in
Shanghai, the Joint Savings Society. While the bottom two floors
were used by the bank and the nineteenth story by the company's
board of directors, the rest of the building was the luxurious Park
Hotel. In the Sky Terrace ballroom on the fourteenth floor, an
upscale Chinese clientele drank and danced as they gazed down
upon the once-segregated racetrack across the street. The club's
hybrid decor employed traditional Chinese red-and-gold pillars to hold up a frescoed Art Deco ceiling mural that celebrated
the dancing world of the Jazz Age in stylized images of dashing
bandleaders amid floating musical notes.

Though not as architecturally elegant as the Cathay, the Park
Hotel, with its massive dark redbrick base and jagged setback
tower, is impressive for its size. When it opened, it dwarfed not
only the other buildings of Shanghai, but all of the buildings of
the Old World, Europe included. At twenty-two stories, it was
the tallest building in the world outside of the Americas. Notably, in the Shanghai boom of the 1920s and '30s, it was Chinese
clients who embraced the modernist architectural style the most
wholeheartedly while Europeans retreated into nostalgia for the
pre–Great War world of unquestioned European dominance.

Though the Chinese could be justly proud of the Park Hotel,
the Park was not strictly Chinese any more than the city itself
was. Instead, the building, like the metropolis itself, expressed
the world's leading architectural, social, and economic trends.
The modernist wonder commissioned by the Joint Savings
Society's directors was, fittingly, designed by an unplaceable,
only-in-Shanghai character, architect Ladislav Hudec. Born in
Austria-Hungary in 1893, Hudec earned an architecture degree
from the Royal University in Budapest in 1914 and was promptly
pressed into the Austro-Hungarian army to fight in World War I.

Captured by the Russians, he was sent as a POW to Siberia, but in 1918, while being transferred by rail between POW camps, he jumped a train near the Chinese border and made his way to Shanghai. There, he found work with an American architecture firm, married a German-British woman, and in 1925 opened his own firm. Flush with commissions, he and his wife lived a luxurious life in a French Concession Tudorbethan mansion he designed himself. A Shanghailander to the core, Hudec wrote, "It doesn't matter where I go. I will always be a stranger, a guest . . . who is at home everywhere he goes but still has no fatherland." Hudec's contradictory thrill at being a citizen of the world and concomitant fear that ultimately he belongs nowhere is the experience of modernity itself.

Cosmopolitan Shanghai was a home for the homeless like Hudec, which Hudec himself helped build. Soon after his return from a 1927–28 tour of the United States, Hudec designed Columbia Circle, an American-style subdivision built on the outskirts of the French Concession that mixed Mediterranean- and Tudor-style single-family homes in the manner of the neighborhoods contemporaneously rising across the Pacific in Los Angeles. Appropriately, the developer behind the project was an American, Frank Jay Raven, head of the Shanghai-based Asia Realty Company and a member of the Shanghai Municipal Council. The stylistic hodgepodge typical of America, a nation of immigrants, where throwing up a Spanish-style house next to an English-style house was no stranger than a Hungarian man marrying a German-British woman, was oddly fitting for Shanghai. With its communities from all over the world, Shanghai was like a New World city randomly parked in the Old World. It was this strange truth that Shanghai-born British novelist J. G. Ballard was referencing when he referred to the Shanghai of his 1930s boyhood as "90 per cent Chinese and 100 per cent Americanised."

Caught up in the excitement of building the most dynamic

city on earth, Frank Jay Raven succumbed to irrational exuberance at the city's prospects. His Asia Realty Company's 1920s survey of the Shanghai real estate market concluded, "The rapid advance of the past few years in building developments [befits Shanghai,] the metropolis of this continent" and optimistically envisaged the city in 1950 with "an increasing number of foreign residents from all parts of the world; a city with constantly improving standards of life."

The undisputed financial capital of Asia, and still posting impressive economic growth even as the West became mired in the Great Depression of the 1930s, Shanghai was in no way second-rate. When London-trained, Shanghai-based architect George Leopold "Tug" Wilson traveled to Europe and America in 1931 to survey the newest buildings on each continent, he wrote home in a letter, "There is not a great deal which Shanghai can today learn from elsewhere which would be in the direction of improving practice here." It was a sentiment on display in an advertisement for the Wilson-designed Cathay Hotel, which crowed, "The two most interesting 'towers' in the world: Eiffel Tower, Paris, of course, and the 'Cathay' Tower, Shanghai." If anything, the claim was an undersell; by the 1930s, the Cathay Hotel was far more interesting than the decades-old steel skeleton on the Seine. The cabaret-and-opium nightlife in the Cathay combined the elegance of Paris with the devil-may-care frisson of Al Capone's Chicago. As the *All About Shanghai* tourist guidebook brazenly declared, "What odds whether Shanghai is the Paris of the East or Paris the Shanghai of the Occident?"

The manic building boom of Jazz Age Shanghai strongly suggests that the Shanghailanders couldn't see the approaching abyss of world war and Maoism. Indeed, the massive new Shanghai Municipal Council building, opened in 1922, with its gray heft and blocky half-carved columns, bespeaks an overweening arrogance. So, too, does the Asia Realty Company's sunny summation, "Even . . . in the midst of chaotic conditions, in the midst of plots and counterplots, Shanghai evidently continues to grow and her business actually increases." And yet, there is a sense in the *All About Shanghai* guidebook of dancing at the end of the world—that the city is unstable, and that is half the fun. The guidebook's wild-eyed paean to the city on the Huangpu revels in its instability. It celebrates the "city of missions . . . and brothels," its "limousines with silk-clad Chinese multi-millionaires surrounded by Chinese and Russian bodyguards bristling with automatics," even its "Communists plotting." This is what makes the city so "vital, vibrant, vivacious . . . cinematographic." This is what makes it "Shanghai the incomparable!" An urgency animates the prose: see it before it dies.

What neither the Shanghailanders nor the Shanghainese could see was the more vibrant and cosmopolitan their city became, the less chance it had of enduring. Its very successes were the seeds of its destruction. For with each new stunning skyscraper and luxurious nightclub, the metropolis on the Huangpu became more estranged from the rest of China. No matter how large Shanghai grew, China's greatest city would always be dwarfed by the countryside's hundreds of millions of peasants, many of whom were now armed under Mao Zedong with China's capitalist heart in their crosshairs.

# THE CITY UNDER PROGRESS'S FEET

## Bombay, 1896–1947

Eros Cinema

On June 22, 1897, Queen Victoria celebrated her Diamond Jubillee, the sixtieth anniversary of her ascension to the throne. The British Empire was at its peak, encompassing fully one-quarter of the world's population. As the new day dawned in each British holding from New Zealand in the east to Canada in the west, carefully coordinated celebrations erupted. In India, the fulsome festivities befit its status as the jewel of the empire. In Hyderabad, every tenth convict was set free; in Bangalore, a new statue of the porcelain-complected Empress of India was unveiled. But the *urbs prima in Indis* was haunted with unease. There was nothing in Bombay to match Victoria's lesser Golden Jubilee, her fiftieth anniversary a decade before, when the city's greatest Gothic edifice, Frederick William Stevens's Great Indian Peninsula Railway station, was named Victoria Terminus in her honor.

In its perfunctory revelry, the city on the Arabian Sea appeared to be just going through the motions. A vicious outbreak of bubonic plague had begun sweeping through the city's impoverished Indian neighborhoods the previous year, and even in the midst of the jubilee celebrations, more Bombayites dropped each day. Alongside *The Times of India*'s laudatory coverage of anniversary events from around the subcontinent ran its latest tally of plague deaths from the previous twenty-four hours in Bombay. As the plague took its course, the *Times'* catalogue of mortality, broken down by fatalities per neighborhood, had become a fixture in the daily, akin to cricket scores, transit information, and the weather forecast.

More than just decimating Bombay's population, the plague had called into question Britain's grandiose claims to be developing India and to be building Bombay as the empire's greatest city. The contradictions of the Raj had long stood out most starkly in the *urbs prima*. Bombay was India's most integrated city, and yet many of its institutions remained for whites only. Nowhere in India were native elites allowed more input into city administration, but this only made the lack of true self-rule more painful. And as Bombay was India's most economically dynamic city, the restrictions the Raj placed on India's economy felt all the more frustrating there. Bombayites smarted at being so tantalizingly close to a dignified existence they could never quite attain. The plague made plain the racial and economic realities of Bombay, exposing the squalor the British tolerated behind the Gothic façades of their model metropolis.

At the time bubonic plague broke out in the city, no one knew how the disease was transmitted—it is spread by rodents and their fleas—but it was obvious to public health officials that the contagion was linked to unsanitary living conditions: the Indian slums were ravaged by the epidemic while the posh British neighborhoods remained unaffected. As one British official explained in a lecture,

> The wonder is not that the death rate is exceedingly high,
> the infant mortality terrible and plague so prevalent, but that
> so many human beings manage to exist at all, and that the
> ravages of disease and pestilence are not far greater. In many

quarters the houses are jammed so closely together that free circulation of air is prevented, the sun can barely get lower down than the roofs and the atmosphere is thick with foul odors. There are no proper roads, only narrow tortuous lanes and passages and horrible gullies and the older houses have generally been built without any regard to light and air.

The abominable living conditions were the flip side of the city's industrial boom. Bombay's Indian merchants, first among them Parsi industrialist Jamsetji Nusserwanji Tata, had learned to shrewdly game the colonial economy by taking advantage of the technologies the British brought to the city while skirting the economic restrictions that used the colony for its raw materials while reserving high-value production processes for the mother country. In 1877, Tata went into the textile manufacturing business, founding his first cotton mill five hundred miles inland, in Nagpur, and using the rail system to ship his product to the Bombay port. The plant, named Empress Mills in honor of Queen Victoria, Empress of India, produced low-count cotton cloth for the Chinese market since the high-count production was reserved for British mills. Other merchants followed suit and soon an industrial belt of mills stretched across the middle of Bombay Island itself, all enjoying direct access to the rail hub and port. By the turn of the twentieth century, Bombay's eighty-two mills employed seventy-three thousand workers, making textiles the city's leading industry.

For the workers who toiled in the mills north of downtown, the modern urban wonders that industrialists like Tata used to their advantage seemed almost a conspiracy against them. The improvements in the city's electricity grid and the introduction of electric lighting just emboldened their bosses to demand a sixteen-hour workday. And the new streetcar system, run by the

Bombay Electric Supply and Tramways Company, registered in London and universally known by its laudatory acronym, BEST, whizzed past them like so many taunts as they trudged to and from jobs that didn't pay enough to cover the fares. Too poor to commute, the laborers lived crowded around the mills where they worked. As demand for housing outstripped supply, rents for proper Bombay apartments were soon on par with London and Paris. In the mainland cities of Calcutta and Madras, villagers who had flocked there for jobs just erected jury-rigged village clusters on whatever land they could, but in the *urbs prima*, housing industrial workers became a big business. Mill owners built a distinctive type of Bombay tenement to house their employees, and private entrepreneurs soon followed suit, seeing profits in packing men into tiny rooms.

The result was a unique Bombay housing form called the *chawl*. Bombay's answer to the Shanghai *lilong* was a wide, squat five- to seven-story building with a central courtyard hosting three to four hundred cell-like eight-foot-by-eight-foot cubicles lined up along breezeways. A 1911 report found that 80 percent of the city's population lived in such single-room tenements. Despite the shocking conditions within, the *chawls* themselves, constructed by Indian craftsmen, often included fine architectural details that lent the structures a touch of dignity. Lovingly carved wooden verandas and louvers were typical. Courtyard entryways were occasionally done up with grand Mughal-style arches that belied the lowly status of the inhabitants within.

Most *chawl* dwellers came to the metropolis as adolescent boys, leaving their villages on the subcontinent and crossing the creek to the island city. A 1921 study showed that fully 84 percent of the city's population had been born elsewhere. It was a journey to a new vision of India, vastly different from the rural settlements of fewer than five thousand people where the overwhelming majority of their countrymen lived. In their *chawls*, Bombay newcomers endeavored to preserve their village traditions. Each building was typically inhabited by members of a single religion or caste, and the weddings and celebrations of that group were held in its courtyard.

But even as craftsmen poured their souls into the buildings and residents kept their traditions alive in the courtyards, the structures' overcrowding smothered their nods to humanity. Often compared to an army barracks, the *chawl* was closer to a human beehive, with single men literally packed on top of each other. Five to ten people shared each room with just a small basin for washing clothes and cooking utensils, and often nothing but wooden planks for sleeping. Common toilets were provided at a rate of one per story at best. As a Scottish urban planning professor at Bombay University aptly put it, *chawls* were not "housing, but warehousing people!"

Some fared even worse. For those who could not afford even a bed slat in a *chawl*, there were the streets. As American writer Mark Twain recorded on his 1896 visit to Bombay, "Everywhere on the ground lay sleeping natives—hundreds and hundreds. They lay stretched at full length and tightly wrapped in blankets, heads and all. Their attitude and rigidity counterfeited death."

The mortality rate from the plague that broke out the year of Twain's visit was so high that the 1901 census showed that the city's population had fallen over the past decade. The *urbs prima in Indis* was in measurable decline. But Bombay, of all cities, could not be permitted to decline. In the ideology of the British Raj, the right of the British to rule India was predicated upon bringing "progress" and development. Bombay was supposed to be the ultimate icon of that progress, a great demonstration of sophisticated Western technology that offered a vision of a prosperous future to the masses of the subcontinent. The model modern metropolis was literally presided over by a fourteen-foot-tall statue of the goddess Progress staring out over the city from the top of Victoria Terminus. Though Bombay was never the political capital of the Raj—that role was assigned to Calcutta and then, in 1911, to Delhi—it was its economic capital and, more important, its ideological capital. To put the city back on the ascendant path, at the turn of the century, the British embarked upon their greatest building boom since Sir Bartle Frere's 1860s spree. Paternalistically viewing their domination of India as a sacred trust—one called into question by Bombay's decline—the British endeavored to bestow upon their Indian charges a healthy, modern city.

The city's redevelopment was presided over by the Bombay City Improvement Trust, created in the wake of the plague to improve public health through architecture and urban planning. From its four-story Gothic headquarters fronted by a massive statue of Queen Victoria, the trust's pith-helmeted army of architects and engineers fanned out across the city. First and foremost, their task was to address conditions in the *chawls*, where population densities ran as high as twelve hundred people per acre. In response, the trust built new model *chawls*. Constructed from brick or concrete rather than the usual wood, the trust's sturdy new three- to five-story structures offered ten-by-twelve-foot rooms—nearly twice the square footage of the slumlord and company-town *chawls* that plagued the city. Through such developments, the trust hoped to reduce population density to five hundred people per acre. The pith-helmet brigades also rebuilt entire neighborhoods, evicting and temporarily rehousing thousands while new *chawls* were built and streets were cut.

In the bazaar area behind Victoria Terminus—the old Native Town in the days of the British East India Company fort, whose haphazard, cheek-by-jowl layout had lost whatever antiquarian charm it possessed with the overcrowding of the industrial age—the trust essentially rebuilt the entire neighborhood between 1901 and 1905. A wide avenue, Princess Street, was cut clean across the

island, allowing breezes from the Arabian Sea to reach Craw-
ford Market, the city's main food mart, whose butcher shops and
produce stalls badly needed the ventilation. The new avenue also
gave inner-city residents direct access to the sea beaches.

The new grand avenues knit the enclaves of Bombay together
into a single city. What urbanist Marshall Berman wrote of Baron
Georges-Eugène Haussmann's Paris could equally stand for trust-
transformed Bombay: "The new construction wrecked hundreds
of buildings, displaced uncounted thousands of people, destroyed
whole neighborhoods . . . but it opened up the whole of the
city, for the first time in its history, to all its inhabitants. Now,
at last, it was possible to move not only within neighborhoods,
but through them. [The city] was becoming a unified physical
and human space." Yet again, grandiose British modernization
plans were unwittingly sowing the seeds of the Raj's destruction;
the trust's boulevards were unifying a multicultural city that the
British could rule only through divide-and-conquer tactics.

Although life in the *chawls* always retained a bit of its village
character, while toiling in the same factories, men from different
regions, with different religious beliefs, began to find a collective
identity as workers. Thrown together in an imperial metropolis
with ultimate power in the hands of the British, they came to
see themselves less as Gujaratis or Tamils, Hindus or Jains and
more as Indians. While Indian nationalism had begun as a relatively timid movement of the university-educated Anglophone
elite who founded the Indian National Congress in Bombay in
1885, by the early twentieth century it was drawing strength from
the industrial workers who labored in the mills and who rallied around the more radical demand for Indian self-rule. When
nationalist Bombay newspaper editor Bal Gangadhar Tilak was
convicted of sedition in 1908 for daring to publish a call for self-
rule, thousands of Bombay mill workers went out on strike in
protest. As tensions escalated, the British resorted to increasingly

reactionary measures, culminating in their granting themselves the power to detain Indians without charge and try them without juries under the archly named World War I–era Defense of India Act.

Yet Bombay City Improvement Trust officials remained largely oblivious to what they were setting in motion by reshaping the social fabric of the city, linking heretofore balkanized worker communities to each other, and building them the avenues they would march down together in protest. Trust officials simply believed they were imposing Western urban order on the disorderly Eastern city that sprawled out around their meticulously planned core. But for all the trust's attempts to impose British propriety and progress on the man-made island, the pith-helmeted imperialists only succeeded in midwifing a new, uniquely Bombay form of unruly, hybrid urbanism.

Along with its primary mission to sanitize the residential districts of Bombay, the trust also endeavored to decongest the city's commercial heart. Fifty years after Sir Bartle Frere had torn down the fort wall, the city's business life remained concentrated in the overcrowded streets just south of Victoria Terminus. Though hardly a trace of the ramparts could be found in Raj-era Bombay, the denizens of the city continued to refer to its downtown as "the Fort" (as Mumbaikars still do today). In an effort to impose order on the commercial spine of the district, Hornby Road, the trust mandated that all of its buildings, no matter their architectural style, be of relatively uniform height and provide a sheltered arcade at ground level. In place of a typical sidewalk, Hornby Road arcades create a shaded pathway continuing from one building to the next, running the entire length of the avenue, protecting pedestrians from the intense sun and the monsoon rains. While leading Western businesses leased offices in Hornby Road buildings—including the British travel agency, Thomas Cook, and the American photography giant, Kodak—Hornby Road's

streetscape was more Indian than Nevsky Prospect's was Russian
or Nanjing Road's was Chinese, as all pretentions to British order
melted away under the arches. In the arcades, Indian vendors held
sway, peddling newspapers, coconuts, samosas, and whatever dry
goods they could get their hands on that week. The street became
a hybrid business district of "bazaars in Victorian arcades," as a
pair of Indian architectural historians so accurately described it—
an eclectic mix of Indian village market and English high street.
Neither the *urbs prima* nor its urbanites could be subdued.

In trying to bestow a healthy city upon their Indian subjects, the
British were hoping to stave off calls for self-rule, but the paternalism that undergirded the trust made it a lightning rod. Many
of the "slum dwellers" that the British wanted to rehouse in their
"improvement" schemes simply wanted to stay put, valuing the
preservation of their communal life over any material benefits
that the trust might offer. Indian tenants and landlords opposed
to the demolitions of their neighborhoods tried to stop the urban
renewal effort through thousands of petitions and court cases. And
many Bombayites spurned the trust's offer of new housing in a new
neighborhood, instead finding or building themselves new accommodations close to their old demolished homes.

To the Bombayites, the trust embodied everything that was
demeaning about British rule. The whole concept behind the
trust—that the colonial authorities paternalistically bestow
modernity upon their charges—crystallized the humiliation of
the Raj. The economic restrictions Britain imposed on India
meant that even in cutting-edge Bombay, the wonders of the
modern world had to be thought up in England rather than created locally. Under this system of constraints, by the early twentieth century, India had become the chief market for British
industrial machinery. And over the creek from Bombay's showcase of up-to-date architecture and urban amenities, the subcontinent was being purposefully underdeveloped. Used solely for

raw materials, Raj-era India was actually becoming more agri-
cultural and less industrial as the decades passed. Whatever the
limited veracity of British claims to be turning Bombay into a
showcase of the future, it was turning the clock back in most of
India.

Taking a page from the British, Bombay's Indian elites began
asserting their ability to govern their own affairs through architecture and urbanism, building themselves their own modern city
rather than graciously accepting the British administrators' self-
regarding infrastructural gifts. First, Indians simply built themselves Indian versions of the institutions the British reserved for
themselves. Ultimately, however, Indian architects would build
whole new swaths of Bombay in their own modern style.

The first major integrated institution of the new century was
J. N. Tata's Taj Mahal Hotel. According to urban legend, Tata had
been turned away on account of his skin color when he tried to
rent a room in one of the city's most elegant hostelries. Smarting
at the slight, he resolved to build his own even more luxurious
integrated hotel. Many believe the story to be apocryphal; after
all, J. N. Tata would surely have known he was too dark skinned
to ever be served in a British-run hotel. What is indisputable is
that he built the city's most luxurious accommodations: the Taj.

To design a hotel worthy of the name of India's greatest building, the white marble mausoleum seventeenth-century Mughal
emperor Shah Jahan built for his favorite wife, Tata tapped Rao-
saheb Sitaram Khanderao Vaidya, an Indian engineer who had
overseen construction on Frederick William Stevens's Bombay
Municipal Corporation building. Like the BMC building, the
Taj's design, modified by English engineer W. A. Chambers
after Vaidya's untimely death in 1900, merged Gothic with Indo-
Saracenic forms. Onion domes at the corners echoed the building's namesake and mashrabiya windows, the Middle Eastern lat-
ticework that allows for cool breezes to penetrate while keeping

out the hot sun, accentuated its Mughal flair. The central ribbed dome, reminiscent of Victoria Terminus's, suggests that the great rail station's design, which could have been dismissed by locals as a European knockoff, had come to be embraced as quintessentially Bombay. Inside, the Taj, which opened in 1903, offered guests of all nationalities, colors, castes, and creeds American fans, German elevators, Turkish baths, and, pointedly, English butlers.

The integrated Taj Mahal Hotel was created by and for the Anglophone Indian elite. Soon the more enlightened among the British population were pushing for integrated institutions as well. The prestigious Willingdon Sports Club was founded in 1917 after Lord Willingdon, the British governor of Bombay, was turned away from the whites-only British-run Bombay Gymkhana club when he went to dine accompanied by a maharajah friend. With its facilities for cricket, polo, golf, and tennis, the Willingdon, whose membership was overwhelmingly Indian, was the equal of Bombay's all-white clubs. It bespoke a stunning transformation for an urban Indian population that, just fifty years earlier, had laughed at sporty Raj officials. As Govind Narayan recorded in 1863, "Our people . . . consider it strange that prominent Englishmen should play a game of toss and catch with a ball. They . . . exclaim, 'Why do the English play like small children?' " The Anglophilic Narayan sagely advised his readers, "This is the reason for their healthy and fit bodies." By the early twentieth century, Narayan's Westernizing outlook had clearly won out.

From early twentieth-century integrated versions of British institutions, like the Willingdon Sports Club, Bombayites progressed in the 1930s to erecting their own modern vision of the city. Appropriately, their new Bombay would be built on new land reclaimed from the sea. Wealthy and confident—even the 1929 crash that sent the Western economies into a decade-long tailspin was just a hiccup in Bombay, whose population increased nearly 30 percent in the 1930s—the city finally completed the unfinished project that had long been an embarrassment: the Back Bay reclamation. Grand plans for a seafront residential district first proposed during the American Civil War–era cotton boom were dusted off and updated. On the land reclaimed from the sea, Indians would for the first time build their own vision of Bombay modernity.

The reenergized construction of Back Bay coincided with the arrival of an architectural style that was sweeping the world: Art Deco. In Bombay, it was the rising generation of Indian architects, many of whom had trained abroad, who pioneered the new style as British firms languished, reeling from the Depression back home, worried about the growing Indian independence movement, and generally hostile to modern forms that broke so radically with the British imperial Gothic traditions of the city. In the span of two decades, Bombay architects would create one of the world's greatest Art Deco districts, a collection of buildings even larger than Shanghai's that is rivaled only by America's Miami Beach.

In 1935, the Back Bay project reclaimed a stretch of land along the western side of the Oval Maidan park. In the 1860s, when Sir Bartle Frere had built his Gothic line of modern institutions along the park's eastern edge, he'd left the western side open to the sea. Now, in the late 1930s, a line of twenty-one Art Deco apartment buildings rose to face them. In a stunning urban panorama that survives to this day, two visions of Bombay modernity stare each other down across the maidan.

Strict design regulations governing the Back Bay development ensured uniform building heights and materials—in particular, reinforced concrete. Within the strictures of the guidelines, creativity flourished. Architects and craftsmen strived to outdo each other in the chic lettering announcing the building names— Palm Court, Oval View, Sunshine, Moonlight—and in the styl-

ized Deco palm trees, sunrays, and ocean waves they created on
the buildings' bas-relief stucco panels and etched-glass doorways.
Inside, the cosmopolitan industrialists, merchants, and professionals of the booming city lived the gracious life of bourgeois apartment dwellers the world over, made possible in the Bombay heat
by the advent of the electric ceiling fan.

The new line of Art Deco buildings on the maidan facing the
Victorian Frere Town announced Bombay's arrival as a pace-
setting city that had transcended its origins in colonial imitation. While the Oxbridge-style university Frere commissioned
arrived in India more than half a millennium after Oxford's
founding in England, Bombay was now on the same schedule
as the world's other leading cities. And while the university was
designed entirely in London by a British architect who didn't
even visit India, the vast majority of Art Deco row was the
work of Indian architects. In contrast to Frere's line of Victorian
Gothic buildings, which reverently looked back to the European
past, Deco row eagerly looked forward to the global future.

The earlier Gothic Revival buildings airlifted into Bombay
were distinctly and purposefully British, but the new Art Deco
buildings transcended any national character. They were Bombay Deco as comfortably as the Miami Beach buildings were
Miami Deco. With their design elements lifted from the ships
and planes that ferried international travelers, the style embodied
a cosmopolitan world of border crossers. Even before the Raj,
Bombay had been a city of peoples thrown together from around
the world. It now finally had an architectural style befitting its
social reality.

The well-to-do Bombayites who lived in the new Art Deco
apartments enjoyed the urbane pleasures the city offered in its
burgeoning array of racially integrated spaces. While in village
India married couples did not traditionally socialize outside the
home, in Bombay a date night out on the town became com-

mon. The neoclassical Royal Opera House, featuring carved Union Jacks and a statue of Shakespeare on its pediment, offered increasingly diverse evening entertainments. Jazz bands played gigs at the Taj Mahal Hotel, often on an international circuit that included nightclub-crazed Shanghai. World-renowned touring artists, like the Petrograd ballerina Anna Pavlova, performed on Bombay's stages.

The ultimate expression of the new Bombay cosmopolitanism was the cinema. In going out for a movie, Bombayites were not only participating in a new urban ritual but, through the films themselves, being exposed to places where they could not afford to travel and learning about cultures and social milieus they might never encounter in their real lives. In time, Bombay would come to produce films as heartily as it consumed them, eventually spawning the world's largest film industry.

The roots of what became known as "Bollywood," today's film-mad, film-producing movie mecca, run deep. Film production began in India in 1896, contemporaneously with the West. The first Indian feature film was made in 1913. In the silent-film era, language was irrelevant, but when the age of the "talkie" arrived, the first Indian entry came out in 1931, just four years after the premier of the American feature, *The Jazz Singer*. As the 1930s rolled on, filmmaking became an integral part of the Bombay economy, eventually rivaling textiles as the most important local industry.

Film going also became big business in Bombay. The first "moving pictures" were projected one evening in 1905 on a screen set up on the maidan. Just two years later, the first movie houses began popping up on Hornby Road. By 1917, the vast Royal Opera House was filling its seats on certain nights by showing films rather than hosting live performances. The city had more than sixty cinemas by 1933; by 1939, nearly three hundred.

Impressive for more than sheer numbers, the city was soon

famous for the quality of its cinemas. In the 1930s, grand Art Deco movie palaces began dotting Bombay. The first was the Regal Cinema, designed by Charles Frederick Stevens, the son of Victoria Terminus architect Frederick William Stevens. Opened in 1933 with a Laurel and Hardy picture, the Regal façade boasts bas-relief masks of tragedy and comedy and a vertical neon sign of its name in lights. Inside, a glass mirror in the stairwell is etched with an Oscar award blown up to human size. Modern in every way, patrons could park in the theater's underground garage and enjoy its luxurious air-conditioning.

In February 1938 an Art Deco ziggurat, the Eros, opened at the end of the Oval Maidan's row of Deco apartments. Designed by architect Sohrabji Bhedwar for a Karachi-based businessman client, the Eros placed its entrance at the rounded edge of its U-shaped site under a cylindrical tower of setbacks that looks like a telescope unfurling. The exterior mixes red sandstone from Agra, the historic Mughal capital, with cream-colored paint typical of other Art Deco structures in Bombay— a fitting palette for the city that blended Indian traditions with trendy global styles. Inside, the rounded atrium of black and gray marble is decorated with silver bas-reliefs of bare-breasted nymphs set against an ethereal blue background. In the theater itself, patrons could recline in cushioned chairs imported from the American Seating Company while the projector, made in Toledo, Ohio, rolled.

Soon after the Eros raised the bar on cinema design, the Metro opened just inland from Marine Drive, a reclamation-built sea-front boulevard lined with Art Deco apartment buildings. While the Regal and the Eros had just a touch of America, with their etched-glass Oscar and imported seats, the Metro was truly a Hollywood production. The cinema was built by the eponymous Metro-Goldwyn-Mayer Corporation of Los Angeles. Seeing India as an emerging market for its films, MGM secured a 999-

year lease on the land, the former site of an anachronism border-ing on the oxymoronic: an air force stables.

To design the project, the California studio, founded by a pair of Jewish emigrants from the Russian Empire (Goldwyn and Mayer were born Gelbfisz and Meir), hired Thomas Lamb, a Scotland-born, New York–based architect who specialized in theater design. With the streamlined metal fin embossed with the word METRO jutting out at the corner and the tapered tower over the theater entrance, Lamb created a sense of vertical-ity, capturing the mystique of American Art Deco skyscrapers of the era like New York's 30 Rockefeller Plaza. Inside, fifteen-foot glass chandeliers, whose blocky setbacks gave them the look of miniature Empire State Buildings, hung from the ceiling. For the Metro, not only the 1,500 leather-upholstered chairs and projec-tion equipment but even the carpeting itself was imported from America.

The print advertisement for the gala opening—a black-and-white image of the theater, flanked by MGM's trademark lions—promised "a cinema for all Bombay" and encouraged patrons to flock to the theater "no matter where you live," quietly telegraph-ing that the cinema was open to all regardless of creed or color. And yet, with its materials and architecture airlifted from the United States and its offerings restricted to MGM's Hollywood-produced fare, the Metro raised doubts about how Indian Bom-bay's version of modernity really was. In fact, Thomas Lamb had been commissioned to design nearly identical theaters for MGM in several other cities, including Calcutta and Cairo, raising the specter that Bombay, rather than being its own unique moder-nity, was just another link in a long chain of Western knockoffs.

Reeling from this fear, the city that had once been captivated by Dadabhai Naoroji's call for British rule in India to be made more truly British was now taken in by a new nationalist leader: Mohandas K. Gandhi. Emulating or inheriting British institutions without question, as so many Bombayites did, would never lead to a truly independent India, Gandhi argued. Even if political independence were achieved, it would amount to nothing but "English rule without the Englishman," a preposterous South Asian "Englistan." Instead, Gandhi urged Indians to breathe new life into their preindustrial traditions. To reclaim their nation, Gandhi taught, Indians must reclaim their indigenous civilization by turning their backs on the *urbs prima* and its seductive, Western delights.

Gandhi's anger at Bombay and what it stood for was the anger of a spurned lover. As a young man enthralled with the metropolis, Gandhi had moved to Bombay soon after graduating from law school in England in the early 1890s. Like so many ambitious Anglophone Indians, he came to the *urbs prima* as an eager worshipper, prostrating himself at the feet of the goddess Progress. With his British education and Bombay dreams, the young Gandhi was a quintessential product of the Raj. But the city rejected him; he found himself outclassed by Bombay's barristers. Unable to succeed in the city's ultracompetitive legal world, Gandhi left to seek his fortune in the British colony of South Africa. By the time he returned to Bombay in 1915, his unrequited love for the city had mutated into disdain. "To me the rise of the cities like . . . Bombay is a matter for sorrow rather than congratulations," the mature Gandhi would lament.

Through the Satyagraha Sabha (Soul Force Council) he founded in Bombay in 1919, Gandhi led his Noncooperation Movement against British colonialism. Gandhi's campaign of nonviolent resistance, which included boycotts of British goods, public violations of British economic and civil liberties restrictions, and refusals to pay bail upon arrest, was met with a level of British violence not seen since the time of the Sepoy Rebellion. The British took to humiliating protestors with public floggings and so-called fancy punishments like rubbing detainees' noses into the ground or forcing men to stand all day in the hot sun. Sedition laws were applied with almost farcical indiscriminateness: an eleven-year-old boy was charged with waging war against the king of England. In the Punjabi city of Amritsar, a thousand miles north of Bombay, the overzealous General Reginald Dyer dispersed an unauthorized nonviolent protest with live rounds, killing 370 protestors he'd cornered in a city square as his troops reloaded again and again. When the general was brought back to England, insisting his only regret was that he'd run out of ammunition, he was given a hero's welcome and awarded thirty thousand pounds sterling. The funds were raised through a donation campaign led by poet Rudyard Kipling, the Bombay-born son of a sculpture professor at the Sir JJ School of Art, who championed imperialism as "the white man's burden" in a poem composed for Queen Victoria's Diamond Jubilee.

For all Gandhi's distress at the bloodshed, passively goading the imperialists into a violent response, drawing out the brutality hidden beneath the elegant clothing of Britain's "civilizing mission" in India and exposing the bloodlust that permeated even its poets, made his points exactly. Despite its claims to be founded on freedom and equality, Gandhi argued, Britain's modern civilization was in fact based on an insatiable thirst for conquest, militarism, and violence. The whole ideology of the Raj had been to earn the right to rule India without resorting to terror. But to Gandhi, imperialism was ultimately based on brutality, whatever its rhetorical cloak.

Gandhi's critique of the Raj had taken decades to develop, and in his leadership of the Indian independence movement, the mahatma ("Great Soul") took his supporters through his own journey of personal development, from infatuation with British progress and the city that embodied it—Bombay—to a rejection of both. As a nattily dressed youth, Gandhi had experimented with the cultivated persona of a Victorian dandy, taking up dancing and learning to play the violin. The lifelong vegetarian also undertook secret experiments in meat eating. (According to British ideology, the English ruled India because they were strong, manly carnivores while the Indians were weak, effeminate vegetarians.) But the experience of living in South Africa made the young Gandhi rethink his Anglophilia.

It was in South Africa, slotted uneasily into the middle of a racial hierarchy that placed whites on top and blacks on the bottom, that Gandhi for the first time felt himself to be "Indian." He became a civil rights activist defending Indians in South Africa against discrimination, but more than that, he began to dwell on what it meant to be Indian. Previously, Gandhi's self-perceptions were as a Gujarati, or as a member of his merchant caste, or as a Hindu, though none of these components of his identity figured prominently in shaping his general outlook, which was that of a modern British subject. It was only in South Africa that Gandhi began to see the value in the Indian traditions he had so purposefully shunned.

In formulating his new philosophy, Gandhi drew primarily on two thinkers—a nineteenth-century British critic who railed against industrial modernity from the heart of the empire, and an elderly Russian who, like Gandhi, had grown up in a country that had had Westernization undemocratically foisted on it from above and had grown similarly disenchanted. The Briton was the late John Ruskin, an art and architecture critic who had sought to defend the value of traditional, culturally rooted arts and crafts in a soulless industrial world of manufactured goods. The Russian was Tolstoy, the great novelist, who saw Christian pacifism as a path of salvation out of a modern world built on violence. In the brief correspondence between the young Gandhi and the aged Tolstoy, the Indian attorney enclosed a copy of his 1909 pamphlet, *Hind Swaraj* (*Indian Self-Rule*), which he'd penned in just nine days on board a ship from London to South

Africa. Tolstoy wished Gandhi well in his anti-imperial struggle and saluted *Hind Swaraj* in a handwritten English-language letter: "I read your book with great interest because I think the question you treat in it: the passive resistance—is a question of the greatest importance, not only for India but for the whole [of] humanity."

Beyond offering a strategy of nonviolent resistance to empire, in *Hind Swaraj* Gandhi sketched out his vision for what true Indian independence would mean. To Gandhi, liberation had to entail more than simply having Indians take over British institutions. Traveling that path would lead to "Englistan," a materialistic, industrialized India dominated by a haughty class of robber barons. "It would be folly to assume an Indian Rockefeller would be better than the American Rockefeller," Gandhi warned. Instead, India must draw on its past and its enduring village traditions of subsistence farming and artisanal production to pioneer a more humane alternative to the system the British had imposed. "India's salvation consists in unlearning what she has learned during the past 50 years," Gandhi taught. "The railways, telegraphs, hospitals, lawyers, doctors and such like have all to go, and the so-called upper class have to learn to live consciously and religiously and deliberately the simple life of a peasant." For Gandhi, the hypocrisy of British imperialism—building modern cities like Bombay while purposefully underdeveloping the rural Indian hinterlands—was a blessing in disguise. By preserving village India, if only for their own resource-extracting gain, the British had kept a glimpse of traditional India alive. If Indians could learn to love India again, rather than the urbanized industrial modernity with which the British had seduced them, they could free their minds and their nation. The way to defeat the Raj was not to smash it but to disavow it.

Disavowing the Raj meant disavowing Bombay. For what was Bombay but the Raj embodied in stone and steel? It was in Bombay, Gandhi wrote, that the enslavement of Indians was greatest.

In the villages—"the interior that has yet not been polluted by the railways"—people were still connected to the land, working just to meet their real human needs. But in the cities, with their ceaseless toil and railway-induced pace of life, all were in bondage. "The workers in the mills of Bombay have become slaves," Gandhi wrote. Even the rich were in bondage, ruled by their insatiable wants. The wealthy barrister's rat race across the maidan, earning money representing clients at the High Court only to spend it at the Eros Cinema, was ultimately no more liberating than the common laborer's commute between satanic mill and pestilent *chawl*. "Formerly, men were made slaves under physical compulsion, now they are enslaved by temptation of money and of the luxuries that money can buy," the mahatma taught. "We cannot condemn mill-owners; we can but pity them." Bombay, with its fantastical edifices, rags-to-riches opportunities, and freedom to reinvent oneself proudly called itself *maya-nagri*, the city of illusion. But Gandhi had seen through its illusions and urged the Indian people to as well.

To rediscover the beauty of village India, Gandhi set his followers along his own path of overcoming the seductions of Bombay and his own youthful Anglophilia. The archetype of the colonial Indian enthralled to all things English was Gandhi's younger self, the impeccably dressed, British-educated aspiring Bombay barrister. "The lawyers have enslaved India . . . we, the English-knowing men," Gandhi confessed. Just as the youthful Gandhi's dress and behavior had embodied the ideology of the Raj, as his ideas changed, so did his physical presentation. The man who once aped fine Savile Row fashion donned a spartan loincloth made of homespun cloth (*khadi*), produced on the simple spinning wheel Indians had used for centuries before British technology birthed massive mills. To Gandhi, homespun cloth struck at the heart of colonialism: it attacked the economic restrictions that required Indian cotton to be processed into clothing in England, but more than that, it challenged the whole edifice of industrial consumer capitalism with self-sufficient artisanal production. "India was prosperous so long as there was spinning. Take up again the work of spinning with a view to make India prosperous again," Gandhi exhorted on a mass-produced political poster that was hung in prominent locations around Bombay.

Setting himself as an example, Gandhi took a public pledge to use only homespun cloth. "With God as my witness, I solemnly declare that from to-day I shall confine myself, for my personal requirements, to the use of cloth manufactured in India from Indian cotton, silk and wool; and I shall altogether abstain from using foreign cloth, and I shall destroy all foreign cloth in my possession. For a proper observance of the pledge it is really necessary to use only handwoven cloth made out of handspun yarn." In 1921, Gandhi announced a national campaign calling on all Indians to use only homespun cloth, holding several meetings and rallies in Bombay.

But in setting himself against the symbolic Bombay that had long captivated the colonial Indian's mind as a vision of a better future, Gandhi also set himself against the real Bombay that was the heart of the Indian economy. Gandhi was upfront about what his homespun campaign entailed for the city that made its money producing fabric in factories and importing finished clothing. "The burden of boycott has to be principally borne by Bombay," he explained, since "Bombay controls the cloth market of India."

Fashionable, cosmopolitan Bombay soon became a source of exasperation for Gandhi as he exhorted his countrymen to make their own goods. "Bombay, which is the first city of India . . . appears to be asleep," the mahatma fumed. "I constantly hear complaints to the effect that spinning-wheels do not ply in Bombay, no one buys *khadi*, the people are not found wearing it." But the heart of the problem was Bombay's global character—here the cosmopolitan felt local and the provincial felt foreign. "Not a single street in Bombay is without a shop selling foreign cloth. On one road, at every step, there are many such shops. A shop selling *khadi* appears to be something foreign, while one selling foreign goods seems like *swadeshi*—our own," Gandhi observed.

Cognizant of the toll the homespun campaign was taking on the city's Indian merchants, Indian National Congress officials gave some ground. While Gandhi urged the exclusive use of homespun cloth, low-quality, mass-produced, Indian-made garments were still better than British ones, so Congress officials met with Bombay mill owners and convinced many to cease importing machinery from Britain. Among the firms that signed the pledge was E. D. Sassoon & Co., owned by the Bombay cousins of Shanghai's Cathay Hotel–building Sir Victor Sassoon. A company print ad from the era shows the map of India with a sari-clad woman superimposed over the subcontinent. The text exhorts, "Buy Indian Cloth," and the fine print explains, "This label is a warranty that the cloth is made from Indian yarn with Indian labour by an Indian company." In the ad, the firm's defensive crouch is palpable. A firm owned by diaspora Jews with roots in Baghdad, part of a family business empire stretching from London to Shanghai, feels forced to assert how purely Indian it is. The firm is quintessentially Bombay—technologically sophisticated, globally oriented, diverse, modern—but it is not quintessentially Indian. For the *urbs prima* more generally, a metropolis that thrived on international commerce, that was always part Indian and part global, Gandhi's push toward indigenous economic independence was a difficult fit.

For all Gandhi's fuming at Bombay, he still used the city where India engaged the world to his advantage. Seizing on Bombay's role as a media and communications hub, Gandhi became a global figure by staging rallies, launching campaigns, and giving interviews in the city. Bombay was Gandhi's chosen site to open his campaign against the salt tax, one of the Indian natural resources controlled and taxed as a government monopoly by the British. When Gandhi was imprisoned for his anti–salt tax civil disobedience in May 1930, a monthly vigil was held in the grassy maidan across the street from Victoria Terminus, under the silent gaze of Progress herself—and the not-so-silent international press corps. As the peaceful demonstrations were routinely broken up by baton-wielding police, they became newsreel footage seen by cinema goers around the world.

The ghastly images out of Bombay began to sway world opinion. While many had initially dismissed Gandhi as a quixotic figure with his loincloth and staff and conviction that the world's greatest empire could be humbled by "soul force," his campaigns proved his mettle. And he showed himself to be a master of public relations with a wit both sharp and disarming: when asked what he thought of Western civilization, Gandhi famously replied, "I think it would be a great idea." In Britain itself, where the political divide had long been over the balance between paternalism and autonomy for a subcontinent that all agreed must be ruled as a colony, more and more figures on the left began supporting outright independence for the subcontinent.

The nonviolent campaigns escalated into a final Quit India Movement, launched in 1942. In 1946, when the seamen of the Royal Indian Navy stationed at the Bombay naval base mutinied against their officers, it was the symbolic death of the Raj. During the 1857 Sepoy Rebellion, Bombay had been quiescent. In the aftermath, the British rewarded the city by building it into the greatest metropolis in their empire. Now, nearly a century later, the Bombay navy was less loyal to the Crown than the Bombay sepoys of the British East India Company era had been.

On August 15, 1947, India achieved independence. On February 28, 1948, the last British troops departed Indian soil through

Bombay's Gateway of India, a ceremonial Indo–Saracenic gateway built in 1920 to commemorate King George V's visit to the jewel of the empire. After nearly a hundred years, the Raj was over. But India had gained its independence by disavowing Bombay, by breaking the spell the city had cast over the subcontinent. The *urbs prima* of the empire seemed destined to become the bane of the republic.

# 7

## CLOSING THREE WINDOWS AND OPENING A FOURTH

## I: THE TWO-FRONT WAR | Leningrad, 1934–1985

Not far from the nationalized Putilov Works, amid Leningrad's greatest showcase of early Soviet avant-garde architecture, the modernist wonders culminate on a square presided over by a statue of Leningrad Party chief Sergei Kirov, on whose watch many of the structures were built. In the quote inscribed on the pedestal, Kirov riffs on Archimedes's aphorism on the power of the lever: "Give me a place to stand and I will move the earth." Here in Leningrad, Kirov suggests, lies the fulcrum point.

On December 1, 1934, Kirov was shot in his office in the Smolny Institute, the tsarist girls' school turned revolutionary headquarters that in the Soviet era had become Leningrad's city hall. When news of the Kirov assassination reached the Kremlin, where Stalin now ruled, the dictator and his entourage of loyal henchmen rushed to Leningrad on the overnight train. To conduct their investigation, the team commandeered the third floor of Smolny. Most historians believe it was a case of the murderer returning to the scene of the crime; the assassination is now widely believed to have been an inside job ordered by Stalin himself. From the cradle of the revolution, Stalin would crush his rivals, the generation of Petrograd radicals who had led the Bolshevik coup.

The triggerman, a disgruntled Party member, was promptly arrested, personally interrogated by Stalin, and executed. But the larger blame for the crime was assigned to Stalin's intra-Party rivals whom he had outflanked for leadership in the 1920s. Initially, fourteen conspirators, the most prominent leaders of the Communist revolution, were accused of plotting to kill Kirov as a prelude to the murders of other Soviet leaders, up to and including Stalin. But soon thousands, and ultimately millions, ended up accused of membership in a vast conspiracy to bring down the Soviet state led by turncoat Bolsheviks in league with the Western capitalist powers.

Using Kirov's murder as a pretext, Stalin issued an order expediting political investigations. The civil liberties guaranteed by the Soviet constitution would not apply on account of the new state of emergency. In political cases, the new rules decreed that the accused would only see the indictment a day before the proceedings; that the accused could not participate in the trial; and that pardon hearings would no longer be held for those sentenced to death. For the secret police in Leningrad, the new procedures were a relief. With so many "enemies of the people" to arrest, jail space was at a premium. Victims of what became known as the Great Purge routinely disappeared into the night in black vans emblazoned with signs reading "Meat" or "Milk." Leningraders came to call them "Black Ravens." Soon the "Big House," the newly opened, imposing Leningrad secret police headquarters, just blocks from its old tsarist-era equivalent, was the site of two hundred executions a night. One by one, prisoners were led to the elevator, taken to the basement, and shot. With factory-like precision, the staff got their turnaround time down to two and a half minutes per victim.

The thoroughness of the purge was astounding. Of the 1,966 delegates to the 1934 Party Congress, 1,108 were subsequently shot as "enemies of the people." But what is most striking about the Great Purge was the toll it took on any Leningrader who was politically or intellectually active—or merely knew someone who was. Through its web of connections, the entire Leningrad intellectual and political elite was targeted for elimination and either deported to labor camps in Siberia or executed outright. The sophisticated, internationally connected Hermitage museum staff was swept up—the curators of the Oriental Department were accused of being Japanese spies—but so were people affiliated with lower-profile institutions. The librarian of the Leningrad Young Communist Club, where Kirov's assassin had been a member in the 1920s, was arrested. So were her sister, her brother-in-law, and everyone who had ever given her a job recommendation. Within months of the Kirov murder, more than thirty thousand Leningraders had been sent to Siberia.

If the Kirov murder was indeed Stalin's plan, it was a darkly brilliant one. Stalin likely admired Hitler's June 1934 Night of the Long Knives, in which the German fascist had orchestrated the murders of his fellow Nazi Party founders, paving the way for his unrivaled rule as führer. To take out the founders of the Bolshevik party, the witch hunt would have to be centered on Leningrad—hence the Kirov assassination pretext—for it was from Leningrad that the revolution had been launched. Indeed it was only in Leningrad, with its worldly intellectuals open to Western ideas, its armies of educated bureaucrats stifled under the tsarist hereditary class system, and its masses of exploited industrial workers, that the Communist revolution could have been launched. A war on the generation who led the revolution would have to be a war on Leningrad.

The Great Purge was both a literal war on Leningrad and a metaphorical one. The purge of Leningrad's revolutionaries was also a purging of the revolutionary values of Russia's gateway—the love of the new and the foreign in architecture, the arts, literature, and politics. The power grab by the Georgian tough in the Kremlin drew on resentments that had simmered in Russia for centuries—the revenge of the illiterate empire on its worldly former capital.

Having launched his investigation and purge from Smolny, Stalin left Leningrad for Moscow. He would rule the Soviet Union as undisputed dictator for two more decades, but he would never return to its second city. Leningrad was dead to him; he had done his best to execute it.

Through his policies, Stalin worked to downgrade Leningrad into just another city. Stalin's forced industrialization of the Russian hinterlands, which begun in earnest with the First Five-Year Plan unveiled in 1928, served twin purposes. It helped Russia catch up technologically and economically with the industrialized West, as Stalin claimed it would, albeit at tremendous human cost, but it also served an ulterior goal: diminishing Leningrad's economic primacy. In the nineteenth century, one would have had to travel to St. Petersburg to find a massive industrial structure like the Putilov Works in Russia, but by the 1930s such factories dotted the Soviet Union.

Stalin was similarly obsessed with reducing the city's position in the Russian mind as the symbol of popular opposition to unaccountable authority. Trying to erase the memories of the revolutionary metropolis, Stalin overturned the Bolshevik edict that had renamed the streets around the Cathedral of Our Savior on Spilt Blood, where Tsar Alexander II had been assassinated, for his assassins. Those who rise up against their leaders ought not be glorified, the dictator felt. And Stalin ordered his officials in Leningrad to build a new downtown district for the city, leaving the historic center where the revolution had been sparked to decay from neglect.

Six miles south of the old imperial center, a new broad avenue named International Prospect was laid out. Plans were made to line it with imposing neoclassical façades in the Stalinist style that was fast replacing the modernist avant-garde as the official face of the Soviet state. Why replace the original neoclassical center with a second neoclassical downtown? For all the formal similarities of the columns and pediments, the style dominating Stalin's new International Prospect would be quite different from that of the imperial center. While the historic city was built on an intimate, human scale—even the Winter Palace for all its one thousand rooms is just three stories tall and decorated with delicate ornamentation—the Stalinist buildings would be massive and imposing. Stalinist architecture symbolized a return to order and authoritarianism reminiscent of the Romanovs but also the arrival of a dehumanizing and unmistakably modern bureaucratic totalitarianism. While Stalin personally interrogated Kirov's assassin, just like Nicholas I had after the Decembrist revolt, most of his repression was carried out by interchangeable bureaucrats in blank-walled interrogation cells and servile judges in Kafkaesque courtrooms. Secret police units were literally given quotas of "enemies of the people" to arrest in each region and ruthlessly held accountable for hitting their numbers. One Stalin biographer has dubbed him the "red tsar," for his rule—and the buildings that symbolized it—embodied both the autocratic nature of tsarism and the bureaucratic nature of Bolshevism's dictatorship by Party flowchart.

The centerpiece of the International Prospect development was the House of the Soviets, a vast, plodding stone neoclassical edifice fronting an enormous square on which a giant statue of Lenin dwarfs the people at his feet. The building, begun in 1936, embodies all the qualities that the modernist architect Mikhail Okhitovich lambasted in a speech the month after the Kirov murder, in which he had called out the nascent Stalinist style for abandoning the egalitarian features of Constructivism and embracing a "cult of hierarchy." With its giant government hall and supersized statue of Lenin looming over the Soviet citizens below, the complex augured the ultimate end of Stalinism, in which adulation of the ruler became a civic religion. Okhitovich was arrested shortly after his speech and died in a labor camp in 1937.

In his fateful speech, Okhitovich had bravely noted that the Nazi rulers of Germany shared Stalin's hostility to modernism. At the time, Hitler's Germany and Stalin's Soviet Union were sworn enemies, but Okhitovich's sense of their similar appetites for dictatorial domination was prescient. In August 1939, the two regimes stunned the world by signing a nonaggression pact. In a secret addendum, they divided Eastern Europe between them. Hitler's Wehrmacht and Stalin's Red Army launched a two-front assault on Poland the following month, beginning World War II.

From the first, Hitler had schemed to break the peace treaty and invade Russia. Most of all, he dreamed of an attack on Leningrad so vicious that it would make Stalin's basement murders and deportations to Siberia look mild by comparison. For the Nazi führer, as for the Soviet Great Leader, the city on the Neva was an idea as much as it was a place. While Peter the Great had founded St. Petersburg to be a gateway through which European technology and culture could flow into his Asian empire, Hitler viewed the city conversely: as a beachhead of Asia's inferior civilization on the European continent. Hitler called the city "the poisonous nest from which, for so long, Asiatic venom has spewed forth into [Europe]." To culturally purify Europe in advance of the Thousand-Year Reich, Leningrad would have to be eliminated. As a Nazi command memo, later entered into evidence at the Nuremberg war crimes trial, stated, "Hitler has decided to wipe St. Petersburg [sic] off the map. . . . If conditions in the city should reach a point that would bring offers of surrender, such offers should be rejected. . . . We are not interested in the survival of even a fraction of the population of so large a city."

When Germany invaded Russia in June 1941, the Nazi Wehrmacht made a beeline for the Venice of the North. While the upper echelons of the Red Army remained paralyzed by shock at Hitler's surprise attack, the cultural guardians of Leningrad got to work. Not waiting for an order from Moscow, the wizened, bald-headed, and white-bearded Hermitage director, Iosif Orbeli, who had survived the Great Purge (he would later be fired in a postwar purge), gathered his staff and ordered them to begin packing up the treasures of the museum for evacuation to the east, away from the front.

Half a million objects were sent on trains mounted with anti-aircraft guns to Sverdlovsk, on the Asian side of the Ural Mountains, just before the Germans severed the railway line. The last Hermitage treasure to be packed up was Jean-Antoine Houdon's sculpture of Voltaire, commissioned by Catherine the Great and then banished to the attic during the French Revolution—the ultimate symbol of the city's possibilities and contradictions.

The Hermitage staff worked day and night as the city collapsed around them. German troops completed their noose around Leningrad in September 1941, requisitioning the suburban palaces of the tsars as their command posts. Food supplies were cut off, and a German napalm and phosphorous attack incinerated the city's flour and sugar warehouses. At first, bakers pulled up bakery floorboards searching for whatever had fallen through the cracks in less-trying times. Once those crumbs were consumed, tens of thousands starved to death each month. The city's few cultivated intellectuals who had survived the Great Purge resorted to eating the binding glue from their book collections. Common laborers boiled their belts into a thin soup. Desperate Leningraders went to the Haymarket to trade wedding rings for black-market bread and mysterious meat patties, which, rumor had it, were made of human flesh. It is likely that over a million people died during Leningrad's nine hundred–day ordeal—the largest city ever under siege in the history of the world.

As the Nazi blockade cut Leningrad off from Moscow and the rest of the Soviet Union, Leningraders began referring to the rest of Russia as "the mainland." Leningrad had always been an island off the coast of Russia metaphorically, an untamable city with independent habits of mind; now the war had made it a literal island, a noncontiguous part of the Soviet Union. In 1941, on the anniversary of the October Revolution, something seemingly unthinkable in Stalin's Russia took place: a protest broke out on Strike Avenue near the nationalized Putilov Works, which had been renamed the Kirov Works for the assassinated Party chief. The assembled workers and young people of the island city boldly demanded the end of the Bolshevik regime. When Soviet troops were ordered to fire on the protestors, they refused. The situation was defused only when Nazi shells happened to fall in the vicinity and the crowd dispersed of its own volition.

While Stalin's secret police never fully lost control of the besieged metropolis, the second city of Stalin's empire edged shockingly close to becoming the free republic of Leningrad. Its Communist leadership was despised by the people. While a day's bread rations were reduced to the size of a dinner roll, the cafeteria at the Party's Smolny headquarters instituted just one wartime rule: no seconds on meat. And Smolny itself was immediately camouflaged from Nazi air raids while the beloved monuments of the imperial city, including St. Isaac's Cathedral and the Admiralty building, went naked for months. It was as if the leadership wanted the old downtown to be destroyed.

Petersburgers speculate to this day that even when the tide of the war turned in 1943, Stalin took his time pushing the Nazis back from Leningrad—the better to bleed the city he so loathed. Speculation aside, Leningrad, whose population, between deaths and evacuations, had dropped from three million to one million during the war, was indisputably rebuilt last of all the major

Soviet cities in the war zone. The memory of the surprise attack, mass starvation, and disloyalty to the regime during the siege did not fit the official Stalinist narrative of the nationalistic "hero city" valiantly defying the fascists. Nor did the inconvenient truth that the Leningraders' indomitable fight for survival was a fight for their city, not their country. The first director of the Blockade Museum, which had opened just three months after the liberation of the city to memorialize the victims of the siege, was shot by the secret police and the museum was shuttered until the Gorbachev era. Even the official Monument to the Heroic Defenders of Leningrad near the House of the Soviets did not open until the 1970s.

The Great Patriotic War, as it came to be called, made Stalin's rule even more nakedly nationalistic as earlier aspirations of Bolshevism to universal human progress—aspirations rooted in the city on the banks of the Neva—were expunged. In 1943, Stalin scrapped "The Internationale," with its call to global proletarian solidarity, as the USSR's national anthem and replaced it with a hypernationalist ballad that personally name-checked Stalin. After the war, the main avenue of Leningrad's alternate downtown, International Prospect, was renamed for the Great Leader. And in his final, paranoid purge, victims sent to Siberia—or worse—were tarred with a new epithet: "cosmopolitan." Embracing the global values that had always defined Peter's city had become grounds for repression.

After Stalin's death in 1953, though Soviet Communism was never again as brutal, Leningrad had accepted its diminished role. As during the reigns of reactionary tsars, the city's greatest talents, like composer Dmitri Shostakovich and poet Anna Akhmatova, poured their efforts into the arts instead of politics, pushing boundaries and embracing the new as much as they could get away with. The most brilliant people often pursued the most menial jobs, where there was no pressure to join the Party and one's mind, at least, was free. A desk job monitoring Leningrad's citywide steam-heat system became a coveted position. As long as the system was functioning normally, a worker was free to punch in and spend the workday writing music or poetry. But life in the economically stagnating and intellectually stifling Soviet system was bleak—a career of commutes from the gray high-rise slab apartments erected around the city to an ossified, bureaucratic workplace via the lavish subway system, opened in 1955, whose marble stations, dubbed "People's Palaces," conjured a bounteous Communist future everyone knew was a lie.

For an alternative future, as always, Leningraders looked westward. The city became a major center for jazz music, recovering from the authorities' draconian 1949 confiscation of all Soviet saxophones. Rock 'n' roll, too, survived the new Soviet leader Nikita Khrushchev's condemnations—he called it "dog shit"—fueled by European tourists who sailed in on summer cruises from Finland and eagerly bartered their vinyl LPs for vodka on the black market. In the growing Leningrad artistic underground, being a "Petersburger," a worldly aesthete/intellectual, became a form of non-Soviet identity. Fittingly, the city's early-1970s pioneering punk band chose as its name the city's original moniker: St. Petersburg. The clueless Communist authorities accused the punk rockers of being monarchists.

The silver lining to the city's demotion during Soviet times was that its historic center was never leveled. Though battered by the war and poorly maintained, it remained one of the most beautiful cities in the world. Officially saluted after the Nazi siege as "the heroic defenders of Leningrad," the people of the city, having survived assaults from Moscow as well as Berlin, became the world's most committed architectural preservationists, with by far the largest local chapter of the official, state-backed Association for the Protection of Monuments in the late Soviet era.

A defensive posture was the only way to endure. But as the city focused on preserving the past rather than building the future, its perennial dreams of remaking Russia in its image lay dormant.

## II: THE DARK AGES | Shanghai, 1937–1989

In the summer of 1937, the militarist empire of Japan, intent on subduing a vast swath of Asia, attacked China. That fall, vicious urban warfare swept Shanghai as the Japanese invaded the Chinese districts of the city. The fighting left some one hundred thousand Chinese dead, many felled in hand-to-hand combat.

For the Western residents of the foreign settlements, it was just more of the same. The key to the Shanghai concessions' success had always been as an island of stability in the midst of chaos. With their nations still at peace with Japan, the Britons, French, and Americans felt themselves to be safely in the eye of the storm. After a night on the town, Shanghailanders in tuxedos and evening gowns would go up to the rooftops of the city's industrial warehouses and watch the fighting less than half a mile away as if it were a fireworks display.

As usual, the instability sent an influx of Chinese refugees to the foreign concessions, boosting their populations and economies. The city similarly benefited from the storm clouds gathering over Europe. In the late 1930s, twenty-five thousand stateless German and Austrian Jews who had been stripped of their citizenship by the Nazi regime poured into Shanghai, the only city in the world where neither passport nor visa were required for entry. While initially a burden on the city—Sir Victor Sassoon turned vacant offices and apartments in his Embankment Building on the Suzhou

Creek into a massive social service agency to aid his desperate coreligionists—the influx of so many Western-educated professionals and entrepreneurs soon proved a boon to the local economy. Ironically, the Jewish refugees who had been told by their government that they were not, and never could be, Germans brought their Germanic culture with them, strengthening the Central European layer of international Shanghai's multicultural stew. Viennese coffeehouses soon sprang up along the avenues of the concessions, and the cabarets that the Nazis had closed down as too "decadent" and "degenerate" for fascist Berlin found a home in a city where "decadent" and "degenerate" were considered high praise for a nightlife act. To oversee entertainment at the Cathay Hotel's Tower Club, Sir Victor hired Fredy Kaufman, a veteran cabaret impresario who had been run out of Hitler's Berlin.

In time, however, the escalating turmoil that became World War II would overwhelm even international Shanghai. As Japanese warplanes launched their surprise attack on Pearl Harbor in 1941, Japanese naval vessels sailed up the Huangpu to attack the Anglo-American International Settlement. The battle was brief. A single British gunboat, no match for the Japanese armada, protected the river. As royal navy sailors jumped overboard and swam for the shore, pajama-clad British guests from the Bund's luxury hotels waded into the mud to aid them. The Japanese took the International Settlement that very day. The French Concession, administered by the Nazi's Vichy France puppet regime since the fall of Paris in 1940, endured until 1943 when the Germans gave it to their Japanese allies outright. To the eternal embarrassment of China, it was the nation's archrivals, the Japanese, who finally ended extraterritoriality and freed Shanghai from a century of Western domination.

Hoping to win over the Chinese with their rhetoric of an "Asian Co-Prosperity Sphere" rather than a "Japanese Empire," the Japanese occupiers humiliated the Western residents of the former International Settlement. Colonial Shanghai was turned upside down as the foreigners were reduced to the second-class citizenship they had foisted on the native Chinese for a century. Citizens of the allied powers were forced to wear red armbands denoting their nationality ("A" for American, "B" for British, etc.), and their bank accounts were frozen with monthly withdrawals limited to the wages of a typical lower-class Chinese laborer. "Enemy aliens" were barred from the hotels, nightclubs, cinemas, restaurants, and bars from which they had once barred the Chinese. Finally, foreigners were rounded up in Holy Trinity Cathedral, just behind the Bund, and relocated to less-desirable parts of the city, with single males forced to live in a British American Tobacco company warehouse in Pudong. Eventually, some eight thousand foreigners were imprisoned in internment camps. In keeping with the wishes of their German allies, the Japanese moved Shanghai's Jewish population to an official ghetto just off Broadway in the former American zone, though they rebuffed Nazi requests for extermination.

While there were Chinese collaborators—and even a Vichy-like Chinese puppet government under Wang Ching wei—the violence with which the Japanese took the Chinese city of Shanghai, let alone their infamous Rape of Nanjing, made it impossible for the empire to win over the Chinese masses. The Japanese occupiers of Shanghai had more luck with the city's other Asian communities. As colonial Indians, the Sikhs, who had been brought to Shanghai to serve as policemen in the International Settlement, were officially British subjects. But the Japanese specifically exempted them, as fellow Asians, from their anti-British regulations and won their loyalty in return.

The Empire of the Sun had grand plans for postvictory Shanghai. They envisioned the city as far more than a minor colonial outpost—it would be the jewel of the empire that dare not speak its name. Japanese city planners debated several different proposals for how Asia's greatest port should be developed in the glorious, imminent future in which Japan would be Asia's unrivaled superpower. Some called for continuing the Chinese Nationalists' strategy of building up the civic center at Jiangwan as an alternate downtown away from the Bund. Others called for leveling the foreign settlements entirely, as well as the industrial district in Pudong, and rebuilding the city's two riverbanks into an ultra-modern metropolis linked together by a network of bridges and broad high-speed roadways. By 1950, imperial planners predicted, Shanghai would have a Japanese population of three hundred thousand. Ultimately, these boosterish Japanese projections were no more accurate than the American Shanghailander real estate firm's 1920s vision of a city at midcentury with "an increasing number of foreign residents from all parts of the world."

Japan's dreams of domination over Asia collapsed as American troops pushed the imperial forces back to their home islands and then won unconditional surrender after twin nuclear attacks obliterated the cities of Hiroshima and Nagasaki. In the aftermath of the war, American troops poured into Shanghai, which, with its history as East Asia's great international hub, became the central processing zone for Americans heading home from the Pacific theater. For the GIs from New York and Chicago, being surrounded by the neon lights of Nanjing Road and the skyscrapers on the Bund was like a homecoming; to the Arkansas and Iowa farm boys who had assumed all of Asia was as undeveloped as the South Pacific atolls where they'd fought, Shanghai was a wonder—the biggest city they had ever seen.

With the Japanese defeat, Chiang Kai-shek and his Nationalists retook control of China and, for the first time, the entire city of Shanghai. But the war for China was not over. The Nationalists and Communists, who had put aside their differences to make common cause against the Japanese "dwarf bandits," now again battled each other for dominion over the world's most populous country. With the Cold War competition between American- and Soviet-aligned blocs getting under way, the Nationalists enjoyed American backing as a bulwark against Mao's Communists, who had won mass support in the countryside for their valiant resistance to the Japanese.

The Nationalist government's reign would be brief. Economic mismanagement led to out-of-control inflation and unemployment. In what had been Asia's leading financial center just a decade before, residents were reduced to bartering for basic goods. The foreign businessmen who had presided over Shanghai's economy began cashing out and abandoning the city. Many returned "home" to the country that had issued their passports but which they had, in many cases, never seen. Sir Victor Sassoon, bon vivant to the core, forsook his ancestral homelands of Baghdad and Bombay, as well as his youthful British stomping grounds, and moved to the Bahamas in 1948.

The following year, with Mao's million-man army closing in from the countryside, the Shanghai bankers did what they always did: they cut a deal. The bankers paid off the People's Liberation Army to enter the city peacefully. While the worldly urbanites of Shanghai and the masses of Mao's peasant army gawked at each other in mutual befuddlement, the Communist conquering of China's capitalist heart on May 27, 1949, was remarkably nonviolent. Mao had long promised his peasant troops that when they conquered Shanghai they would sleep in skyscrapers—and the authorities made good on their promise, requisitioning a handful of French Concession high-rises and billeting soldiers there in shifts. An apocryphal story soon spread among Shanghai sophisticates of the high-rise–dwelling peasant soldier who, never having encountered a commode before, took to washing his rice bowl in the toilet.

Though most of the Chinese business elite stuck it out, some fled. Contemporary Shanghai writer Lynn Pan recalled that when Shanghai fell, her father, a building contractor whose firm built

several of the French Concession's Art Deco apartments including
the Picardie, where peasant soldiers were housed, was on a business trip in British-run Hong Kong. He simply never returned
home. But many wealthy Chinese families blithely continued living their bourgeois lives in the now-Communist city.

Even after Mao's formal announcement of the founding of
the People's Republic of China (PRC) in October 1949, only
American business interests were seized in Shanghai as revenge
for American support of the Nationalists. Despite the revolution,
many of the several hundred Britons who had remained through
the economic chaos of the Nationalist era stayed put. "We will
stand by Shanghai if we possibly can," the British consul general
said at the time. "Shanghai is home to us as a community, not
merely a trading post."

As with the French Concession high-rises, the new Communist leadership seized pieces of the city selectively, taking only
those with the largest propaganda payoff. The Shanghai Race
Club, the long-segregated gambling den in the heart of the city,
was converted into People's Square, making the International
Settlement's largest green space free and open to the general public for the first time. (Betting was banned as a relic of the capitalist past.) The new Communist authorities also requisitioned the
British-owned Hongkong and Shanghai Banking Corporation's
(HSBC) beaux-arts pile on the Bund as their new city hall. A
red star was added to the building's pinnacle. Similar cosmetic
changes were made to other Bund buildings. It was as if the
authorities believed revolution was as simple as slapping a red star
on a capitalist building and calling it communist.

The surprising moderation of the new Shanghai authorities
resulted from the backgrounds of its first Communist leaders.
While Mao's decades-long sojourn in the hills had resulted in
a Party far removed from its sophisticated Shanghai roots, the
two men who led the city administration were part of the old

cosmopolitan Communist clique. Chen Yi, the first Communist mayor of Shanghai, had lived in Paris as a young man and still sported the beret on his head and the cigarette in his mouth to prove it. His right-hand man, Pan Hannian, had been a habitué of Shanghai's avant-garde Jazz Age literary circles. A committed coffee connoisseur, after the revolution he often held Party meetings in the city's elegant cafes. To Chen Yi and Pan Hannian, New China, as the Communists called it, was more about China's emergence on the world stage as a dignified, independent power than about crushing the capitalist class. By early 1951, under the leadership of the cadres holed up in the red-starred HSBC building on the Bund, business was booming in Shanghai once again. The upscale Nanjing Road department stores still did a steady business, even if their displays and advertisements had been toned down a bit. While rickshaws were quickly banned as backward and degrading, the city's red-light districts took longer to shutter. For a time, it seemed like Shanghai, though no longer an autonomous city, might remain China's cosmopolitan trading hub. Then came the first cold wind of Stalinist-style repression from the northern capital.

In April 1951, ten thousand Shanghai "counterrevolutionaries" were arrested and 293 of them executed on orders from Beijing. In fear, many Chinese businessmen fled to British-run Hong Kong, taking their businesses with them. Others lost all hope: men who had once looked down on their industrial holdings in Pudong from their Bund skyscrapers threw themselves from the windows splattering the riverfront pavement with their remains. Lynn Pan, then a little girl, recalled being out for a (supposedly banned) rickshaw ride with her *amah* in those days and being surprised when the governess pulled down the shade. Why, she asked, did she lower the shade under a brilliant blue sky? "Because there are things you mustn't see," came the reply.

The climate for foreigners degenerated rapidly. The bosses of foreign firms, who had already acceded to new requirements by giving Chinese workers job security and massive raises, could no longer feel at home in Shanghai. As in Stalin's Russia, any contact with Westerners became grounds for suspicion; Chinese journalists and teachers who had trained in the West became targets for repression. In such times, how long could people like Chen Yi, who had cavorted in Paris in his youth, stay in charge? Hoping to satisfy Beijing while preserving his leadership position and Shanghai's booming economy, Pan Hannian ordered three hundred of his favorite Shanghai capitalists to meet with him in the Cathay Hotel (renamed the Peace Hotel after the revolution) for a softball session of self-criticism.

As the Shanghai economy began to decline from the trauma, cooler heads in Beijing prevailed and the repression campaign was called off. After all, in the early Communist period, on average, 87 percent of the taxes Shanghai collected went to the central government in Beijing. Under the city's business-friendly leadership, even when Shanghai's businesses were nationalized in 1955, their former owners were put on retainer at large salaries to continue managing the enterprises.

Though the city with the cosmopolitan, entrepreneurial soul could never quite fit into Mao's New China, the Beijing authorities were divided over the role Shanghai would play in the People's Republic. All agreed that Shanghai must play second city to Beijing. (Fortuitously, this policy preserved the historic skyscrapers and *lilongs* of Old Shanghai while the ancient heart of Beijing was leveled and redesigned by Soviet planners, complete with the world's largest square, Tiananmen.) Other Party planners went further, arguing that Shanghai must be made into a "normal" city by moving fully half of its population to the interior. Beginning with China's First Five-Year Plan in the 1950s, a national industrialization program cribbed from Stalin's Russia, 170,000 skilled workers and 30,000 engineers from Shanghai factories were sent to smaller cities. The ultimate end of this vision would be for Shanghai to revert to the regional market town it had been before the Westerners had set eyes on it and developed it into China's most modern metropolis.

To mark China's emulation of Stalin's Soviet Union, with its five-year plans and leader's cult of personality, in the mid-1950s the Bubbling Well Road estate where one of the city's Jewish real estate magnates had built a traditional Chinese garden for his Eurasian wife was turned into the site of the Russian-designed Sino-Soviet Friendship Palace. With the palace unmistakably modeled on Leningrad's Admiralty building, its surging gold spire atop a neoclassical cupola, it is here that China's international gateway tips its hat to its spiritual sister city. But in the 1950s, the two cities were unified only by loss—both demoted and forced into hibernation by new Communist authorities who distrusted the very cities where the dreams of revolution had been born.

For all of Chen Yi and Pan Hannian's efforts at moderation, in 1966 a Chinese purge to rival Stalin's, the Cultural Revolution, would rise out of Shanghai. Today, the Cultural Revolution is seen as a cynical ploy by Mao and the Gang of Four (also known as "the Shanghai group" for their roots in the city) to hold onto power after their 1950s industrialization program failed to deliver on claims that China would economically "surpass England and catch up with America" in fifteen years. And indeed Mao and the Gang did exploit the dissatisfaction of Shanghai's youth for their own ends. But the tensions were real. By the mid-1960s, many in Shanghai had begun to wonder whom the revolution had benefited. On account of Mao's relocations of the city's industries and the Beijing government's siphoning off of the city's remaining bounty, average Shanghai residents had even less housing space per capita than they had had in 1949. The city's people saw Shanghai's overall wealth and prominence declining. Meanwhile, over them, they saw the same Westernized Chinese business class who had held sway in the city before the revolution, as well as a haughty new Party elite. Given these conditions, the rising generation of postrevolutionary youth who had come of age steeped in the Chairman's cult of personality—many of them had been named Chaoying (Surpass England) and Chaomei (Overtake America) in honor of Mao's delusional economic pronouncements—could not help but identify with Mao's new slogan: "To rebel is justified."

Led by the Red Guards, young armed cadres loyal to Mao, the Cultural Revolution was an Oedipal war on a humiliating past. And Shanghai was the foremost symbol of that past, still filled with the churches and skyscrapers the Westerners had built and a Western-dressed, English-speaking business class that still cavorted on Nanjing Road. In the summer of 1966, Red Guards began harassing pedestrians sporting Western fashions and hairdos; soon Mao suits—the gray pants-and-tunic set always buttoned to the very top—were nearly ubiquitous. Red Guards tore down the foreign-language signs that still dotted Shanghai and went to work coining Chinese words for Western manufactured goods. City residents who spoke English—either the rarefied Queen's English version or the near-ubiquitous pidgin—soon pretended to know only Chinese.

Western architecture itself was a target, but in a city so thoroughly Western influenced, there was little the Red Guards could do to purify the metropolis short of leveling it outright. As such, only the most obvious examples of Western influence were trashed. Religious sites, including Holy Trinity Cathedral, were desecrated. And the British Consulate, which occupied the most desirable parcel of land in the whole city, was attacked and its diplomatic staff marched out, beaten, and covered with glue. (A British Foreign Office official later quipped with a last gasp of imperial hauteur, "122 years without rent isn't bad going.")

In the summer of 1966, the Red Guards ransacked the homes of

Shanghai businessmen, searching out "the Four Olds"—old ideas, old culture, old customs, and old habits. While the most notorious Buddha bonfires took place in historic Chinese cities with millennium-old temples, the antique Chinese book and art collections of wealthy Shanghainese were looted and often destroyed on the spot. The Red Guards also found—and confiscated—millions of US dollars in cash stashed away in Chinese businessmen's homes.

In January 1967, the Red Guards' wrath turned on the Shanghai Party itself. One hundred thousand gathered in People's Square to denounce the municipal party committee and overthrow it. Mao praised the rally and backed the Shanghai Party takeover. For the next decade, China withdrew into itself in a violent rejection of the world and even its own past. The nation recalled all but one of its foreign ambassadors. Chinese universities were shuttered. The economy atrophied. Not only were the symbols of a century of foreign domination eradicated but so, too, were relics of China's thousands of years of civilization before the unequal treaties, now tarred as a "feudal" pre-Communist culture irrelevant to New China. Rather than come to terms with its past, China erased it.

With Mao's death in 1976, a nation exhausted and impoverished after a decade adrift sought pragmatic leadership. In 1978, Deng Xiaoping, whose cosmopolitan youth studying in France and working as a Party organizer in Jazz Age Shanghai had led to his tarring as a "capitalist roader" during the Cultural Revolution, took power.

For all his Shanghai values—his gaze fixed on the market and the outside world—Deng was wary of Shanghai itself. The city had been the birthplace of Chinese capitalism but also the cradle of the Cultural Revolution that had destabilized the country. To begin market-oriented reforms, Deng chose to bypass Shanghai. Instead, he would test his policies in an entirely new city of his own creation, called Shenzhen, that he ordered built on the border with Hong Kong, the British colony that had grown rich swiping businesses and businessmen from Shanghai during its Maoist stagnation. Deng designated Shenzhen as China's first "Special Economic Zone," a carve-out area where private enterprise and foreign investment would be encouraged in the Communist state.

To sidestep intra-Party ideological debates about communism and capitalism, East and West, Deng packaged his free-market zone in Shenzhen as a mere "experiment." He was, as he aphoristically put it in a pair of exceedingly famous (if apocryphal) quotes, "crossing the river by feeling the rocks"; he didn't care "if it's a black cat or a white cat as long as it catches mice." But within the wrinkled septuagenarian still lurked the curious teenager who had moved to France with the stated intention "to learn knowledge and truth from the West in order to save China."

For another decade, while Shenzhen boomed, Shanghai remained a somnambulant metropolis. At night, the city that once had been a riot of flashing lights was nearly pitch black. The streets, once packed with honking American automobiles, were now plied by silent bicycles. Squatters occupied the old banking towers on the Bund. And in the nationalized Peace Hotel (née Cathay), the same aging jazz band played the same numbers every night for an audience of handpicked foreign visitors whom Communist authorities trusted enough to grant a heretofore unnecessary document: a visa to visit Shanghai.

## III: LICENSE-PERMIT RAJ | Bombay, 1947–1991

During the British Raj, Bombay had been the hub of the empire—an island off the coast of India linked as much by sea to the mother country as by rail to the subcontinent. Neither fully British nor fully Indian, Bombay was a zone apart. But what would its role be in the new independent India?

Bombay's uncomfortable fit into the federal republic was immediately evident when a postindependence language fight broke out as the government in Delhi carved the subcontinent into states organized by mother tongue. The federal scheme worked well enough for rural areas and even for major cities like Calcutta, where Bengali was the lingua franca, or Madras, where it was Tamil. But in Bombay, with communities from all over India and beyond, English was the closest thing there was to a common language. And English, the language of colonial domination, was a target in the early national period, slated for a fifteen-year phaseout (that never quite took).

In Bombay, at independence, the largest linguistic segment, accounting for 43 percent of the population, was Marathi speakers, who composed most of the city's working class; Gujarati, the main language of the traders and industrialists, came in second. To address this predicament, some argued that Bombay should become a federally administered Union Territory akin to America's District of Columbia, as had been done with the Indian capital, Delhi. Instead, in 1955, the federal government decided to make Bombay the common capital of both Marathi-speaking Maharashtra due east over the creek and Gujarati-speaking Gujarat to the north. The compromise failed to placate the Marathi-speaking plurality who continued to agitate, undeterred by violent crackdowns on their protests, until 1960, when Bombay was made the capital solely of Maharashtra. It was a fateful decision. Henceforth Bombay, lashed to the vast Maharashtrian hinterlands, would be run by politicians who weren't from Bombay and whose constituencies lay elsewhere. Even during the Raj at its most paternalistic, the men who ran Bombay were loyal to the city and wanted to see it live up to its potential as the *urbs prima in Indis*, if only because they knew Bombay's success or failure reflected on the colonial project itself. In the new Indian republic, with the island metropolis run by mainlanders, this was no longer the case.

The challenges of fitting the polyglot trading port of Bombay into an independent India were even starker in economic policy. For Gandhi, who was assassinated by a Hindu nationalist in 1948, just months after India won independence, Bombay's economy had been a symbol of everything that was wrong with modern civilization—infernal mills amid luxurious frippery, a rich city in a poor country. The new postcolonial India, he had argued, would have to decommission the nation's industrial, financial, and commercial hub. Though India's first prime minister, Jawaharlal Nehru, had a different vision—he foresaw a fully industrialized India built by a socialist system that combined the Soviet Union's central planning with Great Britain's rights-based liberalism—his plans dovetailed with Gandhi's anti-Bombay sentiments. While Nehru's methods were incomparably gentler than Stalin's or Mao's, his goal was identical: to demote his nation's most modern city and, through central planning, spread its riches to the rest of the country.

In the lead-up to independence, the top industrialists of Bombay had met to ponder what a post-Raj economy should look like. J. R. D. Tata, the heir to Bombay's greatest commercial dynasty, and the other assembled magnates ceded tremendous power over their businesses to the state. In a surrender to central planning that became known as the "Bombay Plan," the industrialists agreed to limit foreign direct investment in their companies and give the state the power to fix their prices and regulate their production—even seize their companies outright. In 1953, the government used this new authority to nationalize Tata Airways, creating Air India. Similarly, Bombay's landlords acceded to a 1947 rent-control law, capping rents at 1940s levels and destroying the incentive for maintenance and upgrading of properties even as the population of Bombay tripled in the postindependence decades.

Some economic historians remain puzzled as to why Bombay capitalists would surrender so much power to the state. But given the temper of the times, the outcome was all but inevitable. The Raj, they had to acknowledge, had been good for Bombay but bad for India. Even though India produced enough food to feed itself, periodic famines had long plagued the colony. Linking a poor country to the global market had allowed rich cities, like Bombay, and rich, developed countries, like Britain, to siphon off crucial resources as goods sought their highest price. And even when Bombay boomed under the Raj, many Bombayites had been left behind. The Bombay business elite was shrewd enough to realize that maintaining Bombay as a rich and divided island off the coast of an impoverished nation would be untenable in the world's largest democracy.

With the Industries Act of 1951, the government began to put its vision of a less Bombay-centric Indian economy into practice. The stated goal of the new law was to maintain a regional balance when deciding where to locate industries. The meaning, to all who could read between the lines, was to move industry from the island of Bombay to the rest of the nation. To make companies comply, the new law mandated that government agencies sign off on routine corporate decisions. The state meddling soon grew into a stifling bureaucratic system dubbed alternately "red-tapism," as if it were a religion, and the "License-Permit Raj," suggesting that the independent Indian government was as restrictive of Indian businesses as the old British imperialists.

The Gandhian goal of preserving industries whose value was spiritual rather than economic, like handloom weaving, coupled with Nehru's insistence on spreading industry equally throughout the subcontinent developed into a system that quashed Bombay and hamstrung the Indian economy. While Japan and other rapidly developing Asian countries were using protective tariffs to shelter their indigenous industries until they grew strong enough to vanquish their competition in the West, India sheltered its indigenous companies but then regulated them into oblivion— when it didn't nationalize and mismanage them outright. The foibles of the License-Permit Raj were legion but among the most egregious was slapping inexpensive synthetic fabrics with a luxury tax under the misguided presumption that handloom-woven artisanally produced natural fabrics, like silk, were for the poor while high-tech synthetics, like polyester, were for the rich.

To spread the wealth and development of Bombay inland, grand plans were laid during the License-Permit Raj to physically transform the surrounding region. Right at independence in 1947, a master plan proposal for greater Bombay, prepared by a Bombay city planner and a New York–based consultant, endorsed moving industry out of the city. Relocating factories, the thinking went, would eliminate the industrial slums that scarred Bombay Island. Plans were made to build a new bridge across the creek to connect the city to the subcontinent and facilitate the moving of industry from city to countryside. But the inefficiencies of the Indian public sector slowed its grand plans. The bridge, slated to be opened in 1964, was completed in 1972.

As in Nationalist-era Shanghai and Stalinist-era Leningrad, the new Indian authorities hoped to create an alternate downtown away from the impressive but psychologically humiliating edifices of the British colonial center. In 1964, a team headed by the leading Indian architect of his generation, Charles Correa (his Latino surname comes from family roots in the Portuguese colony of Goa), published a vision for New Bombay, a "twin city" to be built across the creek from the original *urbs prima*. With New Bombay, the nation's greatest metropolis would cease to be an island off the coast of India but would be a twin

city with a coequal half on the mainland. In Correa's explana-
tion of the need for New Bombay, it was clear that the practical
considerations—"The development across the water is essential
to the orderly growth of Bombay"—were as important as the
ideological ones. New Bombay, he and his team wrote, "would
give a new image and new vitality to the citizens of the City and
the State. . . . Where new capitals have been created," the authors
concluded, "it has been found that they not only fulfill the functional requirements of creating efficient administrative centres,
but they also become a source of pride for their citizens." Surely
the historic "new capital" foremost in the minds of the planners—
more prominent even than Brasília or Washington DC—was
"Old Bombay" itself. While never the political capital of the Raj,
it was its ideological capital, built as much to be an administrative
center as a source of pride. Fully exorcising the ghosts of the Raj
required building an entirely new Bombay.

According to the plan, overseen by the State Industries and
Investment Corporation of Maharashtra, the government bureau
charged with encouraging a rational distribution of industry over
the entire state, the state government offices were to be moved
from the island city to New Bombay where they would serve
as the anchor tenants of the new development. Using the government as a tenant seemed a wise move at the time; the new
Indian state kept growing and growing as it nationalized more
and more industries and employed a larger and larger proportion of the population. The architects and planners duly drew
the roads, railway stations, and office blocks, all in the slabby
modernism-on-the-cheap that revealed centrally planned Nehruvian India's affinity for the utilitarian socialist ideals of the Cold
War–era Soviet Union. The development that sprung up around
the central rail station, a white concrete structure adrift in a vast
parking lot that looks as if it were constructed out of an enormous
Lego set plagued by a shortage of window pieces, was given the

grandiose name Belapur Central Business District (*belapur* means "city of vines" in Sanskrit, a homage to the lush tropical environment the development paved over). But the state government never moved in, dooming New Bombay to a second-rate status it has never shaken.

Instead, state officials placed themselves in Nariman Point, a new land-reclamation project adjacent to the heart of historic Bombay, a short walk from the Oval Maidan where Sir Bartle Frere's Victorian Gothic government buildings face the Art Deco apartments. The state officials, who constantly harped on the need to redistribute investment from central Bombay to the mainland, had refused to do their part. At Nariman Point, government officials spared no expense to give themselves top-of-the-line design. The headquarters of the nationalized Air India, which was completed in 1974 and looks like a giant white domino or punch card, was designed by the New York firm Johnson/Burgee Architects, where modernist-superstar-cum-Museum-of-Modern-Art-curator Philip Johnson was a partner. The nearby National Centre for the Performing Arts was designed solely by Johnson.

The new "International Style" buildings—a term coined by Johnson to describe the unadorned, blocky, placeless, modernist structures that came to dot the world in the mid-twentieth century—answered Nehru's call for a fresh start for independent India. Rather than draw on indigenous architectural traditions—traditions many felt had been tarnished by the British rulers' appropriation of Indo-Saracenic styles—Nehru called for an Indian modernity "unfettered by the traditions of the past . . . an expression of the nation's faith in the future." But many came to resent the arrogance of public officials who housed themselves in the choicest locations in buildings designed by the highest-profile international architects while relegating others to inhabit the inland redevelopment scheme they touted. Ultimately, the bleakness of places like Belapur CBD, coupled with the sluggish growth of the Indian economy, led more and more Indians to wonder if Nehru's path to a modern India was a road to nowhere.

Though there was no political opposition in the early independence period powerful enough to stop the License-Permit Raj, there were always naysayers against India's state-directed, micromanaged economic development strategy. In the 1950s, a pair of Bombay economists suggested that India put its people to work making low-skill, low-cost consumer goods for the global market rather than building Nehru's heavy-industrial dreams. In 1961, a young Manmohan Singh, the man who would ultimately lead India on a new economic path, wrote his Oxford doctoral dissertation on the need for India to embrace export-led growth.

But beyond the scholastic debates of academics and policy wonks, the real ideological naysayers against Nehruism were the Bollywood studios. To grow in spite of national economic policies that directed the state banks' capital into serious, important industries like steel production rather than showbiz, the movie studios came to rely on Bombay black-market merchants and underworld figures for financing, effectively inoculating their businesses against red-tapism. While some studios dutifully turned out politically correct fare, saluting Nehruvian socialism with tedious documentaries on the openings of rural cement plants and the like, others presented a vision of a vibrant Bombay as an alternative to a staid, self-abnegating, official socialist ideology that ignored the metropolis at best and condemned it at worst. Lacking the vast resources of the Hollywood studios, Bollywood films were often shot on the streets of Bombay rather than on backlots.

The metropolis the studios presented was not the License-Permit Raj–restricted city of office clerks and public employees, but a mythic throwback to the glamorous Bombay of the Jazz Age.

It was not difficult to conjure such a city, for Bombay had been physically frozen in its preindependence, cosmopolitan state. The same rent-control laws that preserved the city's housing stock, albeit in increasing levels of decay as well-to-do homes were converted into de facto *chawls*, provided the city's multinational corporate tenants with an offer they couldn't refuse. Paramount Pictures, the Hollywood studio, maintained the same downtown office it first rented in 1933 right through the socialist period until today, all for a token rent. Similarly, Thomas Cook stayed put on Hornby Road, which was renamed for Indian nationalist Dadabhai Naoroji. And whatever the government's economic program, the citizenry's right to dissent against its policies was always protected; with independence, the full free speech rights that the British had preserved for themselves back home had, at long last, been attained by the Indian people. In Bollywood movies, at least, Bombay remained *maya-nagri*, the city of illusion, a place where peasant farmers migrate to reinvent themselves as business magnates and mafia dons. While in traditional Indian philosophy, it is the goal of the wise and philosophical soul to see beyond the illusion (*maya*) of this world to the ultimate spiritual reality, Bombay's film directors reveled in illusion and glitz. For Bollywood, the city's moniker, *maya-nagri*, was a badge of honor to be worn proudly despite the sneers of stoical Gandhian India.

But when the lights came up and the comforts of the air-conditioned movie palace gave way to the sweltering streets of the metropolis, the denizens of the actual Bombay still had to deal with the realities of a city economy regarded with hostility by its inland rulers and bound with red tape. For many of the ambitious but idle young men who sat along Marine Drive looking out across the Arabian Sea, their backs turned to the once-gracious, now-crumbling Art Deco apartments behind them, the future lay just a short trip across the waters in the booming oil sheikhdoms of Arabia. While Cold War–era Bombay, like Leningrad and Shanghai, seemed to have exhausted the possibilities of its founding, in new regions unbound by the burdens of history the slate was still as blank as that of Bombay Island freshly reclaimed from the sea, the Neva river delta just conquered from the Swedes, or the new treaty port on the Huangpu after the Opium War.

## IV: THE CITY AT THE CENTER OF THE WORLD | Dubai, to 1981

There are many stories of how Dubai got its name. Unlike the fantastical tale of St. Petersburg being built whole in heaven and dropped to earth, the most fitting of Dubai's origin myths may even be true. According to one theory, the name Dubai comes from a physical description of the town. A city along a tidal creek running inland from the Gulf, Dubai may mean "two houses," one on each side of the creek. But the two words come from two different languages. The word *two* (*doh*) is Hindi while the word *house* (*bayt*) is Arabic; they come together to form *doh-bayt*— Dubai. Whatever its literal veracity, this origin story conveys a deeper truth: Dubai has always been a polyglot city.

The reason for Dubai's eternal crossroads status is its location. It is the city at the center of the world. Shards of porcelain unearthed by contemporary archeologists suggest that Dubai merchants were trading with China two thousand years ago. But the geography of Dubai cuts both ways. The centrality of its location, at the crossroads of Europe, Asia, Africa, and the Middle East, is undermined by its climate. The intensity of the summer heat, often reaching 120 degrees Fahrenheit, meant Dubai could never achieve liftoff before the advent of air-conditioning. From the coming of Islam in 630 AD to the dawn of the twentieth century, Dubai and its surrounding region experienced no population growth.

Befitting its status as a trading port, but hardly a boomtown, Dubai was of minor interest to Great Britain in its age of empire. Seeing the centrality of the Gulf for its lucrative trade routes to India, the British East India Company sought to safeguard the region from anti-Western, Islamic fundamentalist pirates in the early nineteenth century. With the help of their intimidating royal navy, the British struck a series of agreements with the local sheikhs beginning in 1820 to keep the region peaceful and the trade routes open. When the Maktoum, a branch of the ruling family of Abu Dhabi, a small trading port seventy-five miles down the coast, took over Dubai in 1833, they duly kept the peace on behalf of the British. The Makhtoums have ruled Dubai as autocrats ever since. The only organized movement for democratic reform was crushed in 1939 with a massacre of conspirators at a royal wedding.

For all the British touting of their "civilizing mission"—the 1930s British representative for the region waxed eloquent about, as he put it, modernizing a people stuck in the seventh century—the colonial power did little to develop Dubai. While Bombay was being rebuilt as a showcase of modernity, Dubai languished with little public investment in infrastructure, like roads and railways, or in institutions, like schools and hospitals. In contrast to the stunning university the British built in Bombay, in Dubai they didn't found a single college. Dubai was seen as junior partner in the empire, a lowly adjunct to the Indian jewel. It wasn't even given its own currency, instead using the imperial Indian rupee as its legal tender. As long as it was peaceful and trading, Dubai was largely ignored by its imperial overlords.

Though Dubai meant little to the British, it meant a lot to its region. In 1900, when Persian authorities raised their port duties, the ruler of Dubai, Sheikh Makhtoum bin Hasher, declared his city a tax-free, customs-free, license-free port. Soon Persian merchants were pouring into the city, relocating from across the Gulf. Dubai's urban structure became a perfect reflection of its name. As the "two houses" grew into two neighborhoods facing each other across the creek, one developed into an Arab neighborhood and the other into a Persian and Indian one; segregation rules privileged Arabs, allowing them to live wherever they pleased while prohibiting Indians from living on the Arab side.

Having established itself as the leading trading center in the Gulf, a British visitor in 1908 recorded that Dubai had a population of ten thousand, drawn from around the Middle East and South Asia. Defined by trade, the city boasted two bazaars, four hundred shops, 385 pearling and fishing boats, 380 donkeys, 960 goats, and 1,650 camels. The Briton concluded, "The trade of Dibai [sic] is considerable and is rapidly expanding, chiefly in consequence of the enlightened policy of the late Shaikh Maktum-bin-Hashar, and the stringency of the Imperial Persian Customs on the opposite coast."

Given their loose ties to the city, people only flocked to Dubai as long as there was economic opportunity. In the early twentieth century, a vogue for pearl jewelry brought tremendous wealth to the Gulf; its warm shallow waters produced the largest pearls in the world. Bombay merchants seized the moment, sailing to Dubai on buying trips and then trading the pearls on the British-dominated global market from Bombay. With the massive boom, pearling soon composed 95 percent of the Gulf economy. But when the Japanese developed a method of culturing pearls by inserting grit into the oyster rather than relying on chance, the Gulf industry went into steep decline. When the 1929 stock market crash sent the Western economies into free fall, demand for pearl jewelry crashed as well. The foreigners who had made

Dubai a booming regional hub went home, and the city looked doomed to revert to its centuries-long stagnation.

Problems elsewhere brought prosperity back to Dubai. In what would become a pattern, the city-state would turn its location in the middle of a troubled region—political instability in the surrounding Middle East, mass poverty in nearby South Asia—into an asset. With the unquestioned rule of the Makhtoum family and a commitment to laissez-faire economics born of trading-port traditions, Dubai became an island of prosperity and stability.

The first large influx of traders came from a newly independent India, particularly from the nation's commercial heart, Bombay. With Nehru's nationalization of the commanding heights of the Indian economy and the strictures of the License-Permit Raj, scores of Indian traders decamped for Dubai. Bombay textile plants, now limited in the amount of product they could sell in India each year by new antimonopoly laws, unloaded their surplus in Dubai for distribution around the region and beyond. In time, Dubai developed into a kind of Bombay-in-exile where Indian merchants participated in the global economy from which they were barred by a government pursuing economic self-sufficiency, not trade links. In Dubai, it was Indians who became the importers for all the leading Japanese electronics companies, including Sony, NEC, and JVC, that were slapped with insurmountable import tariffs at home. A creek-dredging project to accommodate larger ships, launched by royal decree and completed in 1961, helped cement the deal with the regional traders as Dubai now provided both the economic environment and the physical facilities necessary for international commerce.

While many Indian merchants used Dubai as a base to do business with the world's open economies, others used it as a base to illegally do business with their homeland. When a Nehru-ordered tax on precious metals sent the price of gold in India to two times its price on the global market, gold smuggling became a major business in Dubai. With Bombay effectively knocked out of the world's gold market, tiny Dubai became the second-largest destination for gold purchased on British exchanges, surpassed only by Britain's wealthy, luxury-goods-producing neighbor, France. Of course, the Gulf emirate was just a proxy for Bombay, where most of the gold ended up, sold on the black market at a huge markup. The illegal importation of gold into India was masterminded by Bombay underworld figures. At night, ships would sail from both Dubai and Bombay and rendezvous in the Arabian Sea, where they would exchange cash for gold.

With a prosperous Indian merchant class firmly entrenched in Dubai—some above board, others operating in the shadows—Indian professionals, like lawyers and accountants, followed along. Working-class Indians arrived to work as drivers, shopkeepers, and barbers for wages above what they could earn back home. By the late 1960s, one thousand South Asians were arriving in the Arabian Peninsula each week, most of them destined for Dubai. By 1970, foreigners made up the majority of Dubai's population, the largest groups being Iranians, Pakistanis, and Indians.

The Maktoum family had always seen Dubai as a trading port, but with the 1960s influx of guest workers—noncitizens whose presence in the city-state was contingent upon a specific offer of employment—Sheikh Rashid, who had assumed power when his father died in 1958, seized the opportunity to turn Dubai into a fully modern city. While still crown prince, he had embarked on his first public works project: dredging the creek. Seeing infrastructure as a wise investment, requiring capital up front in exchange for long-term returns, Dubai borrowed the money for the dredging from nearby Kuwait, which was growing wealthy from the discovery of oil within its borders. But Rashid's full vision of a modern Dubai only came together after his 1959 trip to Western Europe, his first outside the Gulf, which began in Rome and culminated in London, the capital of the empire that officially still presided over Dubai. The prince, who had grown up in a "palace" with ceilings made of rough-hewn wooden logs and dried palm fronds arranged around a sand courtyard, found himself in a city where even the impoverished residents of public housing projects had plumbing and electricity. The sheikh rode the London Underground like a common commuter and wandered the streets, taking in the grand structures of the city. He was transfixed by the modern metropolis—a diverse, wealthy global hub on an island that was linked to the rest of the world solely by sea and air.

When he returned to Dubai, Sheikh Rashid was determined to bring the city into the modern world. To house his people, as well as the growing numbers of guest workers, Rashid replaced makeshift neighborhoods of palm-frond huts with concrete buildings. Electricity came to the city in 1961. While the superpowers were engaged in the Space Race, Dubai was installing the modern conveniences that London, Paris, and New York as well as Leningrad, Shanghai, and Bombay had all enjoyed since the nineteenth century. Possessed by grand dreams for his city's future, when Rashid began building Dubai's airport in the early 1960s, he ordered up a parking lot with more spaces than Dubai had cars.

Many investors dismissed Rashid's vision for his city's future as preposterous, but in 1966, when oil was discovered in Dubai, it gave Rashid an independent source of capital for further infrastructure improvements. It was not a grand find by Middle Eastern standards: at full levels of production, Dubai would have about $1.5 million in oil per capita—significant, but nothing compared to the oil-rich emirate down the road, Abu Dhabi, with more than ten times that amount. Dubai's relative resource poverty turned out to be a blessing. Rather than view the oil deposits as a giant national trust fund that could allow his people to do nothing but read their bank statements in perpetuity,

Sheikh Rashid viewed the windfall as start-up capital. By invest-ing it wisely in infrastructure, he hoped to set Dubai on a path toward permanent prosperity that could sustain it when the oil ran dry. The sheikh plunged money into building Port Rashid, a new deep-water port to be administered by the state-run com-pany that would one day become DP World, one of the largest port operators on earth. And he also plunged money into recruit-ing talented architects, engineers, and businessmen to Dubai.

Sheikh Rashid's development lodestar was London. As such, he hired a slew of British experts to build his city who, in turn, scoured the globe for fresh talents. One of the recruits was a recent university graduate from the Philippines named Jun Palafox. While eager to put his urban planning education to use, Palafox had never heard of the city-state that was recruiting him. Before his job interview, he pulled out a reasonably up-to-date reference book with basic information on every country in the world and saw that its listing for Dubai included the statistic "Kilometers of Paved Road: 0." What does a city planner do in a city with no paved roads? he wondered. Is it even a city?

Perhaps in an effort to find out, Palafox moved to Dubai in the 1970s. The sheikhdom was small enough that Palafox met the sheikh himself, who personally explained the urban planning office's mandate. "The marching orders," Palafox recalled, were "bring Dubai from the third world—or fourth world—into the first world in fifteen years. Number two: Dubai was only 200,000 in population, design it for one million. Number three: design Dubai as if there's no oil. Number four: make it the center of the Middle East. Number five: go around the world and copy."

For his templates, Palafox was most interested in enduring boomtowns. Traveling the world, he gravitated toward cities like San Francisco, which sprang from the Gold Rush but developed a diversified economy that sustained it long after the gold was gone. By contrast, the sheikh and the British planners in the office were more enamored of London, and newly paved Dubai was soon dotted with British-style traffic roundabouts. Taken with the boxy modernism then in vogue, Sheikh Rashid and his team saw nothing wrong with leveling the Persian-influenced architecture of the old neighborhoods along the creek. The traditional wind towers—essentially a ship's sail within an open cupola that ingeniously catches sea breezes and redirects them down into the house—were replaced by cement boxes with air conditioners hooked up to the new electricity grid.

Rashid assumed complete control of Dubai in 1971, when the newly formed United Arab Emirates (UAE), composed of political capital Abu Dhabi, business capital Dubai, and five lesser nearby city-states, became fully independent of Great Britain. It was not until 1973 that the union had its own flag, postage stamps, and currency. (Even after Indian independence, Dubai initially continued using the Indian rupee issued by the new Republic of India. For a time in the 1960s, the Reserve Bank of India even issued a Gulf Rupee specifically for use in the region.)

With full authority to craft Dubai's modernization, Rashid assumed the curator-in-chief role of the Westernizing autocrat. Under the motto "What's good for the merchants is good for Dubai," Rashid hoped to foster a freewheeling internationally linked economy while monopolizing all political power. He purchased the loyalty of Emirati nationals by providing a lavish welfare state and by granting powerful families lucrative import licenses for coveted Western goods like Mercedes automobiles. In return, he and his fellow UAE sheikhs got the least democratic political structure in the Gulf, with no parliament or political parties at all.

While the social contract in which people traded a vibrant economy and generous welfare benefits for a stagnant political system seemed stable, controlling the cultural environment of the merchant-driven city-state proved more difficult. Though the state maintained an austere version of Islam as its official religion, it could not be open to the world without being open to nonbelievers. While neighboring Saudi Arabia banned all non-Muslim houses of worship, Rashid gave land for churches and carved out exemptions from Islamic religious law for the non-Muslims who called Dubai home. In contrast to Saudi Arabia and even some of the other emirates, hotels were permitted to serve alcohol; drinks were simply slapped with high sin taxes. And despite his own conservative predilections, Rashid made peace with prostitution. In the 1960s, his attempted crackdown on the oldest profession foundered when so many Dubai prostitutes flocked to a British bank to withdraw their savings before leaving the country that it nearly sank the bank. The sheikh relented. The legitimate and illegitimate sectors of Dubai's economy were already so intertwined that it would be impossible to sort them out.

Rashid rolled with his freewheeling boomtown. Many foreign workers came to the city illegally, sneaking in by boat or over land rather than going through the passport control booths at the airport, but Rashid didn't care. "What is the problem, so long as they are paying rent in Dubai?" he asked his advisers rhetorically. The city, which had had just 60,000 people in 1960, grew to 100,000 by 1970 and 276,000 by 1980. With demand for housing and commercial space rising, the physical city grew rapidly as Rashid gave free land to favored developers who agreed to build on it. And the massive infrastructure projects continued. In 1979, Rashid opened the largest man-made harbor ever created: Jebel Ali. The city was spending as much as 25 percent of its gross domestic product on infrastructure each year. And yet it was still largely unknown on the global stage.

Reaching for the now well-worn playbook of upstart global cities, Sheikh Rashid sought recognition through iconic architecture. He commissioned a skyscraper, demanding the tallest tower in the Middle East and embracing an American building form that had rarely been used outside the United States (pre-Communist Shanghai being the most famous exception). In open homage to the West, he gave his building a purposefully unoriginal name, the Dubai World Trade Centre, and had it inaugurated by Queen Elizabeth II, in 1979. From the start, the thirty-nine-story high-rise, clad in a symmetrical metal skin of small Arabian peaked arch windows, proved a highly successful real estate venture. Major Western multinationals including IBM and British Petroleum signed up to rent space, and the US Consulate moved its offices into the building. But a thirty-nine-story tower could only grab local headlines in a world where hundred-story towers were common. To the extent Sheikh Rashid's infrastructure investment garnered any attention in the West, it was to be mocked. In 1980, *The Wall Street Journal* lampooned Rashid's grand outlays, duly cataloguing them and then urging readers to "consider that not one of these investments is in an industrialized country." But Rashid was confident that the city was on the path blazed by other developing world metropolises, and that the Westerners would soon stop snickering.

Rashid would not live to see Dubai become the business hub of the Arab world and a global household name. In May 1981, the sheikh hosted a state visit from Indian prime minister Indira Gandhi, Nehru's daughter and the torchbearer for his socialist vision of a centrally planned India. The schedule of events was grueling, with substantive meetings during the day and lavish banquets running late into the night. It must have been an awkward visit for Rashid. One can imagine the sheikh slyly urging the Indian leader to continue the economic policies that were so disastrous for India and such a boon to Dubai. The morning after Gandhi left, Rashid suffered a debilitating stroke from which he never fully recovered. But he had laid the foundation for modern Dubai, the strange society—cosmopolitan and fundamentalist, authoritarian and libertine—the whole world would come to know.

# FROM PERESTROIKA
# TO PETROLGRAD

Leningrad, 1985–St. Petersburg, Present

Proposed Gazprom tower in architect's rendering

When the reform-minded new Soviet leader Mikhail Gorbachev visited Russia's historic Window on the West in May 1985, his initial itinerary followed that of any Soviet ruler on an official visit. The new general secretary toured factories, met with faculty at the Polytechnical Institute, and attended a Party meeting at Smolny, the revolutionary headquarters turned city hall. Then Gorbachev did something no Soviet leader had ever done: he went to Nevsky Prospect and plunged into the crowds, mixing and chatting with ordinary Leningraders.

Gorbachev, at just fifty-four the youngest member of the Politburo, had been elevated to power in the hope that a youthful reformer could reinvigorate the Soviet system after decades of stagnation and a string of geriatric general secretaries. Now he was in Leningrad to solidify popular support in preparation for unveiling his signature reforms: perestroika (restructuring) and glasnost (openness). Having traveled many times to the West as a rising Soviet official, Gorbachev, like previous Westernizers, cast himself as the Great Curator and hoped to import certain features he had observed abroad—private enterprise, a free press, elections—while still maintaining ultimate control. It was the mission for which the Western-looking city on the Neva stood. As Gorbachev later recalled, "The people of Leningrad . . . listened closely to my explanations, asked questions, gave advice and encouragement. When someone yelled 'Keep it up!' this was indeed heartening."

The people of Leningrad, true to form, were soon pressing even the reformist leader toward further democratization. On March 16, 1987, a rumor spread through the city's preservation-obsessed populace that the Angleterre Hotel, a massive nineteenth-century edifice that stood on the square facing St. Isaac's Cathedral, was about to be razed. In a panic, preservationists massed in front of the hotel while their leader, Alexei Kovalev, went to the relevant city administration building, conveniently located on the same square, to complain. Inside, a high-ranking bureaucrat told him no demolition was planned and exhorted him to "stop misinforming people and spreading panic." A half-hour later, a blast echoed through the square and the hotel imploded.

For seventy years the people of the city had been subjected to the bald-faced lies of the apparatchiks who ruled them, but this time something had changed. Rather than disperse, crestfallen, toward the nearest metro station, the crowd stood its ground, staying to protest in front of the dusty remains of the hotel. The following day hundreds massed and transformed the fence around the demolition site into an informal "information point" for dissidents to post their formerly underground criticisms of the Soviet system in broad daylight. The protest, which came to be known as the Battle of the Angleterre, continued on the square for three days. The information point endured for two and a half months before city authorities shut it down.

The following spring, Leningraders went even further, claiming a section of the Mikhailov Garden, the former home of the grand duke that had become a public park with the revolution, as a free-speech zone. In a public version of Peter's "assemblies" and

Catherine's salons, on Saturday afternoons ordinary citizens could make five-minute speeches on any topic. The activists called their creation "Hyde Park," named for the London greenspace with its famous "Speakers' Corner." When the authorities cracked down on the venue, organizers decamped for an even more public space: Nevsky Prospect. Setting up in front of a former cathedral that had been transformed by the Communists into the Museum of the History of Religion and Atheism, "Hyde Park" now claimed the most visible location in the city. The street that had long offered Russians all the bounty of the West—save its political freedoms—finally seemed to be fulfilling its destiny.

Free speech soon blossomed into free assembly. That summer Leningrad witnessed the first large-scale grassroots political protest in the history of the Soviet Union. On the day the Supreme Court of the USSR posthumously overturned the guilty verdicts in the treason cases that had launched Stalin's 1930s Great Purge out of Leningrad, locals held a memorial gathering to honor the memory of victims of state repression.

Leningrad was rapidly reopening economically and culturally as well, even as reform lagged in the backwaters of the vast Soviet empire. Rediscovering its long-dormant tradition of being Russia's commerical gateway to the world, with perestroika permitting joint ventures with foreign companies, the city again welcomed international businessmen. Foreign languages could again be heard on Leningrad's streets beyond the herds of tourists who were carefully corralled around the city on government-controlled trips. The city's television station, Channel 5, embraced glasnost to pioneer the nation's freest news program, broadcasting muckraking reporting never seen in the city under either the tsars or the commissars. Culturally, Leningrad not only opened up to the world but rediscovered its own long-suppressed avant-garde heritage. Alongside Catherine the Great's imported Western masterpieces at the Hermitage, works by Russian Constructivist artists and architects were again put on display. And Leningrad émigré writers, like Vladimir Nabokov and Joseph Brodsky, were finally published in their hometown.

With Gorbachev's reforms, for the first time, Leningraders were permitted to choose their leaders through free and fair elections with universal suffrage. In 1989, they sent Leningrad State University law professor Anatoly Sobchak to Moscow as their elected representative. Famous as the host of the Channel 5 talk show, *Law and Economic Life*, Sobchak had campaigned tirelessly with his trademark bullhorn outside a metro station not far from the university. Through his connections with Channel 5's management, he convinced the station to host the USSR's first televised political debate. In 1990, Leningraders elected Sobchak to their local council, the Leningrad Soviet, where he became chairman, effectively mayor of the city.

One of the new council's first moves was to allow Leningraders to vote on what their city should be called. A lively debate ensued. Exiled dissident Alexander Solzhenitsyn, who had bravely written about his experiences in Stalin's labor camps, suggested the city be renamed "Svyato-Petrograd"—acknowledging the city's roots while substituting Russian for the original Dutch. But Solzhenitsyn's suggestion never made it onto the ballot. "Leningrad" and "St. Petersburg" were the only choices. In June 1991 voters chose to adopt the original name Peter the Great had given the city. The name-change debate—with its binary choice of a name from 1924 or one from 1703—captured the city's predicament. Rather than conceive of a new role for itself, it simply chose between different types of nostalgia—one for tsarist opulence, the other for Soviet superpowerdom—both of which had stifled the city. In the same vein, while the vote was taking place, the Angleterre Hotel was being rebuilt on-site in a nostalgic style chosen to mimic the building that had been destroyed just four years earlier.

Two months after the referendum, on August 19, conservative Party officials launched a coup against Gorbachev and his fellow reformers. The general secretary was placed under house arrest and arrest warrants were issued for reformist officials, including Sobchak. The St. Petersburg mayor, who was in Moscow, escaped to the airport ten minutes before agents arrived to arrest him. Safely back in St. Petersburg, Sobchak rallied its citizens against the coup, taking full advantage of the historic resonances of his revolutionary hometown. Crowds massed in front of Sobchak's office on the square where both Russia's first liberal insurrection, the Decembrist revolt, and its most recent, the Battle of the Angleterre, had been launched. As barricades rose amid the constructivist buildings near the Kirov Works (the renamed Putilov Works), Sobchak protested with the plant workers who had officially condemned the putsch in the tradition of their forbears who had led the 1905 Revolution.

That night, Sobchak used his connections at Channel 5 to speak out against the coup on national television. It was the first televised statement of open opposition; until that point, Soviet television had been largely controlled by the coup leaders in Moscow. A loop of the ballet *Swan Lake* ran ceaselessly on all channels, interrupted at regular intervals by an announcement of the "state of emergency"—a chilling crystallization of Russia's strange mix of more-Western-than-the-West culture and pre–Magna Carta politics.

The next day, a massive rally was held in front of the Winter Palace. So many Petersburgers turned out—estimates range up to three hundred thousand—that the square, built by the tsars for massive, intimidating military parades, couldn't hold them all. Copies of the nascent glasnost-protected newspapers were defiantly distributed gratis to the crowd with white spaces brazenly showing where the coup's censors had removed content. While the foreign media focused its attention on demonstrations in Moscow where Boris Yeltsin, the first-ever elected president of the Russian Republic, the largest of the USSR's constituent republics, famously stared down the army from atop a tank, the St. Petersburg rally was twice its size—all the more impressive considering that the long-demoted second city was now just half the size of Moscow. But even as massive protests rocked the country's two historic capitals, most of Russia was quiescent. With the exception of St. Petersburg, Moscow, and Yeltsin's hometown of Sverdlovsk, there was no unrest at all. Though the putsch fizzled out when the army units in Moscow defected to Yeltsin's side, the disparate reactions to the state of emergency underscored the enduring differences between urban and rural Russia in general and St. Petersburg and the rest of the nation specifically.

Gorbachev survived the coup and nominally returned to power. But the image of a heroic barrel-chested Yeltsin atop a tank contrasting with a dazed and disheveled Gorbachev returning from his nightmarish summer vacation discredited the Soviet premier's rule. Governed by a leader whose power had been exposed as illusory, the USSR unraveled in the months after the failed coup. The various republics declared independence, and the largest piece of the shattered empire, stretching from St. Petersburg in the west to Siberia in the east, became an independent Russia under Boris Yeltsin.

As Yeltsin struggled with the massive task of moving a vast nation dotted with collective farms and unproductive state-owned factories toward a market economy, Mayor Sobchak rushed ahead with his vision for St. Petersburg. He called his city "the only Russian door to Europe" and dreamed of a St. Petersburg restored to its prerevolutionary role as Russia's banking and financial hub. Sobchak hoped to turn St. Petersburg into a Special Economic Zone (SEZ) of the type he had seen on a trip to Deng Xiaoping's China in his days as a professor—a city with special business regulations to woo foreign investment. The appeal of the

SEZ concept for Sobchak was obvious: his West-facing city could finally be decoupled from Russia's backward hinterlands.

Under Sobchak's leadership, the city privatized its local businesses much faster than the rest of Russia. His old university partnered with the Haas School of Business at the University of California, Berkeley, to open a school of management, and Duke University opened an executive training program for businessmen in the city. Foreign companies soon opened up St. Petersburg offices, including Coca-Cola, Gillette, and Otis Elevator.

As Sobchak focused his efforts locally, a group of St. Petersburg economists and Western experts centered around Anatoly Chubais, who had begun pushing market-based reforms publicly once the space for debate had been opened by the Battle of the Angleterre, embraced a more extreme strand of the Petersburg legacy. The group believed that Russia's most modern city could, through the sheer force of its brilliant imported ideas, wrench all of Russia into the future. Chubais and his crew sold Yeltsin on a strategy for reform known as "shock therapy." Rather than a Chinese-style transition to a market economy, slowly weaning unproductive industries off of state subsidies and only then freeing up prices for basic commodities, the St. Petersburg economists endorsed immediate removal of price controls. Unleashing the forces of supply and demand, they theorized, would immediately remedy the chronic shortages and epic queues that plagued the late-Soviet economy. When they succeeded in applying their shock therapy to the Russian economy, the prices of long-subsidized food staples tripled literally overnight. But since the still-collectivized farms had no incentive to produce more even as the price of their products rose, Russia's people were left to buy the same amount of goods at higher prices. Shock therapy, as the bitter joke of the era went, was all shock and no therapy.

The largest privatization scheme in the history of the world went similarly awry. Per Chubais's plan, the major industries of the old Soviet Union were converted into private companies, and every Russian was given a share worth twenty dollars of the erstwhile state-owned companies. But with prices for staples spiking and ordinary Russians desperate for cash, those with secret fortunes amassed during late Communist times, by definition organized crime associates if not outright gangsters, immediately bought up all the shares. Having seized control of the nation's companies, these new politically connected oligarchs surveyed the broken economic landscape and decided, rather than build up their companies, they would go for the quick buck through asset stripping. Everything that wasn't bolted to the floor in factories all over Russia was sold, and then, to protect the proceeds of the sales from rampant ruble inflation, profits were converted into hard currency and moved to banks in the West.

American economist Joseph Stiglitz, who had just finished serving as chief economist of the World Bank, quipped of the Russian reforms, "Privatization [alone] is no great achievement— it can occur whenever one wants—if only by giving away [public] property to one's friends." The St. Petersburg economists soon came to be compared with another group of vanguardist revolutionaries so taken with the beauty of their imported theories that they were blinded to the damage they wreaked on the ground. They became known as "market Bolsheviks."

The St. Petersburg economists' national plans were disastrous for their hometown. Mayor Sobchak's vision for his city as a business hub foundered as foreign companies realized that doing business in the new Russia would not be like doing business in the West. In Europe, a company could base its operations in a financial center like Frankfurt and station a skeleton staff in Berlin and Brussels to keep an eye on government policies and the regulatory environment. But in Russia, a clique of politically connected Muscovites would control the entire economy. Without access to political power in Moscow, a foreign company didn't stand a chance of success. Soon many corporations that had initially sited their Russian headquarters in St. Petersburg decamped for Moscow. Among them was the French bank Crédit Lyonnais, whose office had been a fixture on Nevsky Prospect before the revolution and had initially been eager to return. Even Danish shipping giant Maersk forsook Peter the Great's city of boats for Russia's landlocked capital.

Soon St. Petersburg's economy—and even its population—was in free fall. Indeed all of Russia, save for a few posh neighborhoods in Moscow where the asset-strippers lived, was collapsing. Between 1990 and 1995, the number of Russians living on four dollars a day or less went from two million to sixty million. The crime rate spiked. Russia became the only industrialized country in history to see its life expectancy go into steady decline, from 68.5 in 1991 to 64.5 in 1994. Overall, in the 1990s, economic inequality doubled while Russia's economy shrank by nearly half. Russians began to quip that everything Marx had said about communism had been wrong—but everything he'd said about capitalism was right.

St. Petersburg became a living symbol of capitalism gone awry. Unregulated gambling parlors sprouted up all over town with flashing neon "*zhakpot*" signs. Side streets, unlit by neon, became muggers' alleys. Organized crime hits plagued the city's top hotels. But since gangsters, rumored to be in league with the city's reconstituted KGB, were their only customers—virtually anyone who had money in the city was, at least to some degree, mixed up with the mob—the hotels simply asked that weapons be checked at the door, like coats. With the economy's productive capacities lower even than during the late-Soviet stagnation and the social safety net in tatters, patients were asked to bring their own syringe to the doctor. On the streets, elderly women, their pensions wiped out by runaway inflation, their husbands wiped out by vodka, hawked their last meager worldly possessions. Shock therapy had turned the whole city into a giant, taw-dry flea-market-cum-casino.

But the "market Bolsheviks" would not be discouraged. When American adviser Jeffrey Sachs, a thirty-seven-year-old Harvard economics professor, was asked by the *Financial Times* in 1992 about the economic catastrophe that was unfolding on his watch, he dismissed complaints as "yak, yak, yak." It was only the financial crisis of 1998, which completely decimated the value of the ruble and emptied St. Petersburg store shelves for a full two weeks, that finally ended the Russian experiment with shock therapy's "free market."

Russians came to associate the poverty, crime, and chaos of the Yeltsin years with democracy. Many yearned for a strong leader to reimpose order. That leader would be Vladimir Putin, Boris Yeltsin's handpicked successor, who would renationalize the commanding heights of the economy and centralize power through an authoritarian system that came to be known as Kremlin, Inc. In the guise of a modern, Westernized nation brimming with profitable multinationals, Putin's Russia would be an autocracy reborn.

Vladimir Putin was born in Leningrad in 1952, the grandson of one of Stalin's cooks. As a teenager, spellbound by Soviet spy movies, Putin went to his local KGB office to sign up. Told that the organization didn't take volunteers—if it wanted him, it would find him—Putin set his sights on Leningrad State University's law school, a well-known KGB feeder. There, he studied under a charismatic young professor named Anatoly Sobchak.

Just as the young Putin had hoped, when he graduated in 1975, the KGB came calling. The newly minted spy was initially stationed in his hometown. While Putin's precise Leningrad assignment has never been conclusively confirmed, he most certainly served as one of the many anonymous henchmen who kept Russia's historic window to the West firmly shut in the pre-Gorbachev era, either monitoring foreigners, domestic dissidents, or both. An excellent student of German, Putin was sent to Dresden in 1985 to work in the KGB branch office across the street from the local headquarters of the Stasi, East Germany's infamous secret police. When the Berlin Wall came down in 1989 and crowds ransacked the Dresden Stasi building, the young Putin dutifully burned documents across the street. When protestors turned on the KGB office, the compact, steely-eyed Putin pulled a gun on them. The crowd backed down.

With the collapse of Russia's East Bloc empire, Putin returned to Leningrad and remained on the KGB payroll even as he landed an administrative job at his alma mater, Leningrad State University. There, he reconnected with his old teacher, Anatoly Sobchak, possibly on a KGB assignment to keep an eye on the reform-minded professor. Sobchak hired Putin as an aide when he became the head of the Leningrad City Council. When the August 1991 coup came, even though the KGB chairman was a leading conspirator, Putin tacked to the prevailing wind, casting his lot with the resistence. Putin caught Sobchak's escape plane to St. Petersburg and helped organize the massive anticoup rally in front of the Winter Palace.

Putin served Sobchak as deputy mayor until 1996 when, plagued by charges of corruption and impotent to halt post-Soviet St. Petersburg's descent into crime and poverty, Sobchak was denied a second term by the voters. (By Sobchak's own admission, he gave formerly state-owned apartments to banker and journalist friends; when Sobchak came under investigation by federal prosecutors for corruption, Putin helped ferry him out of the country to France.) Through connections in Moscow, the out-of-work Putin landed a position as a minor functionary in the Kremlin, where he impressed Boris Yeltsin with his loyalty. Putin became head of the FSB, the successor to the KGB, in 1998 and prime minister in 1999. That New Year's Eve, Yeltsin went on national television with a surprise announcement: he was resigning his office several months early and turning over his powers to Putin. The new president's first major act in office was to grant Yeltsin and his family immunity from prosecution. (The Yeltsins were suspected of taking bribes from a Swiss company that won construction contracts to renovate the Kremlin.)

Putin's main vehicle for recentralizing economic power in the Kremlin was Russia's largest company, the quasi-governmental natural gas monopoly Gazprom. Fossil fuels had always been the secret strength of the Soviet economy. The country's natural gas reserves were so vast that Soviet apartment buildings had no gas gauges, their units had no thermostats, and their radiators had just two settings: on and off. Indeed, it was a drop in global energy prices in the 1980s that, in part, brought on the collapse of the Soviet Union.

When the St. Petersburg economists and their Western advisers were breaking up the old Soviet economy in the 1990s, they made an exception for natural gas. While other industries were spliced into rival companies, they left untouched the old Soviet Ministry of Gas that in 1989 had simply converted itself into a private corporation, with the government as the largest single shareholder.

Under Putin, the government asserted increasing control over the company—and the company, in turn, asserted increasing control over the country. In 2001, government representatives became a majority on the company's corporate board; in 2005, the government used cash to raise its stake in the company above 50 percent. As demand for energy rose in the new century with the stunning growth in China and India, cash poured into the coffers of Kremlin, Inc. By 2011 Gazprom was the fifteenth largest company in the world, bigger than American corporate behemoths like Wal-Mart and Goldman Sachs. As energy prices spiked, Gazprom grew richer, Russia grew powerful, and Putin and his allies grew unassailable.

The key was that under Putin, Gazprom ceased to be just a gas company. Instead, it was transformed into a vast conglomerate that served as the government's vehicle for asserting control over Russia's remaining independent media. In 2001, oligarch Vladimir Gusinsky, imprisoned on tax evasion charges, sold his media empire to Gazprom for a lowball price in exchange for his release. The sale included NTV, Russia's leading independent television station, and *Itogi*, a newsmagazine that had been published in conjunction with the American publication *Newsweek*. Ultimately, all three Russian television networks came under Kremlin control. With television defanged, newspaper censorship could be less strict; the marginalized St. Petersburg and Moscow intelligentsia, though at times openly critical of Putin's regime, was seen as powerless to threaten it. As a Kremlin official put it, "The president has a very clear idea: let them print whatever they want, nobody reads it."

Having established a pliant mass media, after his 2004 election victory Putin executed his most audacious power grab: seizing the authority to choose regional governors from Russian voters. Henceforth, governors, as well as the mayors of St. Petersburg and Moscow, who have governor status by virtue of their cities' size, would be appointed by the president. Putin, the former aide to the democratically elected mayor of St. Petersburg, had taken away the power of his hometown residents to choose their own leaders.

In what would turn out to be St. Petersburg's final mayoral election, in 2003 voters had elected Communist-youth-movement-leader-turned-Putin-protégé Valentina Matviyenko. The state-controlled television news stations had heavily favored Matviyenko, who appeared side by side with Putin on billboards around the city. Suspecting Putin had things rigged, few Petersburgers even bothered to vote. Turnout was just 29 percent. Matviyenko's closest rival, Anna Markova, could only mock the absurdity of the "free and fair" election: in the highlight of the campaign, she posed with a horse on Nevsky Prospect with a sign reading, "Would you vote for a horse if the president asked you to?"

When Putin proposed doing away with gubernatorial elections altogether in 2004, not a single governor spoke out against the proposal. Instead, a pair of American correspondents reported, the governors issued "statements so fawning that even a tsarist courtier might have blushed." Many were surely cowed by fears of a politically motivated federal investigation like those that plagued some of their less-loyal colleagues. But Putin's closest allies were true authoritarians—none more so than St. Petersburg mayor Matviyenko. On the day Putin announced his proposal, Matviyenko appeared with him on state television to endorse it. A few weeks later, Matviyenko baldly told the now-docile, reconstituted Gazprom-owned magazine, *Itogi*, "The Russian mentality needs a baron, a tsar, a president . . . in one word, a boss."

In Putin's Russia, St. Petersburg would no longer be a symbol of cosmopolitan modernity but a symbol of repression, the cradle of Putin's KGB–alumni association regime. And critics of the regime began to see the mobbed-up, corrupt, dangerous St. Petersburg of the 1990s as a kind of embryonic version of Putin's Russia—not Mayor Sobchak's city gone awry but his underling Putin's city operating according to plan. A joke began spreading around Russia that attested to the new reality: A phone rings in Moscow. The man picks up to hear, "I'm calling from St. Petersburg." He responds, "Don't begin by threatening me!"

With Matviyenko ensconced in the mayor's office, never to have to face the voters again, she and her patron in the Kremlin were free to advance their vision of St. Petersburg as a Potemkin village. While major planned infrastructure improvements like a high-speed rail connection to Moscow and a beltway around the city were downsized, delayed, and plagued by pilfered funds, Putin shined up central St. Petersburg. Putin envisioned his rehabilitated hometown as a window through which Westerners could gaze at Russia, be reassured by how European it looked, and return home confident that the great empire to the east has finally become a "normal" European country. St. Petersburg was to be a cynical stage set of a Westernized Russia that Putin had no intention of fostering beyond the city's boundaries.

Like a true Potemkin village, the authorities cleaned up the front façades of the city's historic imperial center while allowing the backs of the buildings to rot, a shambles of peeling paint, broken windows, and cracking stucco. The Kunstkamera's rear wall, safely hidden from its riverfront viewers, is sloppily painted two noticeably different tones of flaking blue paint. Inside, the stodgy museum exhibits are like a time warp to the American Museum of Natural History in the 1950s. An institution that once offered a vision of the future that the West couldn't match is now a tunnel burrowing into the past. The historical marker plaque on the building identifies the institution only as "Russia's first science museum," not the world's first. Having turned inward from Peter the Great's broad-minded era, at the Kunstkamera, one of the city's greatest triumphs is not even a distant memory; its global significance has been completely forgotten.

A few blocks from the Kunstkamera, the university that Peter the Great built—Putin's alma mater—is similarly a scandal. The meticulously restored third-of-a-mile-long eighteenth-century façade is just that: a façade. Those who enter the university's interior courtyard find a central quadrangle where virtually every structure is in some state of dilapidation. Poorly funded and subject to censorship in Putin's Russia, the university is no longer considered a place to make a career. Professors follow their students to the greener pastures on the Kremlin, Inc., payroll.

To lure tourist dollars without the destabilizing influence of a large foreign community, the authorities have made obtaining a visa to enter Russia a long, arduous, and expensive process while exempting short-term Petersburg-only cruise-ship tourists from the red tape. In summer, hundreds of thousands of Westerners pour in on luxury liners, generally seeing nothing of Russia beyond the shined-up façades fronting the Neva and the suburban imperial palaces. Finding, often to their surprise, that St. Petersburg doesn't look Russian—so European; so civilized!—tourists stock up on postcards of the Muscovite-style Cathedral of Our Savior on Spilt Blood, lest confused relatives back home think their aunt went to Amsterdam or Venice.

This is the face of Russia that Putin is eager to show foreign dignitaries as well. In suburban Strelna, Putin had the vast baroque Constantine Palace, begun under Peter the Great but trashed by the Nazis and left unrestored by the Soviets, returned to its former glory to host diplomatic conferences. It is a luxurious little world of Versailles-worthy topiary gardens, Dutch-style billiard rooms bedecked with blue and white porcelain tiles, and statues of Peter the Great, all safely quarantined away from the real Russia. Along the seaside, Putin had luxurious retro-style "cottages" built for the foreign heads of state who visited for the 2006 meeting of the G8, an organization of the world's largest economies plus Russia, its leading nuclear-armed petrostate.

Putin is always eager to keep up a cynical façade of Westernness in his policies as well. "Russia is a diverse country," Putin publicly pontificated, "but we are part of Western European culture. No matter where our people live, in the Far East or in the South, we are Europeans." Even his most brazen power grabs were always cloaked in the trappings of Western-style legitimacy. By controlling the media through state-controlled companies rather than a state propaganda ministry, Putin ensured that the arrangement, on the surface, looked similar to General Electric's ownership of NBC in the United States. And controlling the media in turn made more overtly totalitarian methods unnecessary. In today's Russia, only the largest protests must be banned outright or violently broken up. Smaller ones can just be purposefully misreported. When green-clad environmental activists protested a vote on a bill in the St. Petersburg city council to open one thousand city parks, gardens, and green spaces to real estate development, they were shown on the nightly news—but identified as supporters of the bill rather than opponents.

But even in St. Petersburg, Putin is not alone in his authoritarian sympathies. The humiliations of the loss of superpower status has pushed many Petersburgers into a defensive crouch against the outside world. A city that once yearned for progress now searches for scapegoats. In St. Petersburg a proud devotion to European high culture that outstrips any actual European city now coexists with the routine voicing of illiberal attitudes that would be considered backward in Europe's capitals. St. Petersburg is a city where an otherwise liberal academic, so enamored of European high culture that she attended Richard Wagner's complete four-opera Ring Cycle at the Mariinsky Theater night after night while seven-months pregnant, rails against Western feminism and openly yearns for the reconquest of the Russian empire. The careful political correctness of genteel European society does not exist in St. Petersburg where racial slurs, particularly against Asian migrant workers, are used in polite company.

The sense of masquerade so salient in the eighteenth century with its printed soirée manuals is still palpable in the city today. At a rooftop summertime barbeque, mediocre imported wine rather than excellent local beer is served because, as one guest puts it, "St. Petersburg is always trying to be European." But a few glasses later, a distinctly un-European conversation breaks out filled with homophobic vitriol justified by Russia's religious conservatism and apologetics for post-Soviet corruption. One young lawyer, a graduate of Putin's local alma mater, whose firm, as he puts it, "represents the monopolies," defends his clients as the only firms capable of getting the job done—a rather circular argument in an economy without open competition. The attorney praises Putin for cleaning up downtown, but for the city's founder, he has less fulsome praise: "Peter the Great is a very controversial figure in Russian history."

As the crowning glory of Putin's shiny new Petrolgrad, a giant symbol of the petroleum-based power of the Petersburger in the Kremlin was proposed: a Gazprom office tower that would be, at over 1,300 feet, Europe's tallest skyscraper. Sited just across the river from a Rastrelli–designed Russian baroque cathedral, the tower would dwarf the historic city. Though Gazprom had obtained a special exemption from the historic neighborhood's height limit, the UN cultural agency, UNESCO, threatened to remove St. Petersburg from its list of World Heritage sites if the tower were built. To preservationists locally and at UNESCO, the unity of the city's church spire–dominated skyline would be destroyed by inserting the tallest building in Europe along the Neva.

The design for the Gazprom tower was chosen in 2006 through an international competition marred by controversy. International starchitects Sir Norman Foster and Rafael Viñoly, who had been enlisted as judges, resigned from the committee in protest. While neither architect explained his reasons publicly, speculation was rampant that they quit over preservation concerns as well as pressure from Mayor Matviyenko to pick her favorite design, that of London-based architecture firm, RMJM. Competitors complained as well. Swiss architecture firm Herzog & de Meuron, which submitted a design to the competition, put out a statement saying that the process "seemed to confirm the clichés about Russia, which we are reluctant to believe."

Amid the controversy, RMJM's proposal for a translucent, twisting, tapering design that echoed the blue gas flame of the Gazprom corporate logo was chosen. Philip Nikandrov, a native St. Petersburg architect who had launched his career in Dubai, became the firm's point man in the city. He served as the public face of the protower forces from his office in the Singer Building on Nevsky Prospect—a building that itself had been initially proposed to tower over the street at sixteen stories, only to be cut down to six by decree of the tsar.

From the start, the project had powerful backers in Putin, Matviyenko, and Dmitri Medvedev, the chairman of Gazprom's board of directors who, in 2008, became Putin's handpicked successor as Russian president. (Putin would reclaim the presidency in 2012, demoting Medvedev to prime minister.) But the people of St. Petersburg, from the architectural elite down to workaday residents, were hostile to the tower. The skyscraper debate was an issue where dissent could not be covered up by the authorities. How could a Petersburger not have an opinion on whether the tallest tower in Europe should be built over their city? En masse, residents returned to the defensive preservationist stance they had held to in the Soviet period, with popular opposition to the tower spearheaded by Living City, an activist group made up of architects and historians as well as ordinary citizens. Members of the city's architects' union were almost universally opposed to the project, which they felt violated the architectural traditions of the old capital—its sense of proportion, balance, and horizontality. There was even talk of expelling Nikandrov from the union, but with the unsavory historical resonance—in Stalin's time, being expelled from your professional organization was typically a prelude to being arrested and executed—the group decided simply to issue a formal statement of opposition.

Critics of the skyscraper found themselves up against an almost tsar-like arrogance. When several leading St. Petersburg cultural figures secured a meeting with Gazprom executives to air their objections, the company's St. Petersburg chief assumed from their impertinence that they must be missing something. Public opinion was irrelevant, the executive explained, because, as he put it simply, "We are Gazprom."

And yet for all its arrogance, the new regime was keen to keep up appearances of democratic legitimacy. Even if the outcomes were fixed, a show of proper procedure was made. Public hearings were duly held on the Gazprom tower albeit with riot police present to intimidate opponents. But the hearings themselves were a kind of kabuki theater. In 2008, antitower activists surreptitiously attended and filmed a casting call for actors hired to support the project at public meetings. And a scrappy local English-language newspaper reported that after the hearing, protower actors had lined up around the corner to collect their pay, reportedly four hundred rubles (seventeen US dollars). As with Catherine the Great's assemblies, the Western-style ritual was performed but drained of its meaning in a masquerade of political equality and democratic openness.

Architect Nikandrov himself was unfazed by the allegation that project supporters were paid actors. Even if the protower members of the audience were paid, he explained, this would still be in keeping with the letter of the law. "Even if it was done, it wouldn't be a breach [of the law] because [in] a public hearing, anybody can come. An artist [or actor] can come. There are no limitations, [to] an open public hearing, anybody can come." In Putin's Petersburg, as everyone understands, democracy is just a show. So why should it matter if some of the actors are paid and others are volunteers?

As usual, it was left to Matviyenko to play the open authoritarian. After visiting Dubai to sign up Arabtec, the contractor that built the world's tallest building, the Burj Khalifa, for the Gazprom job, she gushed, "Of course, it's summer there year round. Of course, they have a cheap workforce there, and there is the sheik, who signs off on a project one day and the next day building begins. We don't have that here *yet*. Nevertheless, it should give us pause for thought. We should carefully study this know-how and use all the positive elements in our work."

With near-unanimous public opposition to a project backed by a mayor who would never have to run for reelection and the man who put her in office, the public fight over the tower became a proxy war over the city and nation's turn toward authoritarianism under Putin. Being a proxy war, the stakes were much higher than just whether the tower would be built. If the project went through, opposition figures in St. Petersburg felt, activism on all fronts in the city would collapse as Petersburgers would be forced to conclude that they had been demoted from the citizens of the early post-Soviet period to mere petitioners again, as they had been in tsarist and Communist times.

In the winter of 2010, something surprising happened: Mayor Matviyenko announced that the tower project would be moved to the outskirts of the city where it wouldn't mar views of the historic center. Many observers believed that the relocation plan was just a face-saving measure, that the tower would never be built at all. Regardless, it was a stunning victory for the tower's opponents.

The people of St. Petersburg had proven that they could, together, still veto their unaccountable leaders' vision for their city—but they still felt impotent to propose what their city should become. The leading opposition group in the tower fight may have been called Living City, but it had no vision for the future of St. Petersburg. It just wanted to protect the existing city from those who would destroy it. (The activists' critique

without a constructive project would be echoed in the rallying
cry of the 2012 protests: "Russia Without Putin.") The leaders
who were proposing the tallest tower in Europe had little vision
either. The tower wasn't the symbol of a dynamic global hub
or even of a St. Petersburg that again aspired to become one.
It wasn't the pinnacle of a vast program of urban development,
a worthy heir to Peter the Great's ambitions. It was a one-off
vanity project—a monument to the petrochemical wealth that
bubbles up from Russian soil and the Petersburg clique in the
Kremlin that shrewdly seized it. Ultimately, the Gazprom tower
was just a twenty-first-century Ice Palace, a monument to what
leaders can buy, not what they can build.

For all its failure to live up to its potential today, St. Petersburg
proves that Peter the Great was right about something: geography matters. In the post-Soviet era, being a short drive from the
European Union border has again made St. Petersburg Russia's
Window on the West, even if its rulers would prefer otherwise.
While the new Russia retains the Soviet-era internal passport
system that tracks its people despite the freedom of movement
ostensibly guaranteed by its constitution, the end of the Cold War
led Western Europe to loosen its restrictions on Russian visitors.
To reap the benefits of Russia's new petroleum wealth, Finland
provides its neighbors to the east with tourist visas almost on
demand. Today, even workaday Petersburgers have all been to
Europe, if only to Finland for a day trip to the mall.

But even a shopping trip to Finland, makes an impression.
When you get pulled over for speeding in Scandinavia, Russians
notice, the cops don't demand a bribe. In scrupulously honest
Finland, the former prime minister was arrested for drunk driving, while in Russia, the concept of a leader bound by law seems
hopelessly utopian. Just 120 miles from the European Union border, St. Petersburg is where the status quo in today's Russia gets

questioned. While the rest of the country generally accepts the way things are done in Russia, Petersburgers ask why.

The specter haunting Russia today is that St. Petersburg gives up—that the city stops trying to influence the larger nation and retreats into its cocoon. It is a lovely cocoon, nicer than it has been in a century. The Petersburgers who run Russia make sure the façades of the Winter Palace get a new coat of paint every summer and the parks get freshly planted flowers. Nevsky Prospect today is once again a thoroughfare where the most luxurious goods in the world are available for purchase by wealthy locals—the pride of a city that is, as it was in the nineteenth century, open to foreign products, if not foreign ideas. In the 24/7 sunlight of the summer months, fashionable young Russians riding the fossil fuels gravy train—Gazprom employees and the lawyers, accountants, real estate agents, public relations managers, and bankers who serve them—line the cafes enjoying international delights, sushi and mojitos being the trendiest of late, after a night at the theater. Institutions catering to tourists, including the Hermitage museum and the Mariinsky Theater, have all been shined up to a polish not seen since tsarist times. The city built out of an inferiority complex is now firmly a world capital of high culture, and it revels in its ability to look down on upstart Eastern metropolises as Western Europeans once looked down on it. Of his time in Dubai, architect Philip Nikandrov sneered, "It's a depressing place, if you're a civilized person."

But not everyone is drawn in by the bread and circus of Petrolgrad. While some young Petersburgers drink cosmopolitans in Nevsky Prospect cafes, others walk the streets in English-language T-shirts bearing tongue-in-cheek slogans like "Politicians Never Lie" and "Follow Your Leader." Again, just as they did during the reigns of the most reactionary tsars and commissars, St. Petersburg's artists create a realm of freedom in an unfree city, blurring the lines between art and politics. When Putin and

Medvedev welcomed dignitaries to the International Economic Forum at the height of the White Nights in 2010, the radical art collective Voina (Russian for "war"), which is run from shifting undisclosed locations, mounted a protest of sorts. During St. Petersburg summers, tourists gather after midnight to watch the drawbridges on the Neva rise to accommodate barge and ship traffic. In a perfectly timed assault on the bridge in front of St. Petersburg's "Big House," the KGB-turned-FSB headquarters, artists scrambled out to paint a giant phallus, which duly rose in salute to the office where Vladimir Putin and his cronies got their start. Rising up along the Neva, it conjured the Gazprom tower, mocked the Napoleon complexes of the pint-sized Putin and Medvedev, and underscored that the petty authoritarians who so often run this city were, yet again, unworthy of its sophisticated, worldly populace. Whether that populace can seize the reins and build the future is unclear. But one thing is certain: despite the miserable slog of Russian history, as long as there is St. Petersburg—a city where even at midnight, a glimmer of sunlight still peeks out over the horizon—there is hope.

# THE HEAD OF THE DRAGON

## Shanghai, 1989–Present

Pudong skyline, seen from a demolition site in the
former French Concession

When Shanghai's leaders looked out over the new New China born of Deng Xiaoping's economic reforms, it seemed history had gone off the rails. It wasn't Shanghai, the city that invented Chinese capitalism, but Deng's new experimental instant metropolis, Shenzhen, on the border with Hong Kong, that was brimming with factories and drawing thousands of ambitious young people from across the country. It was as if Deng had held a great national casting call for China's next business hub and upstart Shenzhen had gotten the part Shanghai assumed she was destined to play. Hoping to set things right, Shanghai officials lobbied their superiors in Beijing, urging them to reopen to the world China's historic global gateway city and financial center.

Even Deng's promarket political allies were wary of Shanghai. Some officials worried that unleashing China's cradle of cosmopolitanism and revolution could upend their rule. Others fretted that the symbolism alone would aid their ideological enemies. Deng was already beset by antimarket factions within the Party who warned that his new Special Economic Zones for international investment would become "foreign concession zones" reborn. Though Deng had been able to overrule them in creating

Shenzhen, the symbolism of their critique would be much more salient in Shanghai, a city that had actually been a grouping of foreign concessions during China's "Century of Humiliation," from the Opium War through World War II.

But the Shanghai city government kept pushing. In the 1980s, "when we prepared the master plan," Zhang Rufei, a former Shanghai city planning official, explained, "we had the idea to build the [Pudong] side of the river [and] we tried to sell [the central government on] this idea." The ambitious plans for Pudong were seemingly the perfect antidote to the charge that the new Shanghai would be a revival of the foreign concessions of the old. Shanghai planners called for building a sparkling new downtown directly across from the Jazz Age skyline that the British and American Shanghailanders had erected on the Bund. By towering over the edifices of foreign-dominated Shanghai, the new development would symbolize the rise of a powerful, independent China. And beyond just dwarfing the foreign-built city, the new downtown would literally rise above Old Shanghai's shame. The skyscrapers would sprout from the mud of Pudong, the notorious district of foreign-owned factories and Chinese workers' shacks, where the Chinese had toiled for a pittance to enrich Western companies like British American Tobacco and Standard Oil.

For all the ideological allure of the proposals, time and again the ambitious plans were scuttled by the central authorities in Beijing. If Shanghai wanted to open up economically, its leaders would first have to reassure the Politburo that they could keep the lid on. The opportunity to prove their authoritarian credentials came with the Tiananmen Square movement of 1989.

The massacre in Beijing is well known. Yet in hindsight, the relative order that prevailed in Shanghai during the unrest may have been even more important. It was Shanghai's composure during the Tiananmen movement that finally won it the go-ahead to develop Pudong—and ultimately shift all of China to its model of economic openness and political deep freeze, when the ruthlessly efficient pair who ran Shanghai, Jiang Zemin and Zhu Rongji, were given the keys to the Middle Kingdom. Just as Bombay's quiescence during the Sepoy Rebellion of 1857 convinced authorities in London to unleash its development and made the city a model for all of India, so Shanghai's relative tranquility in 1989 convinced the rulers in Beijing to reopen the city as the archetypal Chinese metropolis.

The Tiananmen Square crisis seemed to come out of nowhere. On April 15, 1989, news of the reformist Politburo member Hu Yaobang's fatal heart attack spread across China. While committed to one-party rule, Hu had been a strong supporter of Westernization. He was the first top official to mothball his Mao suit in favor of Western business attire and even urged people to start using forks and knives, arguing (erroneously) that chopsticks were unsanitary and spread disease. But he crossed the line when he suggested in a 1986 interview with a Hong Kong journalist that China switch from its last-comrade-standing gerontocracy, which generally allowed top cadres to serve till the day they died, to a system of orderly succession. The implication that the octogenarian Deng ought to retire did not go over well. A few months later, when Hu refused to stifle a series of minor student protests for political liberalization, he was ousted.

In China, a tradition of over-the-top mourning to express political dissent had been established in 1976, when diplomat Zhou Enlai's death was met with vociferous public lamentations as a tacit criticism of Mao's erratic rule. Sensing an opportunity to register their discontent, Beijing students were soon massing on Tiananmen Square. In a similar vein, Shanghai's *World Economic Herald* newspaper held a laudatory commemorative symposium on Hu's life and work in Beijing on April 19.

Two days later, the Shanghai Party Committee got wind that the *Herald*'s editor in chief, Qin Benli, planned to devote several pages of his next issue to a recap of the forum. With commemorations of Hu's death already a flash point in Beijing, Shanghai Party secretary Jiang Zemin personally went to the newspaper's offices and ordered Qin to delete one symposium panelist's critical quotes about Deng from the section. Qin agreed—and then ran the full, unedited text in the paper the next day. Meanwhile, reporters in the *Herald*'s Beijing bureau leaked the story of the Shanghai Party's censorship demands and Qin's wily defiance to friends in the foreign media. Qin Benli's game of bait and switch went on for a few more days. Each day, he promised to run the censored edition of the paper with a correction. And each day he didn't. Finally on April 27, the Leading Group for Discipline of the Shanghai Party Committee arrived at Qin's office and "rectified" the *Herald*, removing Qin as editor.

While the Shanghai Party, under local chief Jiang Zemin and his protégé, Shanghai mayor Zhu Rongji, presented a united front against "the turmoil," as it came to be officially known, the Politburo in Beijing was tearing itself apart. General Secretary Zhao Ziyang publicly endorsed "dialogue," but paramount leader Deng Xiaoping wanted a crackdown, violent if necessary, against the now tens of thousands of Tiananmen Square demonstrators. A mix of workers and students, the protestors rallied around a handmade torch-bearing "Goddess of Democracy" that looked uncannily like America's Statue of Liberty—hardly the Western import Deng hoped to encourage with his reforms. Though intra-Party disagreements were not unusual, the public daylight between Deng and Zhao was unprecedented.

Escalating the situation was Soviet leader Mikhail Gorbachev's long-planned May 15 state visit. "How big is this square?" the USSR's general secretary asked en route, high over Mongolia, when his advance team reported there were now, a full month after Hu's death, well over a hundred thousand protestors in Tiananmen. Ironically, it was Soviet urban planners who had helped expand Tiananmen in the 1950s, but Sino-Soviet relations had so soured over the intervening decades that this would be Gorbachev's first visit to the world's largest Communist country.

When Gorbachev's jet landed at noon, the Soviet premier was welcomed at the airport rather than in Tiananmen Square, as had been planned. The next day Gorbachev was spirited into the square-fronting Great Hall of the People through the back door, two hours behind schedule. Beijing's leaders had doubted that the path to the front door could be cleared without the use of force. As Gorbachev spoke inside, the crowds outside welcomed him with shouts of his name in Chinese and handmade banners reading "Welcome the initiator of *glasnost*."

On May 18, the Soviet general secretary escaped the chaos engulfing Beijing and flew to Shanghai for the second leg of his state visit. While roughly seven thousand protestors had rallied on People's Square, the former racetrack, and then marched to the front of Mayor Zhu's office, the former HSBC building on the Bund, the city never descended into the kind of anarchy seen in the capital. In contrast to Beijing, Gorbachev's trip to Shanghai came off exactly as planned. The Soviet leader met with local officials and laid a wreath at a statue of the nineteenth-century St. Petersburg poet, Alexander Pushkin, in the former French Concession. On the tree-lined streets of the old French district, Gorbachev paid quiet homage to the Russian writer who had described St. Petersburg as "a window cut through to Europe." As part of the Sino-Soviet thaw, China's historic Window on the West, Shanghai, had fittingly become an official sister city to Russia's Leningrad in 1988.

For all the viciousness of the restoration of order in Beijing, with the People's Liberation Army opening fire on its own people in the early morning hours of June 4, the most enduring image of the crackdown betrayed the hesitation of the People's Liberation

Army: the famed defenseless "Tank Man" stopping a column of armor simply by standing in front of it. In Shanghai, there was no such hesitation. Upon hearing news of the massacre in Beijing, Shanghai protestors began massing and erecting barricades along the main train tracks connecting Shanghai to the capital. On the evening of June 6, as a passenger train from Beijing came careening down the tracks toward protestors atop their barricade, which included an entire locomotive, the demonstrators anticipated a Tank Man–style hesitation. Instead, the train plowed right into the barricade, mowing down nine people, five of whom died. When the train finally came to a halt, enraged protestors pulled the train's engineer from his cab and beat him before setting several train cars on fire. It took seven hundred police sent by the municipal government to restore order.

The next night, Shanghai mayor Zhu Rongji gave a televised speech. "Shanghai cannot afford any turmoil," he intoned, invoking the official euphemism for the protest movement. "Many comrades have asked us to call in the People's Armed Police, and some have even suggested bringing in the army. As mayor, I solemnly declare that neither the Party Committee nor the Municipal Government has considered calling in the army. We have never envisaged military control or martial law; we seek only to stabilize Shanghai, to steady the situations, to insist on production, and to ensure normal life." A master of public relations, Zhu created a sympathetic public persona in his speech before spending the rest of the week playing the remorseless commissar behind the scenes. In short order, he oversaw the arrest, conviction, and execution of three people who had beaten the train conductor.

Mayor Zhu's public statement on the need to "insist on production"—that the business of Shanghai was business—echoed a private statement that his mentor, Jiang Zemin, had made at a Politburo meeting weeks earlier, in the thick of the crisis. "We will never allow protests to disrupt Shanghai's production routine or social order," Jiang had declared. "[We] will never permit the rise of illegal organizations, will ban all illegal demonstrations and marches, will forbid all forms of networking. . . . In particular, we will strive to win over the masses in the middle, to defuse confrontations, and to get things settled down as quickly as possible." This strategy of caring less about hearts and minds than about actions, of preferring intimidation to violence, and, above all, of keeping the economy humming would become, in time, the governing philosophy for the whole of China. When General Secretary Zhao Ziyang refused to declare martial law even after the diplomatic humiliation of Gorbachev's state visit to an out-of-control capital, Deng had him replaced. On May 27 Jiang Zemin became general secretary, and he ultimately supported the June 4 crackdown. Having proven themselves during the Tiananmen crisis, the Deng-backed "Shanghai clique" of Jiang and Zhu took over China, and the Shanghai model became the nation's model. But before joining General Secretary Jiang in Beijing, Mayor Zhu would lay the foundations for the new Pudong, a shimmering glass-and-steel vision of the new authoritarian capitalist China.

The Tiananmen crackdown initially appeared to slow down Shanghai's reopening. Following the massacre, a development loan for the construction of Shanghai's new subway system got held up for six months. Work stalled, as well, on Atlanta architect and developer John Portman's Shanghai Centre, an office, shopping mall, and hotel complex that constituted the first foray by an American architect into the city since the days of the international settlements. But seven months after the crisis, during his Chinese New Year visit, Deng told Shanghai's authorities to fast-track the development of Pudong. Two months later, the State Council approved the Pudong New Area as a Special Economic

Zone. And Deng himself christened the city the "Head of the Dragon," reanointing Shanghai as China's economic hub. The following year, Mayor Zhu convinced the visiting Deng to support his ambitious plan to turn Pudong into far more than just another manufacturing SEZ. Zhu envisioned the new Shanghai as the trade and finance capital of Asia, the Wall Street of the East. The possibility of supplanting the soon-to-be-returned but frustratingly free city of Hong Kong as China's financial hub greatly appealed to Deng.

With Communism collapsing in Eastern Europe and then in Russia itself, the Chinese Communist Party wagered that only massive economic growth fueled by foreign investment could keep it in power. Modernizing Shanghai would be the centerpiece of the Party's project. "Before liberation," ousted General Secretary Zhao Ziyang wrote in his memoir, "Shanghai was a highly developed metropolis in the Asia Pacific Region, more advanced than Hong Kong, let alone Singapore or Taiwan. But after a couple of decades, Shanghai had become run-down and had fallen far behind Hong Kong, Singapore, and Taiwan. This made people ask, 'What exactly is the advantage of socialism?'" Only by turning Shanghai into a showcase of its authoritarian development model could the Party reassert its right to rule. Much as the British felt they could vindicate their colonial domination over India through the awe-inspiring edifices of Bombay, so the Chinese Communist Party felt it could win adherents to the system it called "the people's democratic dictatorship" by rebuilding Shanghai as the world's most futuristic city.

The speed and efficiency with which the Communist authorities would move Shanghai from mothballed relic of the past to stunning vision of the future would rattle the world. In just twenty years, the city's people would go from commuting to run-down factories by bicycle to riding to the city's new international airport on the fastest train on earth. Makeshift huts would be replaced by a high-rise cityscape boasting more skyscrapers than Manhattan. And the Shanghainese would go from agonizing over each year's rice harvest to enjoying a life expectancy higher than America's. Looking to Shanghai, the masses of China's interior finally had evidence that, as Mao famously declared upon taking power but never quite proved, "China has stood up." And the world would again have to reckon with we-will-bury-you Communism—the ruthless efficiency of a system of rule by fiat, where people build wonders by shutting up and doing what they're told.

The man who would launch the building of the new Shanghai, Mayor Zhu Rongji, like all of history's authoritarian city builders, had the mind of an engineer. As one famous anecdote has it, at a state dinner in Australia, Zhu went to the bathroom and was gone for so long that his worried hosts went to check on him. Found in his shirtsleeves tinkering with the toilet tank, Zhu embarrassingly explained that he had grown so fascinated by the Australian water-conserving commode that he couldn't resist taking apart its dual-flush system and putting it back together again. "We must introduce this toilet to China," Zhu gushed in his fluent English. But the engineer-mayor's ultimate passion wasn't for minor advances in toilet hydraulics. He preferred civil engineering on a pharaonic scale.

Soon after Deng approved his Wall Street of the East plan, Zhu held a meeting with Western financial executives at the top of the Peace Hotel (formerly the Cathay) on the Bund. Zhu directed the assembled bankers to look out across the Huangpu to Pudong. The blighted spit of land they looked down on, he explained with the calm assurance of the certifiably insane, would become the world's leading financial center. "It was just warehouses and shacks and rice paddies," a Wall Street executive in attendance later recalled. "And there were people living there. So I asked

Zhu, 'What are you going to do about all of those people?' And he just said, 'We'll move them.' "

And move them he did. In Pudong, three hundred thousand residents were pushed out of their homes and relocated to high-rise apartments. The repetitive rehousing slabs—just stacks of simple rooms rising twenty-five stories in the air—may have been a physical improvement over the shacks of the old Pudong, but many inhabitants were loath to move, fearing the destruction of their village-like neighborhoods' sense of community. Those who failed to appreciate their government's largesse were forcibly evicted by armed police and hired goons. Oftentimes, the authorities would cut off water and electricity to neighborhoods they were clearing to convince the hesitant. Overall, a million families were moved in the effort to remake Shanghai.

The new slab high-rises hardly presaged the ultramodern neighborhood Pudong would become. The rehousing developments looked like something out of the Eastern Europe of the 1960s and '70s, the years China was busy tearing itself apart with the Cultural Revolution, not building. But Zhu envisioned Pudong as much more than an East Bloc–style residential improvement scheme. The real purpose of the evictions was to clear land for new, quasi-private real estate development—the first permitted in Shanghai since the revolution. Stacking people vertically who had been spread out horizontally opened up land that the authorities then leased to wealthy real estate developers often based in Hong Kong or Taiwan. These leases brought the government a windfall that it plowed into building the world's greatest civic infrastructure, including the brand new international airport linked to the financial district by maglev train, a new subway system larger than New York's or London's, and a plethora of bridges and tunnels connecting the historic center of Shanghai in the former foreign concessions to its new financial center in Pudong. In the first decade of developing Pudong, Chinese authorities spent over US$10 billion on the neighborhood's infrastructure.

The Chinese government moved companies into Pudong as easily as it moved people out of it. Bringing in domestic financial firms was just a matter of telling them to move. China's state-run banks soon erected skyscrapers along the Pudong riverfront. With each company wanting a signature Shanghai headquarters to brand its business, the towers of Pudong became a kind of fashion-show runway of recent skyscraper designs. "It's like ladies' outfits at the opera," a German architect working in Shanghai explained. The key is being unique—standing out from the crowd—even if it means being outrageous, over-the-top, or downright ugly. "Shanghai clients really will object if they think the design for their building looks like another building. That's why the city has no unified style," the modern-day Shanghailander explained.

But spending billions on infrastructure with no guarantee that foreign private companies would set up shop in Pudong was a risky development strategy. When critics argued that the state-sponsored building boom in Pudong wasn't justified by market demand, a successor of Zhu Rongji's, Mayor Xu Kuangdi, replied that building Pudong was like buying a suit for a growing boy: you get one a few sizes too big and he grows into it.

To lure foreign businesses to Pudong, the Chinese government offered tax incentives and launched a savvy starchitecture-based marketing strategy. For the first of three supertall skyscrapers planned for Pudong, an international competition was held in 1993 with Western and Japanese firms competing to design an eighty-eight-story tower—eighty-eight being an auspicious number in Chinese numerology, since the word for "eight" in Chinese sounds like the word for "wealth." "The whole concept behind the tower was to create an element that would give the property developers [in] the area, a comfort level that this would become . . . the financial center of the East," explained Adrian Smith, the Chicago-based architect who won the commission despite having never been to Shanghai.

As in the city's previous Jazz Age building boom, the pace of construction was as stunning as the backwardness of its methods. Sleek skyscrapers rose up behind bamboo scaffolding on a round-the-clock building schedule as workers moved bricks by hand-pushed wheelbarrow. Speaking about his eighty-eight-story Jin Mao Tower, Smith said, "The first time I saw the site, it was all squatter villages . . . and the next week I went there, it was cleaned off completely, with a brick wall around the site. . . . It was flat. It wasn't piles of rubble. . . . It was flat." Today, with Pudong's financial district almost completely built out, only the trees lining its main boulevard, Century Avenue, just spindly saplings still held up by stakes, bring home how new the development is.

But the fast-forward timescale of Pudong is the same one on which Chinese Communism has reinvented itself—a reinvention written into the cityscape itself. At one end of Century Avenue stands the last Soviet building: the Shanghai Oriental Pearl Radio and Broadcasting Tower, which is anchored by a plodding concrete tripod and punctuated by a series of bulbous pink spheres (the "pearls"). Conceived in 1988, a year before the Tiananmen Square protests and the fall of the Berlin Wall, the tower, which opened in 1995, was built to broadcast television and radio programs. Symbolizing the state's power to control the masses through propaganda, such towers were staples of East Bloc cities, and they dominated Communist-era skylines everywhere from Leningrad to East Berlin. That it took China's leading city until 1995 to erect its TV tower bears witness to how stunted China was, even by East Bloc standards. Most Chinese lacked TVs long after East Germans and even Russians took them for granted. By the time it opened, Shanghai's TV tower already had the feel of a building that is supposed to look futuristic but instead evokes some now-defunct conception of what the future would look like.

At the other end of Century Avenue sits Shanghai's new civic plaza, with a stunning concert hall, science museum, and new administration building. As in its sister city on the Neva, the concert hall exposes locals to foreign cultures, the science museum encourages them to think for themselves—and the administration building stifles the worldly, free-thinking urbanites the other two institutions breed. The administration building's style can only be called the architecture of intimidation. Its squat gray appearance echoes the old Shanghai Municipal Council building near the Bund, a plodding stone symbol of a colonial government that thought it would rule for centuries even as its days were numbered. Save for the red-and-gold seal of the Communist regime, the building is entirely unadorned. Its gray glass is completely reflective: the cadres inside the building can observe Pudong, but the denizens of Pudong cannot observe the cadres.

That the people cannot even know *if* they're being watched is the essence of China's new Communism. In the old Communism embodied by the Pearl TV Tower, the authorities proudly hurled their propaganda down upon the people; today, Chinese Communism operates on a kind of secret society model. While it is estimated that tens of thousands of Chinese bureaucrats work day and night to censor the Internet, there is no official acknowledgment in China that the web is censored at all beyond vague statements about ensuring that online information is "wholesome." Blocked websites are disguised with the routine Internet error message, "The connection has been reset." The secret of power in post-Tiananmen China is its invisibility.

The ultimate invisible power is the power to design the

structures in which people live their lives. The authorities in contemporary Shanghai clearly understand how architecture structures the human experience of the city, how it sets the terms on which people are brought together in urban space. The monumental, alienating feel of Pudong, with its mismatched office-atop-shopping-mall towers set back from the speeding multilane traffic, is no accident. There are several factors why this style predominates: the dominance of Hong Kong and Taiwan developers who build as if they're in their stiflingly hot home climates where an air-conditioned mall is a seductive place to hang out; the speed with which unimaginative boilerplate designs can be transformed from blueprints to reality in an environment where time is money for developers as well as for government officials on the make and on the take; and the legacy of Soviet planning, with its penchant for monumental buildings, squares, and avenues passable on foot only via underground passageways. But the ultimate factor is the government's social engineering scheme. Wide boulevards are nearly impossible to shut down with street protests; allowing crowds to gather only when engaged in the solipsistic activity of shopping is a recipe for a depoliticized city.

While Pudong represents a tabula rasa where the authorities have been able to build their dream city, across the river the former foreign concessions have been retrofitted to bring them into accord with this vision. Innumerable *lilongs* have been demolished and replaced with Pudong-style skyscraper-topped shopping malls set in concrete plazas. And People's Square, the former racetrack that became the city's leading site for staging officially sponsored political rallies during the Maoist era, has been filled up with civic buildings. In addition to a new city hall, a theater, and a museum is Reform-era Shanghai's salute to itself, the Shanghai Urban Planning Exhibition Hall, an official "Patriotic Promotion Site" that boasts a Socialist Realist bronze sculpture of heroic muscle-bound workers erecting Pudong's banking towers. Filling up the square with these imposing new buildings allows the authorities to shrewdly herald the city's revival while simultaneously rendering its main green space unusable for demonstrations. The only place the people can congregate in the renovated People's Square is in its underground shopping mall.

The new Shanghai is as much a testament to social engineering as it is to civil engineering. A complete inversion of the historic city where anyone in the world was welcome to move at any time, the new Shanghai centrally planned the composition of its population as much as its bridges and buildings. The authorities' power to curate their city's populace was well established. Since the late 1950s, China has had a system of local residency registration, complete with IDs that function as internal passports, affording the government discretion over who lives where. To create the new Shanghai, the authorities brought in several different types of people—a working class of imported rural laborers to physically build the city, a class of foreign experts to advise its multinational businesses, and a white-collar class of university-educated, English-speaking Chinese professionals to staff its companies. Taken together, the different housing forms used by each group created the disparate urban fabric of the rebuilt Pudong.

Throughout the metropolis, at the bases of the most sophisticated corporate office towers, modular dorm trailers hung with laundry house migrant workers, the new class of coolies building contemporary Shanghai. Lured by work as well as the opportunity to live in China's greatest city, a laborer with a documented offer from a Shanghai employer is permitted to relocate from his rural area for the duration of the job. Once in Shanghai, he is housed in the dorm on his worksite. Given the staggering scope of the construction boom in Shanghai, temporary trailer dorms have become a near-ubiquitous housing form in the city, akin to the *lilongs* of Old Shanghai. But unlike the *lilongs*, the trailers, like their inhabitants, are temporary.

The employment requirement for city residence allows newly capitalist Shanghai to present an image of the perfect socialist city where there are no beggars. The poor of Shanghai are all disguised, invariably dressed in their work uniforms. While rural people often stay illegally in the city after the temporary job for which they were brought in is completed, they need to find new jobs fast. Indigent, unemployed rural people routinely get sent home in sweeps, especially before high-profile events like Shanghai's World Expo, the 2010 world's fair that served as reopened Shanghai's international coming-out party. And police harassing guest workers, standing over them examining their ID cards and barking questions, is a common sight on Shanghai's streets. The official 2008 Shanghai Demographic Survey reported that fully one-third of Shanghai's overall population is composed of domestic migrant workers. But the real numbers may be even higher. After all, the survey listed the city's total population as 18.88 million, a number likely chosen for its string of auspicious number 8s, not its statistical accuracy.

Inland from the financial district's office towers and their modular coolie dorms, Western-style housing developments dot Pudong that eerily resemble the 1920s developments still standing in the former foreign concessions across the river. The gated communities house the foreign experts who have been imported to manage the new businesses of Shanghai after a forty-year gap that wiped out most Chinese people's knowledge of the basics of corporate capitalism. The authorities have set an official goal that Shanghai aim for a foreign population of 5 percent—enough to help manage the city's global businesses but not enough to threaten stability. (Citizens of Hong Kong and Taiwan, both major presences in Shanghai, are not counted as "foreign" because of the "One-China" ideology of the People's Republic.) When Shanghai first reopened for international business in the early 1990s, foreigners could only live in hotels; in the mid-1990s, an official list of (presumably bugged) apartments were opened up to foreign renters. Finally, in 1999, the authorities dropped even that requirement and began relying on a state-influenced market system to corral foreigners with carrots rather than sticks. Pudong's Western-style suburbs are the final result of the authorities' strategy for luring expatriates to live and work in the city.

Green Villas, a Pudong gated community of single-family homes that opened in 1999, is one such development designed to woo foreign professionals and their families. The neighborhood was explicitly modeled on the houses built for Westerners in the old foreign concessions, as Star Chen, an executive at the state-backed real estate firm that developed Green Villas, explained. At the outset of the project, said Chen, "I would take every weekend to go look at all these old single houses in [the former foreign concessions of] Shanghai. And I would take notes." Chen completed her research by traveling beyond the west bank of the Huangpu—to the actual West.

For Green Villas, Chen's primary model was a Vancouver subdivision. To create the neighborhood of single-family houses with the typical West Coast suburban mix of Tudor- and Mediterranean-style homes, her company imported all of its materials from Canada—right down to the plumbing and electrical wiring, and even the construction equipment. Her company imported the designers, as well. Three Canadian architects were brought to Shanghai to draw up plans for the neighborhood. To further woo foreign families, Chen helped open up two international schools, one British and one American. The British school, Dulwich College, an overseas branch of the prestigious boys school outside of London, was all but flown in from England. To build Dulwich, Chen explained,

"We went to London, to the real Dulwich College, the original one, and we hired the staff architect."

Not far from Dulwich College Shanghai, Star Chen's real estate firm commissioned an Australian architect to design a new shopping mall. With its black-and-white-striped façade, inspired according to its soul-patch-sporting designer by the bar code, a nod to the impersonal global capitalism for which it stands, the mall offers the area's expatriates a taste of home, much as the foreign department stores of Old Shanghai did a century ago. Inside the mall, a multicultural mix of American bankers' and German engineers' wives hop from the health club to the Starbucks. The mall is anchored by a supermarket where all of the exotic luxuries of home—cheese, bread, and breakfast cereal—can be had at a shocking markup. In the mall's Indian restaurant, turbaned Sikh teenagers enjoy a taste of home. While in Old Shanghai, Sikhs were imported for their skills in law enforcement, in today's reglobalized Shanghai, they are prized as computer programmers. Outside, on the mall's grounds, white children play under the watchful eyes of Chinese *amahs* as they did a century ago in the Public Garden.

As in the early twentieth century, the English-speaking Shanghai Chinese professional elite favor Western-style homes; a belt of ersatz Western developments has duly sprouted on former farmland around the city, now linked to Pudong's financial district via the massive new subway system. Shanghai's authorities have consciously built up this class of Chinese professionals to staff the city's global businesses. Today's Shanghai is essentially run like a college with a competitive admissions process, with city residency permits given to those who hold a degree from a national-level university and have passed tests in computer literacy and English fluency. The system also allows well-to-do Chinese to buy a Shanghai residence permit outright: in 1996, the Shanghai municipal government began bestowing local residency on anyone who purchased an apartment in Pudong worth at least US$60,000. Goosed by the policy-augmented demand, the reintroduction of market-based real estate development has led to a building frenzy for Western-style housing as real estate developers catered to this growing class's tastes.

The 2009 Holiday Real Estate Market expo, held in the old Sino-Soviet Friendship Palace (now a rentable exhibition hall), hawked developments modeled on all of Shanghai's former colonial powers to the professional newcomers. American-themed projects included Park Avenue, a high-rise luxury apartment building; for an ersatz France, buyers could choose between La Vill (*sic*) de Fontainebleau and 16ème Arrondissement; Anglophiles could opt for a Tudor-style cottage in Cambridge Village or British Manor. Many of the projects being touted at the expo were still under construction, but Thames Town, opened for business in 2006, had long ago proved the model a great success. Channeling a complete English country town, the development is centered around a typical High Street lined with redbrick buildings and even a statue of Winston Churchill. The town square has a full-scale fake church whose grounds are popular with a new generation of Shanghai Girls taking wedding photos, decked out in white wedding dresses, part of a vogue for what can only be called "white weddings" that has swept Reform-era China.

For all Pudong's metropolitan might, the new Shanghai has yet to live up to the city's historic promise—to sort out what it means to be Chinese and modern. The experiments of the 1930s that worked to combine traditional Chinese forms with modern institutions and technology are conspicuously absent from reopened Shanghai. In Jiangwan, Dong Dayou's library sits empty in a weed lot, its windows broken and boarded up, its façade still marred by remnants of Red Guard graffiti. With the Cultural Revolution having destroyed so much knowledge of traditional Chinese culture, the forms airlifted in from the West face little resistance from indigenous styles. This may be a key to China's rapid economic growth: there are few traditional ways of life militating against the new life of feverish work and consumption. The questions of cultural authenticity that dog other developing countries and once dogged Shanghai itself are largely absent. To the extent that there is interest in integrating and updating traditional Chinese forms in contemporary Shanghai architecture, it comes from foreigners, sometimes non-Chinese Sinophiles following in the footsteps of Henry Killam Murphy, but more often from diaspora Chinese raised in Hong Kong or Taiwan, where Chinese culture escaped the ravages of Maoism on the mainland.

The extinction of historical knowledge among even educated mainlanders is stunning. As real estate executive Star Chen explained of the wood-framed houses typical of American suburbs, "Green Villas uses a timber structure. This suits the tastes of the foreigners. Chinese live in concrete houses and the Americans live in timber houses." In fact, historically, it was precisely the reverse. When the Americans, British, and French first came to Shanghai in the 1840s, the Chinese lived in wooden houses and it was the stone lintels of the Westerners' homes that marked them, to Chinese eyes, as foreign. Only after the revolution, with the construction of Soviet-style apartment blocks, themselves a take on the modernist style pioneered in Western Europe, did the Shanghainese start living in concrete homes. But the frightening success of the Cultural Revolution in stamping out historical memory of traditional Chinese architecture means that today even educated Chinese have come to think of concrete architecture as authentically Chinese while wooden homes have come to seem foreign.

This strange mix of pride in China's new wealth and ignorance of China's traditional civilization is the great contradiction of China's rise. When an American reporter asked a Beijing man on the street—a fruit vendor—to explain China's core values on the eve of National Day, the anniversary of the founding of the People's Republic, he replied, "The ability of China to adapt . . . to learn from the West." In his estimation, the essence of the new China was that it knew to stop being so Chinese. Amazingly, in Pudong, filled with Western-style homes, malls, and office buildings often housing foreigners and Western companies, the obvious question of whether this is a disturbing redux of the foreign concessions—of whether China is, in some sense, assisting in its own recolonization—is never raised. And it is not merely that such a question is politically taboo or that in contemporary China there is no incentive to have strong opinions (and lots of incentives not to have them). It is that Chinese-ness has been so gutted of meaning. The social tabula rasa the philosophes dreamed they'd find in eighteenth-century St. Petersburg really exists in twenty-first-century Shanghai.

Under these conditions, even the return of forms of extraterritorial privilege is rarely discussed. Unlike the Chinese, the new Shanghailanders enjoy freedom of worship and some freedom to organize independent nongovernmental organizations. Satellite television is allowed in hotels catering to international travelers but prohibited in private homes. Moreover, is the new Dulwich College really that different from the Oxbridge-style Cathedral School for British boys, built in 1929 a block behind the Bund, or the colonial revival Shanghai American School, built in the French Concession in 1923? After all, when Chinese professionals take jobs in Britain or America, they send their children to the local vernacular schools—something foreign residents of Shanghai would never deign to do.

The wholesale abandonment of traditional Chinese forms and culture renders the world's largest rising power strangely absent from a global conversation that, as in the last era of globalization, hinges on forging a global culture that is more than just a universalization of Western culture. For all the global links made possible by the new Shanghai Pudong International Airport, which opened in 1999 and already has annual passenger traffic comparable to New York's JFK, the city remains oddly cut off from global debates. In a telling example, Chinese officials were dumbfounded when the Indian architects responsible for designing their country's pavilion at Shanghai's 2010 World Expo wanted to top their building with the world's largest bamboo roof. The Indian architects had hoped their innovative dome would send a goodwill message to their fellow rising Asian power: by choosing bamboo, a local Chinese material, the Indians were respectfully acknowledging the host country and positing a world that can be environmentally sustainable even with a developed China and India. But when the Indian architects requested to see the section of Shanghai's building code governing bamboo structures, they were told there was none. While the wider world wrestles with issues of site-specific sustainability, the Chinese, so eager to build Western structures, rarely use local materials like bamboo for anything other than scaffolding. It is the disconnect of a country whose leaders have culturally cut it off from the wider world even as they have linked it to the global economy, and who use the phrase "global values" as an epithet to mean "not ours." It is the curious face of China that foreign visitors glimpse when they are invariably asked how many children their government permits them to have.

Amid the financial towers and luxury shopping malls of Pudong sits the Stellar International Cineplex. It is a preposterously grandiose name for a movie theater, since no movie house in China can legitimately be described as "international." Only twenty foreign films a year are permitted to be shown in Chinese theaters, and even those are censored. In recent years, China's government has privatized its movie production sector, but this just means that the predictable propaganda has higher production values than under Mao; the days of ham-fisted Socialist Realism have given way to glitzy historical thrillers in which crafty, dashing Communist agents outflank savage Japanese occupiers and bloodthirsty Nationalist officials.

Out on the streets, of course, vendors hawk bootleg DVDs of anything and everything. It's evidence of Reform-era China's de facto social contract: what you do in the privacy of your own home is your own business, but what you do in public, in large groups, is a different story. Under this philosophy, the wide-ranging civic conversations that are a hallmark of the world's great cities, which rely on publications, panels, exhibitions, and performances, cannot take place. Nowhere are the film restrictions more jarring than in Shanghai, where the former foreign concessions are studded with stunning Art Deco cinemas from the prewar period, reminiscent of Bombay. Between 1931 and 1941, fourteen cinemas were built in Shanghai, among them the Grand, by Ladislav Hudec, and the Majestic, by Fan Wenzhao, who had been among a cohort of Chinese architects trained at the University of Pennsylvania in the early 1920s. As in Bombay, Hollywood studios flocked to Jazz Age Shanghai, where Metro-Goldwyn-Mayer, United Artists, and Warner Bros. all rented offices on the ground floor of Sir Victor Sassoon's Embankment Building. Today, Shanghai's theaters remain, but they show fluff and propaganda. Live theater in Shanghai is similarly unstimulating. As the organizers of the nascent Shanghai Fringe Festival complained on the web in 2009, they had been forced to move its international performances to smaller peripheral cities because "the SH [Shanghai] government culture department has some nonsense issues with our foreign performancer [sic] this year."

In its de facto deal with the central government, Shanghai's economic openness is contingent upon the authorities keeping the city's cultural and intellectual life under wraps. Even apparatchik-packed Beijing lets more cultural flowers bloom. Notably, dissident artist Ai Weiwei was held under house arrest in his Beijing studio, but his Shanghai studio was demolished outright. In music, too, Beijing now hosts a burgeoning scene, while Shanghai is held back. "Shanghai is more restricted than Beijing," said Zhang Shouwang, the lead singer of Beijing rock band Carsick Cars, who was anointed an "indie-rock wunderkind" by *New Yorker* music critic Alex Ross. "Once, when we played there, someone called the police. That kind of thing always happens in Shanghai." In September 2006, several of the city's leading indie rock clubs were simultaneously shut down by the Ministry of Culture, all cited for the same lack of "performance licenses." Zhang explained that the restrictions on venues have stunted Shanghai's music scene. "In Shanghai, there's no space for local bands to get good crowds," he said, "so they don't have good local bands." Though top international orchestras perform regularly at Shanghai's stunning Oriental Art Center, a Paul Andreu–designed complex of glass lobes arranged like the petals of a flower in Pudong's civic plaza, international pop music acts have trouble getting visas, especially since Björk's 2008 Shanghai concert in which the Icelandic superstar ended her song "Declare Independence" with shouts of "Tibet! Tibet!"

But for all the restrictions, there are signs that the worldly, sophisticated people that the reinvigorated city is assembling and forging are demanding a voice. The Fringe Festival organizers couldn't thwart the government's edict—but they did have the audacity to call it "nonsense" on their (eventually censored) web posting. Similarly, Shanghai residents now resist evictions in ways that would have been unthinkable just two decades ago. Faced with the public embarrassment of homeowners who refuse to move and their so-called stubborn nail houses, in 2005 the Shanghai government forbade developers from cutting off water and electricity to pressure people to leave. Today, the unpopularity of the evictions has slowed development in Shanghai as residents hold out for fair market value of their land. "It costs enough to have a nice two-bedroom apartment in New York to get some-one out of a rowhouse," complained one American architect who has been engaged in Shanghai projects for nearly a decade. His shock that people are getting anything approaching fair market value for their homes—which really do sit on plots worth mil-lions—bespeaks his experiences in the not-so-distant era of forced blackouts. In 2009, residents of historic homes near Nanjing Road put up protest signs against an American firm's high-rise project simply because it would block their sunlight and violate the city's own stated height limits for the district. Not even threatened with eviction, these Shanghai residents were willing to mount a protest solely over rule of law and quality of life.

As in nineteenth-century St. Petersburg, if you're with-it enough to be a worldly resident of your nation's most interna-tional city, you're also knowledgeable enough to understand that, through happenstance of history, your society remains yoked to an antiquated political system, a bizarre holdover from the previ-ous century. Walking down Nanjing Road today, with all the world's products for sale and all the world's peoples assembled in the context of political deep freeze, is the closest one can get to strolling down Gogol's Nevsky Prospect in nineteenth-century St. Petersburg.

Interspersed among the international businessmen and wealthy Chinese shoppers are rural migrant workers. Called out by their leathery skin and ill-fitting, raggedy sport coats, they are the great human contradiction of the new Shanghai. Surrounded by the modern world, the migrants are in the city but not of it, second-class citizens too poor to enjoy many of the city's ameni-ties. In colonial Shanghai, the parks of the foreign concessions were famously closed to Chinese and to dogs. Today, Pudong's newly built Century Park proudly proclaims on a sign, "You are all invited to Century Park!" but charges ten yuan admis-sion (US$1.50)—enough to make migrant workers think twice.

Will the millions of migrant workers who live in Shanghai accept such status forever? Or will the city again face the instability that rocked it during its last coolie-powered economic boom in the 1920s and '30s?

China's authorities are betting that Shanghai matters more as a symbol than as an actual city—a wager reminiscent of the one the British rulers of Bombay made and came to regret. In the new master-planned Pudong financial district, each of the stylistically mismatched skyscrapers sits on a pedestal set in a vast, empty plaza, pulled back from the massive avenues. With few traffic lights, limousines and taxicabs speed down the broad streets, making them all but impassable for pedestrians. Built to be impressive, not enjoyable, Pudong is meant to be viewed from across the river on the Bund—and in photos or films shot from the Bund—rather than from its own streets, for Pudong is less a city than an ad for a city.

For the 98 percent of the Chinese population that doesn't live in Shanghai, the official images of the city present an urban perfection airbrushed of any social tensions. In 2006, film censors chose *Mission Impossible III*, which had been filmed on location in Shanghai, as one of the twenty foreign films to be shown in Chinese cinemas. But before granting the film a license, they cut out shots of Shanghai buildings hung with drying laundry. To the Chinese masses, Shanghai had to be portrayed as the pinnacle of modernity. The skyscrapers that dwarf contemporary Manhattan could be shown but the laundry lines, reminiscent of Manhattan's tenements from a hundred years ago, could not. Any images of Shanghai as anything but the most modern city in the world had to be excised.

In 2009, on the sixtieth anniversary of the Communist revolution, posters of Shanghai's imposing skyline were featured in the official celebration in Beijing as a vindication of China's authoritarian system. And on one level, of course, Shanghai's breakneck redevelopment constitutes the perfect ad for the Party's authoritarian rule: the ability to move a million families, order companies to relocate, and devote resources on the basis of a long-term investment strategy rather than the short-term profit motive has made the city's global reemergence possible. But on another level, opening up a great global city in a bid for stability betrays a stunning hubris. Historically, global Shanghai brought many things to China—technology, culture, ideas, trade—but the one thing it never brought was stability.

As it did a hundred years ago, the city's embrace of modernity is breeding groups that will be hard to control. There is only so far the gap between the migrant workers and the local Shanghainese they serve can grow before the foundations of the city buckle—and only so many well-educated, English-speaking, computer-literate, world-traveling young people the city can welcome before they demand change. Modernity is about more than fast trains and tall buildings. Despite the authorities' strict controls, some among Shanghai's millions have surely figured this out.

# SLUMDOGS AND MILLIONAIRES

## Bombay, 1991–Mumbai, Present

Hiranandani Gardens

After completing his Oxford PhD in 1962, Manmohan Singh funneled through various bureaucracies, among them the Indian Ministry of Foreign Trade, the Planning Commission of India, and the United Nations. Singh's doctoral dissertation had argued that India embrace export-led growth rather than the Nehru- and Gandhi-endorsed goal of economic self-sufficiency. In his various job titles, Singh pushed his ideas as much as he could—a tweak to a report here, a modification of a policy goal there—but there were limits to a lone dissident's influence, even a powerful one like Singh who, in 1982, became the head of the Bombay-based Reserve Bank of India. The lifelong bureaucrat's fortunes changed abruptly in 1991 when Prime Minister Narasimha Rao called the mild-mannered, blue-turbaned, fifty-eight-year-old to New Delhi, where he was thrust into the spotlight by a crisis.

For decades, License-Permit Raj India's support for a bloated, unprofitable public industrial sector had resulted in anemic economic growth, typically around 3.5 percent a year. In a famous quip, Delhi School of Economics professor Raj Krishna dubbed it India's "Hindu rate of growth"—a level of economic output befitting a nation whose principal religious tradition taught that the material world is an illusion best treated with indifference. As the information age dawned, India levied tariffs on imported computer software that topped 100 percent and employed an army of 250,000 bureaucrats to oversee its mere 2.5 million telephones. Even so, for decades the nation's economic problems had been partially masked by a favorable barter trade with a friendly Soviet Union that sought to project its influence into South Asia. But with the erstwhile superpower teetering after the fall of the Berlin Wall, India was nearly broke and the bankers who had sustained the country on credit were growing nervous. The Washington-based International Monetary Fund, spawned in the wake of World War II to oversee the financial system of the non-Communist world, agreed to provide a bailout—but only in return for major structural changes to the Indian economy. Washington decreed that India would have to shift from a variant of the planning-based Soviet model to a variant of the market-driven American system. For over forty years, India had pursued an economic strategy that was supposed to produce self-sufficiency and independence from the West. Now the republic was beholden to international development bureaucrats in Washington who were demanding that Indian gold be flown to London, the former imperial capital, as collateral for a $2.2 billion emergency loan.

The newly appointed Finance Minister Singh went to work immediately. Having been sworn in on June 21, by early July he had instructed the government to devalue the Indian rupee by 20 percent against the dollar. With the lower value of the rupee, export subsidies designed to make Indian goods more competitive on international markets became moot and were abolished. The capital markets were unleashed by a reform to the rules governing initial public offerings (IPOs). Under the License-Permit Raj, a government agency dictated share prices for new companies—usually at a lowball figure—but now stock prices would be determined by market demand for shares. Requirements that

Indian firms obtain special licenses to import foreign equipment or expand their operations were similarly scrapped, as were limits on foreign direct investment and foreign ownership. The pillars of the License-Permit Raj, which had been built up over decades, were dismantled in days. Almost immediately, foreign companies like IBM and Coca-Cola that had pulled out of India over License-Permit Raj requirements poured back in.

The reforms not only reopened the country to foreign products, they also reopened the world to Indians with the wherewithal to travel. Before Singh's reforms, converting rupees to foreign currency had required the approval of the Reserve Bank of India; now, converting enough for a trip abroad meant a visit to the local Thomas Cook office.

With the end of the License-Permit Raj, the spiritual India of Gandhi and the socialist India of Nehru was razed and rebuilt in Bombay's image: energetic, acquisitive, worldly. But no place in India was transformed by the reforms as much as Bombay itself, the home of India's stock exchange, its film industry, and its international air hub. In the postreform era, Bombay would reclaim its historic role as a showcase of, and yardstick for, a developing India, piling up triumphs and failures on each side of the scale. As Manmohan Singh, who rose to become India's prime minister in 2004, summed up the stakes, "If Mumbai fails, then India fails."

The initial euphoria among well-to-do Bombayites after what they called "the golden summer of 1991" did not last. The astounding early 1992 Bombay Stock Exchange boom, in which the Indian stock index, the SENSEX, doubled in three months, proved to be powered by more than just the IPO reforms. In a cycle reminiscent of the 1860s "Share Mania," the stock market collapsed just as spectacularly as it had risen when self-made Jain stockbroker, Harshad Mehta, was exposed for goosing share prices by illegally buying massive quantities of stock with commercial bank deposits. But in the gold rush environment, the obvious lesson that India had swung wildly from a system of stifling overregulation to one of dangerous underregulation went unheeded.

The following year, a series of coordinated bomb attacks rocked the city. The most deadly struck the Bombay Stock Exchange itself, killing several dozen traders and clerks. With the 1993 bombings, Bombay's international elite, sipping their Cokes and calling their stockbrokers and travel agents on their brand-new telephones, could no longer take solace in being insulated from the problems of the rural migrants who made up the majority of their city's population. Hindu-Muslim tension had long plagued India, but in the new world of Bombay, as the English-speaking globalized elite pulled away, enjoying Western consumer goods like computers that cost more than they paid their maids and drivers in a year, the tensions became especially acute. Frustrations simmered in the *chawls* where lifelong jobs in the unionized mills and formerly state-owned enterprises were disappearing. Laid-off industrial workers invariably lacked the English skills needed for the new business process outsourcing jobs that soon multiplied as Western multinationals sent back-office work to the cheapest English-speaking workforce on earth.

Once organized as industrial workers into unions affiliated with various left-wing political parties, working-class Bombayites were now organized along ethnic and religious lines into criminal gangs and political parties that often crossed the line into being hate groups. In the Nehruvian period, for all its practical failures, there was a sense that Indians would rise or fall as one people. Now narrower definitions of peoplehood—ethnic and religious—were reasserting themselves. Though the beginnings of this transformation were evident as early as the 1950s in linguistic battles that set Marathi-speaking workers against their Gujarati-speaking bosses, only in the postreform period was the transition "from red to saffron," the signature colors of left-wing radicalism and Hindu nationalism, completed.

The era's communal tensions had begun inland, in Uttar Pradesh, one of the least developed states in India, when in 1992 a mob of Hindus destroyed a mosque built, according to their beliefs, atop the birthplace of the Hindu god Ram. Hindu-Muslim rioting soon spread to cities across India, including Bombay, where hundreds were killed, the majority of them Muslims. To avenge the massacre of his Muslim coreligionists, Bombay mob boss Dawood Ibrahim, head of the eponymous D-Company, had plotted the Stock Exchange bombing from his safe haven in Dubai, where he had amassed an illicit billion-dollar fortune smuggling gold to Bombay during the License-Permit Raj. In the freewheeling Gulf city-state, Ibrahim had become famous for using his connections as an underworld Bollywood film financier to recreate glamorous Bombay at lavish parties studded with Bollywood starlets.

With communal tensions rising, in 1995 the Marathi nationalist party, Shiv Sena, won control of both the Bombay city and Maharashtra state government with a xenophobic message of Maharashtra for the Marathis, the ethno-linguistic group indigenous to the region just over the creek. The party, with its trademark saffron banners, was the brainchild of Bal Thackeray, a political cartoonist, ethnic chauvinist, and open admirer of Hitler. Bal's father had anglicized the family name to that of the Victorian novelist, William Makepeace Thackeray, out of a desire to make the family more modern. In an act of posthumous revenge, Bal Thackeray renamed his father's city, replacing the Anglo-Portuguese name, Bombay, with the Marathi name, Mumbai, derived from the locally worshipped Hindu goddess Mumba Devi.

While Shiv Sena offered little vision for remaking the economic and social fabric of the city on behalf of its struggling constituents, it had an inexhaustible imagination for renaming it.

All across the metropolis, British colonial names were replaced with Indian ones. By the late 1990s, the city was entertaining fifty road-renaming proposals a month. Major landmarks were also renamed, the most prominent for Chhatrapati Shivaji, a local Marathi hero who retook the region from the Muslim Mughal emperors in the seventeenth century. Victoria Terminus was renamed Chhatrapati Shivaji Terminus; the Prince of Wales Museum of Indian antiquities became the Chhatrapati Shivaji Museum; and both the domestic and international airports were renamed after Chhatrapati Shivaji.

Clearly the people who would support a harebrained scheme to give both airports the same name didn't fly very often. Indeed, Shiv Sena was a movement more deeply driven by class resentments than ethno-linguistic and religious identity. Maharashtrians had always made up the majority of Bombay's working class, while other ethnic and religious groups, notably Parsis, Jains, and Gujaratis, were typically the traders and industrialists. Fifty years after independence, the prime target of these anticolonial name changes was not the long-departed British but the Anglophone Mumbai elite that was reascendant in Singh's era of economic reform. And though many educated Mumbaikars would continue to call the city Bombay, noting the inanity of Shiv Sena's claim to a membership base of "sons of the soil" in a city where so much of the soil was reclaimed from the sea by the British, the elites were similarly at a loss to propose plans for healing the city's divisions. For all the bluster of a rising global India, few had faith in the notion that the city could be made to work for everyone. Even the former head of the chamber of commerce group, Bombay First, whose public relations materials proudly boast that though the city accounts for just 2 percent of India's population, it generates 38 percent of the nation's GDP, conceded that a Mumbai where every resident had electricity and running water was a utopian idea.

During the Nehruvian period, Bollywood's images of a glamorous Bombay had served as the de facto political opposition. But once that opposition triumphed with the 1991 reforms, the Bollywood vision was enacted all too literally. Rather than envisaging a new iteration of global Mumbai, a worthy heir to Governor Frere's nineteenth-century Victorian Gothic city and the Indian-designed Art Deco reclamation neighborhoods of the preindependence period, the self-proclaimed "global Indians" of today have contented themselves to live in real-life Bollywood sets. Rather than remake their city, they have built walled luxury zones where they can hide from the poverty, decay, and dysfunction that all the new finance and showbiz wealth at the top has done nothing to ameliorate. To build the great Mumbai modernities of the past, the city had channeled the market's bounty into a cohesive vision via government planning and private philanthropy. But in reaction against decades of Nehruvian stagnation, planning has become a dirty word in contemporary Mumbai. And rebelling against decades of Gandhian self-abnegation, philanthropy has become a lost art as Mumbai's new class of superrich compete to build helipad-topped skyscrapers for themselves rather than a stunning modern city for their nation.

In *Slumdog Millionaire*, the 2008 blockbuster film that reintroduced Mumbai to the world, the protagonist, Jamal, and his brother, Salim, gasp at the prowess of neocapitalist India while looking out across a development of neoclassical high-rise towers. To a Western audience, the development looks like Caesars Palace in Las Vegas—only much, much bigger. "Can you believe it?" Salim asks. "This was our slum. We lived just there, huh? Now it is business, apartments, call centres. . . . Fuck USA, fuck China. India is at the centre of the world now."

The fantastical cluster of thirty-story columned high-rises, looking like ancient Greek temples stretched into modern skyscrapers, is no computer-generated image. It is an actual real estate development set on parkland abutting a British-built reservoir several miles north of the historic heart of the city. Called Hiranandani Gardens, it is named for the real estate developers who built it, the billionaire Hiranandani brothers. The location scouts for *Slumdog* surely picked the project for its stunning size and flamboyant architecture. But the choice was also historically astute for a representation of postreform Mumbai. The development's first building was begun in the "golden" year of 1991. Since then, as India's economy has boomed, scrapping the "Hindu rate of growth" for blistering figures that have run as high as 8.9 percent a year, dozens of buildings, with names like the Sovereign, the Brentwood, and Evita, have been added to the development, with still more under construction. Real estate is big business in India's financial hub, where office rents run twice Manhattan's rates and apartment rents fall in between London and Paris. In addition to housing one hundred thousand well-to-do Mumbaikars, Hiranandani Gardens hosts the satellite offices of 150 multinational corporations, including J. P. Morgan, Credit Suisse, and Colgate-Palmolive, all testament to the flood of international investment that has swept Mumbai since 1991. If Victorian Frere Town embodied early Raj-era Bombay and Art Deco row the global Bombay of the first half of the twentieth century, the island within the island city that is Hiranandani Gardens embodies the reglobalizing Mumbai of today.

Reforms to unleash the real estate market have so empowered developers that comprehensive planning has become all but illegal. Meanwhile, the city's Shiv Sena–led government has happily washed its hands of the responsibility for providing public services. As a result, on greenfield development like Hiranandani Gardens, the developer, not the government, is responsible for building the infrastructure, like streets and sanitation systems, and even social institutions like schools and hospitals.

At the center of Hiranandani Gardens sits Nirvana Park, a

landscaped green space boasting palm trees and a koi pond. But even the park is not a public institution; it is a private facility that charges admission and, according to a sign, "reserves the right to deny admission to anybody." And all its amenities can't quite make up for the stench emanating from the sewage treatment plant at its center. Because the development is responsible for its own waste management, the dirty work of sewage treatment is done, malodorously, on-site.

Even in central Mumbai, every new high-rise building is required to have, essentially, its own private park; zoning rules mandate that each tower be set back from the street in green space. The idea that the government would plan the city and build public parks at reasonable intervals for everyone to enjoy is now seen as a quixotic, antiquated notion. The city has gone from a system in which it expected the government to plan everything and the private sector to provide nothing to one in which it expects the private sector to provide everything and the government to plan nothing. In the throes of a postsocialist purge, Mumbai's vision of the future is a city with no vision at all—nothing more than the sum of its real estate deals.

The architect behind so many of the one-off Bollywood-set spectacles that now dot contemporary Mumbai, including Hiranandani Gardens, is Hafeez Contractor, a locally born Parsi who trained at Columbia University in New York and operates out of a cramped office in Mumbai's historic downtown financial district. (The surname "Contractor" suggests a family background in the building trades.) Contractor first made a name for himself during the License-Permit Raj, devising ingenious solutions for developers hemmed in by the square footage limits then in place on luxury apartments. To skirt the regulations, Contractor would add balconies, which were exempted from the rules, and skillfully arrange rooms to create the impression of vast spaces.

When the reforms removed those limits, Contractor quickly

adapted to the new market conditions. An architectural Zelig, Contractor's buildings have no defined style. If the man has opinions on matters of taste, he keeps them to himself. He has designed everything from a contemporary campus for a tech company that looks like a UFO has landed in Maharashtra to a corporate educational facility that cribs St. Peter's Cathedral at the Vatican, right down to the colonnade-encircled square. Touring Washington DC, Surendra Hiranandani, of the family real estate firm Hiranandani Upscale, saw a new Georgetown University law school building and reportedly raved to his host, "I'll have Hafeez build me one of those."

Contractor's philosophy is market nihilism—he will build anything, for anyone, in any style, as long as the checks clear. And what his clients typically want is a funhouse-mirror image of the West transposed onto the East—like Carlo Rossi's more-Western-than-the-West neoclassical St. Petersburg edifices taken to their most unhinged extreme. Even as the Hiranandani brothers' tastes have developed since the 1990s, they're still building stretch-limo Greek temples to suit customers' demands. If the newer buildings didn't look like the older buildings, Surendra Hiranandani explained, customers will complain, "Their building has Doric columns and mine does not."

The archetypal customer who makes such demands is the new "global Indian"—someone with cousins in Singapore and Houston who often feels more at ease shopping on the streets of London and New York than in the bazaars of the subcontinent across the creek. Rather than clean the streets of Mumbai to even a New York standard of "cleanliness," a task routinely dismissed as impossible, the Mumbai elite buys itself snippets of sanitation and functionality in compounds like Hiranandani Gardens. Unlike in congested central Mumbai, where rich and poor live cheek by jowl, in Hiranandani Gardens the entire development is solely for the well-to-do. The slum that is home to the development's gardeners and drivers and maids is out of sight, hidden behind the hill that rises alongside the development. As one global Indian, an architect who had studied in Colorado and worked in California, gushed, "Hiranandani Gardens makes me feel like I'm back in L.A. with the wide streets and the shops and everything so clean."

In Hiranandani Gardens, the raucous street life that typifies Mumbai is excised. There is not a single hawker on the streets selling *vada pao*, the city's signature vegetarian street snack that combines the archetypal Indian appetizer, a chutney-topped *vada* potato fritter, with the archetypal Western staple, bread, called *pao* in Portuguese. Three-wheeled auto-rickshaws incongruously roll down Technology Street past the Rolls-Royce dealership and circle roundabouts with green landscaping topped by triumphal Roman columns and carved Pacific Northwestern totem poles. Prosperous Mumbaikars dine in a spotless, air-conditioned Pizza Hut that occupies the ground floor of a four-story Roman temple–inspired shopping mall that looks like a set from the movie *Gladiator*. While Sir Bartle Frere once demanded a university to rival Oxford and Cambridge for his global economic and cultural hub, today's Mumbai builders content themselves with a Bollywood-backlot Pizza Hut that outdoes the strip malls of Phoenix and Atlanta.

Of course in the West, Pizza Huts are not located in ersatz Roman temples—not even in Las Vegas. The development is less a copy of the West than a fantasy of the West whose totemic power of modernity—even in its most mundane incarnations— appeals to its upscale Indian customers. It is a West as experienced by the global Indian, where all its differences from India rise to the fore and the distinctness of the Indian city, most notably its vibrant informal commerce, is dismissed as an embarrassment that must be expunged. Hiranandani Gardens conjures the West as experienced by its creator, Hafeez Contractor, who waxes nostalgic about driving—not walking—past Hyde Park in London and enjoying unimpeded views of the park, in contrast to the sidewalks along the maidans in central Mumbai, which are dotted with hawkers: "You go to London . . . you drive past Hyde Park you say 'wow.' . . . You see the beautiful Hyde Park. Today I pass by all the maidans, I see only shop, shop, shop, shop. All illegal shops. I go down[stairs from my office], the guy's selling *vada pao*. Illegal shop."

The question of how to forge an Indian architecture for a modern India does not seem to preoccupy either architect or client. In the age of globalization, with an Indian diaspora numbering in the tens of millions, opting to live in Mumbai in itself has become an assertion of Indian identity. For most of the city's history, moving from one's native village to the great international metropolis was a way to turn one's back on India. Today, moving to (or staying in) Mumbai is a way for global Indians, enamored with the West but rooted in India, to approximate a Western standard of living in their homeland. Even as they are shuttled from ersatz Western space to ersatz Western space, chauffeured from an apartment in Hiranandani Gardens to an office in Mindspace, an antiseptic outsourcing business development, to an upscale mall and then to a nightclub to spend in a night what their driver makes in a month, it is a life indisputably more Indian than that of their Singapore-based cousins.

For the Mumbai elite, it is the enduring traditions of personal life—most centrally marriage—not public life that are seen as the key to identity. While so-called cosmopolitan personal ads, where caste and religion are not specified, are more common in Mumbai than in other cities, arranged marriages are still the norm even for Mumbai's global Indians. The rise of women in the workplace and the university, where women now make up 42 percent of graduates, has done little to erode the traditional marriage system; female graduates of prestigious universities simply list their degrees in their matrimonial ads and expect a lower dowry demand in return. While Valentine's Day has caught on in Mumbai—to the dismay of Shiv Sena, which has taken to torching pink paper hearts in protest—much of the dating is a form of playacting, a Western rite drained of its actual meaning. Couples out on "dates" are often betrothed in all but name. Only the most cosmopolitan Mumbaikars engage in what Westerners would recognize as dating.

Hafeez Contractor's developments provide global Indians with the perfect sets on which to stage their playacting versions of Western life—Hiranandani Gardens' imperial Roman Pizza Hut is an ideal place for a nondate date on Valentine's Day. As Dhiru Thadani, a Bombay-born-and-raised, Washington DC–based urban planner who worked with Contractor on Hiranandani Gardens, explained, "He [Contractor] really plays into the Indian ego that it has to be the tallest, it has to be the most outrageous, the most colorful, whatever the theme is. Like in every developing country, you don't appreciate what you've got, you think what's outside there is good stuff—what they're doing in America—and there's this real fear of appearing backwards [that] no one admits." But as Thadani rightly pointed out, you don't have to be a trained architect to sense the fakeness of Contractor's buildings. Anyone seeing a column going up thirty stories knows intuitively that it's not actually holding up the building, that it's just wallpaper on a steel-and-concrete structure. "I'm not a stickler on these things but these are so bad, this is so much of a cartoon, I think it's quite jarring. . . . I don't consider what he [Contractor] does architecture. I consider it fashion." Fashion though it may be, in contemporary Mumbai, it is very much in vogue.

The allure of the global Indian's retreat into fantasy can only be understood by walking the streets of Mumbai, whose unique form of filth constitutes a parable of postreform India's failures.

The changes of 1991 opened India up to all manner of foreign consumer goods while simultaneously allowing the government to wash its hands of the responsibility for creating a sanitation system to deal with all the waste. While traditionally, Indian street snacks came in easily biodegradable materials—simple bowls crafted from a banana leaf and toothpicks, clay teacups that could be dropped, stepped on, and returned dust-to-dust—the branded snack packaging produced by Western corporations and their local imitators lasts much longer. The streets of Mumbai are now strewn with bags from long-ago-eaten potato chips and wrappers from long-ago-spitted *paan*, a chewing tobacco–like betel-nut derivative that was once leaf wrapped but is now sold in shiny foil packaging. The only real sanitation system, such as it is, is homeless street children, known as ragpickers, who collect the trash, sort it, and sell the raw materials.

The street children are the collateral damage of the human flood that had hit Mumbai. The economic boom that has birthed a new moneyed class has also attracted newcomers from the countryside to the city, seeking to serve them. In the decade after the reforms, the overall metropolitan region grew by a third. The Indian constitution guarantees all Indians freedom of movement throughout the country, and subsidized interstate rail rates mean that one can travel from one end of the subcontinent to another in the lowest class (open to both human and animal passengers) for about ten US dollars. Armies of three-dollar-a-day maids and drivers—or those who simply hope to become them—have flocked into Mumbai. Being so impoverished, while living in one of the world's most expensive cities, they have nowhere to go but the slums. Even the lowest-end "hotels"—two-dollar-a-night bunk beds packed into decrepit building hallways—are beyond their means.

It is telling that Mumbaikars will only use the term *slum* to describe homemade housing jury-rigged by the inhabitants. No formally built structures, no matter how run down, are ever tarred with the term. And the handmade housing that Mumbaikars term slums is where most Mumbaikars live. With their open sewers and inadequate facilities, illness is rampant. In Dharavi, Mumbai's (and indeed Asia's) largest slum, home to between six hundred thousand and a million people, it is estimated that there is one working toilet for every one thousand residents. Life expectancy in Mumbai is a full seven years below the already-bleak Indian average, not even in the top one hundred countries worldwide. Even in the city's poshest districts, shantytowns fill any available unclaimed space. A small informal settlement shockingly sits on the same street as the most expensive private home in the world, oil refinery baron Mukesh Ambani's recently completed, American-designed, twenty-seven-story personal high-rise that cost an estimated $1 billion to build.

Ambani's vertical mansion, named Antilia, looks down on the seafront, the site of both the city's best sunset views and its most debased phantasmagoria of desperation, the Haji Ali shrine. A Muslim monument on a small offshore island, Haji Ali, becomes the site of a kind of inverse beauty contest each day when it is connected to the main island of Mumbai by a causeway at low tide. As the tide goes out, deformed beggars soliciting zakat, the charitable contributions required of all believing Muslims, line up on the causeway, publicly displaying their ailments in de facto free market competition. As the pilgrim progresses toward the shrine, elephantiasis and late-stage leprosy are set against the self-inflicted wounds of the career beggar. The dark man with the quivering leg stump baking facedown in the sun as he fervently repeats the first Arabic phrase of the Muslim declaration of faith, "There is no god but God, there is no god but God," makes one wonder if there even is a God looking down on all of this. Or just Mukesh Ambani.

Zakat is no substitute for a functional city administration.

Mumbai groans under the weight of more and more people and more and more stuff. While major cities in other developing countries, most notably Shanghai, have made massive infrastructure improvements, in Mumbai little has been improved since the days of the Raj, despite now supporting a metropolitan population of twenty million, up from four million at independence. The train from Chhatrapati Shivaji Terminus (formerly Victoria Terminus) to Thane, a city on the mainland just over the creek, takes fifty-five minutes today, a scant improvement over 1869, when it took one hour and twenty minutes. In the time Mumbai has struggled to plan and build a single new metro line, Shanghai has built the world's largest subway system.

Every year, the local commuter trains are overwhelmed by more passengers. In the 1990s alone, the average number of passengers on the system's nine-car trains increased by a third, to 4,500 per train. The cars, which have no air-conditioning despite the tropical heat, have their doors bolted open for ventilation. At rush hour, people are so packed in that they become a single organic mass, swaying with the train car as foolhardy young men hang out of the doors for relief. Each day, nearly a dozen people are killed on the train system, typically by hanging out of open doors with too much abandon or underestimating the time it takes to scurry across the tracks before an approaching train. Since the land along the tracks is Mumbai's most significant strip of unclaimed space, it is covered from end to end with slums.

Deaths are so routine on the system that the cleanup procedure works with at least as much precision as the transit system itself. Stations are equipped with gurneys and staff whose responsibilities include removing bodies from the tracks. A local kite dealer provides major stations with free clean white shrouds as a philanthropic gesture. An utterly mundane occurrence, passengers do not even comment, sweltering in the stagnant air of the stopped train in silence. It is bad form—and bad karma—to grumble about being late. Besides, everyone in Mumbai has had the experience of being late on account of a train death, so the tardiness is easily forgiven.

Even the city's proudest contemporary infrastructure improvements betray a deeper sense of hopelessness. In a city where visitors are advised deadpan that rush hour lasts from 9:00 a.m. to 1:00 p.m. and from 4:00 p.m. to 11:00 p.m., the city's most highly touted new public works project is the $350 million Rajiv Gandhi Sea Link, a sleek white bridge to nowhere that connects two contiguous pieces of land. The bridge, essentially an offshore connector road, is the traffic circulation equivalent of a heart bypass, where an existing artery is so clogged that an alternate route is added. The efficient solution—building an onshore expressway—was off the table because it would involve evictions, an impossibility in a country whose judicial system assiduously protects squatters' rights. The "slumdogs" are someone's constituents, called "vote banks," and decades-long lawsuits are generally necessary to evict them. Cognizant that their power comes from the ballot box, Mumbai's slum dwellers have near-perfect voter turnout while the city's rich all but boycott elections and rely on their wealth to protect them. Of course, the preposterous bridge boondoggle is wildly popular with the nonvoting chauffeured class of Mumbaikars, as it has cut nearly an hour off the habitual global Indian's journey from the airport to the financial district.

For humble pedestrians, the city has likewise built humbler bridges to nowhere. In a new office district built on former industrial land dotted with immovable slums, the city has erected "skywalks"—essentially elevated sidewalks. The skywalks connect the different parts of the office district that are already connected by streets. The key is that they allow pedestrians to walk in a shaded, elevated walkway over the slums rather than through them. Two flights of stairs up in the air, the walkways afford views of tarp shantytown roofs; goats picking through makeshift garbage dumps; a fetid, trash-strewn river of sewage; and a slum main street of three-story handmade buildings, strewn with green streamers to mark it as a Muslim slum rather than a Hindu one. The bridges to nowhere bespeak a strategy of urban triage, a dispiriting sense that twenty-first-century Mumbai's problems cannot be solved—only cauterized.

Embodying Mumbai at its most bizarre are building projects that mix slum redevelopment with luxury housing, combining the city's immovable poverty with its unfathomable wealth. For these urban infill projects, a developer is given a plot covered in shantytowns and the right to clear it for market-rate luxury housing in exchange for rehousing the slum dwellers on-site in tiny two-room, midrise apartments—one room for sitting and sleeping, the other, a kitchen-cum-bathroom, for everything else. It is a "solution" that could only be born in Mumbai, where democracy means that no one can ever be moved and where the legacy of the caste system means that living next to a slum doesn't necessarily diminish the status of the wealthy any more than living next to a luxury tower raises the status of the poor.

The most famous of these developments are the twin missile-shaped high-rises that are currently the tallest buildings on the Mumbai skyline. They rise up like a vision of Oz at the end of Falkland Road, the city's most notorious red-light district where each night women, some in the district's infamous viewing cages, engage in the world's oldest profession for rates beginning at fifty rupees (US$1). Designed by Hafeez Contractor and given a retro name—Imperial Towers—the apartments go for as much as $20 million. The floor-to-ceiling windows in the multi-million-dollar units look down on the bare-bones concrete slabs of the slum redevelopment housing below. The rain- and filth-stained rehousing towers, arranged around a barren dirt courtyard with a rickety slide and jungle gym, already look decades old. In the last remnants of the soon-to-be-leveled slum, the dark little girl clutching the white doll in an alleyway covered with saffron Shiv

Sena posters undercuts the hopes that any of this offers a real solution to the city's problems. So do the jobless boys playing cricket in the courtyard—and the employed boys who work construction, shoveling earth while standing atop a pile of mud in flip-flops.

The popularity of these slum redevelopment projects has birthed a larger ambition to remake entire neighborhoods on the same ad hoc model, the sum of several contiguous parcel-by-parcel redevelopments. A newly passed Mumbai exemption from India's politically untouchable rent-control rules established the neighborhood redevelopment process: if 70 percent of tenants in a building agree, a real estate developer can demolish their building and rehouse them in new apartments on-site in exchange for the opportunity to build new market-rate units. The larger the plot, the higher the developers can build, so there is an incentive to assemble large parcels out of several contiguous buildings. The wheels of the democratic process among the tenants are widely reputed to be greased with developers' bribes.

The Princess Street corridor (now renamed Shamaldas Gandhi Marg), a mix of bazaars, working-class *chawls*, and middle-class apartments just north of downtown that had been built in the early twentieth century by the Bombay City Improvement Trust, is being used as the guinea pig for the redevelopment process. It is an elegant neighborhood despite the disrepair, built on the historic "black town" that has hosted the city's busiest bazaars since the days of the fort. The neighborhood's incongruous mix of European buildings and Indian commerce is quintessentially Mumbai. Each day, when traders flock into the markets by train, the neighborhood becomes, for the duration of the workday, the most crowded place on the planet. Cars honk incessantly as they crawl down alleyways packed with handcarts piled high with sacks of goods—one man pulling from the front, two others pushing from the rear. The buildings are covered with hand-painted billboards for the various shops, but peeking out between the signs are glimpses of the elegant balconies and neoclassical stone-carved façades of the century-old buildings.

The renderings of the proposed redevelopment prepared by the Remaking of Mumbai Federation, a developer-backed nongovernmental organization, look like Pudong on the Arabian Sea. Inside the redevelopment group's office, a giant poster of the iconic skyscrapers of Pudong is tacked to the wall next to a map depicting plans for this section of Mumbai, similarly filled with skyscrapers isolated from the street on superblocks. Though the plans call for preserving individual historic buildings and religious sites, the vibrant life of the streets—the urban phenomenon that makes Mumbai Mumbai—is slated to be excised. Skywalks will keep the streets safe and empty for cars. Tragically, the city's historic buildings and street life have become inexorably linked in most Mumbaikars' minds with the filth and dilapidation that currently accompany them, and rehabilitation has become synonymous with demolition. Few have any vision of the city improved without being destroyed. Besides, there is less money in that.

Dissenting voices, like the architecture trainees at the Sir JJ School of Art, whose nineteenth-century students carved the decorative sculptures on the great Victorian Gothic edifices of the city, are largely ignored. A pair of students, Harshavardhan Jatkar and Priyanka Talreja, who were given a class assignment to create an alternate redevelopment plan for the area, surveyed the people in the neighborhood and created detailed maps illustrating the patchwork diversity of the area's religions, classes, and languages. The pair suggested restoring the historic structures of the Princess Street corridor and encouraging high-rise development in less historic, suburban areas. "We understand it's a little utopian," Jatkar conceded, "because it would give less benefit to the builders." But, the pair pointed out, the official plan pushed by the Remaking of Mumbai Federation is quixotic in its own way. Imitating Pudong ignores the character of the people who inhabit the city. "Our culture is about street commerce," Talreja said, noting that Mumbai's shopping malls, "which are merely copied from the West," are relatively empty compared to its teeming street bazaars. In the city's last era of globalization, it took the younger generation to forge an Indian vision of modernity. If these Sir JJ School architecture students are any indication, perhaps history will repeat itself and Mumbaikars will stop fighting about whether to copy China or America and instead reinvent what it means to be Indian.

What is ultimately so dispiriting about the self-regarding plans for contemporary Mumbai—Hiranandani Gardens, the Rajiv Gandhi Sea Link, the redevelopment of the Princess Street neighborhood—is how unambitious they ultimately are. What impresses in Pudong is not merely its skyscrapers—cities all over the world have skyscrapers—but its infrastructure of trains and bridges, the best in the world. And what is most remarkable about the cities of the West is not that they have multi-million-dollar apartments—Mumbai has those, too—it is that you can drink the tap water. While neocapitalist Mumbai has endless blueprints for luxury housing and corporate offices, it has no workable plan to give all of its people toilets. In reform-era Mumbai, the whole concept of public investment has been lost. Neighborhood redevelopment just means a series of contiguous private redevelopments; green space does not mean public parks but rather the private lawns around apartment buildings. The contemporary city, seen as nothing more than a series of privately held parcels, has devolved back to its pre-Raj roots when it was a socially dynamic place, but as French visitor Louis Rousselet complained in the early 1860s, "It cannot be considered a city, in the full acceptation of the term; it is rather a conglomeration of vast districts, situated a short distance from each other, on an island which gives them a generic name."

In 2003, a report commissioned by Bombay First, the business group, and issued by the US-based consulting firm McKinsey & Company, entitled *Vision Mumbai: Transforming Mumbai into a World-Class City*, sparked controversy for suggesting that Mumbai get back on track by modeling its growth on Shanghai's. Indian pundits and intellectuals pilloried the report as a blueprint for authoritarianism and argued that India's democratic traditions meant it could never model its development on a city, however impressive, built by Communist Party fiat. Touching the raw nerve of the India-China rivalry, the report's other key model city—Cleveland—got almost no notice. But as the report clearly explained, Mumbai would be wise to study "the efforts of two international cities—Cleveland and Shanghai—that became world-class." Alongside the building of Pudong, the McKinsey report touted a generation of waterfront and downtown redevelopment projects in Cleveland.

Just months after the McKinsey report was issued, the US Census Bureau announced that Cleveland had become America's poorest city, with nearly one in three residents living in poverty. For all of the prominence of its world-class institutions—the Cleveland Clinic and the Cleveland Symphony among them—and its stable, democratic governance, Cleveland was failing its people. The truly frightening possibility for Mumbai, the financial hub of a stable democracy, is that it become a city of world-class institutions walled off behind fences where unconscionable numbers of people live in poverty. The specter haunting Mumbai is not that it trades efficiency for authoritarianism like Shanghai, but that it trades its historic ambitions to be the *urbs prima in Indis* and contents itself with being "the Cleveland of the East."

Just as the American census bureau's pronouncement had shocked Cleveland, in 2011 an announcement from the Indian census bureau stunned Mumbai: the population of Mumbai island, it found, was in decline. While growth in the wider suburban region continued, the migratory tides lapping up against the man-made island city had reversed. Presumably word had reached village India that the glowing vision of Mumbai they saw in Bollywood movies didn't stack up with "Slumbay" realities.

The 2011 census recalls that of 1901, under the Raj, which similarly showed a shocking decline in the population of Bombay island. Back then, the authorities responded with a comprehensive plan of urban improvements to bring the *urbs prima* into the new century and put it back on the ascent. The current Mumbai government has yet to propose anything comparable. But the slowing of migration does provide the city with an opportunity to figure out what twenty-first-century Mumbai should look like, and its tremendous new wealth provides the resources to make those plans a reality, if only the city will seize it.

Even in Mumbai's current beleaguered state, the idea of the city remains a powerful one. South Asia still looks to Mumbai as a symbol of modernity, cosmopolitanism, and the region's engagement with the wider world—for both good and ill, as the 2008 Mumbai terrorist attacks showed. More than just an attack on Mumbaikars, the coordinated strikes by Islamist radicals were an attack on the urban fabric of Mumbai: terrorists targeted the city's greatest icons, including Chhatrapati Shivaji Terminus (formerly Victoria Terminus) and the Taj Mahal Hotel. Notably, the marauders did not strike at a single post-1991 monument, like the Imperial Towers or the Rajiv Gandhi Sea Link. Utterly uninspiring, these landmarks fail to give voice to the ambitions and meaning of Mumbai. To the terrorists, they were not even worth destroying. But Mumbai—the idea as much as the city itself—still drew their fire. With its unique history, Mumbai long ago had greatness thrust upon it. The only question is whether the metropolis can yet again build the Indian future, whether the *urbs prima in Indis* will live up to its destiny.

# DUBAI INC. PROUDLY PRESENTS THE INTERNATIONAL CITY™

## Dubai, 1981–Present

"Downtown Dubai" development, seen from the Burj Khalifa

With Sheikh Rashid sidelined by his debilitating 1981 stroke, it was left to his sons, chief among them his third born, Sheikh Mohammed (then thirty-one), to transform Dubai from a regional hub into a global one. Dubai had been a majority foreign born city since the 1970s, but under Sheikh Mohammed's leadership, it would become the ultimate city of immigrants, where fully 96 percent of the population came from somewhere else. Mohammed dreamed Dubai into a pinnacle of modernity: the entire world in one city.

A tireless, media-obsessed booster for Dubai, Mohammed outdid his father, Rashid, through a scarcely concealed edifice complex. First, Mohammed demanded a building taller than any in Europe—the silvery, triangle-peaked Emirates Towers, completed in 2000—and then the tallest tower in the world, the Burj Khalifa, opened in 2010. A compulsive, hands-on manager, Sheikh Mohammed became known for keeping tabs on his city by driving around (sans chauffeur) in a white Mercedes SUV bearing the license plate "DUBAI 1." His vanity plate summed up his goal for Dubai. "I want it to be number one," he told an American television reporter in 2007. "Not in the region, but in the world." More specifically, in his 2006 book, with its inspirational business-lit title *My Vision: Challenges in the Race for Excellence*, Mohammed declared that Dubai should elevate itself to "a par with the world's most prestigious financial centers, including London and New York." While these statements smack of hubris and pride before the fall, there is merit in having outsized aims. As the early twentieth-century planner who mapped out Chicago—another upstart city that went on to build the world's tallest building—famously said, "Make no little plans; they have no magic to stir men's blood and probably themselves will not be realized. Make big plans; aim high in hope and work."

As the locomotive built Daniel Burnham's Chicago, the jetliner built Sheikh Mohammed's Dubai. In 1974, Sheikh Rashid tasked the young Mohammed with overseeing the growth of Dubai International Airport. In the 1980s, Mohammed tapped British Airways veteran Maurice Flanagan to launch Emirates airline, which would become an archetype of the Dubai model: a state-owned company managed by Western experts that would thrive in open international competition.

In the early years, Emirates just linked Dubai to its surrounding region. Saudis and Iranians came to shop and enjoy the libertine nightlife banned in their native theocracies. Entrepreneurial Russians arrived to empty Dubai's store shelves and resell the items back home during the chaos of the Soviet collapse and post-Soviet free fall. By 1990, Emirates was flying to major hubs like London, Frankfurt, and Singapore, taking advantage of the fact that most of the world's population lives within a reasonable flying time of the city-state. As Emirates grew, it became a kind of octopus, grabbing ever more far-flung parts of the world and drawing them to Dubai. Lured by the prospect of tax-free salaries, some of the international businessmen who visited, stayed. (Many countries, including the United Kingdom, do not tax their expatriate nationals' earnings; the United States taxes foreign-earned incomes above $91,500.) By 1995, roughly twenty thousand Britons lived in the emirate, enjoying the familiarity of a former colony as the first wave of expatriate "Dubailanders" that would become a flood of First World consultants, architects, and bankers in the new century.

Of course, aviation in the world's least stable region could never just be about route maps and stewardess uniforms. (As the UAE has no antidiscrimination law, by company policy, Emirates prefers not to hire male flight attendants.) Dubai was a common refueling stop for hijacked jets, and Sheikh Mohammed became one of the world's most experienced hostage negotiators. In dealings with fearsome groups including the (pre-Oslo) Palestine Liberation Organization, Japanese Red Army, and Baader-Meinhof Gang, an underground cell of West German radicals, Mohammed never lost a passenger. The young sheikh's triumphs barely made the international news, but they foreshadowed a development strategy that would serve his city well: Dubai would be an island of stability in a wealthy but volatile region, headed by a businessman/autocrat who thrived on high-stakes negotiations. To achieve liftoff, Dubai just needed a spark. That spark would be the most devastating hijacking of them all: 9/11.

Though only a sole Emirati was among the 9/11 hijackers, Dubai was crucial to the attacks. Since Dubai is the air hub of the Middle East, the majority of the perpetrators entered the United States via Dubai. And because Dubai is the financial hub of the Gulf, the money that funded the plot flowed through its banks. Moreover, in the run-up to the attacks, the Emirati elite had protected al-Qaeda founder Osama bin Laden, if, perhaps, unwittingly. In 1999, the CIA abandoned an opportunity to execute bin Laden on a hunting trip because they believed Emirati royalty were leading the expedition. A cruise missile attack "might have wiped out half of the UAE royal family," CIA chief George Tenet later testified. Indeed, until President George W. Bush's post-9/11 declaration—"Either you are with us or you are with the terrorists"—the Emirati royals really were with both; the UAE played the seemingly impossible game of being friends with both the Americans, for whom Dubai serves as the largest overseas naval port, and the man who had declared war on America. Hardly dyed-in-the-wool jihadis, the Emirati royals likely saw bin Laden as an eccentric buddy—part of their social milieu of Gulf Arab millionaire heirs but with an added frisson of radical chic.

Considering the UAE's less-than-hostile relationship with bin Laden as well as the Taliban (the UAE was one of just three countries that recognized the Taliban as the legitimate rulers of Afghanistan), the 9/11 attacks might have been a blow to Dubai's global reputation. Instead, it was a boon, setting off massive growth that was only halted by the global financial crisis. The anti-money-laundering provisions of the Patriot Act, passed in the wake of 9/11, made investing in the United States less appealing to wealthy Gulf Arabs. Saudis alone are estimated to have pulled over $300 billion in assets out of the United States. At the same time, the instability in the Middle East set off by the attacks and the subsequent American invasions of Afghanistan and Iraq helped raise the price of oil, which already had been creeping upward in response to increasing demand in developing economies like China and India. Thus, 9/11 both showered oil profits on the Gulf and ensured that those profits would be invested close to home. As the regional financial center, Dubai was the logical place to invest locally. Sheikh Mohammed moved quickly to turn the increasing capital flows into a gusher.

In 2002, Mohammed issued a land reform decree allowing foreigners to own real estate in Dubai—a first in any Gulf state. Before the reforms, Dubai had no real estate market. Land was given out under a quasi-feudal system; all land was held by the sheikhs or by favored Emirati friends upon whom the sheikhs had bestowed parcels. Everyone else—including every foreigner— was a renter. With the 2002 reform, anyone could buy a home in Dubai—an opportunity with particular appeal to wealthy families in unstable countries nearby. Loaded Lebanese afraid of another civil war back home, Indian nouveaux riches seeking respite from the poverty at their doorsteps, and Russian oligarchs banking assets stripped from operations in their decaying motherland all poured cash into Dubai properties. What Miami had long been for the elite of Latin America—a place to park wealth too risky to keep back home—Dubai became for the magnates and kleptocrats of the Middle East, North Africa, South Asia, and the former Soviet Union. The apotheosis of this trend would come in 2009, when the dictator of Azerbaijan amassed nine waterfront mansions during a two-week, $44 million buying spree—all purchased in the name of his eleven-year-old son.

With the unprecedented land reform in place, the global real estate consulting firm Jones Lang LaSalle touted Dubai, along with Dublin and Las Vegas, as its "World Winning Cities" for 2002. The report put Dubai on global investors' maps alongside the better-known capital of the Celtic Tiger and the Mojave Desert outpost that was then the fastest-growing city in the world's largest economy. All three cities experienced massive booms, but Dubai's was the most explosive.

If early St. Petersburg was a Renaissance perspective drawing brought to life on a marshy tabula rasa, Dubai was a real-life SimCity, a fantastical metropolis that looked as if it had magically leapt from an architect's laptop running the latest computer-assisted design software out onto the pristine desert. Housing developments sprouted up along the beachfront, and office towers rose along the city's massive freeway spine, Sheikh Zayed Road, in the most outlandish shapes: an enormous golf tee, a silvery sandworm, even a proposed spherical "Dubai Death Star." Architecture firms struggled to keep up with demand, importing new employees so fast that they could scarcely find desks for them all. Between 2002 and 2008, the city's population doubled and its urbanized footprint quadrupled—in part from speculation-driven land-reclamation projects reminiscent of the nineteenth-century Bombay boom, albeit in outlandish shapes of palm trees and maps of the world. In 2008, Dubai experienced as much property development as Shanghai, a city with thirteen times its population.

Through a parallel strategy designed to lure multinational companies, Sheikh Mohammed successfully turned Dubai into the global business hub of the Middle East. In the early 1980s, Mohammed had breathed new life into the languishing Jebel Ali port by declaring it Dubai's first "free zone." The term was something of a misnomer. Free zones in many countries were simply areas where companies were exempt from taxation. But in Dubai, there were no corporate or income taxes to begin with; the government was funded largely with the profits of state-owned enterprises, oil revenues, and sin taxes on alcohol. Jebel Ali Free Zone was more like a Special Economic Zone in Deng Xiaoping's China, where separate laws applied within the SEZ than beyond the gates. Beyond the borders of Jebel Ali, strict, traditional Shariah law would still govern business relations (under Shariah, for instance, those who can't pay their debts are imprisoned). But inside the new free zone, business could be done much as it was done in the West, according to a specially crafted civil legal code geared specifically toward port businesses. Jebel Ali thrived under the new regime, becoming one of the busiest ports on the planet. Today, it processes over ten million shipping containers annually.

With the success of Jebel Ali, Sheikh Mohammed began carving other free zones out of the desert, each specifically designed to woo an industry he felt would benefit Dubai. But carving Dubai up into free zones was more than just an economic development strategy. Being a single city governed under multiple legal regimes would come to define Dubai. Global cities have always struggled with how to apply laws to their diverse assemblages of people. Through its patchwork of free zones, Dubai had come up with a new answer. While in the foreign concessions of Shanghai, different people were bound by different legal codes based on their nationality, in Dubai the same people would be governed by different legal codes depending on where they were within the city. In Shanghai, extraterritoriality meant that no matter where you were in the treaty port, you were, in a legal sense, always back home; in Dubai, the free zones made traveling from neighborhood to neighborhood, in a legal sense, like moving from country to country.

The Dubai International Financial Centre (DIFC) free zone, opened in 2002, is physically set on a block of desert off of Sheikh Zayed Road. The DIFC complex, designed by San Francisco architecture firm Gensler as a massive horseshoe-shaped office building wrapped around a central twelve-story arch, soon filled up with the giants of global banking, including Citibank, HSBC, Standard Chartered, and Credit Suisse.

As with the architectural blueprints, the intellectual blueprints for the DIFC had been drawn up for the monarch by an American firm—consulting behemoth McKinsey—which advised the Dubai government to create a financial district governed by Western-style business regulations. It fell to veteran finance regulator Errol Hoopmann, who was hired away from the Australian Securities and Investments Commission in 2003, to write the legal code. "The whole concept here was to vacate 110 acres of [land of UAE] laws, just empty it of civil and commercial laws," Hoopmann explained in his Australian accent, wearing a pinstriped suit in his office atop the arch. "And then we had to write our own laws to fill up that vacuum. And those laws are based on mainly UK [regulations]—though there's an awful lot of Australian because I wrote it."

Hoopmann called the DIFC "a state within a state. . . . We compare it to the Vatican." It is a geographically accurate anal-

ogy, though in Europe, it is the tiny Vatican that is run according to religious law and the larger Italian state that surrounds it
that is secular—the precise opposite of the situation in Dubai.
Like a state, the DIFC has its own court system, presided over
by an imported British judge, to enforce its laws. The DIFC
even has its own official currency—the US dollar rather than the
UAE dirham—and its own official language. "English is the official language, in a sense, of the country we've got here," Hoopmann said.

By building a separate international financial zone operating by
its own rules rather than reforming Dubai's economy more generally, Hoopmann explained, "you don't upend all the relation-
ships and the way business was done for many, many hundreds
of years in the UAE under . . . Shariah." Beyond the 110 acres of
the DIFC lies the realm of debtors' prisons—about 40 percent of
Dubai's prisoners are in jail on debt charges—but inside, business
can be done as it's done in New York, with dollars and English
and lawsuits.

In addition to making Dubai the financial hub of the Middle
East, Sheikh Mohammed sought to make it the technology and
media capital—pursuing glamorous industries whose viability in
an autocracy seemed dubious. In 1999, saltwater-inundated low-
lands along Sheikh Zayed Road were drained and set aside to
become two contiguous free zones, Internet City and Media City.
Today, the fifty-three-story twin Chrysler Buildings standing
next to each other along the expressway mark the development.

The SimCity Chryslers are a fitting icon for the Internet and
Media City free zones, since the zones themselves mimic America on a deeper level, hoping to approximate the constitutionally
protected free inquiry that has helped make the United States
a global leader in media and technology. To entice companies
to locate in Internet City and Media City, Dubai's authorities
exempted the contiguous free zones from the UAE's strict Inter-

net censorship policy. In the twin zones, the government promised, the Internet would be fully searchable (except for sites based in Israel, which would remain blocked).

The government of Dubai could be open about the special Internet City and Media City regulations because, unlike other authoritarian countries, notably China, the UAE is completely transparent about its Internet censorship. In the UAE, censored sites are blocked not with the message "The connection has been reset" but with "We apologize the site you are attempting to visit has been blocked due to its content being inconsistent with the religious, cultural, political, and moral values of the United Arab Emirates." A few more clicks and Emirati Internet users can read the official criteria for blocking sites, which prohibits, among other sites, web pages with instructions for computer hacking and bomb making and sites that offer Internet gambling and Internet dating, which, according to the regulations, "contradicts with the ethics and morals of the UAE." The openly closed system even allows appeals to the censorship authorities if a user believes a site was blocked in error—assuming the user is willing to give her name and contact information to the authorities on the reporting form.

To kick off the Internet City development, the state-owned real estate company behind the project cut a loss-leader deal with Microsoft: in exchange for locating in the development and putting the world's largest Microsoft sign on its new building, the Washington State–based software giant could lease space rent-free for fifty years. With Microsoft signed up, other companies soon followed. Today, Internet City hosts the Middle East headquarters of not only Microsoft but Hewlett-Packard, Dell, and Canon, among others. Hundreds of smaller companies employing thousands of workers occupy a series of sleek, if less-showy, low-slung office buildings set amid manicured grounds and parking lots. But despite its big corporate names, Dubai has only been able to lure the finance and marketing departments of the tech companies. Assurance of free thought in one designated neighborhood has not been enough to woo the creative research and development and programming departments, which remain clustered in the more liberal nearby nations of India and Israel. Internet City, for all its successes, is still hamstrung by the lack of intellectual freedom in the wider city-state of Dubai.

With similar guarantees of freedom of information, the adjacent Media City development successfully attracted foreign bureaus of leading Western news services, including the BBC, CNN, and Reuters as well as the top Arabic stations, al-Jazeera and al-Arabiya. To the companies, Dubai offered a quiet location in the eye of the Middle Eastern storm. The city-state was an ideal place from which to cover the American wars in Afghanistan and Iraq. Journalists could hop on a plane for a short flight into the war zones, do their reporting, and then return to their office in rich, peaceful, stable Dubai.

To Sheikh Mohammed, part of the allure of building Media City was free publicity. Bringing major bureaus to the city helped make Dubai a global household name as locally based journalists ended up covering fluffy stories in the city-state that they would never have covered farther afield. Dubai's over-the-top real estate projects—a shopping mall with an enormous indoor ski slope, giant man-made islands shaped like palm trees—became world famous. Many Dubai developments seem to have been conceived with just such stories in mind.

But as with Internet City, the degree of intellectual freedom in a Gulf autocracy remained an issue for the media companies. Their initial assumption that uncensored reporting by foreign media operating in Dubai would be tolerated as long as it focused on the wider region rather than the internal affairs of the UAE has been called into question. In 2007, at the request of fellow regional autocrat, Pakistani strongman General Pervez Musharraf, Dubai shut down two independent Pakistani media outlets that were reporting on unrest in their home country from Media City. That said, in 2011, Google's Middle East marketing director, Wael Ghonim, openly organized revolutionary protests in his native Egypt via uncensored Facebook from his Internet City office. Despite some drawbacks, media and tech companies continue to operate out of Dubai for its many advantages, but should the Arab Spring—launched in part from Dubai—ultimately birth any stable Arab democracies, they may give the emirate serious competition as the Arab world's media and technology hub.

With Microsoft and Google in the bag, it was left to Dubai's Healthcare City development, spearheaded by a Dubai Holding subsidiary best known for its theme parks, to attempt Dubai's greatest brand-name educational coup: luring Harvard. Dubai Inc. came to Massachusetts in 2004 with a fully funded proposal that Harvard Medical School embark on its first overseas venture since its short lived campus in pre-Communist Shanghai. As a Harvard official involved in the venture explained, the Dubai authorities envisioned Healthcare City as a medical tourism facility where wealthy Arabs would fly in for treatment just as they did for shopping. Wedged between the upscale Wafi City shopping complex and a Hyatt hotel, the development needed a brand-name anchor tenant—hence, Harvard. As the Harvard official put it, Dubai Inc.'s thinking was, "We want a [jewelry store] so we're gonna get Tiffany's here; we want a university, so we'll get Harvard."

Harvard officials drafted regulations and credentialing standards for all future tenants in Healthcare City that were, as the official put it, "comparable to Western standards"—the medical equivalent of the financial regulations Errol Hoopmann had written across town for the DIFC—but they balked at opening a Middle Eastern branch of its prized medical school. Instead, they proposed to set up a Harvard-affiliated teaching hospital in Dubai that would help to train graduates of a new, independent medical school to be created and administered by local authorities. In the end, plans for a Harvard teaching hospital in Dubai were a casualty of the global economic downturn, just like Harvard's ambitious expansion scheme back home in Boston, where plans for a $1 billion science complex were shelved in 2009. In this case, at least, early twenty-first-century Dubai would not be able to match early twentieth-century Shanghai as a global hub.

As Dubai became the most diverse city on earth, with foreigners flocking in from every country and ranging from the richest people on the planet to the poorest, the city came to look like a microcosm of the earth itself. With no attempt from the municipality to enforce uniform standards, some Dubai neighborhoods look to be right out of America; others, out of Bangladesh. The patchwork urbanism of twenty-first-century Dubai is as evident in the city's residential neighborhoods as in its business-oriented free zones.

Beachfront high-rise apartments and inland gated communities of single-family houses cater to the expatriate professionals brought in to manage the city's multinationals. The serried high-rise Jumeirah Beach Residences and the towers clustered around the man-made Dubai Marina inlet look like sleek condominium developments out of Miami. Deeper in the desert, the Arabian Ranches gated community, developed by Emaar Properties, the state-backed developer behind the Burj Khalifa, conjures Orange County, California, with its large single-family homes in styles ranging from Mediterranean to Santa Fe neopueblo and its traffic circles planted with palms and bougainvillea and crowded with SUVs.

Dubai's reputation for letting Western expatriates live much like they do back home goes far beyond ersatz American subdivisions. If anything, the city-state has developed a reputation as a place where even guest workers from libertine Western countries can let their hair down. The first day of Dubai's Friday-Saturday weekend is known as the day when Muslims pray and Westerners party, all-you-can-drink brunch being a staple of Dubailander culture. To please Western expatriate professionals and fuel tourism while touting its conservative Islamic credentials, Dubai officially only permits the consumption of alcohol in hotels. It just defines hotels exceedingly broadly as any real estate project that contains a hotel. Thus, because several floors of the Burj Khalifa are home to the Armani Hotel, and another hotel adjoins the mall at the base of the tower, any venue in the entire "Downtown Dubai" project, including the world's largest shopping mall, is permitted to serve alcohol.

In the interest of business travel and tourism, the city also famously turns a blind eye to prostitution. With an economy so heavy on construction and finance and fueled by get-rich-quick dreams, the vast majority of guest workers are young men. Overall the city is more than three-quarters male. But the city's gender imbalance only provides a potential market for prostitution. It is Dubai's authorities' lax attitude toward the oldest profession that allows it to thrive. In nightlife venues that don't adhere to a couples-only admission rule, most women present are prostitutes, typically from East Asia, sub-Saharan Africa, and Eastern Europe. Specific clubs like the Rattlesnake, a saloon with an American Wild West theme located in the Metropolitan Hotel on Sheikh Zayed Road, exist solely to unite an international array of prostitutes with an international array of johns. Even during Ramadan, when Dubai's nightlife is strictly circumscribed by the austere no-music dictates of Shariah, prostitution thrives in silent nightclubs.

Dubai is like a city-sized version of Sir Victor Sassoon's Cathay Hotel in Old Shanghai—not only in its libertinism but in its multicultural urbanism. In the Cathay Hotel, each suite was done up in the style of a different culture; in Dubai, each neighborhood, even each building, looks like it came from a different part of the world. Dubai hosts Filipino supermarkets right out of Manila, Indian markets right out of Mumbai, and British markets right out of Liverpool. Of course, similar urban spaces exist in any global city, but what makes Dubai unique is that none of them are mainstream and, thus, none of them marginalized. In London, Tesco is the mainstream supermarket and the Filipino market is not. In Dubai, there is no mainstream supermarket. To the extent that there is a leading supermarket in Dubai, it is Carrefour, the French chain. It succeeds in Dubai not because French culture is the norm but because the French know food—and the store is happy to make the relatively minor concessions to Muslim dietary laws that Dubai demands by not selling alcohol and walling off its pork products in a section specifically marked "for non-Muslims" that operates on the honor system.

Just as Dubai has no mainstream supermarket, it has no mainstream culture. If an observant Pakistani Muslim moves to London, she is faced with the dilemma of whether she will remain veiled or join mainstream British society. In Dubai, there is no dominant culture to conform to. In Britain, no matter how good her English becomes, she will always "speak with an accent." In a city where nearly everyone speaks English as his or her second language, it doesn't matter if one speaks with a Pakistani accent or a Filipino one.

Because there is no dominant culture one feels pressured to join, Dubai is a cosmopolitan city where most people are not cosmopolitans. As a London banker posted to Dubai put it, "In London, your eye would find same diversity on the streets but beneath the surface everyone's a Londoner. Here the Indians really are Indian, the Egyptians really are Egyptian." One Moroccan-born, US-educated architecture professor expressed frustration that he kept inviting an Indian colleague to lunch to try his Moroccan foods but the man refused to eat anything but biryani, the fragrant subcontinental basmati rice pilaf. For many in the developing world, however, the ability to move to a wealthy country without the pressure to change or conform is precisely Dubai's appeal.

But there is a dark side to Dubai's come-as-you-are ethos. Just as Dubai has no universal cultural or legal norms, it has no universal ethical norms, either. Unlike other wealthy societies, Dubai makes no effort to provide a developed-world standard of living for all. The housing developments of Dubai are similar to the supermarkets. And while having Pakistani foods available in Dubai is a boon, having Pakistani-level worker housing in one of the world's richest cities is a scandal.

On a parcel of land that was once no different than the desert superblock where the luxurious Arabian Ranches was built sits the Sonapur labor camp (meaning "City of Gold" in Hindi). In Sonapur, the construction workers of Dubai—the ragged army of brown-skinned men in blue suits who, numbering close to half a million, constitute roughly a quarter of the city's population—are housed in a string of twenty-first-century company towns. In Sonapur, with its trash-strewn paths of packed dust in place of sidewalks, the vaunted ultramodern Dubai infrastructure of superhighways and computerized, conductorless metro trains seems in another country rather than another neighborhood. And all of the lifestyle freedoms that Dubai markets to tourists and professionals are nowhere to be found. A series of threatening signs lays down rules: guests are only permitted in the camp on Fridays from 3:00 p.m. to 6:00 p.m. Another sign reads, "Important notice: The following items are strictly prohibited within the camp: Alcoholic drinks; cigaratte [sic] smoking; pan [betel nut] chewing; illegal CD's [sic]. Contravention could lead to a fine, suspension or in some cases contract termination." If the upscale hotels that serve alcohol and prostitutes are Dubai's ultimate "free zone," Sonapur is the opposite.

In Sonapur, men live bunked up in dorms with the names and logos of the global companies they work for—Arabtec, Emirates airline, Chili's—on the side of the cinder-block slabs. The workers are, in some sense, owned by the companies, since workers are brought to Dubai to work for the specific employer who sponsors their visa. Losing a job, either by quitting or being fired (the ominous "contract termination" mentioned on the sign), typically means having to leave the country. A similar sign in the service elevator of the Burj Khalifa threatened construction workers with termination (i.e., deportation) for smoking. In this respect, Dubai, for all its diversity, is the opposite of Old Shanghai, where all were welcome to stay, with neither passport nor visa nor job offer required.

Dubai's guest worker system places limits on social mobility that other wealthy countries do not. Dubai workers not only lack the right to a minimum wage or to collectively bargain, they lack the freedom to take a better job offer should one come along. Workers can only legally change jobs by obtaining a "No Objection Certificate" from their employer. In Dubai, there is no driving a cab until you find something better: once a cabdriver, always a cabdriver. Even a rudimentary speaker of English among Dubai's cabbies used the erudite phrase "second-class citizen" to describe his status. In 2007, these frustrations bubbled over when forty thousand Dubai construction workers mounted an illegal strike at top projects, including the new airport terminal and the Burj Khalifa.

Even the Dubai-born children of guest workers remain just that—guests—because it is virtually impossible to become a naturalized citizen of the UAE. A self-described "Indian businessman who's lived in Dubai for 26 years" is actually a twenty-six-year-old who was born in the city-state and who has never lived anywhere else. Though he uses the first person plural to refer to Dubai ("We need to attract more multinationals," he offered at a forum in the wake of the economic crisis), every three years he must reapply for a work visa simply to remain in his home-town. With its unreflective assumptions of white supremacy, Old Shanghai once exalted its tiny foreign population over the indigenous Chinese majority; today, undergirded by postcolonial self-righteousness, Dubai has turned this system on its head, disenfranchising its foreign majority—including many, like this "Indian" businessman, who are indigenous to the city.

Even with non-Emiratis demoted to second-class citizenship, Dubai's authorities struggle to manage tensions with their own people, who feel alienated from a city overrun by expatriates. As the foreign population has grown, many locals have moved deep into the desert. Georgetown-educated Emirates University professor Abdulkhaleq Abdulla is one of the few Emiratis who publicly voices locals' frustrations—frustrations that eerily echo both the Decembrists' resentment of the foreign experts who ordered around St. Petersburg's native Russians and that of colonial-era nationalists in Bombay and Shanghai who turned the Western-ers' political value of democratic self-determination against them. Looking courtly in his white robe and white beard at Dôme, an Australian chain that miraculously transforms Dubai shopping mall food courts into Parisian cafés, Abdulla says bluntly, with Emiratis so outnumbered by foreigners, "you feel like you're losing your society." In Abdulla's view, high-earning Western experts shipped in to run global companies have monopolized the most desirable sections of the city, all to power a massive boom that was totally unnecessary. While China and India need breakneck development to lift hundreds of millions of people out of poverty, Dubai, blessed with $1.5 million in oil per Emirati, does not. In Dubai, there was no problem to be solved—and yet the city was thrown open to the world and turned upside down as Emiratis became a tiny minority in their hometown. "This is not the US, Canada, or Australia," Abdulla says pointedly, referring to former English colonies where the indigenous populations were ethnically cleansed to make way for societies where, today, over 95 percent of the people have roots elsewhere.

While the precise percentage of Emiratis in Dubai is a matter of dispute—the government does not publish reliable demographic data—it now rivals the meager percentages of indigenous North Americans and aboriginal Australians. Academic estimates of the percentage of Emiratis in Dubai range from 5 percent to as low as 3 percent. While the city contains an estimated 150,000 expatriate Arabs, often educated professionals from impoverished countries like Morocco or Egypt, Sheikh Mohammed's full-on embrace of globalization has rendered Dubai demographically less Arab than Dearborn, Michigan, or Marseilles, France, let alone other Middle Eastern cities. South Asians are by far the majority of Dubai's population, likely numbering over a million and performing a full range of jobs from doctors and lawyers to construction workers and hotel clerks. Britons, numbering approximately one hundred thousand, make up the largest contingent of expatriate Westerners. Dubai is so devoid of natives that, in 2007, the Department of Tourism and Commerce Marketing sponsored a series of "Talk to a Local" booths in Dubai shopping malls so tourists could meet a real-life Emirati. Today, at the Sheikh Mohammed Centre for Cultural Understanding, visitors can meet a local—but only one day a week. On other days, guests are treated to traditional Arabian coffee and fresh dates served by an Indian.

The UAE authorities try to placate their people through a system that explicitly exalts them over the guest workers they host. As a sop to Emirati capitalists, the government mandates that all businesses outside of the free zones be majority owned by Emiratis. This means that the Bangladeshi barber working dawn till dusk and the Filipino on the night shift at the noodle shop toil to further enrich the locals. In the private sector, where foreigners make up 99 percent of the workforce, the rare Emirati enjoys tremendous job security, since firing a local could get a company in trouble with the authorities. As an expatriate American manager in an urban planning firm put it, describing the firm's sole Emirati employee, "She gets to play by different rules." Emiratis more commonly work in the public sector where they are openly paid higher wages than their guest worker counterparts for doing the same job. In the public schools, for example, Emirati teachers are paid more than twice what expatriates make. And public sector management jobs are often reserved for Emiratis. Imperious robe-clad Emiratis earning princely sums as make-work "supervisors" peering over the shoulders of Malaysian ticket sellers is a common sight on the Dubai metro system. Routine jobs involving national security are similarly reserved for Emiratis and are generally done poorly. At the Dubai International Airport, the border guards fiddle with their cell phones between stamping passports and take impromptu snack breaks, throwing back handfuls of candy while weary travelers wait for service helplessly. More complex, high-level national security jobs are outsourced to skilled foreigners. The elite special forces unit trained to protect the Burj Khalifa from terror attacks is staffed by Columbian and South African mercenaries trained by American, British, French, and German experts.

For Emiratis who don't work, the welfare safety net is lavish. The average man collecting welfare benefits receives $55,000 a year—equivalent to a lifetime's earnings for a Dubai guest worker on a construction site. To be an Emirati is to be high born; even Dubai's public housing flats include a servant's room.

While benefits are generous, the ruling bargain essentially states, "No taxation therefore no representation." Government efforts to make the locals feel like partners in the administration of the UAE have thus far failed. In 2006, the country for the first time went through the motions of democratic procedure, allowing voters to elect half of the members of the UAE's powerless "advisory" parliament. While having candidates handpicked by the rulers is common in the pseudoelections of authoritarian states, the UAE leadership went ahead and handpicked the voters as well. From the qualified voter pool of the roughly 350,000 UAE nationals over age eighteen, the leadership gave ballots to just 7,000. Sensing a sham, many didn't even bother to vote, prompting a high-ranking government official to give the Gilbert-and-Sullivan-worthy quote, "This is particularly disappointing given that all of the candidates and participants were from very good families, and were all personally approved by the UAE's rulers." Apparently too few appreciated what an honor it was to be asked to participate in a meaningless election.

As the larger UAE federation has pursued such "democracy" schemes, in Dubai, Sheikh Mohammed has worked to transform his city-state from a feudal hereditary autocracy to a corporate state with Mohammed as CEO-for-life. Rather than a cabinet, Dubai is administered by the Executive Council, which is made up of the CEOs of Dubai's state-owned enterprises, like Emirates airline and Emaar Properties. The Executive Council chambers sit near the top of the Emirates Towers. At the very top is the office of Sheikh Mohammed himself, ruling not from a palace like a king, but from the top of a Class A office building, like a corporate titan.

As with a corporation, rather than a country, policy is ultimately made by diktat from the top, and when advice is solicited, it generally comes not from the powerless parliament but from Western consulting firms like McKinsey and Booz Allen Hamilton. According to a UAE-based PricewaterhouseCoopers consultant, the firms give only advice on means, not ends—the government sets a goal, and the consulting firms offer plans to achieve that goal. Today's Dubai operates much like tsarist St. Petersburg, where Western advisers were brought in to modernize systems of governance without challenging the autocratic system itself. As in St. Petersburg, the extent to which Dubai can welcome Westerners without destabilizing the regime remains an open question. Certainly the Emiratis of Dubai find their government's reliance on Western experts to be humiliating.

Sheikh Mohammed's strategy of using wealth derived from Dubai's globalization to placate Emiratis who feel marginalized by that same globalization is increasingly written into the urban fabric of the city. Architecturally, Sheikh Mohammed has gone from simply proclaiming that Dubai's success as a global hub is, in and of itself, a triumph for the Arab people to embracing traditional Arab architectural forms in major city icons. This accounts for the strange fact that as Dubai has become more global, it has come to look more overtly Arabian. In the 1990s, Sheikh Mohammed was content merely to name the superdeluxe hotel he'd commissioned, the Burj al-Arab (Tower of the Arabs), even though it was designed by a white man in London in the universal maritime shape of a sail. But in the Burj Khalifa development, built a decade later, the Arabian architectural influence is unmistakable.

As with the Burj al-Arab, the tallest building in the world was designed by a white Westerner, Adrian Smith, the same American architect who had designed Shanghai's eighty-eight-story Jin Mao Tower. Smith's Dubai design, which won an international competition in 2003, called for a multishafted silvery skyscraper like the Emerald City turned a blue-gray moonstone. The design, Smith admitted, was loosely based on a black, three-lobed 1960s skyscraper he saw out of his office window in Chicago, but he insisted it also drew on the pointed arch found in Islamic architecture over the centuries. "When you look up at the building, if you think about it as a pointed arch, you get it," Smith explained. In a less subtle nod to its Middle East location, the building includes "the world's highest mosque" on the 158th floor. Often dismissed as a glorified prayer room, some speculate that it was built more to make Islamist terrorists think twice about attacking the building rather than to placate religious Emiratis. (Rumors also abound that the UAE royals have taken out a more ironclad insurance policy against an attack: paying protection money to terrorist groups.)

Whether visitors to Smith's tower will discern its Islamic inspiration will likely vary, but the Arabic influence at the base of the building is, to put it mildly, unsubtle. The shopping mall on an island in the man-made lake at the tower's base, called Souk Al Bahar (The Sailor's Bazaar), is touted in the skyscraper's visitors' center as an "Arabian-inspired . . . pedestrian-only island . . . with its traditional architecture of natural stone corridors [and] high archways." The Souk, which provides a traditional counterpoint to the contemporary architecture of the Burj, is quintessential Dubai, with over-the-top production values for its exquisitely crafted Syrian-style chandeliers. Like the larger development, its stores are a mix of local and Western, with a Dean and Deluca, the upscale New York grocer, at one end and a series of shops selling Arabian souvenirs, from Orientalist paintings to stuffed camels, at the other. Being Dubai, the role of traditional Arab merchant is assigned to Filipinos.

The Souk Al Bahar is just the most recent in a series of Arab pride malls that now dot the city-state. The most elaborate is the Ibn Battuta Mall, named for the medieval Arab travel writer. Sections of the complex are based on different places Ibn Battuta visited: Andalusia, Tunisia, Egypt, Persia, India, and China. Lavish even by Dubai standards, the Mughal emperor's court, cribbed from seventeenth-century Indian ruler Shah Jahan's royal residence in Agra, is built to a scale that rivals the original. And the blue-and-gold tiled ersatz Persian mosque is home to what is surely the world's most luxurious Starbucks. Sensibly, on his journey, the real-life Ibn Battuta skipped the barren desert that is today the United Arab Emirates. But through Islam, Dubai claims a heritage from the larger region—and even formerly Muslim locales like Moorish Spain and Mughal India. In a corridor channeling the bazaars of Cairo, an educational exhibit on Ibn Battuta constitutes a minimuseum of Arab chauvinism. The display recounts Battuta's travels and exalts a time when the Islamic world excelled while Europe was mired in the Dark Ages.

For all their "local" bells and whistles, Dubai's Arab pride malls are Western shopping malls filled with Western stores that fail to respond to the complexities of their location, environmentally as well as culturally. Environmentally, Dubai's air-conditioned megamalls only fulfill Sheikh Mohammed's desire to be number one in one respect: they have helped make the UAE the only country on earth to top America in energy use and carbon footprint per capita. Culturally, such malls are just multi-million-dollar exercises in psychological overcompensation for the least Arab city in Arabia. As the late Arab-American journalist Anthony Shadid wrote in *The Washington Post*, Dubai's globalization strategy is to "[bring] success to an Arab city by shearing away the qualities that have long defined it as Arab." Indian expats knowingly call Dubai "the best city in India" while Iranians dub it "the best city in Iran." Even as the state-backed real estate companies pander to the locals with Arab pride malls, de-Arabianizing Dubai to further open the city to the world remains an obvious if unstated policy goal. English is more than just the city's lingua franca; it is a semienforced official language. Dubai has no requirement that shop signs include Arabic translations of their invariably English names, and the municipality actually imposes fines on taxis if their rooftop signs are in Arabic rather than English. In 2006, the government changed the public sector weekend from the Islamic Thursday-Friday to Friday-Saturday to bring it closer to norms of the West. And there is talk of shifting it to Saturday-Sunday despite the Muslim Friday Sabbath.

This blatant embrace of un-Islamic mores fuels an equal and opposite reaction. Dubai is a schizophrenic metropolis where the dialectic of local and global engage in a kind of arms race, each ratcheting the other up. Feeling under siege in a sea of expatriates, many locals have sought shelter in Muslim traditions. Gender segregation among Emiratis has become stricter in recent years, and the Emirati dress code—a white dishdasha robe for men and a black abaya robe for women—has become much more universal of late in part because it distinguishes locals from foreigners.

Even as Muslims have become a smaller and smaller percentage of Dubai's total population, Islam's status as an official state religion has remained in place. The public schools still teach children that all non-Muslims will burn in hell. Dubai's urban planning regulations require a mosque to be built every three hundred meters to make a Muslim house of worship accessible on foot even to the old and infirm. The zoning law, coupled with the relative dearth of Muslims in many Dubai neighborhoods, creates a bizarre cityscape dotted by often lavish, invariably empty mosques. In a state-run religion museum geared toward tourists called the Guiding Light, nonbelievers are taught about Islam with a mix of newfangled technology and old-time religion. High-tech computer displays and deftly designed text panels offer Quranic quotes like "Those who disbelieve . . . are the dwellers of the Fire. They shall abide therein forever" and traditional Muslim descriptions of hell: "If a stone as big as seven pregnant camels was thrown from the edge of Hell, it would fly through it for seventy years, and yet it would not reach the bottom."

For its part, the government makes a show of trying to keep the seven million tourists who visit Dubai each year from offending local sensibilities. Signs posted at hotel pools in Dubai inform guests that management will "turn over" to the Dubai police any guests not abiding by the UAE swimsuit-modesty law. Occasional arrests of expatriates for sex on the beach make international headlines. In the geopolitical sphere, even as Dubai routinely, albeit quietly, admits Israeli businessmen on special visas and plays host to the US Navy, serving as a staging ground for American wars in the region, the UAE loudly proclaims a foreign policy that keeps it in good stead with neighbors like Iran and Saudi Arabia.

For all the Emiratis' misgivings about Dubai's internationalism and the difficulties of containing the pressures generated by its unusual social structure, Dubai's leaders have proudly turned Dubai's internationalism into a brand. Emirates airlines flights begin with an announcement of the obscure non-English, non-Arabic languages spoken by a flight crew assembled from all over the world—Malay, Latvian, Serbian. Signs on Dubai bus shelters crow that the city's people come from nearly every country on earth. And many of Dubai's state-backed real estate ventures are purposefully branded as international—as if it isn't enough that they are international but must proclaim themselves to be so.

Since Dubai is one of the world's leading cargo ports, it follows that it is home to the largest trading center for Chinese goods outside of China. But for Dubai Inc., this is not enough. The center for Chinese goods must be located in a giant themed building called Dragon Mart, shaped, the state-backed developer claims, like a dragon. In truth, the building, which stretches the length of nearly a dozen football fields and attracts nineteen million visits a year, looks more like an enormous caterpillar. Inside, the mall—really a cavernous warehouse cut up into shops, like an open-plan office with cubicles—is organized by wares, with an electronics section, a furniture section, and a tea section, among others. At the Shanghai Hailiang International Trading FZCO, a husband-and-wife team from a factory town near Shanghai sells toys, barrettes, and watches from back home. One Bangladeshi-run shop specializes in plug-in revolving lamps with flashing portraits of Jesus, Mary, the Hindu god Ganesh, or a panorama of the Kaaba in Mecca—Dubai's kitschy ecumenical capitalism at its most endearing and discomfiting. Far off of tourist itineraries, many stores are down-at-heels affairs where merchants cut wholesale deals rather than cater to the general public. Dubai Inc.

markets the Ibn Battuta Mall as a multi-million-dollar monument to non-Western capitalism, sparing no expense to highlight the historical trade links between China, South Asia, and
the Middle East before the rise of Europe—and yet it is filled
with Western stores like Starbucks, Nike, and H&M. Meanwhile,
the actual site of this revived trade that is reshaping the world is
hidden in a glorified warehouse off the beaten path. Dynamic,
profane, decidedly unglamorous, Dragon Mart is the true monument to the global market's capacity to draw together people and
goods from all over the world. This is the real wonder of Dubai.

Bordering Dragon Mart is perhaps Dubai's most ham-fisted
and contradictory attempt at grabbing the mantle of global
metropolis: a 387-building housing development called International City made up of a series of interlinked apartment complexes, each with a different national theme (including China,
Russia, France, England, Persia, Greece, and Italy). In an unde-
sirable section of the city, far from the beach, the tight budgets
allowed for only the most perfunctory nods to the architectural
distinctions between the regions. A whitewashed Orthodox
church–style cupola signals Greece; a blue-green peaked arch
halfheartedly conjures Persia. Anyone can live in any section,
but the state-backed developer encourages prospective residents
to rent or buy in their national section should they happen to
be Chinese, Russian, French, English, Persian, Greek, or Italian. Certainly the China section, with its Chinese restaurants and
supermarkets (and over a billion potential tenants), has achieved
the developer's vision for a kind of live-in Epcot World Showcase
open 24/7.

But in International City, Dubai Inc.'s anodyne vision of wel-
coming the world while preserving an upscale Islamo-suburban
sense of order and propriety crashes and burns. The Chinese restaurants in the Chinese section of the city have the feel of Chinese restaurants the world over, with red lanterns out front and

lazy Susans on the tables. But they are a little too insistent on being like Chinese restaurants around the world in that they illegally sell off-menu beer when asked. More troubling, Chinese gang-related crime, including a number of kidnappings for ransom, has plagued the China section of the development.

When critics compare Dubai to a Disney park, like Epcot, Dubai's builders take it as a compliment. As an executive at Nakheel, the real estate development firm responsible for International City, Dragon Mart, the Palm islands, and the Ibn Battuta Mall, put it, "I think it's a flattering statement." But while there is indeed a strong dose of Disney in Dubai, the city-state is much more than just a series of sanitized imitations of other places. While for Nakheel even Dubai's most appealing aspect— its internationalism—must be packaged in a Disneyfied environment of International City (capital *I*, capital *C*) and its status as a trading hub logoed and branded in Dragon Mart, the international dynamism of Dubai is real.

And it isn't just Chinese gangsters in International City who deviate from Dubai's official script. The wonder of a city that sprang from the desert in a decade cannot help but empower, even if the authorities do not want it to. An expatriate financial regulator who was born and raised in Finland, moved to London, and now lives and works in Dubai said it is in Dubai that he feels most compelled to shape the city. In the Gulf city-state, the new metro system has just opened, and the Finn feels he can suggest a new line to a new part of the city. By contrast, in London, where the Tube has run the same routes for a hundred years, the map is essentially set.

The legal realities of Dubai don't seem to have sunk in for the Finn. In Finland, he is a citizen, entitled to vote on matters of public import; in Britain, he is protected by a right to free speech. In Dubai, he is a guest worker. Present at the pleasure of the authorities, he has no fundamental right to be there. He can be deported at any time for any reason. And yet, it is in Dubai that he feels empowered to give his opinion because Dubai is a work in progress—a city that we build rather than inherit, where the most fantastical drawings architects can imagine spring to life, where the fingerprints of the construction workers are still visible on the buildings. Still busy being born, the city of Dubai begs for its residents' input even if its rulers, most emphatically, do not.

Conclusion

# GLIMPSES OF UTOPIA

Guest worker, Dubai

In 2009, the global financial panic rippled through Dubai. Like its historic sister cities, the Gulf's instant global metropolis had implemented the West's latest architectural and intellectual fashions in the most extreme manner on its blank slate. While cities the world over gorged on debt-financed real estate speculation, ostensibly made safe through the financial innovations of collateralized debt obligations and credit-default swaps, Dubai topped them all. At the most insane heights of the bubble, Dubai was, to a large extent, a casino posing as a city: owner-occupied units accounted for just 30 percent of its housing market. When the music stopped, Dubai had the farthest to fall. Only an emergency $10 billion bailout by its oil-rich neighboring emirate Abu Dhabi saved Dubai Inc.'s real estate arm from defaulting on its bonds. Humbled and grateful, Dubai's authorities opened the world's tallest building, long planned as Burj Dubai, as Burj Khalifa to honor Sheikh Khalifa, Emir of Abu Dhabi. Designed as a monument to Dubai's ambition, the tower now stands as a monument to its hubris—the world's tallest metaphor.

As construction on lower-profile skyscrapers came to a standstill and Ozymandian skeletons of steel came to litter the desert, thousands of expatriate professionals fled the emirate. Wary of debtors' prison, many famously abandoned their late-model automobiles in the airport parking lot. "Bye-bye Dubai" glee ran rampant in the Western press coverage as readers were told of an "unprecedented" crash to go along with Dubai's "unprecedented" rise. But just as the rise of Dubai was prefigured by the rise of other instant East-meets-West cities, so was its crash. In the halting of construction on Dubai's offshore reclamation projects, including a man-made archipelago in the shape of a global map called The World, the echoes of the collapse of nineteenth-century Bombay's Back Bay Reclamation Company are all too clear. And yet Bombay's reclamation project was ultimately restarted and, in the early twentieth century, became Bombay's remarkable Art Deco district, a far more sophisticated vision of Indian modernity than what had originally been planned for the site. Similarly, the specter of sovereign default that hung over Dubai in 2009 hung over the International Settlement of Shanghai during its nineteenth-century bust. And yet reports of that city's death—both in the nineteenth century and again during the Maoist reign of the twentieth century—were greatly exaggerated.

Even postcrash, there is still great potential in Dubai—and even greater potential in the idea of Dubai. Sadly, many can only see the draw of Dubai or its drawbacks, not both. Apologists for Dubai, like architect Rem Koolhaas, who salivates over the city-state as "the ultimate tabula rasa on which new identities can be inscribed," cannot explain away the barbarism of its system: one that assembles all the world's people but makes no attempt to treat them all like people. Those who condemn Dubai, like urban theorist Mike Davis who tars it as an "evil paradise," cannot explain the allure of the city for the hundreds of thousands of low-wage guest workers who have migrated there. They cannot see that the draw of Dubai in the twenty-first century—as the draw of St. Petersburg, Shanghai, and Mumbai historically—is

more than just the lure of great wealth; it is the lure of participating in modernity. To go from being a South Indian rice farmer to
a construction worker who erects the tallest building on earth is
to untether oneself from the past and build the future. The apologists act as if Dubai has already delivered on its promise, while
those who rail against it deny that the city offers any promise at
all. But if anything is clear from the histories of its historic sister cities, it is that understanding Dubai requires acknowledging
both its opportunities and pitfalls, keeping one's eyes open to the
wonder and the horror.

Dubai represents the world as it is. It is a living version of the
leftist parable "If the World Were a Village of 100 People" that
begins "Fifty-nine of them would be Asian" and ends "and two
white guys and an Arab would own virtually everything." Apologizing for Dubai is apologizing for the world as it is. But writing off Dubai is writing off the world as it might be. It is writing
off modernity itself, smothering the hope that in the age of jet-
powered globalization, we can all learn to live together as a community, sharing a single city and, ultimately, a single world.

To fully grasp Dubai, one must catch the glimpses of utopia
within the dystopia. As Disneyfied as the developer's concept for
the Ibn Battuta Mall may be, the mall's panorama of humanity
testifies to the wonder of twenty-first-century border crossing
in ways that could never be planned or "imagineered." In the
mall's corridors, people from all over the world come together
and people who have never before been out of their native villages encounter the modern world. That they are drawn by shopping and air-conditioning does not fully undo the wonder of the
whole world under one roof—the wonder of the human traffic jam that breaks out when a group of Afghan village men,
all in their characteristic headdresses, crane their necks to see
their tribesman miraculously draw money from an ATM. Where
else would Korean engineers, Moroccan accountants, Pakistani

bricklayers, British bankers, and American journalists all cross paths? Though they are lured by trade, there is the potential for a deeper global exchange. Though Dubai's lingua franca is that of the Western world's greatest imperial power, that common language provides a universal means of communication. That few seize Dubai's opportunities for cross-cultural communication is a shame; shame on Sheikh Mohammed for banning so many topics of discussion, yes, but shame on us as well for letting him get away with it. Yet if Dubai is truly the latest chapter in a tale begun in St. Petersburg, Shanghai, and Mumbai, the only question is when, not if, its people will seize the opportunity its autocrats have unwittingly created. As with the great East-meets-West cities before it, ultramodern metropolises built by dictatorial fiat with coolies and serfs, Dubai has assembled a stunningly diverse cast of characters who can seize the reins and build a true city of the future.

The true city of the future is not simply the city with the tallest tower or the most stunning skyline but one that is piloted by the diverse, worldly, intelligent people it assembles and forges. As a British statesman sagely observed in an 1870 lecture in London, "We were very apt to decry our own City of London as inferior to the capital cities of the despotic powers of Europe, but in London was to be seen the impress of an architecture that grows from within—an architecture that expresses what the people think, and feel, and mean, and not what they are told to think, feel, or mean, as was too often the case in despotic capitals of Europe." The lecturer was Sir Bartle Frere, the retired governor of Bombay. The irony that Frere, having built the architecture of imperialism, would salute the architecture of democracy is rich. But it is also fitting, for the breakneck modernization Frere unleashed on Bombay unwittingly laid the groundwork for a democratic India. Even the most autocratic modern global cities offer democratic vistas despite the assiduous efforts of their autocrats to block them from view.

Whatever becomes of Dubai, it has rivals for the title of great developing-world metropolis of the twenty-first century. What was once an unusual phenomenon—the modern city dropped into an agrarian society—is now common. While it was once a tiny, largely self-selected percentage of Russians who moved to St. Petersburg, Chinese who moved to Shanghai, and Indians who moved to Bombay, the journey from developing-world hinterland to globalizing city has become the defining journey of the twenty-first century. Whether or not Dubai itself endures, the idea of Dubai will endure.

Burgeoning developing-world metropolises like Lagos, Nigeria, or Dhaka, Bangladesh, now the fastest-growing cities on earth, may not have the rich histories or the towering ambitions of the cities detailed in this book, but the social fabric of those cities and the initiation into the modern world that they embody for their people are yet more chapters in the story begun in St. Petersburg in 1703. Whether they will be more successful at managing the distance between city and countryside, rich and poor, foreigner and local, migrant and native, and East and West than the cities that have gone before them remains an open question. But the stakes could not be higher. When St. Petersburg ran aground in the early twentieth century, it shook the world. When Shanghai reengaged with the global economy in recent decades, it reshaped the world. Today, more than ever, the fate of the world will be decided in the rising metropolitan hubs of the developing world, in places like Mumbai, Lagos, and Dhaka. Whether they can deliver on their promise is a pressing question not just for them but for us all.

---

# FROM WINDOWS ON THE WEST
# TO WINDOWS OF THE WORLD

Man and metropolis, Century Park, Pudong

On the bottom floor of the thousand-gallery Hermitage museum, far from the crowds craning their necks to glimpse a Raphael or a Rembrandt, are a series of rooms designed by a German architect in the mid-nineteenth century. A marriage of tsarist opulence and neoclassical order—like a Greek temple built with an unlimited budget—each room places the visitor in a different symmetrical space defined by columns, arches, and pilasters of richly polished marble, one room a somber gray, the next an arresting red, another a flighty pink. In each of these pseudo-Greek rooms stand pseudo-Greek statues: Roman copies of Greek originals.

The wall labels next to the sculptures proudly proclaim their pilfered provenance: "Apollo, Marble, Roman work. 1st c. A.D. After the Greek original of the 4th c. B.C."; "Eros, Marble, Roman work. 2nd c. A.D. After the Greek original of the first half of the 4th c. B.C."; "Athena, Marble, Roman work. 2nd c. A.D. After the Greek original of the late 5th c. B.C." In these neoclassical rooms of the Hermitage, as in the larger neoclassical city that surrounds it, the Russians lay claim to the glories of Western civilization through impersonation, desperately trying to write themselves into the history of the West. And yet in these statues, we see the Romans, seemingly the font of Western civilization, doing exactly the same thing. By copying the glories of ancient Greece, they, too, are willing themselves heirs to its culture.

That the Romans copied the Greeks hardly means that their civilization was a fraud. The Romans went on to make their own contributions, far surpassing the Greeks in fields like engineering and logistics. That the Romans copied does not mean that history is nothing but copying. But it does mean that copying is an integral part of history.

If even the Romans needed to will themselves Western, what does the vaunted East-West distinction even mean? If Westernness or Easternness is a choice rather than an immutable fact, what power does it really have? Though it feels like an immutable inheritance, whether a people sees itself as Eastern or Western is actually a conscious decision that only later becomes an unconscious patrimony. Many of the Egyptians and Syrians of today are the descendants of Roman citizens, and yet they see themselves as non-Western peoples. Many even consider themselves to be in a struggle against the West. Meanwhile the Germans, descended from the barbarians who sacked Rome, consider themselves heirs to Western civilization. A city like Berlin, with its neoclassical parliament and museum buildings, is no different than St. Petersburg in its ex post facto writing of its people into the Western tradition. Berlin feels less Disneyfied than St. Petersburg only because the ruse has worked. While only 12 percent of Russians tell pollsters that they "always feel European," no pollster would even think to ask the Germans if they felt that way. It's just accepted that Germans *are* Europeans.

But the entire Europe-Asia distinction is a mental one, not a geographic one. The distinction began with the ancient Greeks, who used it to distinguish their civilized European selves from the Asian barbarians to the East, across the Aegean Sea. Medieval scholars assumed there must be some narrow isthmus separating Europe and Asia, but when no such natural feature was found, in the early modern period, geographers seized on the Ural Mountains as the dividing line. But the Ural Mountains are not much of a barrier. No higher than the Appalachians of North America, they were easily crossable long before the advent of trains, automobiles, and airplanes. Ukrainian Cossacks invaded Siberia in the late sixteenth century by carrying their riverboats in a brief portage over the Urals.

Though the physical barrier is chimerical, the mental barrier has had real effects. Looking backward, we cannot understand world history without the East-West distinction, whatever we may think of it today. That would be like an atheist studying the history of medieval Europe and ignoring Christianity because she is not a believer. But looking forward, if there is any hope for the world, we must see beyond the notions of East and West that have long divided us. The divisions themselves are arbitrary, and they were created for a world dominated by Europe—a world that is no longer with us. The proposed Gazprom tower in St. Petersburg looked for inspiration not to Amsterdam but to Dubai, where its architect began his career. In America's burgeoning Chinatowns, high-rise buildings that stack offices atop a karaoke parlor atop a restaurant atop a shopping mall bring the distinctive urbanism of twenty-first-century China to the United States just as Americans brought their architecture to their Shanghai concession 150 years before. This is not to deny that the skyscraper was initially an American innovation, but as with Art Deco, born in Paris during that last great age of globalization, in a porous world styles can transcend their birthplaces. And in this Asian Century, no doubt, forms originating in Asia will be imported to—or perhaps even foisted on—the West. The hope, however, is that as Asia rises, the thinking-makes-it-so distinction between East and West can fade, that we can will ourselves from rivalry and resentment to amity and understanding. But only free minds can think themselves to freedom.

At first glance, the Chinese boomtown of Shenzhen does not inspire much hope. The instant metropolis of fourteen million people and counting seems a self-inflicted redux of the most imitative aspects of nineteenth-century colonial Shanghai. Among Shenzhen's tallest structures is a 1:3 scale replica of the Eiffel Tower, less innovative even than Old Shanghai's "Big Ching." In a downtown city park, a massive photomontage shows Deng Xiaoping, the Communist ruler who in his youth had lived in France and in his old age founded this experimental city, admiring its skyline, complete with fake Parisian tower. Frozen posthumously by photography, the grandfatherly Deng keeps a straight face; Western visitors taking in the display typically do not.

The Eiffel Tower replica is the centerpiece of a Shenzhen theme park, called Window of the World, which offers visitors scale-model replicas of all the globe's architectural masterpieces. "See The World Landmarks In One Day!" a poster on the ticket booth crows. The park embodies contemporary China at its tawdriest. Guests who grow bored of the park's architectural wonders can amuse themselves by renting human-sized clear plastic hamster balls, locking themselves in, and taking them out for a spin on a man-made lake.

And yet the theme park is actually quite inspiring. While its central replica of the Eiffel Tower is its most famous attraction, the park gives the wonders of Asia, including Angkor Wat and the Taj Mahal, equal billing with the monuments of the West. And in its replica of the Washington DC monuments, the plaque for the 1:15 scale model of the Lincoln Memorial reads, "Completed in 1922, this white marble building resembles the Parthenon of Greece," a humbling reminder that the United States, too, like the Germans and the Romans, consciously wrote itself into the Western tradition. Placing all of the world's architectural wonders on an equal platform breaks down the distinctions between peoples and inspires a cosmopolitan, human pride in visitors.

As Syrian-born MIT architecture professor Nasser Rabbat has observed, "All architecture is the heritage of all people, although some architecture is the heritage of some people more so than others. It's only a question of degree. But there is no exclusionary architecture that says that you do not belong." The theme park is a paean to the wonders we have made—not we the Chinese, or we the Americans, or we the Asians, or we the Westerners, but we the human race. We build our world—and our future.

The Russia section of the Window of the World park includes a 1:15 scale model of the Hermitage museum in St. Petersburg, but it is the sculpture garden, set off in a quiet green section of the park away from the crowds, that holds the copy of its masterpiece, Houdon's sculpture of Voltaire. In the heart of Deng Xiaoping's instant city of skyscrapers sits the elderly philosophe, draped in a robe, his aged face enlightened by his mercurial grin. The awkward English of the plaque reads, "Author: Antoine Houdon, Imitator: Da Liusheng. Voltaire was the spiritual leader in the French Enlightenment. The statue reflects the humorous and harsh individualities of this sagacious philosopher who had to endure many hardships." Voltaire, the hardship-enduring dissident, stares out silently at "the people's democratic dictatorship" all around him. From the grin Houdon so masterfully captured and Da Liusheng so proficiently channeled, it is clear that Voltaire would appreciate the humor of the situation.

Catherine the Great, of course, had Houdon's Voltaire banished to an attic after the French Revolution. But she could never fully exorcize his spirit. Even at the height of Stalin's repression, the little marble man sitting in the Hermitage never lost the gleam in his eye or the wry smile on his face. He continues to haunt St. Petersburg to this day. That a copy of him now silently haunts Shenzhen as well means that though this book is at its end, its story will continue.

# ACKNOWLEDGMENTS

A pair of magazine assignments helped plant the seeds for this book, and their editors deserve my thanks. Lincoln Caplan, editor of the late, great *Legal Affairs*, graciously gave me the assignment in India that allowed me to travel to Mumbai for the first time; Siobhan O'Connor of *GOOD* magazine dispatched me to Orange County, China, where I learned through a fortuitous conversation with my translator that American-style suburban subdivisions had a hundred-year pedigree in Shanghai.

This book would never have been published without the unflagging support of my literary agent, Larry Weissman, who gave it the push it needed to get commissioned in the thick of the Panic of 2008. Larry sagely got the project in front of Brendan Curry, an editor with the right admixture of left brain and right brain for the project and the adventurous spirit to see a "high-wire act," as he called it, and sign up to act as safety net. In addition to serving as coach and confidant, Brendan has proved an able ringmaster at Norton, getting an excellent team behind the book. I will forever be grateful to him for the book's title.

My preliminary research was greatly enhanced by professors David Brownlee and Holly Pittman's commitment to making the resources of the University of Pennsylvania available to the wider community. I can't thank them enough for giving me access to the university's excellent libraries by making me a visiting scholar in the Department of the History of Art from 2008 to 2010.

Scores of people in St. Petersburg, Shanghai, Mumbai, and Dubai made my month-long research trips to each city both useful and enjoyable. Many of my sources bravely spoke their minds to an American writer despite the potential drawbacks, and all gave me the gift of their time. In particular, the late Erach Viccajee, a nonagenarian Mumbai Parsi raised in Old Shanghai, who continued to e-mail reminiscences of his Shanghai youth even as his terminal illness took its course, embodied the spirit of generosity found in so many sources all over the world. The following individuals deserve thanks: PVG, CC, BM, BK, ZM, DJB, LB, PTB, GG, LM, DF, LPP, SZ, GG, SD, AW, AR, LJ, DYH, PM, ABY, EL, ZR, JB, MG, JC, GY, TJ, AY, RC, PH, LP, MB, ZZ, LN, ZM, BOM, ANL, NF, AB, MG, PM, PK, CL, SD, NR, AW, UDC, GDC, PK, AV, AL, AKRB, DXB, AH, JP, HR, AMS, JS, KL, AA, SB, AF, PB, EK, AA, IU, RH, JP, RW, AS, RM, MR, DK, AI, EH, FE, YE, LED, PM, NB, TC, SG, PN, OR, MT, AV, LK.

In drafting the manuscript, my joint fellowship between the Kluge Center at the Library of Congress in Washington DC and the Black Mountain Institute at the University of Nevada, Las Vegas, provided much-needed time and resources—both archival and financial. Dr. James Billington, Dr. Carolyn Brown, Mary Lou Reker, and C. Ford Peatross at the Library of Congress and Dr. Carol Harter at UNLV as well as their staffs have created a wonderful pair of oases for thirsty minds in forbidding environments. My fellow fellows at both institutions were a collection of tremendously talented writers and scholars. In particular, I would like to thank Uwem Akpan, Mary-Ann Tirone Smith, Nicholas Jackson, Toni Baum, Chris Chekuri, and Naomi Wood for their friendship.

Several wise people with expertise in the history and culture of the cities detailed in this book—Christine Evans, Philip Tinari, and Naresh Fernandez—graciously agreed to read relevant sections and offer advice. Elizabeth Blazevich kindly applied her knowledge of the history of architecture and urban planning to the manuscript. This talented quartet has saved me from several cases of generalist's embarrassment. A trio of gifted readers with a keen sense of history and style—Astra Taylor, Daniel Kurtz-Phelan, and John Swansburg—agreed to read the manuscript as a whole and give feedback. I finally understand that the usual disclaimer "The mistakes that remain are solely my own" is no cliché. Can't say I wasn't warned.

Finally, this book is dedicated to my parents who raised me in the largest metropolis in the Western world and took me at an impressionable age to St. Petersburg. Though they couldn't have known quite what they were setting in motion, I will be forever grateful to them for their love and for presenting me with a world of opportunity.

# BIBLIOGRAPHIC NOTE

As a work of synthesis intended for a general audience, this book is deeply indebted to the scholars who have chronicled St. Petersburg, Shanghai, Mumbai, and Dubai in detailed single-volume histories. Particularly useful for St. Petersburg were W. Bruce Lincoln's *Sunlight at Midnight: St. Petersburg and the Rise of Modern Russia* (Basic Books, 2000) and Arthur George's *St. Petersburg: Russia's Window to the Future* (Taylor Trade Publishing, 2003). On Shanghai, Edward Denison and Guang Yu Ren's *Building Shanghai: The Story of China's Gateway* (Wiley-Academy, 2006) and Marie-Claire Bergère's *Shanghai: China's Gateway to Modernity* (Stanford University Press, 2010), translated by Janet Lloyd, were invaluable. On the history and architecture of Mumbai, perennial coauthors Sharada Dwivedi and Rahul Mehrotra tower over the field. Among their many works, *Bombay: The Cities Within* (Eminence Designs, 2001) was the most indispensable. While one could spend a lifetime solely reading books on the history of St. Petersburg—in English, let alone Russian or French—Dubai, a newly prominent city, has thus far spawned just a handful of works. The most comprehensive among them is Christopher Davidson's *Dubai: The Vulnerability of Success* (Columbia University Press, 2008).

Journeying to each of these cities, I was fortunate that two of them—Shanghai and St. Petersburg—have been meticulously catalogued in building-by-building architecture guides: Anne Warr's English-language *Shanghai Architecture* (Watermark Press, 2007) and Leonid Lavrov's Russian-language *1,000 Addresses* (Eclectic Publishing Center, 2008). Walking the streets of these cities armed with these guides was a pleasure, and having so much information already organized made writing about them that much easier.

A key contention of this book is that the cities portrayed have forever been unofficial sister cities. I have been consistently surprised by how rarely they are compared with each other beyond the Shanghai/Mumbai "Chindia" white papers that have been issued by international organizations and consultancies as both have reengaged with the global economy over the past two decades. One important exception to this blind spot is Marshall Berman's *All That Is Solid Melts into Air: The Experience of Modernity* (Simon and Schuster, 1982), which examines the histories of Paris, New York, and St. Petersburg in comparative perspective. In Berman's work on St. Petersburg's "modernism of underdevelopment," he offers the insight that "we can see nineteenth-century Russia as an archetype of the emerging twentieth-century Third World" (page 175). At the time of publication, neither Berman nor his readers could have understood just how prophetic a statement this was.

The concept of cosmopolitan modernity—a concept more given to trenchant questions than definitive answers—undergirds this book. I am indebted to many writers who have bravely engaged this slippery topic head-on, most notably William Leach in *Land of Desire* (Pantheon, 1993) and Yuri Slezkine in *The Jewish Century* (Princeton University Press, 2004).

# NOTES

## Introduction: The Twenty-First Century: An Orientation

*page*

5    **"This house believes Dubai is a bad idea":** Doha Debates, December 14, 2009 (transcript), accessed August 20, 2012, http://www.thedohadebates.com/debates/debate.asp?d=67&s =6&mode=transcript.

5    **"skyline on crack":** Nick Tosches, "Dubai's the Limit," *Vanity Fair,* June 2006, 156.

5    **96 percent of its population:** Christopher Davidson, *Dubai: The Vulnerability of Success* (New York: Columbia University Press, 2008), 190.

5    **37 percent are immigrants:** "New York (City), New York," U.S. Census Bureau, last modified January 31, 2012, accessed April 20, 2012, http://quickfacts.census.gov/qfd/states/36/3651000.html.

5    **"everyone and everything in it":** John Kasarda and Greg Lindsay, *Aerotropolis: The Way We'll Live Next* (New York: Farrar, Straus and Giroux, 2011), 290.

10   **five million people move:** Edward Glaeser, *Triumph of the City* (New York: Penguin, 2011), 1.

12   **90 percent owned by an Emirati sovereign wealth fund:** Charles Bagli, "Abu Dhabi Buys 90% Stake in Chrysler Building," *New York Times,* July 10, 2008.

12   **"the most abstract and intentional city":** Fyodor Dostoevsky, *Notes from the Underground,* chapter 2.

## Chapter 1: New Amsterdam—St. Petersburg, 1703–1825

15   **world's second-largest navy and more merchant ships:** Robert K. Massie, *Peter the Great: His Life and World* (New York: Ballantine Books, 1980), 178–179.

16   **"St. Petersburg was built to order":** James Cracraft, *The Petrine Revolution in Russian Architecture* (Chicago: University of Chicago Press, 1988), 173.

16   **"as you or I would order lunch":** John Baehrend, dir., *Hermitage—a Russian Odyssey: Catherine the Great—a Lust for Art,* WETA-TV, PBS, Washington DC, 1994, film.

16   **"If God will prolong my life":** Arthur George, *St. Petersburg: Russia's Window to the Future—the First Three Centuries* (Lanham, MD: Taylor Trade Publishing, 2003), 41.

16   **fewer than ten secular Russian books:** Lindsey Hughes, *Russia in the Age of Peter the Great* (New Haven, CT: Yale University Press, 1998), 5.

17   **"We need Europe for a few decades":** Solomon Volkov, *St. Petersburg: A Cultural History* (New York: Free Press, 1995), 10.

17   **"My rank is that of a student":** Henri Troyat, *Peter the Great,* trans. Joan Pinkham (New York: E. P. Dutton, 1989), 90.

18   **"Piter has shown himself":** Troyat, *Peter the Great,* 100.

21   **"These things are in your way":** George, *St. Petersburg,* 9.

25   **shifts from 5:00 a.m. to 10:00 p.m.:** ibid., 35; Massie, *Peter the Great,* 360.

25   **boasted that one hundred thousand:** Baehrend, *Hermitage.*

26   **"architectural books from which this art can be learned":** Cracraft, *The Petrine Revolution in Russian Architecture,* 150–151.

26   **Hundreds of foreign architects:** Massie, *Peter the Great,* 602.

28   **Roughly a third of the students:** Kyril Zinovieff and Jenny Hughes, *Companion Guide to St. Petersburg* (Rochester, NY: Companion Guides, 2003), 319–320.

28   **four hundred rubles a year:** George, *St. Petersburg,* 74.

29   **"Assembly is a French word":** ibid., 82.

30   **population at forty thousand:** ibid., 39.

30   **"Who among you, my brothers":** ibid., 87–88.

31   **"I cannot help writing you":** George, *St. Petersburg,* 31.

32   **"Petersburg is like a part":** George, *St. Petersburg,* 89.

32   **"I shall bring back the old people":** Lindsay Hughes, *Peter the Great: A Biography* (New Haven, CT: Yale University Press, 2002), 127.

33   **"overrun with French as with locusts":** Inna Gorbatov, *Catherine the Great and the French Philosophers of the Enlightenment* (Bethesda, MD: Academica Press, 2006), 15–16.

34   **"The more you build":** W. Bruce Lincoln, *Sunlight at Midnight: St. Petersburg and the Rise of Modern Russia* (New York: Basic Books, 2002), 45–46.

34   **one hundred thousand mark:** Lincoln, *Sunlight at Midnight,* 42.

36   **Catherine's collection of four thousand paintings:** Katia Dianina, "Art and Authority: The Hermitage of Catherine the Great," *Russian Review* 63 (2004): 632–633.

36   **just two Russian paintings:** ibid., 637.

37   **"civilized so many people":** Voltaire, *The Life of Peter the Great, Emperor of Russia*, trans. William F. Fleming (Paris: E. R. DuMont, 1901), 12.

37   **"man's emergence from his self-imposed":** Immanuel Kant, *Perpetual Peace and Other Essays*, trans. Ted Humphrey (Indianapolis, IN: Hackett Publishing Company, 1983), 41.

39   **"I have listened with the greatest pleasure":** Henri Troyat, *Catherine the Great*, trans. Joan Pinkham (New York: E. P. Dutton, 1980), 207.

39   **"On entering, titles and rank":** Zinovieff and Hughes, *Companion Guide to St. Petersburg*, 149.

40   **"I cannot describe the enthusiasm":** George, *St. Petersburg*, 203.

40   **"The hand trembles":** Isabel de Madariaga, *Catherine the Great: A Short History* (New Haven, CT: Yale University Press, 1990), 189.

40   **"the frivolous and flighty spirit":** Lindsey Hughes, *The Romanovs* (London: Hambledon Continuum, 2008), 128.

41   **"The questions brought up here":** George, *St. Petersburg*, 208.

42   **"filled with the most mischievous doctrines":** de Madariaga, *Catherine the Great*, 195.

43   **"that the late King of Prussia":** ibid., 201.

43   **population was roughly two hundred thousand:** George, *St. Petersburg*, 182–183.

43   **between 2 and 7 percent:** Adam Ulam, *Russia's Failed Revolutions: From the Decembrists to the Dissidents* (New York: Basic Books, 1981), 11; Hughes, *The Romanovs*, 119, 122.

44   **most commoners were illiterate:** George, *St. Petersburg*, 193.

45   **"fear to be compared":** Lincoln, *Sunlight at Midnight*, 112.

45   **"During the period":** Yuri Egorov, *The Architectural Planning of St. Petersburg*, trans. Eric Dluhosch (Athens: Ohio University Press, 1969), 121–122.

47   **cites all the great domes of Europe:** Auguste Ricard de Montferrand, *Église Cathédrale de Saint-Isaac*, (St. Petersburg, Russia: Chez F. Bellizard et Co., 1845), 1–4.

48   **"During the campaigns":** George, *St. Petersburg*, 259.

48   **"There was only one subject":** Christine Sutherland, *The Princess of Siberia: The Story of Maria Volkonsky and the Decembrist Exiles* (New York: Farrar, Straus and Giroux, 1984), 53.

50   **"divine liberty and sacred justice":** ibid., 104.

50   **"Long live Constantine and his wife, Constitution!":** Ulam, *Russia's Failed Revolutions*, 53.

50   **"I'm all for a republic":** Peter Julicher, *Renegades, Rebels and Rogues under the Tsars* (Jefferson, NC: McFarland, 2003), 172.

50 **official death toll:** George, *St. Petersburg*, 276.

51 **"that of all nations":** ibid., 178.

52 **"return from [Europe] with a spirit of criticism":** ibid., 288.


## Chapter 2: Shanghai Race Club—Shanghai, 1842-1911

55 **"above the sea":** Ernest O. Hauser, *Shanghai: City for Sale* (New York: Harcourt, Brace, and Company, 1940), 7.

55 **regional market town of around two hundred thousand:** Marie-Claire Bergère, *Shanghai: China's Gateway to Modernity*, trans. Janet Lloyd (Stanford, CA: Stanford University Press, 2010), 23.

56 **"The advantages which foreigners":** Hauser, *Shanghai*, 4–5.

56 **"We possess all things":** Stella Dong, *Shanghai: The Rise and Fall of a Decadent City* (New York: William Morrow, 2000), 5.

58 **"the demands of the foreigners":** Pankaj Mishra, *From the Ruins of Empire* (New York: Farrar, Straus and Giroux, 2012), 29.

59 **"whatever personnel the merchants":** Betty Wei, *Shanghai: Crucible of Modern China* (Hong Kong: Oxford University Press, 1987), 29.

59 **"The number cannot be limited":** ibid., 30.

59 **"Citizens of the United States":** Edward Denison and Guang Yu Ren, *Building Shanghai: The Story of China's Gateway* (West Sussex, UK: Wiley-Academy, 2006), 39.

60 **140-acre British settlement:** Dong, *Shanghai*, 10.

60 **twenty-six different Chinese regional guilds:** Bergère, *Shanghai*, 67.

61 **"dirge-like chorus":** Dong, *Shanghai*, 10.

62 **12.5 percent of all goods:** Jeffrey Wasserstrom, *Global Shanghai, 1850–2010: A History in Fragments* (London: Routledge, 2009), 28.

62 **"Shanghae [sic] is by far the most important station":** Denison and Guang Yu, *Building Shanghai*, 30.

62 **expand their settlement to 470 acres:** ibid., 46.

62 **"Canton has been the cradle":** Wasserstrom, *Global Shanghai*, 32.

63 **fastest-growing city on earth:** Dong, *Shanghai*, 16.

63 **"My problem is how to amass":** Bergère, *Shanghai*, 45.

64 **by 1854 there were twenty thousand Chinese:** ibid., 44.

64 **8,740 *lilongs*:** ibid.

65 **"Until such time":** ibid., 47.

65 **"consent[ing] to the abrogation":** ibid., 78–79.

66 **excluded over 80 percent of the foreigners:** ibid., 112.

67 **"from mere residential zones":** ibid., 47.

67 **"Commerce was the beginning":** Dong, *Shanghai*, 19.

67 **"You must not expect men":** ibid., 15.

67  **Austrians, Prussians, Swedes:** Wasserstrom, *Global Shanghai*, 40.

68  **"Shanghai is tolerant":** Dong, *Shanghai*, 30.

68  **"most gentleman-like speculation":** ibid., 7.

68  **status lasted for one year:** Peter Hibbard, *The Bund Shanghai: China Faces West* (Hong Kong: Odyssey Books, 2007), 93.

69  **linking themselves to the Iberian Peninsula:** Maisie Meyer, "The Sephardi Jewish Community of Shanghai and the Question of Identity," in *From Kaifeng to Shanghai: Jews in China*, ed. Roman Malik (Nettetal, Germany: Steyler Verlag, 2000), 345–346.

70  **"Peruvians do not behave like Germans":** Dong, *Shanghai*, 30.

70  **"just like home":** Anne Warr, *Shanghai Architecture* (Sydney, Australia: Watermark Press, 2007), 171.

70  **"A complete line of American Products and Manufactures":** The Hotel Metropole, *Guide Book to Shanghai and Environs* (Shanghai: Oriental Press, 1903), advertisements addendum.

71  **110 feet long:** Denison and Guang Yu, *Building Shanghai*, 102.

71  **"the social heart of British Shanghai":** Warr, *Shanghai Architecture*, 157.

71  **third-wealthiest foreign corporation in China:** ibid., 157–158.

71  **over 90 percent male:** Dong, *Shanghai*, 28.

71  **688 brothels:** ibid., 44.

72  **"opening up" Shanghai for "intercourse":** "The Past and Future of China," *North China Herald*, March 18, 1854; James Farrer, *Opening Up: Youth Sex Culture and Market Reform in Shanghai* (Chicago: University of Chicago Press, 2002).

72  **"no can do":** *All About Shanghai: A Standard Guidebook* (Shanghai: University Press, 1934; repr., Hong Kong: Oxford University Press, 1986), 120–121.

72  **"How fashion that chow-chow":** Dong, *Shanghai*, 32–33.

73  **"Land mania":** Montalto de Jesus, *Historic Shanghai* (Shanghai: The Shanghai Mercury, 1909), 206.

73  **hectare of land increased 3,000 percent:** Bergère, *Shanghai*, 44–45.

74  **from over five hundred thousand to seventy-seven thousand:** Denison and Guang Yu, *Building Shanghai*, 66.

74  **"the paternal government":** "Retrospect of Events in the North of China during the Year 1864," *North China Herald*, Jan. 28, 1865, 14.

74  **"The bulk of the population":** Denison and Guang Yu Ren, *Building Shanghai*, 66.

74  **"land speculators, some of whom":** "Retrospect of Events in the North of China during the Year 1864," *North China Herald*, January 28, 1865, 14.

75  **"Building operations were suddenly stopped":** ibid.

75  **"The Council have got into a sad mess":** Dong, *Shanghai*, 64.

76  **"At Shanghai on race-days":** "Derby-Day at Shanghai," *Harper's Weekly*, June 14, 1879, 468–469.

77 **"spurious imitations of their celebrated Worcestershire":** Lea & Perrins advertisement, *North China Herald*, September 5, 1863.

77 **one-third of the capital:** Bergère, *Shanghai*, 74.

78 **"spoke English like a Briton":** Dong, *Shanghai*, 67.

78 **over two thousand rental properties:** Wei, *Shanghai*, 126.

78 **eighteen servants:** ibid.

79 **"Celestial beauties drive along this road":** Dong, *Shanghai*, 36.

79 **"learn the superior techniques of the barbarians":** Wei, *Shanghai*, 145.

81 **"every modern convenience, except sewerage":** Denison and Guang Yu, *Building Shanghai*, 128.

84 **"proposed that a voluntary militia":** Wei, *Shanghai*, 193.

84 **"When strangers first come to Shanghai":** Dong, *Shanghai*, 88–89.

86 **"All press ahead!":** Bergère, *Shanghai*, 130.

86 **"Revolution, revolution!":** ibid, 131.

87 **ten times its cover price:** Wei, *Shanghai*, 199.

88 **"Many a poor innocent farmer":** Dong, *Shanghai*, 88.

89 **"As Shanghai is a trading port":** Bergère, *Shanghai*, 143.

## Chapter 3: *Urbs Prima in Indis*—Bombay, 1857–1896

93 **"Then was seen a flash":** Teresa Albuquerque, *Urbs Prima in Indis: An Epoch in the History of Bombay, 1840–1865* (New Delhi: Promilla, 1985), 121–122.

94 **Mohammed cartoon riot:** ibid., 106.

94 **"Wahhabi phobia":** ibid., 112.

94 **"members of all communities offered prayers":** Murali Ranganathan, ed., *Govind Narayan's Mumbai: An Urban Biography from 1863* (London: Anthem Press, 2008), 143.

96 **"God Save the Queen" rang out:** Albuquerque, *Urbs Prima in Indis*, 122–123.

97 **"turned the Seven Isles":** Salman Rushdie, *Midnight's Children*, 25th anniversary edition (New York: Random House Trade Paperbacks, 2006), 101.

97 **100,000-rupee price tag:** James Grant Duff, *A History of the Maharattas, Volume II* (Oxford, UK: Oxford University Press, 1921), 23.

97 **two-thirds male:** Albuquerque, *Urbs Prima in Indis*, 182.

98 **"Those who used to do odd jobs":** Ranganathan, *Govind Narayan's Mumbai*, 197.

99 **46 percent of the walled town's population:** Sharada Dwivedi and Rahul Mehrotra, *Bombay: The Cities Within*, 2nd ed. (Bombay: Eminence Designs, 2001), 56.

99 **"In the hours that follow dawn":** Ranganathan, *Govind Narayan's Mumbai*, 53.

99 **"Clocks and watches":** ibid., 54.

100 **"the hatted races":** ibid., 52.

100 **"world of peoples and races":** Louis Rousselet, *India and Its Native Princes: Travels in Central India and in the Presidencies of Bombay and Bengal* (London: Chapman and Hall, 1875; repr., New Delhi: Asian Educational Services, 2005), 8–9. Citations refer to the reprinted edition.

100 **"The refreshment-rooms":** ibid., 12.

100 **"Not only is one entertained":** Ranganathan, *Govind Narayan's Mumbai*, 53–54.

100 **"The rich Hindoos":** Rousselet, *India and Its Native Princes*, 24.

101 **"It cannot be considered a city":** ibid., 6.

101 **"in the course of demolition":** ibid., 5.

102 **"long colonnades, with open porticoes":** Thomas R. Metcalf, *An Imperial Vision: Indian Architecture and Britain's Raj* (New Delhi: Oxford University Press, 1989) 14.

102 **"be ruled from a palace":** ibid., 13.

103 **"a class of persons":** G. H. R. Tillotson, *The Tradition of Indian Architecture: Continuity, Controversy and Change since 1850* (New Haven, CT: Yale University Press, 1989), 33.

103 **"The classes most advanced in English education":** Thomas Metcalf, *Ideologies of the Raj* (Cambridge, UK: Cambridge University Press, 1997), 49.

103 **"the admission to the legislative body":** Basil Worsfold, *Sir Bartle Frere: A Footnote to the History of the British Empire* (London: Thornton Butterworth, 1923), 29.

104 **before him there was no British architecture:** Christopher London, *Bombay Gothic* (Mumbai: India Book House, 2002), 129.

105 **"a trust from God":** Worsfold, *Sir Bartle Frere*, 40.

105 **"meet the most pressing wants":** London, *Bombay Gothic*, 28.

105 **"As our administration":** Metcalf, *An Imperial Vision*, 1.

106 **"grown up in sunshiny regions":** ibid., 98.

107 **"one long line of array":** Norma Evenson, "An Architectural Hybrid," in *Bombay: Mosaic of Modern Culture*, ed. Sujata Patel and Alice Thorner (Bombay: Oxford University Press, 1995), 168.

107 **"a most powerful lever":** Albuquerque, *Urbs Prima in Indis*, 161.

107 **"Remember, I pray you":** Vijay Tapas, ed., *University of Mumbai, 1857–2000: At the Dawn of a New Century* (Mumbai: University of Mumbai, 1999), 5.

108 **"The number of native people":** Ranganathan, *Govind Narayan's Mumbai*, 228.

109 **Architectural historians surmise:** Andreas Volwahsen, *Splendours of Imperial India: British Architecture in the 18th and 19th Centuries* (Munich: Prestel Verlag, 2004), 149.

109 **"cultures that overlap":** Edward Said, *Orientalism*, rev. ed. (New York: Penguin Classics, 2003), xxii.

110  **"joint enterprise":** Preeti Chopra, *A Joint Enterprise: Indian Elites and the Making of British Bombay* (Minneapolis: University of Minnesota Press, 2011).

111  **"As the lamp-lighters":** Albuquerque, *Urbs Prima in Indis*, 191–192.

111  **"700,000 human beings":** ibid., 174.

111  **"Bombay has had a lower death-rate":** Worsfold, *Sir Bartle Frere*, 35.

112  **"Aerated waters, in bottles":** Great Indian Peninsula Railway Company, *Railway Goods Traffic Classification Adopted by Great Indian Peninsula and Bombay Baroda & Central India Railways* (Bombay: "Bombay Gazette" Press, 1865).

112  **"The 'difficulty' of America":** Albuquerque, *Urbs Prima in Indis*, 13.

112  **"Splendid buildings sprang up":** J. M. Maclean, *Recollections of Westminster and India* (Manchester: Sherratt & Hughes, 1902), 30.

112  **the price of cotton surged fourfold:** Rekha Ranade, *Sir Bartle Frere and His Times: A Study of His Bombay Years, 1862–1867* (New Delhi: Mittal Publications, 1990), 64–65.

112  **the city's population more than doubled:** Albuquerque, *Urbs Prima in Indis*, 174–175.

113  **plots that went for less than five hundred rupees:** Dwivedi and Mehrotra, *Bombay: The Cities Within*, 80.

113  **sold for fifteen times:** Albuquerque, *Urbs Prima in Indis*, 175.

113  **"The whole community":** Maclean, *Recollections of Westminster and India*, 31.

114  **"Supreme Pontiff of Share Speculation":** Albuquerque, *Urbs Prima in Indis*, 19.

114  **sixty-two joint stock companies:** Ranade, *Sir Bartle Frere and His Times*, 80.

114  **"Everyone became suddenly a millionaire":** Maclean, *Recollections of Westminster and India*, 30–31.

115  **price of Indian cotton immediately collapsed to a quarter of its war-time value:** ibid., 32.

115  **"'Woe to the last holder'":** "The Crisis at Bombay," *The Economist*, June 10, 1865, 686.

115  **"Men who had been reputed millionaires":** Maclean, *Recollections of Westminster and India*, 32.

115  **"the best abused man in Bombay":** Albuquerque, *Urbs Prima in Indis*, 26.

116  **"To the present generation":** Ranganathan, *Govind Narayan's Mumbai*, 3.

116  **"His profession":** Rahul Mehrotra and Sharada Dwivedi, *A City Icon: Victoria Terminus, Bombay, 1887, Now Chhatrapati Shivaji Terminus, Mumbai, 1996* (Mumbai: Eminence Designs, 2006), 93–95.

117  **£45 million a year:** Dwivedi and Mehrotra, *Bombay: The Cities Within*, 138.

118  **"The viewer's eye":** Mehrotra and Dwivedi, *A City Icon*, 168.

119  **fourteen-foot-tall goddess:** London, *Bombay Gothic*, 92.

120  **"That there should be one law":** B. N. Pande, ed., *Concise History of the Indian National Congress: 1885–1947* (New Delhi: Vikas Publishing House, 1985), 21.

121  **"form the germ of a Native Parliament":** ibid., 30.

121 **"social and political progress in India"**: ibid., 29.

121 **dozens in Bombay alone:** Ranganathan, *Govind Narayan's Mumbai*, 205.

121 **"discuss questions of national importance"**: Pande, *Concise History of the Indian National Congress*, 13.

122 **over a hundred newspapers:** Barbara Metcalf and Thomas Metcalf, *A Concise History of Modern India*, 2nd ed. (Cambridge, UK: Cambridge University Press, 2006), 136.

122 **"order, . . . the Railways"**: P. N. Chopra, Ram Gopal, and M. L. Bhargava, *A Century of Indian National Congress*, 23.

122 **"according to the ideas of government prevalent in Europe"**: Pande, *Concise History of the Indian National Congress*, 31.

122 **"Un-British Rule in India"**: Dadabhai Naoroji, *Poverty and Un-British Rule in India* (London: S. Sonnenschein, 1901; repr., New Delhi: Commonwealth Publishers, 1988).

122 **"nonofficial parliament"**: Chopra, Gopal, and Bhargava, *A Century of Indian National Congress*, 13.

123 **"It is by force"**: Pande, *Concise History of the Indian National Congress*, 18.

123 **"If India can govern itself"**: Chopra, Gopal, and Bhargava, *A Century of Indian National Congress*, 23–24.

125 **"A man dressed in a coarse homespun coat"**: St. Nihal Singh, *India: Old and New* (Bombay: Great Indian Peninsula Railway, 1900), 1–2.

## Chapter 4: City on Spilt Blood—
## St. Petersburg/Petrograd/Leningrad, 1825–1934

129 **"the capital with the cabaret"**: Lincoln, *Sunlight at Midnight*, 138.

130 **"frequent purposeless travel"**: George, *St. Petersburg*, 294.

131 **more than half of the signs:** Marshall Berman, *All That Is Solid Melts into Air: The Experience of Modernity* (New York: Simon and Schuster, 1982), 194.

131 **nearly twice that of Moscow:** Lincoln, *Sunlight at Midnight*, 130.

131 **the city remained 10 percent foreign:** George, *St. Petersburg*, 290.

131 **fifty thousand aristocrats:** Lincoln, *Sunlight at Midnight*, 131.

132 **over 40 percent of the population:** ibid., 130.

132 **bureaucracy increased fivefold:** George, *St. Petersburg*, 289.

132 **thirty-one million official documents:** ibid.

132 **seven in ten city residents were male:** Lincoln, *Sunlight at Midnight*, 130.

132 **"We provincials"**: George, *St. Petersburg*, 289.

132 **"Theater, exhibitions, shopping mall"**: Volkov, *St. Petersburg*, 27.

133 **"Oh, do not believe this Nevsky Prospect!"**: Nikolai Gogol, *The Collected Tales of Nikolai Gogol*, trans. Richard Pevear and Larissa Volokhonsky (New York: Pantheon Books, 1998), 277.

133 **"Here you will meet"**: Gogol, *The Collected Tales of Nikolai Gogol*, 248.

135 **freed twenty-two million people:** Julicher, *Renegades, Rebels and Rogues*, 184.

136 **first German free city:** W. R. Brownlow, *Lectures on Slavery and Serfdom in Europe* (London: Burns and Oates, 1892; repr., New York: Negro Universities Press, 1969), 218.

136 **"We do not need either a Tsar":** Berman, *All That Is Solid Melts into Air*, 214.

137 **"A sight like it":** ibid., 214–215.

137 **over two thousand students:** Julicher, *Renegades, Rebels and Rogues*, 200.

138 **sixteen hundred students had been arrested:** ibid.

140 **"The people were completely indifferent":** Edvard Radzinsky. *Alexander II: The Last Great Tsar* (New York: Free Press, 2005), 423.

142 **"the weakness, the tolerance":** Richard Wortman, "The 'Russian Style' in Church Architecture as Imperial Symbol after 1881," in *Architectures of Russian Identity*, ed. James Cracraft and Daniel Rowland (Ithaca, NY: Cornell University Press, 2003), 105.

142 **"a notoriously out-of-place landmark":** Michael S. Flier, "At Daggers Drawn: The Competition for the Church of the Savior on the Blood," in *For SK: In Celebration of the Life and Career of Simon Karlinsky*, ed. Michael S. Flier and Robert P. Hughes (Berkeley, CA: Berkeley Slavic Specialties, 1994), 97.

143 **"a deliberate intrusion":** Michael S. Flier, "The Church of the Savior on the Blood: Projection, Rejection, Resurrection," in *Christianity and the Eastern Slavs: Volume II, Russian Culture in Modern Times, California Slavic Studies XVII*, ed. Robert P. Hughes and Irina Paperno (Berkeley: University of California Press, 1994), 30.

143 **over a million people:** Lincoln, *Sunlight at Midnight*, 153.

143 **two out of three Petersburgers:** ibid., 153–154.

143 **ten times higher:** George, *St. Petersburg*, 334.

143 **averaged 8 percent growth per year:** ibid., 373.

144 **eleven thousand workers:** ibid.

144 **thirty thousand people:** ibid., 337.

144 **fifty men, women, and children:** Lincoln, *Sunlight at Midnight*, 134.

145 **twice that in Paris:** ibid., 154.

145 **12,000 factory workers in 1840:** ibid., 145.

145 **three times higher:** ibid., 146.

145 **highest death rate of any major city:** W. Bruce Lincoln, *The Romanovs: Autocrats of All the Russias* (New York: Anchor, 1983), 479.

145 **one resident in fourteen:** Lincoln, *Sunlight at Midnight*, 151.

145 **thirty thousand tons:** ibid., 134–135.

145 **1,840 taverns:** George, *St. Petersburg*, 338.

145 **per capita vodka consumption:** ibid.

145 **"There have been cases of fatal alcohol poisoning":** Lincoln, *Sunlight at Midnight*, 135.

145 **35,000 arrests for drunkenness:** George, *St. Petersburg*, 338.

145 **130,000 Petersburgers were arrested and jailed:** ibid.

146 **150 officially licensed brothels:** Lincoln, *Sunlight at Midnight*, 135.

146 **registered sex workers topped 4,400:** George, *St. Petersburg*, 338.

146 **roughly one in every forty Petersburgers:** Lincoln, *Sunlight at Midnight*, 214.

146 **literacy in St. Petersburg stood at nearly 80 percent:** George, *St. Petersburg*, 338.

146 **well ahead of Moscow:** Charles Clark, *Uprooting Otherness: The Literacy Campaign in NEP-Era Russia* (Cranbury, NJ: Associated University Presses, 2000), 17.

147 **more than a mansion in Paris or New York:** Lincoln, *Sunlight at Midnight*, 12.

147 **lined with twenty-eight banks:** George, *St. Petersburg*, 334.

148 **over twelve thousand workers:** Lincoln, *Sunlight at Midnight*, 156.

149 **12,500 Putilov workers went on strike:** George, *St. Petersburg*, 397.

149 **One hundred twenty thousand Petersburgers refused to report to work:** ibid.

149 **"We, workers and residents":** ibid.

150 **"There is no tsar!":** ibid, 399.

150 **five thousand marchers:** ibid.

150 **sixty thousand people:** ibid., 400.

151 **nearly a thousand men, women, and children:** Lincoln, *Sunlight at Midnight*, 190.

152 **"a gathering of savages":** George, *St. Petersburg*, 404.

152 **"the ancestor I like least":** ibid., 410.

153 **"As if by magic":** Richard Wortman, *Scenarios of Power: Myth and Ceremony in Russian Monarchy, Volume II* (Princeton, NJ: Princeton University Press, 2000), 412.

153 **"The idea was to create":** Wortman, "The 'Russian Style' in Church Architecture," 115.

154 **nearly four million Russian casualties:** George, *St. Petersburg*, 411.

154 **"Down with the autocracy!":** ibid., 435.

155 **thirty thousand gold rubles:** Lincoln, *Sunlight at Midnight*, 228–229.

155 **"Autocratic Russia was collapsing":** George, *St. Petersburg*, 437.

155 **"I beg you to inform":** Lincoln, *Sunlight at Midnight*, 230.

155 **"no more Romanovs":** George, *St. Petersburg*, 442.

156 **forty thousand Petrograd workers were unemployed:** Ronald Grigor Suny, "Toward a Social History of the October Revolution," *American Historical Review* 88, no. 1 (1983): 48, 51.

157 **"economically most backward":** Vladimir Lenin, *Imperialism* (New York: International Publishers, 1939), 81.

159  **"embittered bourgeois intelligentsia"**: George, *St. Petersburg*, 449.

159  **dropped from 2.3 million**: George, *St. Petersburg*, 452.

159  **"Workers and peasants need freedom"**: ibid., 453–454.

160  **Cheka arrested hundreds**: ibid., 453.

160  **"the pride and flower of the Revolution"**: ibid., 454.

160  **"In carrying out the October Revolution"**: ibid., 454.

161  **"the line of advance of free humanity"**: Anatole Kopp, *Town and Revolution: Soviet Architecture and City Planning, 1917–1935*, trans. Thomas E. Burton (New York, George Braziller, 1970), 52.

164  **"Gropius is back from Leningrad"**: Oskar Beyer, ed., *Erich Mendelsohn: Letters of an Architect* (London: Abelard-Schuman Limited, 1967), 125–126.

## Chapter 5: Great World—Shanghai, 1911–1937

167  **"Shanghai, the Paris of the East!"**: *All About Shanghai*, 1.

169  **"modern skyscrapers [and] straw huts"**: ibid., 43.

169  **"carry on trade"**: Denison and Guang Yu, *Building Shanghai*, 72.

169  **doubled the city's population in fifteen years**: Dong, *Shanghai*, 75.

170  **numbering nearly fourteen thousand**: Wasserstrom, *Global Shanghai*, 159.

170  **one in four Russian women**: Warr, *Shanghai Architecture*, 132.

171  **"confiscating all the real and personal property"**: Sean McMeekin, *History's Greatest Heist: The Looting of Russia by the Bolsheviks* (New Haven, CT: Yale University Press, 2009), 26.

172  **two hundred thousand pedestrians a day**: Denison and Guang Yu, *Building Shanghai*, 93.

172  **"To call Wing On's a department store"**: Dong, *Shanghai*, 97.

173  **"accustomed to foreign manners"**: Denison and Guang Yu, *Building Shanghai*, 92, 94.

173  **"a department store for amusement"**: Warr, *Shanghai Architecture*, 162.

173  **"hodgepodge of the most déclassé elements"**: Dong, *Shanghai*, 205.

175  **"I am the splendor of the moon"**: Bergère, *Shanghai*, 273.

176  **"cosmopolitan nationalists"**: Wasserstrom, *Global Shanghai*, 66.

176  **"fifteen minutes one can"**: Denison and Guang Yu, *Building Shanghai*, 135.

177  **"number 11 bus"**: Bergère, *Shanghai*, 261.

177  **bought from their parents for twenty dollars**: Denison and Guang Yu, *Building Shanghai*, 118.

177  **"look round on their magnificent buildings"**: Dong, *Shanghai*, 175.

177  **twenty-one thousand such hovels dotted the city**: Denison and Guang Yu, *Building Shanghai*, 165.

178  **just twenty-seven**: Bradley Mayhew, *Shanghai*, 2nd ed. (Oakland, CA: Lonely Planet, 2004), 52.

178 **only four years:** Dong, *Shanghai*, 163.

178 **"that the ricsha [*sic*] coolies be strong":** The Hotel Metropole, *Guide Book to Shanghai and Environs*, 32.

178 **ten cents a day:** Dong, *Shanghai*, 163.

179 **with 3,350,570 people, was the sixth-largest city:** *All About Shanghai*, 33.

179 **600 people per acre:** Denison and Guang Yu, *Building Shanghai*, 159–161.

182 **three thousand protestors:** Dong, *Shanghai*, 165.

182 **"Take Back the Concessions":** ibid.

182 **"the shooting had the immediate effect":** Wei, *Shanghai*, 224.

183 **over one hundred thousand workers:** Wei, *Shanghai*, 224.

183 **"I could not believe it":** Dong, *Shanghai*, 167.

184 **forty thousand American, British, French, Japanese, and Italian troops:** Denison and Guang Yu, *Building Shanghai*, 131.

184 **"city for sale":** Hauser, *Shanghai*.

187 **"scientific principles developed from Europe and America":** Warr, *Shanghai Architecture*, 266.

189 **"Shanghai can only stand six floors":** Hibbard, *The Bund Shanghai*, 67.

190 **"When a traveler arrives in Shanghai":** F. L. Hawks Pott, *A Short History of Shanghai: Being an Account of the Growth and Development of the International Settlement* (Shanghai: Kelly & Walsh, 1928), 1.

191 **three thousand brothels:** Bergère, *Shanghai*, 270.

191 **more prostitutes per capita of the female population:** Denison and Guang Yu, *Building Shanghai*, 169.

191 **"an Art Deco rocket ship":** Hibbard, *The Bund Shanghai*, 227.

194 **"According to crowd psychology":** Andrew David Field, *Shanghai's Dancing World: Cabaret Culture and Urban Politics, 1919–1954* (Hong Kong: Chinese University Press, 2010), 102.

196 **"It doesn't matter where I go":** Ladislav Kabos, *The Man Who Changed Shanghai* (film trailer), 2010, http://www.ladislavhudec.eu/.

196 **"90 per cent Chinese":** J. G. Ballard, *Miracles of Life: Shanghai to Shepperton, an Autobiography* (London: Fourth Estate, 2008), 4.

197 **"The rapid advance":** J. S. Potter, *Shanghai Realty: The Position at the Close of 1926* (Shanghai: Asia Realty Company, 1927), 1.

197 **"an increasing number of foreign residents":** ibid., 21.

197 **"There is not a great deal":** Hibbard, *The Bund Shanghai*, 75.

197 **"The two most interesting 'towers' in the world":** ibid., 17.

197 **"What odds whether Shanghai is the Paris of the East":** *All About Shanghai*, 73.

198 **"Even . . . in the midst of chaotic conditions":** Potter, *Shanghai Realty*, 21–22.

198 **"city of missions . . . and bothels":** *All About Shanghai*, 43–44.

## Chapter 6: The City under Progress's Feet—Bombay, 1896–1947

201 **one-quarter of the world's population:** Fareed Zakaria, *The Post-American World* (New York: W. W. Norton, 2008), 167.

202 **"The wonder is not that the death rate is exceedingly high":** Dwivedi and Mehrotra, *Bombay: The Cities Within*, 166.

203 **eighty-two mills employed seventy-three thousand workers:** Gillian Tindall, *City of Gold: The Biography of Bombay* (London: Temple Smith, 1982), 239.

203 **sixteen-hour workday:** Sumit Sarkar, *Modern India, 1885–1947* (New York: St. Martin's Press, 1989), 133.

204 **on par with London and Paris:** Everson, "An Architectural Hybrid," 176.

204 **80 percent of the city's population:** ibid., 174.

204 **84 percent of the city's population had been born elsewhere:** Rajnarayan Chandavarkar, *History, Culture and the Indian City* (Cambridge, UK: Cambridge University Press, 2009), 59.

204 **settlements of fewer than five thousand people:** Metcalf and Metcalf, *A Concise History of Modern India*, 138.

205 **Five to ten people shared:** Dwivedi and Mehrotra, *Bombay: The Cities Within*, 208–209.

205 **Common toilets were provided at a rate of one per story:** ibid.

205 **"housing, but warehousing people!":** ibid.

205 **"Everywhere on the ground":** ibid., 165.

206 **twelve hundred people per acre:** Evenson, "An Architectural Hybrid," 173–174.

206 **ten-by-twelve-foot rooms:** ibid., 174.

206 **five hundred people per acre:** Dwivedi and Mehrotra, *Bombay: The Cities Within*, 169.

207 **"The new construction wrecked hundreds":** Berman, *All That Is Solid Melts into Air*, 150–151.

207 **thousands of Bombay mill workers went out on strike:** Dwivedi and Mehrotra, *Bombay: The Cities Within*, 232.

209 **"bazaars in Victorian arcades":** ibid., 323.

209 **thousands of petitions and court cases:** Chopra, *A Joint Enterprise*, 26.

211 **"Our people . . . consider it strange":** Ranganathan, *Govind Narayan's Mumbai*, 252.

211 **whose population increased nearly 30 percent:** Sharada Dwivedi and Rahul Mehrotra, *Bombay Deco* (Mumbai: Eminence Designs, 2008), 15.

212 **a line of twenty-one Art Deco apartment buildings:** ibid., 124.

214 **by 1939, nearly three hundred:** ibid., 47.

216 **1,500 leather-upholstered chairs:** ibid., 78.

216 **"a cinema for all Bombay":** ibid., 76.

217 **"English rule without the Englishman":** Mohandas K. Gandhi, *"Hind Swa-*

*raj" and Other Writings*, ed. Anthony Parel (Cambridge, UK: Cambridge University Press, 2009), 27.

217 **"Englistan":** ibid.

217 **"To me the rise of the cities":** ibid., 67.

218 **killing 370 protestors:** Metcalf and Metcalf, *A Concise History of Modern India*, 168.

218 **awarded thirty thousand pounds sterling:** ibid., 169.

219 **penned in just nine days:** Pankaj Mishra, "The Inner Voice," *New Yorker*. May 2, 2011.

220 **"I read your book with great interest":** Leo Tolstoy to Gandhi, May 8, 1910, Gandhi Book Centre, reproduction of original letter, Mumbai website, accessed on August 24, 2011, http://mkgandhi-sarvodaya.org/biography/tolstoy_letter.gif.

220 **"It would be folly":** Gandhi, *"Hind Swaraj" and Other Writings*, 106.

220 **"India's salvation consists in unlearning":** Sarkar, *Modern India*, 180.

221 **"the interior that has yet not been polluted":** Gandhi, *"Hind Swaraj" and Other Writings*, 68.

221 **"The workers in the mills of Bombay have become slaves":** ibid., 106.

221 **"Formerly, men were made slaves":** ibid., 35.

221 **"We cannot condemn mill-owners":** ibid., 107.

221 **"The lawyers have enslaved India":** ibid., 56, 102.

222 **"India was prosperous so long as there was spinning":** K. Gopalaswami, *Gandhi and Bombay* (Bombay: Gandhi Smarak Nidhi, 1965), 143–144.

222 **"With God as my witness":** ibid., 51.

222 **"The burden of boycott":** Dwivedi and Mehrotra, *Bombay: The Cities Within*, 234.

222 **"Bombay, which is the first city of India":** K. Gopalaswami, *Gandhi and Bombay*, 224.

223 **"Not a single street in Bombay":** ibid.

223 **"This label is a warranty":** Metcalf and Metcalf, *A Concise History of Modern India*, 200.

224 **"I think it would be a great idea":** Salman Rushdie, "Mohandas Gandhi," *Time*, August 13, 1998, 129.

## Chapter 7: Closing Three Windows and Opening a Fourth
### I: The Two-Front War—Leningrad, 1934–1985

230 **"Black Ravens":** Volkov, *St. Petersburg*, 418.

230 **two and a half minutes per victim:** Robert Conquest, *The Great Terror: Stalin's Purge of the Thirties*, rev. ed. (New York: Macmillan, 1973), 84.

230 **1,108 were subsequently shot:** Robert Conquest, *Stalin and the Kirov Murder* (New York: Oxford University Press, 1989), 29.

231 **more than thirty thousand Leningraders:** Lincoln, *Sunlight at Midnight*, 263.

232 **would never return to its second city:** Helen Rappaport, *Joseph Stalin: A Biographical Companion* (Santa Barbara, CA: ABC-CLIO, 1999), 171.

233 **"red tsar":** Simon Sebag Montefiore, *Stalin: The Court of the Red Tsar* (New York: Knopf, 2004).

233 **"cult of hierarchy":** Hugh D. Hudson Jr., "Terror in Soviet Architecture: The Murder of Mikhail Okhitovich," *Slavic Review* 51 (1992): 458.

234 **"the poisonous nest":** Michael Jones, *Leningrad: State of Siege* (New York: Basic Books, 2008), 39.

234 **"Hitler has decided":** Sergei Varshavsky and Boris Rest, *The Ordeal of the Hermitage: The Siege of Leningrad, 1941–1944* (Leningrad: Aurora Art Publishers, 1985), 272.

235 **Half a million objects:** ibid., 68.

235 **tens of thousands starved to death each month:** George, *St. Petersburg*, 518.

235 **over a million:** Lincoln, *Sunlight at Midnight*, 290.

235 **largest city ever under siege in the history of the world:** ibid., 277.

236 **"the mainland":** Jones, *Leningrad*, 277.

236 **size of a dinner roll:** Monument to the Heroic Defenders of Leningrad, permanent exhibition, St. Petersburg, visited July 6, 2010.

236 **from three million to one million:** Lincoln, *Sunlight at Midnight*, 287.

238 **"dog shit":** ibid., 325.

238 **by far the largest local chapter:** Thomas Campbell interview with author, St. Petersburg, June 23, 2010.

### II: The Dark Ages—Shanghai, 1937–1989

239 **left some one hundred thousand Chinese dead:** Bergère, *Shanghai*, 289.

239 **twenty-five thousand stateless German and Austrian Jews:** Bergère, *Shanghai*, 297.

241 **eight thousand foreigners:** Dong, *Shanghai*, 274.

242 **Japanese population of three hundred thousand:** Denison and Guang Yu, *Building Shanghai*, 199.

242 **"an increasing number of foreign residents":** Potter, *Shanghai Realty*, 21.

242 **"dwarf bandits":** Dong, *Shanghai*, 211.

243 **million-man army:** Denison and Guang Yu, *Building Shanghai*, 201.

244 **"We will stand by Shanghai":** Bergère, *Shanghai*, 347.

245 **ten thousand Shanghai "counterrevolutionaries" were arrested:** ibid., 359.

246 **three hundred of his favorite Shanghai capitalists:** ibid., 362.

246 **87 percent of the taxes:** ibid., 370.

246 **170,000 skilled workers:** ibid., 371.

247 **"surpass England and catch up with America"**: Perry Link, "China: From Famine to Oslo," *New York Review of Books*, January 13, 2011.

247 **less housing space per capita**: Bergère, *Shanghai*, 382.

248 **named Chaoying (Surpass England) and Chaomei (Overtake America)**: Rebecca Karl, *Mao Zedong and China in the Twentieth Century: A Concise History* (Durham, NC: Duke University Press, 2010), 103.

248 **"122 years without rent"**: Denison and Guang Yu, *Building Shanghai*, 206.

249 **One hundred thousand gathered in People's Square**: Roderick MacFarquhar and Michael Schoenhals, *Mao's Last Revolution* (Cambridge, MA: Harvard University Press, 2006), 165.

250 **"to learn knowledge and truth from the West"**: Whitney Steward, *Deng Xiaoping: Leader in a Changing China* (Minneapolis: Lerner Publications, 2001), 23.

### III: License-Permit Raj—Bombay, 1947–1991

251 **the largest linguistic segment**: Ramachandra Guha, *India after Gandhi: The History of the World's Largest Democracy* (New York: Ecco, 2007), 198.

251 **came in second**: Metcalf and Metcalf, *A Concise History of Modern India*, 241.

253 **The population of Bombay tripled**: Wendell Cox, "The Evolving Urban Form: Mumbai," *New Geography*, April 5, 2011. website accessed June 18, 2012, http://www.newgeography.com/content/002172 -the-evolving-urban-form-mumbai.

255 **"The development across the water"**: Dwivedi and Mehrotra, *Bombay: The Cities Within*, 302.

256 **"unfettered by the traditions of the past"**: Metcalf and Metcalf, *A Concise History of Modern India*, 235.

### IV: The City at the Center of the World—Dubai, to 1981

260 **no population growth**: Jim Krane, *City of Gold: Dubai and the Dream of Capitalism* (New York: St. Martin's Press, 2009), 3–4.

260 **modernizing a people stuck in the seventh century**: ibid., 34.

261 **two bazaars, four hundred shops**: Sheikh Jumah al-Maktoum House museum, permanent exhibition, Dubai, visited January 16, 2010.

261 **"The trade of Dibai [*sic*] is considerable"**: ibid.

261 **95 percent of the Gulf economy**: Krane, *City of Gold*, 26.

262 **two times its price**: Davidson, *Dubai*, 70; Krane, *City of Gold*, 72.

263 **wealthy, luxury-goods-producing neighbor, France**: Davidson, *Dubai*, 70.

263 **one thousand South Asians**: ibid., 91.

263 **foreigners made up the majority**: Syed Ali, *Dubai: Gilded Cage* (New Haven, CT: Yale University Press, 2010), 18.

264 **more spaces than Dubai had cars:** Davidson, *Dubai*, 95.

264 **about $1.5 million in oil per capita:** ibid., 101, 103.

266 **"What's good for the merchants is good for Dubai":** Krane, *City of Gold*, 75.

267 **"What is the problem":** Davidson, *Dubai*, 91.

267 **60,000 people in 1960:** Krane, *City of Gold*, 76–77.

267 **largest man-made harbor ever created:** Kasarda and Lindsay, *Aerotropolis*, 294.

267 **25 percent of its gross domestic product on infrastructure:** Davidson, *Dubai*, 107.

268 **"consider that not one of these investments":** Krane, *City of Gold*, 78–79.

## Chapter 8: From Perestroika to Petrolgrad—
## Leningrad, 1985-St. Petersburg, Present

272 **"The people of Leningrad":** George, *St. Petersburg*, 558.

272 **"stop misinforming people":** Masha Gessen, *The Man Without a Face: The Unlikely Rise of Vladimir Putin* (New York: Riverhead Books, 2012), 75.

274 **"Svyato-Petrograd":** George, *St. Petersburg*, 564.

275 **estimates range up to three hundred thousand:** ibid., 571.

276 **twice its size:** ibid., 571.

276 **"the only Russian door to Europe":** Lincoln, *Sunlight at Midnight*, 343.

277 **largest privatization scheme in the history of the world:** Peter Baker and Susan Glasser, *Kremlin Rising: Vladimir Putin's Russia and the End of Revolution* (New York: Scribner, 2005), 48.

278 **"Privatization [alone] is no great achievement":** Joseph Stiglitz, "Preface," in *The New Russia: Transition Gone Awry*, ed. Lawrence Klein and Marshall Pomer (Stanford, CA: Stanford University Press, 2001), xxi.

278 **"market Bolsheviks":** ibid., xxii.

279 **even its population:** George, *St. Petersburg*, 580.

279 **living on four dollars a day:** Stiglitz, "Preface," xviii.

279 **crime rate:** Marshall Goldman, *Lost Opportunity: Why Economic Reforms in Russia Have Not Worked* (New York: W. W. Norton, 1994), 4.

279 **life expectancy:** Michael Specter, "Kremlin, Inc.," *New Yorker*, January 29, 2007; World Bank, Russian Federation Data website, accessed June 18, 2012, http://data.worldbank.org/country/russian-federation?display=default.

279 **economic inequality doubled:** Stiglitz, "Preface," xviii.

279 **economy shrank by nearly half:** ibid., xvii.

280 **"yak, yak, yak":** Goldman, *Lost Opportunity*, 105.

282 **the fifteenth largest company in the world:** "The World's Biggest Public Companies," *Forbes*, April 2011, accessed July 21, 2011, http://www.forbes.com/global2000/#p_2_s_acompanyRankOverall_All_All_All.

283 **"The president has a very clear idea":** Baker and Glasser, *Kremlin Rising*, 96.

284 **"Would you vote for a horse":** "Putin Ally Leads Petersburg Poll" *BBC News*, September 22, 2003.

284 **"statements so fawning":** Baker and Susan, *Kremlin Rising*, 9.

284 **"The Russian mentality needs a baron":** ibid., 377.

284 **"I'm calling from St. Petersburg":** George, *St. Petersburg*, 589.

285 **"Russia's first science museum":** plaque on exterior, Kunstkamera, visited June 19, 2010.

286 **hundreds of thousands of Westerners:** Yelena Zborovskaya, "More Tourists Choose to Arrive by Sea," *St. Petersburg Times*, October 6, 2009.

286 **"Russia is a diverse country":** George, *St. Petersburg*, 588.

287 **one thousand city parks:** Galina Stolyarova, "Bill Threatens 40 Percent of Green Spaces," *St. Petersburg Times*, June 25, 2010.

288 **"seemed to confirm the clichés about Russia":** Ellen Bennett, "Gazprom Jury Walk-Out," *Building Design* (UK), December 8, 2006.

290 **four hundred rubles:** Sergey Chernov, "Farce Hits Tower Hearing," *St. Petersburg Times*, July 1, 2008.

290 **"of course, it's summer there":** *The Potosi Principle*, Alice Creischer, Andreas Siekmann, and Max Jorge Hinderer, eds. (Cologne, Germany: Walther König, 2011).

### Chapter 9: The Head of the Dragon—Shanghai, 1989–Present

300 **"How big is this square?":** Michael Fathers and Andrew Higgins, *Tiananmen: The Rape of Peking* (London: Transworld Publishers, 1989), 60.

300 **well over a hundred thousand protestors:** ibid.

301 **"Welcome the initiator of *glasnost*":** ibid., 61.

301 **roughly seven thousand protestors:** Zhang Liang, *The Tiananmen Papers* (New York: PublicAffairs, 2001), 110.

301 **"a window cut through to Europe":** Dmitry Shvidkovsky, *Russian Architecture and the West* (New Haven, CT: Yale University Press, 2007), 196.

302 **seven hundred police:** Zhang, *The Tiananmen Papers*, 403.

302 **"Many comrades have asked us":** Zhang, *The Tiananmen Papers*, 410.

302 **"We will never allow protests":** Zhang, *The Tiananmen Papers*, 135.

304 **"Head of the Dragon":** Thomas J. Campanella, *The Concrete Dragon: China's Urban Revolution and What It Means for the World* (New York: Princeton Architectural Press, 2008), 71.

304 **"Shanghai was a highly developed metropolis":** Zhao Ziyang, *Prisoner of the State: The Secret Journals of Zhao Ziyang* (Cambridge, MA: Harvard University Press, 2009), 151–152.

305 **life expectancy higher than America's:** Nicholas D. Kristof, "Where China Outpaces America," *New York Times*, May 1, 2011.

305 **"We must introduce this toilet to China":** "Dear John: Tapping into China's Toilet Revolution," *ChinaOnline*, December 18, 2000.

306 **three hundred thousand residents:** Tarun Khanna, *Billions of Entrepreneurs* (Cambridge, MA: Harvard Business Press, 2008), 72.

306 **million families:** Philip Pan, *Out of Mao's Shadow: The Struggle for the Soul of a New China* (New York: Simon & Schuster, 2008), 164.

307 **over US$10 billion:** Yawei Chen, *Shanghai Pudong: Urban Development in an Era of Global-Local Interaction* (Delft, Netherlands: Delft University of Technology, 2007), 150.

307 **Pudong was like buying a suit:** Trish Saywell, "Pudong Rises to the Task," *Far Eastern Economic Review*, November 2, 2000.

309 **"The connection has been reset":** James Fallows, "The Connection Has Been Reset," *Atlantic*, March 2008.

312 **city's total population as 18.88 million:** Xinhua News Agency, "Shanghai's Registered Population Grows," *China Daily*, March 14, 2009.

312 **foreign population of 5 percent:** James Farrer, "Shanghai: A Global City's Mixed Loyalties," *New York Times*, May 19, 2005.

317 **"The ability of China to adapt":** Michael Wines, "On Day for China Pride, Little Interest in Ideology," *New York Times*, September 30, 2009.

318 **"global values":** Nicholas Bequelin, "Crackdown in China," *New York Times*, April 7, 2011.

318 **Only twenty foreign films a year:** "Bigger Abroad," *The Economist*, February 17, 2011.

319 **"the SH [Shanghai] government culture department has some non-sense issues":** *City Weekend* (Shanghai) website, accessed September 29, 2009, dead link, http://www.cityweekend.com/cn/shanghai/events/52749/.

320 **"indie-rock wunderkind":** Alex Ross, "Symphony of Millions," *New Yorker*, July 7, 2008.

320 **lack of "performance licenses":** Zachary Mexico, *China Underground* (Brooklyn, NY: Soft Skull Press, 2009), 113.

320 **"Tibet! Tibet!":** Tania Branigan, "Bjork's Shanghai Surprise: A Cry of 'Tibet,' " *Guardian* (UK), March 4, 2008.

320 **"It costs enough to have a nice two-bedroom apartment":** James von Klemperer, "KPF in Shanghai" (lecture, Kohn Pedersen Fox, the Skyscraper Museum, New York, October 27, 2009).

### Chapter 10: Slumdogs and Millionaires—Bombay, 1991–Mumbai, Present

327 **"Hindu rate of growth":** Robyn Meredith, *The Elephant and the Dragon: The Rise of India and China and What It Means for All of Us* (New York: W. W. Norton, 2008), 50.

328 **topped 100 percent:** ibid., 47.

328 **army of 250,000 bureaucrats:** Gurcharan Das, *India Unbound* (New York: Knopf, 2001), 208.

329 **"If Mumbai fails, then India fails":** Michel St. Pierre, "Sustainable Cities— Shanghai Looking Forward" (presentation, Council on Tall Buildings and Urban Habitat Conference, Mumbai, February 3–5, 2010).

329 **"the golden summer of 1991":** Das, *India Unbound*, 213.

329 **doubled in three months:** Bombay Stock Exchange Historical Data, BSE website, accessed July 24, 2011, http://www.bseindia.com/histdata/hindices .asp.

330 **several dozen traders:** Sanjoy Hazarika, "200 Killed as Bombings Sweep Bombay," *New York Times*, March 13, 1993.

331 **"from red to saffron":** Gyan Prakash, *Mumbai Fables* (Princeton, NJ: Princeton University Press, 2010), 204.

331 **hundreds were killed:** Edward Gargan, "After Bombay's Violence, Fear and Finger-Pointing," *New York Times*, November 19, 1993.

332 **fifty road-renaming proposals a month:** Suketu Mehta, *Maximum City: Bombay Lost and Found* (New York: Knopf, 2004), 129.

332 **38 percent of the nation's GDP:** *Mumbai: First among Equals*, Bombay First brochure, Mumbai, 2010.

333 **"Can you believe it?":** Simon Beaufoy, *Slumdog Millionaire* screenplay (New York: Newmarket Press, 2008), 95.

334 **billionaire Hiranandani brothers:** "India's Richest," *Forbes*, September 29, 2010, accessed on July 26, 2011, http://www.forbes.com/lists/2010/77/india-rich-10_Indias-Richest_Rank.html.

334 **as high as 8.9 percent:** Meredith, *The Elephant and the Dragon*, 89.

334 **office rents run twice Manhattan's rates:** "Mumbai Office Rents Twice of Manhattan," *Times of India*, February 23, 2010.

334 **apartment rents fall in between London and Paris:** "Mumbai Home Rentals Third Highest in Asia," Press Trust of India, New Delhi, April 17, 2008.

334 **150 multinational corporations:** Surendra Hiranandani, speech, Mumbai, February 24, 2010.

335 **"reserves the right to deny admission to anybody":** Hiranandani Gardens, tour, Mumbai, February 24, 2010.

336 **"Their building has Doric columns":** Surendra Hiranandani, speech, Mumbai, February 24, 2010.

338 **42 percent of graduates:** Mehul Srivastava, "Keeping Women on the Job in India," *Bloomberg Businessweek*, March 3, 2011.

340 **grew by a third:** Wendell Cox, "The Evolving Urban Form: Mumbai," *New Geography*, April 5, 2011, accessed on June 18, 2012, http://www.newgeography .com/content/002172-the-evolving-urban-form-mumbai.

340 **for about ten US dollars:** *Trains at a Glance* (New Delhi: Indian Railways, 2012), 290 (fare table).

341 **where most Mumbaikars live:** Darryl D'Monte, "Bridges That Widen the Gap," *The Hindu* (India), August 17, 2012.

341 **for every one thousand residents:** Glaeser, *Triumph of the City*, 93.

341 **seven years below the already-bleak Indian average:** ibid., 94.

341 **not even in the top one hundred countries:** *The World Fact Book 2011* (Washington DC: Central Intelligence Agency, 2011), https://www.cia.gov/library/publications/the-world-factbook/rankorder/2102rank.html, accessed June 18, 2012.

341 **estimated $1 billion:** Jim Yardly, "Soaring above India's Poverty, a 27-Story Home," *New York Times*, October 28, 2010; personal observation, Mumbai, February 12, 2010.

342 **metropolitan population of twenty million:** *CIA World Fact Book 2011*.

342 **one hour and twenty minutes:** permanent exhibition, Chhatrapati Shivaji Terminus Heritage Gallery, Mumbai, visited February 26, 2010.

342 **to 4,500 per train:** Mehta, *Maximum City*, 493.

342 **nearly a dozen people are killed:** ibid., 495.

343 **$350 million Rajiv Gandhi Sea Link:** "Mumbai on the Growth Path," *Economic Times* (Mumbai), January 21, 2010.

343 **near-perfect voter turnout:** Mehta, *Maximum City*, 68.

345 **most crowded place on the planet:** Mayank Gandhi, Secretary (Remaking of Mumbai Federation), interview with author, Mumbai, February 9, 2010.

347 **"It cannot be considered a city":** Rousselet, *India and Its Native Princes*, 6.

348 **"the efforts of two international cities":** McKinsey & Company, *Vision Mumbai: Transforming Mumbai into a World-Class City* (Mumbai: McKinsey & Company, 2003), 10.

348 **America's poorest city:** "Cleveland Rated Poorest Big City in America," Associated Press, September 23, 2004.

348 **population of Mumbai island, it found, was in decline:** Sharad Vyas, Sukhada Tatke, and Madhavi Rajadhyaksha, "Dense Mumbai Packs 20K Individuals Per Sq Km," *Times of India*, April 2, 2011.

### Chapter 11: Dubai Inc. Proudly Presents the International City™— Dubai, 1981–Present

353 **fully 96 percent of the population:** Davidson, *Dubai*, 190.

353 **"I want it to be number one":** CBS News, "A Visit to Dubai Inc.," *60 Minutes*, 2008, accessed September 14, 2012, http://cbsnews.com/2100-18560_162-3361753.

354 **"a par with the world's most prestigious financial centers":** Krane, *City of Gold*, 147.

354 **"Make no little plans":** Charles Moore, *Daniel Burnham, Architect, Planner of Cities, Volume II* (Boston: Houghton Mifflin, 1921), 147.

354 **United States taxes foreign-earned incomes above $91,500:** Internal Revenue Service, *Tax Guide for U.S. Citizens and Resident Aliens Abroad* (Washington DC: Internal Revenue Service, 2010), accessed July 25, 2011, http://www.irs.gov/publications/p54/ar01.html.

354 **twenty thousand Britons:** Ali, *Dubai: Gilded Cage*, 30.

355 **"might have wiped out half of the UAE royal family":** Davidson, *Dubai*, 293.

356 **largest overseas naval port:** Krane, *City of Gold*, 79.

356 **over $300 billion:** Mike Davis, "Fear and Money in Dubai," *New Left Review* 41 (2006): 59.

357 **$44 million buying spree:** Andrew Higgins, "Pricey Real Estate Deals in Dubai Raise Questions about Azerbaijan's President," *Washington Post*, March 5, 2010.

357 **"World Winning Cities":** Krane, *City of Gold*, 121–122.

358 **urbanized footprint quadrupled:** ibid., 301.

358 **as much property development as Shanghai:** ibid., 297.

358 **over ten million shipping containers:** American Association of Port Authorities, 2009 rankings, accessed June 18, 2012, http://aapa.files.cms-plus.com/Statistics/WORLD%20PORT%20RANKINGS%202010.pdf.

360 **40 percent of Dubai's prisoners:** "Debtors Languishing in Dubai Prisons," Associated Press, June 11, 2007.

361 **"We apologize the site you are attempting to visit":** Fallows, "The Connection Has Been Reset."

361 **"contradicts with the ethics and morals of the UAE":** Prohibited Content Categories, UAE, accessed January 13, 2010.

361 **thousands of workers:** Davidson, *Dubai*, 117.

364 **$1 billion science complex:** Abby Goodnough, "Slowing Expansion, Harvard Suspends Work on Complex," *New York Times*, December 10, 2009.

365 **more than three-quarters male:** Krane, *City of Gold*, 254.

367 **"City of Gold" in Hindi:** ibid., 209.

367 **roughly a quarter of the city's population:** Ali, *Dubai: Gilded Cage*, 83.

367 **"Important notice":** Sonapur visit, Dubai, January 29, 2010.

368 **termination (i.e., deportation) for smoking:** Burj Khalifa tour, Dubai, January 14, 2010.

368 **forty thousand Dubai construction workers mounted an illegal strike:** Krane, *City of Gold*, 209.

370 **5 percent:** Yasser Elsheshtawy, *Dubai: Behind an Urban Spectacle* (New York: Routledge, 2010), 213.

370 **3 percent:** Ali, *Dubai: Gilded Cage*, 178.

370 **150,000 expatriate Arabs:** ibid., 113.

370 **numbering over a million:** Krane, *City of Gold*, 199.

370 **approximately one hundred thousand:** Ali, *Dubai: Gilded Cage*, 112.

370 **"Talk to a Local" booths:** Davidson, *Dubai*, 203.

370 **foreigners make up 99 percent of the workforce:** Ali, *Dubai: Gilded Cage*, 7.

371 **Emirati teachers are paid more than twice what expatriates make:** Kathryn Lewis and Kareem Shaheen, "Low-Wage Teachers Take on Second Jobs," *The National* (Abu Dhabi), January 30, 2010.

371 **receives $55,000 a year:** Ali, *Dubai: Gilded Cage*, 168.

372 **"This is particularly disappointing":** Davidson, *Dubai*, 166.

374 **"Arabian-inspired":** permanent exhibition, Burj Khalifa visitors' center, Dubai, visited January 14, 2010.

375 **energy use and carbon footprint per capita:** Krane, *City of Gold*, 223–224.

375 **"success to an Arab city":** Anthony Shadid, "The Towering Dream of Dubai," *Washington Post Foreign Service*, April 30, 2006.

375 **"the best city in India":** Raymond Barrett, *Dubai Dreams: Inside the Kingdom of Bling* (London: Nicholas Brealey Publishing, 2010), 61.

375 **"the best city in Iran":** Vali Nasr, *Forces of Fortune: The Rise of the New Muslim Middle Class and What It Will Mean for Our World* (New York: Free Press, 2009), 46.

376 **every three hundred meters:** Doug Kelbaugh, executive director of Design and Planning, Limitless, interview with author, Dubai, January 22, 2010.

376 **"If a stone as big as seven pregnant camels":** permanent exhibition, Siraaj: The Guiding Light, Dubai, visited January 16, 2010.

376 **seven million tourists:** Ali, *Dubai: Gilded Cage*, 8.

377 **attracts nineteen million visits a year:** Simeon Kerr, "How Developer Weathered the Storm," *Financial Times* (UK), July 2, 2012.

378 **387-building housing development:** Nakheel, "Nakheel Hands Over First Building at International City," press release, October 5, 2005, accessed June 18, 2012, http://www.dubaicity.com/news/Nakheel-hands-over-first-building 10-5.htm.

379 **"I think it's a flattering statement":** Krane, *City of Gold*, 304.

### Conclusion: Glimpses of Utopia

383 **just 30 percent:** Ali, *Dubai: Gilded Cage*, 41.

383 **$10 billion bailout:** Landon Thomas Jr., "Abu Dhabi Tightens Its Grip as It Offers Help to Dubai," *New York Times*, December 14, 2009.

383 **thousands of expatriate professionals:** Robert F. Worth, "Laid-Off Foreigners Flee as Dubai Spirals Down," *New York Times*, February 11, 2009.

384 **"the ultimate tabula rasa":** Mitra Khoubrou, Ole Bouman, and Rem Koolhaas, eds., *Al Manakh* (Amsterdam: Archis, 2007), 7.

384 **"evil paradise":** Mike Davis and Daniel Bertrand Monk, eds., *Evil Paradises: Dreamworlds of Neoliberalism* (New York: New Press, 2007).

386 **"We were very apt to decry":** Chopra, *A Joint Enterprise*, 38.

387 **fastest-growing cities on earth:** Population Division, Department of Economic and Social Affairs, United Nations, *World Urbanization Prospects* (New York: United Nations, 2003).

## Coda: From Windows on the West to Windows of the World

391 **"Apollo, Marble, Roman work":** permanent exhibition, Hermitage museum, St. Petersburg, visited July 9, 2010.

392 **12 percent of Russians:** Richard Pipes, "Flight from Freedom: What Russians Think and Want," *Foreign Affairs*, May/June 2004.

394 **"See The World Landmarks In One Day!":** Window of the World, tour, Shenzhen, September 13, 2009.

394 **"Completed in 1922":** ibid.

395 **"All architecture is the heritage of all people":** Jeff Stein, "Who, What, When, Where, Why, How," *ArchitectureBoston*, September/October 2005, 45.

395 **"Author: Antoine Houdon":** Window of the World, tour, Shenzhen, September 13, 2009.

# IMAGE CREDITS

**Map 1** (The world, 1840): The Lionel Pincus and Princess Firyal Map Division, The New York Public Library, Astor, Lenox and Tilden Foundations

**Map 2** (St. Petersburg, 1776): Library of Congress

**Map 3** (Shanghai, 1862): The National Archives (UK)

**Map 4** (Bombay 1909): *Imperial Gazetteer of India*, new edition, held by University of Chicago Library

**Map 5** (Dubai 2010): Syed Ali, *Dubai: Gilded Cage*, Yale University Press, 2010

**Introduction**: Daniel Brook

**Chapter 1**: Peter the Great Museum of Anthropology and Ethnography (Kunstkamera), Russian Academy of Sciences, Coll. Number МЛ-890 and МЛ-891

**Chapter 2**: Martyn Gregory Gallery, London

**Chapter 3**: Sharada Dwivedi and Rahul Mehrotra, *Bombay: The Cities Within*, Eminence Designs, 2001

**Chapter 4**: Library of Congress; Mike Tomshinsky

**Chapter 5**: Picture This Gallery, Hong Kong

**Chapter 6**: Sharada Dwivedi and Rahul Mehrotra, *Bombay: The Cities Within*, Eminence Designs, 2001

**Chapter 8**: RMJM

**Chapter 9**: Greg Girard and Monte Clark Gallery, Toronto

**Chapter 10**: Hiranandani Upscale

**Chapter 11**: Michael Curry

**Conclusion**: Daniel Brook

**Coda**: Daniel Brook

429

# INDEX

Page numbers in *italics* refer to illustrations.

# ABOUT THE AUTHOR

Daniel Brook is a journalist whose work has appeared in publications including *Harper's*, *The Nation*, *Foreign Policy*, and *Slate*, and the author of *The Trap: Selling Out to Stay Afloat in Winner-Take-All America*. His architecture writing was awarded the 2010 Winterhouse Award for Design Writing and Criticism. To research *A History of Future Cities*, Brook lived for a month each in St. Petersburg, Shanghai, Mumbai, and Dubai and conducted archival research on a semester-long fellowship at the Library of Congress. Originally from New York and educated at Yale University, Brook lives in New Orleans.